WESTMAR COLLEGE

W9-BOA-251

the regulatory regime is weak and is not greatly concerned with the economic welfare of Third World states.

Presenting several novel ideas on the regulation of international commodity markets, the authors show why a rather weak regulatory structure has existed since the end of World War II and why this situation is unlikely to change.

The Political Economy of International Change
John Gerard Ruggie, General Editor

Jock A. Finlayson is currently a management consultant. A graduate of the University of British Columbia and the Yale School of Management, he was, from 1983 to 1986, Director of Policy at the Business Council on National Issues in Ottawa. He has published widely in such areas as international trade and Canada-U.S. economic relations. **Mark W. Zacher** is Director of the Institute of International Relations and Professor in the Department of Political Science at the University of British Columbia. His previous books include *International Conflicts and Collective Security, 1946–1977, Pollution, Politics, and International Law: Tankers at Sea,* and *Dag Hammarskjold's United Nations* (published by Columbia University Press).

MANAGING INTERNATIONAL MARKETS

The Political Economy of International Change
John Gerard Ruggie, General Editor

MANAGING INTERNATIONAL MARKETS

Developing Countries and the Commodity Trade Regime

Jock A. Finlayson and Mark W. Zacher

Columbia University Press
New York   1988

Library of Congress Cataloging-in-Publication Data

Finlayson, Jock A.
　　Managing international markets.

　　(Political economy of international change)
　　Includes bibliographical references and index.
　　1. Commodity control. 2. Developing countries—
Commerce. I. Zacher, Mark W.　II. Title. III. Series:
Political economy of international change series.
HF1428.F56　　1988　　　382′.3′091724　　　87-27849
ISBN 0-231-06574-4 (alk. paper)

Columbia University Press
New York　　Guildford, Surrey
Copyright © 1988 Columbia University Press
All rights reserved
Printed in the United States of America

Harback editions of Columbia University Press books are Smyth-sewn
and are printed on permanent and durable acid-free paper

Book design by Ken Venezio

To Our Families

THE POLITICAL ECONOMY OF INTERNATIONAL CHANGE
John Gerard Ruggie, General Editor

CONTENTS

ACKNOWLEDGEMENTS

During the course of the research on this book many people have helped us, and to all of them we are most grateful. We interviewed over 200 individuals who have worked on international commodity trade problems in governments and international organizations (with a guarantee of anonymity). Many officials in the Canadian and U.S. governments provided invaluable assistance. We also benefited greatly from discussions with members of the staffs of the United Nations Conference on Trade and Development, the Food and Agriculture Organization, the World Bank, the International Monetary Fund, the International Tin Council, the International Sugar Organization, the International Coffee Organization and the International Cocoa Organization. Many of those interviewed also read drafts of various parts of the manuscript. Even when their views differed from our own, they were most generous with their time and insights.

We would like to thank a number of people who read all or parts of the manuscript and whose comments proved especially helpful. Jere Behrman and Gerald Helleiner reviewed our treatment of the economic literature. John Ruggie, Ralph Ives, Karen Mingst, Brent Sutton, and Alfred Maizels read and commented on all or large parts of the manuscript. The assistance of Kate Wittenberg and Karen Mitchell of the Columbia University Press is also greatly appreciated.

During our work on this study a number of individuals served as research assistants. We would like to thank Michael Webb, Rene Cremonese, Janis Doran, Nukhet Kardam, Jeffrey Pentland, Larry Woods, and Ernest Yee. Our research could not have been completed without financial support from the Donner Canadian Foundation, the Social Sciences and Humanities Research Council of Canada, and the Canadian Department of Energy, Mines, and Resources. The Faculty of Graduate Studies' support for the Institute of International Relations at the University of British Columbia was also important to the successful completion of this study.

One other person provided enormous assistance in completing this study—the secretary of the Institute of International Relations, Betty Greig. A friend to researchers in the institute for more than ten years, Betty has made welcome contributions to the academic and social lives of all associated with it.

Finally, we would like to thank our families for the many kindnesses they have shown while we have worked on this and other research endeavors.

Jock A. Finlayson
Mark W. Zacher

1

INTERNATIONAL COMMODITY POLICY AND THE NORTH-SOUTH DIALOGUE

International trade in primary commodities has been the focus of extensive intergovernmental negotiation throughout the twentieth century. This has been particularly true in the period since World War II, when the number of sovereign nations increased dramatically as Third World countries gradually gained political independence. Developing countries have been the principal advocates of intervention by the international community into global commodity markets. They have been responsible for the prominence that issues of commodity policy have acquired in international forums and in North-South relations since the early 1960s.

This book is concerned with North-South bargaining over those commodities of which developing countries are major exporters and on which meetings have occurred to negotiate producer-consumer agreements. All these commodities were included in the Integrated Program for Commodities (IPC) launched by the United Nations Conference on Trade and Development (UNCTAD) in 1976. A central purpose of the book is to explain the policies of Third World commodity-producing states toward both general guidelines for the management of international markets and specific regulatory schemes for individual commodities. A second purpose is to explore the nature of the bargaining outcomes on commodity issues and to explain why they occurred. A final focus of the book is the character of the international regulatory arrangements (or the "regime") that have prevailed in this issue-area. Before discussing the postwar North-South negotiations on general normative issues (chapter 2) and the negotiations held on commodity-specific agreements (chapters 3 to 5), we provide some relevant background on commodity trade patterns, policy issues, and market control mechanisms, as well as a brief overview of international commodity diplomacy during the past four decades.

COMMODITY TRADE PATTERNS AND POLICY ISSUES

There is no question that developing countries are highly dependent on exports of primary commodities for their foreign exchange earnings. In the late 1970s, primary commodities accounted for over 80 percent (in value) of less-developed country (LDC) exports, and for about 60 percent of the export earnings of non-oil-exporting LDCs.[1]

With the worldwide depression in commodity prices during the first half of the 1980s, these figures have declined significantly. The Third World, excluding oil-exporting countries, now obtains less than 40 percent of its aggregate export earnings from commodities. But the aggregate figures conceal important differences among countries. In 1982, for example, nonfuel commodities still provided more than 60 percent of the export earnings of African developing countries, and more than 50 percent of the earnings of South and Central American countries. Despite their continuing dependence on commodities, however, developing countries are not typically the predominant suppliers of most raw materials. In the early 1980s the developed market economies accounted for almost 40 percent (in value) of world primary commodity exports, and for more than 60 percent exclusive of fuels.[2]

On the level of individual commodities, two facts must be stressed. First, in spite of their modest share of world exports in many cases, less-developed countries loom very large in many individual commodity markets. In particular, they account for a majority of world exports of most of the primary commodities that have been subject to intergovernmental negotiations on some form of market control since 1945 (wheat being a notable exception). Table 1.1 provides an overview of the share of (noncommunist) developing countries in total world exports of 33 commodities in the late 1970s. Later chapters will highlight the dominance of particular countries in particular markets.

Second, as is well known, many developing countries depend heavily on primary commodities to generate foreign exchange. Table 1.2, based on United Nations data, sketches Third World dependence on commodities for export earnings over the decade 1970–80.[3] Although there has been a

TABLE 1.1

Developing Countries' Share of Global Exports (by Value) of Thirty-Three
Commodities (Averages 1980–1982)

	Commodity	*% of Exports*
1	Sisal	98.7
2	Rubber	98.3
3	Jute	95.8
4	Cocoa	92.7
5	Copra	91.0
6	Coffee	92.0
7	Bananas	87.5
8	Coconut oil	86.0
9	Tea	84.2
10	Bauxite	84.1
11	Manganese ore	79.4
12	Palm oil	78.1
13	Tin	75.9
14	Groundnut oil	70.5
15	Phosphate rock	66.8
16	Sugar	66.5
17	Linseed oil	64.1
18	Copper	61.5
19	Groundnuts	60.3
20	Rice	54.6
21	Fishmeal	52.4
22	Tobacco	50.9
23	Iron ore	49.1
24	Cotton	44.0
25	Petroleum[a]	36.7
26	Lead	30.5
27	Timber	29.1
28	Zinc	24.1
29	Wool	18.6
30	Maize	17.5
31	Hides and skins	17.0
32	Beef	16.4
33	Wheat and meslin	5.2

[a]The World Bank excludes the Arab members of OPEC except Algeria from the category of "developing country." In this category it includes Cyprus, Greece, Israel, Malta, Portugal, Turkey, Yugoslavia, and South Africa.

Source: World Bank, *Commodity Trade and Price Trends* (1985), table 8.

TABLE 1.2

Importance of Primary Commodities in the Export Earnings of Developing Countries[a]

	Number of Countries	
Percentage Share of Export Earnings	*1970*	*1980*
90–100	36	29
70–90	26	21
50–70	6	14
10–50	9	12
0–10	1	2
Total	78	78

[a]Excluding countries for which exports or reexports of fuels exceeded 10 percent of total exports.
Source: UN Doc. TD/273 (1983), "Commodity Issues: A Review and Proposals for Further Action," Annex, Table 6.

modest decline in the Third World's reliance on commodities, 50 LDCs still depended on nonfuel primary products for at least 70 percent of their foreign exchange in 1980. Many of these countries export a very narrow range of products, and are thus extremely vulnerable to changes in individual markets. With respect to the commodities included in UNCTAD's Integrated Program during the mid-1970s, more than 50 LDCs derived 40 percent or more of their export earnings from these commodities, with about 75 LDCs obtaining at least 20 percent.[4] Although the so-called newly industrializing countries are now major participants in world manufactures trade and account for a growing share of total Third World exports, the number of countries falling into this category is not large.[5] For the bulk of developing countries, primary commodities remain the chief source of badly needed foreign exchange earnings. Average annual LDC earnings from 33 commodities during the late 1970s are presented in table 1.3.

Over the past three decades, the developing countries have focused their criticisms of commodity market performance on a small number of key issues, the most important being unstable prices, fluctuations in producer earnings, and the declining real prices of most primary commodities relative to those of manufactured goods (the "terms of trade" issue). This does not, of course, exhaust the list of Third World concerns. For example, LDCs have complained about the role of multinational corporations in structuring commodity markets in ways that are often inimical to the welfare of producing countries. But it is clear that the major issues of international com-

TABLE 1.3
Average Annual Earnings of Developing Countries from the Export of
Thirty-Three Commodities, 1977–1979 (billions of U.S. dollars)[a]

1	Petroleum	113.46
2	Coffee	9.34
3	Sugar	8.87
4	Copper	5.56
5	Timber	5.24
6	Rubber	3.35
7	Iron ore	3.29
8	Cotton	3.16
9	Rice	2.72
10	Tin	2.29
11	Cocoa	2.18
12	Tobacco	2.18
13	Maize	1.94
14	Tea	1.54
15	Palm oil	1.41
16	Beef	1.37
17	Phosphate rock	1.35
18	Bananas	1.20
19	Wheat and meslin	0.88
20	Wool	0.72
21	Bauxite	0.69
22	Coconut oil	0.60
23	Zinc	0.54
24	Fish meal	0.52
25	Hides and skins	0.42
26	Lead	0.41
27	Groundnuts	0.38
28	Manganese ore	0.32
29	Groundnut oil	0.22
30	Jute	0.16
31	Copra	0.13
32	Linseed oil	0.12
33	Sisal	0.11
	Total	$176.64 billion

[a]The World Bank excludes the Arab members of OPEC except Algeria from the category of "developing country." In this category it includes Cyprus, Greece, Israel, Malta, Portugal, Turkey, Yugoslavia and South Africa.
Source: World Bank, *Commodity Trade and Price Trends* (1985), table 7.

modity policy from the perspective of the South have been price instability and declines in real prices and producer export earnings.

Instability in Prices and Export Earnings

That the prices of many internationally traded primary commodities tend to vary more than the prices of manufactures appears to be accepted by most experts, governments, and international economic organizations.[6] A few studies have challenged this orthodox view,[7] but the proposition that price instability is marked for many resource exports crucial for the Third World is not itself a source of serious dispute by scholars or governments. Innumerable studies have been done on commodity price instability. For the 1951–75 period, David McNicol calculated that variations in the prices of several major LDC commodity exports were more than twice as great as variations for a sample of manufactured products.[8] Another analysis found that over the two decades 1954–73 only 2 of 20 commodities important to LDC exporters exhibited less price instability than manufactures.[9] Table 1.4 lists the changes in real (or constant) prices for the major LDC commodity exports (excluding fuels) between 1955 and 1981.

In considering commodity price instability, the rather unsurprising fact that declines rather than increases in price typically cause concern for LDC producers merits emphasis, since producers' interest in international regulation tends to vary inversely with market trends. But this is not to say that price instability per se is not a real problem. In many cases, rising commodity prices are soon followed by precipitous declines and a period of severely depressed prices. Most of the commodities discussed later in this book have been subject to considerable price instability. The so-called "core" commodities identified in the IPC included several important LDC exports that have "experienced relatively high price instability in the past quarter century."[10]

Explanations of such price instability begin with the apparently low responsiveness of supply and demand to price changes, especially over the short run.[11] Given the general pattern of short-run supply-and-demand price inelasticity that appears to exist for many primary commodities, relatively small shifts in demand or supply will tend to generate relatively large changes in price. Variations in supply conditions are quite common for many agricultural commodities, which are susceptible to the vagaries of weather and disease. For mineral commodities, on the other hand, the main causes of price fluctuations are demand changes due to the business cycle

TABLE 1.4

Average Annual Percentage Change in Commodity Prices (Constant Dollars), 1955–1981[a]

Sugar	41.6
Cocoa	25.3
Copper	18.5
Coffee	17.8
Phosphate rock	17.4
Rubber	16.3
Oils and oilseeds[b]	15.8
Jute	15.6
Tropical timber (logs—lauan)	14.0
Beef	11.8
Tin	10.4
Manganese ore	10.3
Cotton	10.1
Tea	9.7
Iron ore	8.4
Bauxite	8.0
Bananas	7.0

[a]Average of annual percentage changes, devoid of sign.
[b]Figure is an average of percentage changes for palm oil (13.9), coconut oil (20.3), groundnut oil (14.2), soybeans (10.8), copra (22.8), and groundnuts (12.6).
Source: Table provided by World Bank, Commodities and Export Projections Division.

in the developed economies that are the major markets for LDC exports, although supply disruptions are also far from rare. Price instability occasioned by demand and/or supply shifts is certainly not an equally serious problem for all commodities, but it is a problem endemic to many commodity markets.

As was mentioned earlier, much of the debate concerning instability and commodity trade focuses not on price fluctuations per se but rather on the effect of market instability on export earnings. It is widely believed that many LDCs experience severe fluctuations in their total export revenues. This "conventional wisdom" was attacked in the 1960s by Joseph Coppock and Alasdair MacBean, who found that the developing countries they studied (a group much smaller than the total number of LDCs) did not actually suffer from export earnings instability significantly greater than that experienced by developed countries.[12] However, more recent empirical analyses have "produced something of a consensus that the export earnings of the less developed countries are indeed more unstable than those of industrial countries, although the extent to which this greater instability is due to greater dependence on raw materials exports is uncertain."[13] Moreover, it has become "almost an article of faith among many policy-makers and economists in the developing countries that these countries suffer particularly violent fluctuations in their export earnings" because of a concentration on primary exports.[14]

Price and earnings instability should be distinguished when discussing international commodity policy. Most commodity control schemes—including those subject to intensive negotiations in the latter half of the 1970s—tend to focus on the supply of commodities and/or the prices at which they are traded. But if prices are unstable because of shifts in supply, as with many agricultural commodities, the impact on producer revenue may be offset by the fact that prices and volumes of exports will typically move in opposite directions, thus moderating the variations in earnings. (However, for the overwhelming majority of LDCs, their own individual supplies of commodities have little effect on world prices.) On the other hand, where shifts in demand are the basic cause of price fluctuations, prices and volumes of exports will move in the same direction, exacerbating earnings variations.[15]

The question of the relationship between prices and earnings arises in connection with proposals to stabilize prices through, for example, the use of internationally financed or national buffer stocks (discussed below). Under certain conditions, there will be a trade-off between price stabilization and total earnings; under other conditions, price stabilization may actually precipitate unstable earnings. The effect of stabilization on earnings depends ultimately on the underlying elasticities of demand and supply and cannot be pursued here.[16] It must be noted, however, not only that reliable data concerning these elasticities are often difficult to obtain, but that the economic models from which various analytical conclusions are drawn are always premised on restrictive assumptions that proponents of other models can portray as inadequate.[17] For present purposes, what must be borne in mind is the complexity of the debate and the fact that different actors have divergent *perceptions* about the appropriate means for tackling the key problem of earnings instability. Some have wished to address it by affecting prices and supplies, others by implementing schemes to ensure against shortfalls in actual export receipts.[18]

Terms of Trade

Instability of commodity prices and export earnings is basically a short-run, albeit frequently encountered, problem for LDC commodity producers. The other central issue those producers have identified is long term. According to the UNCTAD Secretariat and many LDC governments, the terms of trade of the developing countries have tended inexorably to deteriorate, in large part because of these countries' heavy dependence on exports of primary commodities. Put simply, the "terms of trade" can be understood as the buying power, in imports, of a given volume of exports over time. If revenue from a given volume of a country's exports purchases a diminishing quantity of imports, then that country's terms of trade may be said to have worsened. Many Third World countries claim that this is precisely what has happened to them over the past few decades.

Controversy has long swirled around the debates on this issue, both academic and intergovernmental. For many years, most economists "believed that the terms of trade would move in favor of natural resources over time because they would become scarce as nonrenewable resources were depleted and as agricultural land diminished with increased population and hence was used more intensively."[19] In the 1950s and 1960s, Raul Prebisch, then executive director of the UN Economic Commission for Latin America, disputed this view; he and others encouraged LDCs to reduce their dependence on commodity exports and to develop their manufacturing industries through policies of domestic industrialization.[20] They claimed that several structural factors pointed to a continuing deterioration in the buying power of primary commodity exports. First, in developed countries long-term demand for most primary commodities is income inelastic, and thus rising income levels will not lead to significantly increased demand for many LDC commodity exports.[21] Second, also depressing demand and prices is the long-run trend toward the development of synthetics that partially supplant markets for primary commodities. Finally, Prebisch and his intellectual allies suggested that a basic asymmetry in bargaining power exists that favors the industrial countries. This asymmetry derives from the monopoly of rich countries over technological change and from the fact that large enterprises from the industrial countries can dominate and structure international markets in ways that deny small, unorganized LDC commodity producers the gains that ought rightfully to accrue to them through trade.[22]

Many Western economists and governments have criticized the theory of declining terms of trade.[23] One common criticism concerns the time period for which price trends are mapped. Some studies begin with the years 1950–51, when the scramble for supplies occasioned by the Korean War exerted strong upward pressure on markets. "Proving" that commodity prices declined relative to manufactures prices after this unusual period is simple but introduces a patent bias into the analysis. Several analytically defensible measurements of the terms of trade do not necessarily yield the same results. Difficulties always arise when an attempt is made to construct a price index, since such factors as transportation charges and variations in quality are often not included.[24]

Nonetheless, numerous scholarly analyses have covered the post-Korean War period. According to one widely respected economist, Paul Bairoch, developing countries' terms of trade fell significantly after the Korean War until about 1962, but the situation then stabilized for the remainder of the 1960s.[25] Other studies also show that LDCs' terms of trade fell in the decade following the Korean War and that the real prices of commodities declined steadily throughout most of the 1950s and 1960s. A 1974 Brookings report by 15 economists concluded: "For more than a decade after 1951 . . . the United Nations price index for all primary commodities drifted downward. Periods of scattered and short-lived recovery followed, but in 1968 primary product prices were still below the pre-Korean level."[26] For the 1950–75 period, Jere Behrman found significantly negative trends in real prices for a number of Third World commodity exports, including 6 of the 10 "core" commodities in the UNCTAD IPC and 10 of the 17 commodities originally covered by the IPC.[27] The early 1980s, of course, brought a dramatic decline in the real prices of most Third World commodity exports.

If a longer period is examined, many economists argue, the evidence does not support the contention that there is an inherent tendency for the terms of trade to move against producers of primary commodities.[28] Relative prices have not been inexorably declining for all commodities; nor have all LDCs that depend heavily on commodity exports experienced a deterioration in their terms of trade. But it is unquestionably the case that many countries, especially those without petroleum and those that depend heavily on agricultural exports, have seen their terms of trade worsen over time. Table 1.5 indicates that the Third World as a whole experienced a significant improvement in its terms of trade as a consequence of the OPEC-engineered quadrupling of petroleum prices in 1973–74 and the further rise in petroleum prices in 1979–80; these developments were also reflected in the falling terms of trade of the industrial countries as a group during the same periods. However, as table 1.6 makes clear, the purchasing power of non-oil commodities important to the Third World declined over much of the 1970s and 1980s. Indeed, the vast majority of non-oil LDCs suffered, many severely, because of the sharp increases in petroleum prices since 1973. The political salience of the terms-of-trade

TABLE 1.5
Terms of Trade of Developing and Industrial Countries[a] (1975 = 100)

Year	Developing Countries	Industrial Countries
1960	74	107
1965	71	109
1970	71	111
1972	73	111
1973	80	110
1974	111	97
1975	100	100
1976	105	99
1977	106	98
1978	100	100
1979	109	98
1980	124	90
1981	128	90

[a]Terms of trade is the unit value index of exports divided by the unit value index of imports. "Developing" countries exclude developing communist countries, but include Third World oil exporters. "Industrial" countries exclude communist industrial countries.
Source: World Bank, *Commodity Trade and Price Trends* (1985), table 4.

TABLE 1.6
Purchasing Power of Primary Commodities Exported by Developing Countries in Terms of Imported Manufactures (1977–79 = 100)[a]

Year	Petroleum	33 Commodities Excluding Petroleum
1950	41	146
1955	39	130
1960	29	107
1965	24	107
1970	20	102
1974	108	157
1976	100	109
1978	87	93
1980	166	113
1981	186	91
1982	186	77
1983	165	82
1984	164	81
1985	159	73

[a]Figures are based on annual averages and constant dollars.
Source: World Bank, *Commodity Trade and Price Trends (1986)*, table 21.

issue in the 1970s derived in large part from the experiences of these countries.

MARKET CONTROL MECHANISMS

Much of the international bargaining over commodity policies centers on the feasibility of, and the costs associated with, a number of regulatory instruments that operate on commodity markets. Although a detailed discussion of these instruments cannot be undertaken here, a brief overview is in order.

International and National Buffer Stocks

Individual producers and consumers often elect to hold stocks of a commodity as a normal commercial practice. Governments may also decide to stockpile a particular commodity at one point and sell it off at another. In the absence of a producer-consumer commodity accord, stockpiling will occur as a result of decisions reached by individual importers and exporters. These national stocks can be used to affect the market price for a commodity. Many national governments regularly purchase large volumes of various agricultural commodities grown by domestic farmers as a normal part of their agricultural support policies; the surpluses thus acquired are destroyed, distributed on a concessional basis to poor countries, or disposed of in some other fashion.

A more important technique for present purposes is stockpiling carried out in accordance with a producer-consumer international commodity agreement (ICA). The most frequently discussed instrument is an international buffer stock, administered by an international commodity organization (ICO) according to rules set out in an ICA. The principle behind a buffer stock is very simple: by purchasing quantities of a commodity when prices are falling, one can lessen the extent of the price decline compared to what would happen in the absence of the buffer stock; concomitantly, by selling off accumulated stocks when prices are increasing, one can moderate the extent of the price rise. In theory, an international buffer stock can *always* keep market prices within an agreed price range, *provided* the buffer-stock manager has unlimited funds to purchase the commodity in the event of falling prices and an unlimited quantity to sell in the event of a price rise.

In practice several problems must be overcome before a viable international buffer stock can be established for a commodity. One stumbling block derives from the fact that many commodities are unsuitable for stocking. For example, beef, bananas, and some other agricultural commodities are perishable, and so a buffer stock is not appropriate. Other commodities that are storable in the short run will suffer varying degrees of deterioration as time passes.[29] Costs of storage and handling (including insurance and pilferage) must also be taken into account. A second problem stems from the heterogeneous physical character of some primary commodities. The existence of distinct grades (e.g., of tea or coffee) requires difficult decisions regarding the composition of a buffer stock. Third, an organized and open commodity exchange, where transactions can take place, is critical to the success of a buffer stock. A buffer-stock manager must be cognizant of price movements in order to know when to buy and sell. Commodities such as bauxite and bananas are "traded" within essentially closed market structures because of the dominant role, in both buying and selling, of vertically integrated multinational enterprises.[30] Other commodities, such as manganese ore and iron ore, are sold through yearly or long-term contracts.

If the technical conditions are met, other problems remain. As will be amply demonstrated later in this book, discussion of an appropriate price range for a commodity quickly brings into sharp relief conflicts of interest both between producers and consumers and among producers with divergent priorities and perspectives. Producing countries normally seek as high a price range as possible, preferably one where even the agreed floor price is regarded as remunerative. Consuming countries are usually anxious to ensure that an ICA does not force prices higher, and thus will argue for a lower price range, one that respects underlying market trends. Over the long term prices can be stabilized only if some way is found to ensure that the output of the industry rises and falls in accordance with evolving market trends.[31]

Export Quotas and Production Controls

Although much attention has recently been paid to buffer-stock proposals, a survey of past experiences with commodity control shows that restrictions on exports or production have been a much more popular regulatory instrument.[32] Export quotas are the primary means by which cartels and producers' associations seek to maintain prices at a desired level. Such quotas have also been employed extensively by joint producer-consumer ICAs. Export quotas are designed to control the supply of a commodity by limiting exports to a volume sufficient to meet demand *at some agreed price*. Export quotas can be used in conjunction with a buffer stock to effect longer term adjustments in output that the buffer stock by definition cannot bring about. In the event of a secular downward trend in demand, some form of permanent reduction in production itself is required to hold price within a desired range.[33]

Not surprisingly, construction of a viable export-quota scheme in connection with an ICA typically encounters several problems. The central problem is the allocation of quotas. Rarely will an exporter reduce its existing capacity or its share of the market without a protracted period of hard bargaining.[34] Yet often some cut in total exports is required to attain the desired price and to guard against oversupply. Countries anxious to increase their shares of the market will be especially reluctant to agree to any reduction in exports, as will countries whose production costs are significantly lower than those of other exporters.[35]

The participation of importing countries in export-quota arrangements revolves around the determination of the price range, the rules that govern the use of quotas, and the enforcement mechanisms. Importers and exporters must agree at what pace quotas are to be adjusted in the event of price change. Importing members will tend to favor quick relaxation of quotas as the price approaches the ceiling of the range, while in such an instance exporting countries' enthusiasm for upward revision of quotas may not be great. For exporting countries one of the major incentives to create ICAs stems from the role of importers in enforcing quota allocations, usually by means of a certificate system. Importing countries in effect agree to limit purchases of the commodity from countries that fail to abide by the rules outlined in the ICA.[36]

Many economists express concern at the prospect of export quotas or production controls being incorporated into ICAs.[37] They fear that supply reductions will be used to support and, over the longer term, to raise prices of primary commodities, even though in principle supply manipulation may be used simply to moderate price fluctuations. In the actual operation and negotiation of ICAs, "Stabilization has frequently simply served as a convenient euphemism for [price] support—the fundamental issue manifesting itself as soon as the negotiations concerning the price range within which stability is to be sought begin."[38] Developing countries have seen in supply restrictions a possible way to improve their terms of trade by increasing commodity prices. On the other hand, developed consumer nations have been critical of supply restrictions because of the fear that they may freeze production patterns and misallocate world resources.[39]

Multilateral Contracts

Another technique to stabilize markets is the multilateral commitment or contract, under which exporters agree to provide a certain minimum quantity of a commodity to importers while the latter commit themselves to purchase a negotiated minimum amount of the commodity from exporter signatories. Such commitments are meant to assure exporters of a market for their commodity and importers of supplies, in both cases normally within a predetermined price range. A multilateral contract agreement imposes reciprocal obligations. In a time of shortage, exporters are required to hold their prices within the range, even though the free market price may be substantially higher. In times of excess supply, importers are required to purchase specified minimum amounts at a predetermined price that may well be significantly higher than the market price. The International Wheat Agreements (which are not explored here) are the only ICAs that have relied on multilateral contracts. The major wheat exporters, except Argentina, are developed states.[40]

Indexation

Brief mention should be made of another technique that can be used to influence commodity prices, namely, indexation. Many developing countries have proposed that the prices of their commodity exports be indexed in some way to the prices of their imports. Prebisch and others had broached the idea of indexation early in the UN's history, but only since the 1970s has it been given serious attention. Third World support for indexation led to the passage of various resolutions by the General Assembly and the nonaligned countries in the first half of the 1970s. Later, indexation became a particularly important issue during the protracted IPC negotiations in the last half of the 1970s. Indexation has always been firmly rejected by developed countries and has earned harsh criticism from most economists who have examined the question. Even if an agreement were somehow reached to index commodity prices, a host of difficulties would remain. For example, problems would arise in deciding which manufactured goods should be included in an indexation scheme, in seeking appropriate price quotations for commodities—many of which are not traded on open markets—and in taking account of such factors as differences in quality and competitive relationships among commodities.[41] Some proponents of indexation also overlook the fact that many developing countries are now large importers of commodities, while several Western countries (as well as the Soviet Union) are major commodity exporters. As one Third World expert on commodity policy has bluntly stated: "The assumption that indexation will benefit *all* developing countries is false."[42]

Compensatory Financing

As noted earlier, stabilization of commodity prices does not necessarily imply stabilization of export earnings. Recognition of this, coupled with the reluctance of some countries to support schemes that intervene directly in commodity markets, has generated considerable interest in plans that provide loans or grants to states with temporary decreases in export earnings. The most important is the International Monetary Fund's Compensatory Financing Facility (CFF), first created in 1963, which provides loans to countries with decreased export earnings if they also experience balance-of-payments deficits. Another is the Stabilization Fund for Export Earnings (STABEX) created by an accord between the European Community (EC)[43] and a large number of African, Caribbean, and Pacific states (1975); it compensates LDC signatories for declines in earnings from particular commodity exports. These schemes have been periodically reviewed and revised.

Most developed countries have viewed compensatory financing as a better way to stabilize LDC export earnings than direct controls over price and supply. Rather than intervening in markets to stabilize prices, compensatory financing works to mitigate the effects of instability for producing countries that experience a significant decline in earnings. Because measures to affect prices and supplies are not required under compensatory financing, market forces are allowed to operate and the often cumbersome apparatus of regulation is avoided.

The desire to exert some measure of control over primary commodity markets has been characteristic of governments and industries in producing countries for most of this century. Most of the schemes designed to implement control have been suggested by producers and/or the governments of producing countries. In virtually all instances, the light on the horizon that attracts producers toward control schemes is the prospect of higher prices, although during depression periods, such as the 1930s and early 1980s, the basic goal may be to forestall precipitous declines.[44] Producers acting alone normally have been unable to achieve either price stability or price increases. Part of the explanation for such a pattern stems from difficulties that plague all attempts at collective producer action, such as rivalry among producers for larger market shares or higher earnings. Because of the improbability of success through unilateral action, during the postwar period most producing-country governments have sought joint producer-consumer commodity control. Consumer participation in commodity control arrangements promises at least a chance that producer behavior can be adequately policed—the key requirement of any export or production control agreement. Consumers may also be induced to provide funds for such purposes as buffer stocks, research and development, or diversification activities.

OVERVIEW OF POSTWAR COMMODITY DIPLOMACY

International commodity negotiations have been an important chapter in postwar relations between the developed and developing countries. When the institutional arrangements and rules to govern the postwar international economy were devised in the 1940s, commodity trade was one of several significant issues on the global agenda.

A useful way to examine the evolution of institutions and rules concerned with commodity trade is to consider them as a distinct international *regime*. An international regime can be defined broadly as a set of regulatory arrangements developed by governments to constrain and guide their behavior and interactions in a particular issue area. Scholars employing the concept have analyzed regimes by exploring their norms and rules, which concern both substantive and procedural issues.[45] In considering global commodity arrangements through the lens provided by the regime concept, this book will mainly focus on the norms of the regime, since they constitute its most general injunctions and provide the most important insights into its character and programmatic content. Substantive and procedural rules are basically designed to implement various norms. Nonetheless, conflict over both norms and rules has been an important part of the North-South dialogue.

The economic regimes put in place in the late 1940s were almost entirely a result of negotiations among a small number of industrial democracies, with the United States and the United Kingdom wielding the most influence.[46] The underdeveloped nations, as they were then called, were effectively excluded from a meaningful role and were therefore unable to shape the character of the regime established to govern commodity trade.

Some treatments of the North-South dialogue of the 1970s assume or imply that the confrontation on commodity issues between developed and developing nations began in the mid-1960s, with the birth of UNCTAD, and that international discussions did not reach a serious stage until after the OPEC oil price increase of late 1973. There is certainly some truth to this view. The rapid acceleration of decolonization in the early 1960s and the OPEC revolution of the mid-1970s did indeed spur negotiations on commodity questions and raise their political profile. However, the confrontation between developing exporters and developed importers actually began in the immediate postwar years, with some antecedents in the pre–World War II era.

Immediately after the war intermittent discussions occurred between the exporters and importers of individual commodities (such as tin and sugar) in established international forums. More important, however, were the deliberations aimed at drawing up a charter for an International Trade Organization (ITO) in the late 1940s. Negotiations held between 1946 and 1948 succeeded in producing a constitution for the ITO, often known as the Havana Charter. Not until the latter stages of the discussions did the developing countries of the time—largely from Latin America—participate actively, and for the most part they had little impact on the document. Contrary to their stated wishes, the Havana Charter espoused the free market principle with respect to commodity trade. Only in rather extreme situations of producer distress was intergovernmental action sanctioned to affect prices. When it became clear in 1949 that the ITO charter would not come into force, the responsibility for promoting commodity policies along the lines spelled out in the charter fell by default to the United Nations and the Food and Agriculture Organization (FAO).

Most international discussions of possible commodity–market regulation took place from the late 1940s until the early 1960s in UN and FAO bodies. In these settings producer-consumer regulatory accords were accepted for tin and sugar in 1953 and for coffee in 1962. But despite pressure from developing-country producers, no progress was made in securing agreement on new norms or guidelines that would expand both the scope for intergovernmental intervention in commodity markets and the goals of international commodity agreements.

In 1961 and 1963 two global bodies that would soon become critically important for the Third World were founded—the Conference of Non-aligned States and the Group of 77 (G77). The G77 quickly emerged as the principal LDC voice on international economic matters.[47] Also, in the early 1960s the developing countries came to constitute over two-thirds of the UN's membership, allowing them to pass UN resolutions virtually at will. Seventeen new states came into existence in 1960 alone, with another fifteen territories throwing off their colonial status between 1961 and 1964.

A major onslaught by the Third World on the norms guiding international economic relations was signaled by the UN General Assembly's decision in 1962 to convene a UN Conference on Trade and Development and the holding of the conference in the spring of 1964. The three major goals pressed by the developing countries at this conference were more stable and remunerative commodity prices, improved access for their exports to developed-country markets, and an increased flow of capital to developing nations.[48] The first issue (and the focus of this book) was clearly the most important topic of discussion. This was due in part to the choice of Dr. Raul Prebisch as Secretary General for the conference.

As noted earlier, Prebisch claimed that the prices of LDC commodity exports were highly unstable and that the purchasing power of LDC earnings from these exports had steadily eroded. His views heralded what was soon to become "a widespread belief in the developing world that intervention into market conditions is required to change the adverse terms of trade."[49] Not only did UNCTAD I help to crystallize normative guidelines and policy goals for the Third World, but it also converted UNCTAD into a permanent body within the UN and saw the Group of 77 develop as a coordinating mechanism for the developing countries. These have been identified as the most important accomplishments of UNCTAD I.[50]

The years from the creation of UNCTAD through 1973 witnessed continuing debates over international commodity issues. Until the early 1970s the only concrete successes to which UNCTAD could point were the renegotiation of agreements on tin, coffee, and sugar and, after several negotiating sessions, the conclusion of the International Cocoa Agreement in 1972. The developed countries remained reluctant to support regulatory schemes for most commodities.

The entire climate surrounding the commodity debate changed in the autumn of 1973 with the Arab oil embargo during the war between Israel and its Arab combatants and OPEC's subsequent quadrupling of oil prices. The commodity price boom that started in 1972 fueled the optimism of Third World commodity producers and convinced many that they now possessed "commodity power." The year 1974 saw numerous efforts by Third World producers of various commodities to emulate OPEC's spectacular example. The fact that these attempts at producer collaboration were largely failures did nothing to detract from the enthusiasm with which they were undertaken. In addition to activities occurring at the level of specific commodities, in the mid-1970s the G77 sought to bring together its disparate demands for major changes in the international economic system into two sets of negotiations—the UN General Assembly's Sixth Special Session, held in April 1974, and the meetings to draw up a Charter of Economic Rights and Duties of States held in the autumn of the same year. Commodity policy figured prominently in both sessions. Out of the Sixth Special Session came two important documents—the Declaration and the Program of Action, respectively, for a New International Economic Order (NIEO), a term that quickly became synonymous with the ambitious LDC plans for international economic change.

Since their new sense of economic power derived in large part from their perception that the industrialized nations were now greatly concerned about continued access to Third World commodities, it is not surprising that the developing countries included many specific demands on commodity issues in their campaign for a New International Economic Order. In particular, the G77 called for explicit international recognition of the legitimacy of producer cartels, for the creation of a host of new producer-consumer ICAs, and for the indexing of commodity prices to those of manufactured goods. At the Sixth Special Session the G77 asked the UNCTAD Secretariat to develop "an integrated program for commodities" that would include a number of proposals designed to improve the welfare of LDC commodity producers. The Secretariat quickly proceeded to act on this request. The resulting Integrated Program for Commodities (IPC)— finally accepted by the fourth UNCTAD conference in 1976—featured proposals to negotiate international commodity agreements for 18 commodities (including the four for which ICAs already existed) and to create a Common Fund to finance the buffer stocks of the ICAs. Both UNCTAD and the FAO had previously sponsored meetings between commodity producers and consumers to consider the formulation of ICAs, but the IPC envisaged more extensive negotiations that would be conducted interdependently and that would have a much higher political profile. The G77 and the Secretariat hoped that the OPEC states would lend support to LDC producers of other commodities and that threats to use "the oil weapon" against the industrialized nations would persuade the latter to accept new arrangements to regulate markets.

When the IPC negotiations commenced in the latter half of 1976, the Third World's optimism had declined. The commodity price boom that began in 1971–72 had ended by late 1974. The developed countries had displayed a lack of interest in, and sometimes outright opposition to, intervention in commodity markets at United Nations meetings and at the 1975–77 Conference on International Economic Cooperation. They were, however, more supportive of compensatory financing, and also called for increased investments in technical assistance to LDC commodity industries.

Negotiations on the 14 IPC commodities for which ICAs did not already exist commenced in late 1976 and lasted until the early 1980s. The scores of meetings held led to the publication of numerous lengthy studies of commodity markets and witnessed many conflicts between developed and developing participants as well as within each group. After years of discussions, only a single new ICA emerged from these negotiations, the International Natural Rubber Agreement, signed in 1979. Supplementing this rather meager result was an agreement reached in 1980 to establish a Common Fund to provide loans to international commodity organizations in connection with buffer-stocking operations carried out in pursuit of price stabilization. The fund that was negotiated was in fact a far cry from the ambitious scheme originally proposed by the developing world in the mid-1970s. It will probably enter into force by early 1988.

By 1981, the largely unsuccessful negotiations on price regulation had prompted the G77 and the UNCTAD Secretariat to switch the focus of their reform efforts away from regulating commodity prices to providing more generous compensatory financing to LDC commodity exporters. It seems unlikely, however, that the developed nations will be prepared to countenance major changes in the existing practices and policies of the IMF's Compensatory Financing Facility. And, as if to underline the failure of the South's ambitious campaign to change the international commodity regime in the 1970s, the early 1980s saw the onset of the worst slump in global commodity markets since the 1930s. In this most recent period even existing agreements for such key LDC exports as tin, sugar, and cocoa have proved unable to prevent what for many Third World producers have been truly disastrous price and earnings declines.

POLICIES AND BARGAINING OUTCOMES: SOME KEY THEMES

In recent years some valuable studies have been published on international commodity policy and diplomacy. Many of them have been authored by economists interested in the feasibility, costs, and benefits of different international arrangements to regulate commodity markets.[51] Some address the long-standing debates over the extent of price instability and declining terms of trade and their impact on the Third World.[52] A few authors have also sought to probe the politics of recent international commodity diplomacy.[53]

The present study differs from these others in several respects. It seeks, first, to provide a fairly detailed historical treatment of international negotiations on commodity issues during the entire postwar period, beginning with the abortive effort to establish an International Trade Organization in the 1940s. Second, it analyzes the politics of international regulatory arrangements at two distinct levels: that of general norms and programs and that of specific rules relating to individual commodities or financial programs. As will soon become apparent, the issues and outcomes at these two levels were quite different. Our analysis also highlights some of the most important factors that influence collaboration in this and other international issue-areas. Finally, this book is written from the perspective of international politics rather than international economics. Although key economic issues relevent to commodity markets are touched on, the focus of the book is on the political, diplomatic, and institutional aspects of commodity market regulation.

A few comments on some matters not addressed in the book are in order. The study clearly takes a state-centric approach to the analysis of international negotiations. Although divisions within particular national governments and the activities of interest groups within countries are occasionally noted, the discussion of negotiations generally assumes that national governments are unified actors that speak authoritatively for states on commodity issues. The principal justification for this approach is that a broad survey of a large number of separate negotiating settings over a period of some four decades would not have been feasible if analysis of national decision-making processes had been included. Related to this point, the decision to focus on states' policies and intergovernmental agreements means that the book does not focus in depth on multinational corporations and other nongovernmental actors in world resource markets. Multinationals are discussed in several places, but from the perspective of their influence on states' policies.

The analysis of commodity diplomacy explores a small number of key themes, which are highlighted in Chapter 6. These themes are often treated in existing writings of political scientists, economists, and policy specialists interested in international political economy, North-South relations, and commodity trade.[54] First, there has been a notable disparity between the unity displayed by Third World states in supporting the general objective of intergovernmental management of commodity markets, on the one hand, and on the other, their frequent opposition to specific schemes and their divergences of views in negotiations on specific commodities. Their policies on the latter have been influenced both by characteristics of particular markets and by conflicting interests within their own grouping. The unity of the Third World has often been more apparent than real. And, the oft-attributed preference of developing countries for authoritative as opposed to market allocation of economic rewards has not always been evident.

Second, developing–country commodity producers have enjoyed only limited bargaining leverage in their economic interactions with the developed world. In part this situation is a product of the diverse interests of states in individual markets, but more fundamentally it flows from such factors as the elasticities of supply and demand in commodity markets and the inability or reluctance of producers to contemplate declines in export earnings and economic activity. The vulnerabilities of Third World producers to disruptions in their international economic ties are very real.

Third, despite many statements and studies proclaiming the mutuality of economic interests between the North and South in creating ICAs, the developed nations have seldom perceived such common interests. Insofar as they have been willing to support ICAs, it has been largely for political reasons extrinsic to the markets under consideration. Uppermost in the minds of policymakers from the developed world has been the goal of maintaining general politico-security and economic links with producing states or, on occasion, with the Third World in general. The economic gains that may be derived from ICAs have been viewed as marginal.

Fourth, the international regime in the commodity trade field has not been, and certainly is not now, a particularly strong one. The Western industrialized nations, which have possessed overriding economic power in most commodity markets, have not been prone to accept injunctions that tied them to particular courses of action. On the whole they have favored competitive markets, but they have also insisted on considerable leeway to support collusive arrangements. At least in this area, the hegemony of a group of states with comparable interests has not led to a strong regime.

A final and related theme is the difficulty of establishing strong regimes to govern behavior in issue-areas that are highly salient to the competition among states for wealth and economic advantage. Commodity trade is an important arena of international economic competition. Because of this, states have been reluctant to accept the restrictions on their latitude for independent action that would necessarily inhere in a strong regime. This is probably more true of powerful states that are less vulnerable to external economic shocks than of the weaker, less diversified states that still constitute the bulk of the developing world.

2

NEGOTIATIONS ON COMMODITY TRADE NORMS AND PROGRAMS

THE ITO NEGOTIATIONS AND DEVELOPMENTS IN THE 1950s

Efforts to fashion a global commodity regime in the early postwar years were closely linked to the broader negotiations to create a comprehensive International Trade Organization. The ITO was expected to provide a framework to govern trade relations and serve as a forum in which states could conduct ongoing discussions on trade matters. Intergovernmental action to affect primary commodity markets was one of the many issues discussed between 1946 and 1948, and a separate chapter of the ITO charter was eventually devoted to commodity control schemes. At least until the final ITO bargaining session before the 1948 Havana Conference, the major division among the states participating in the talks was between the United States, which favored rapid liberalization of trade and the introduction of rigorous "law" into international relations, and Britain and other industrial nations, which tended to be less enthusiastic about immediate liberalization and were anxious to maintain many existing preference schemes and trade controls.[1] By the time of the Havana Conference, the underdeveloped countries, which constituted over half the participants at the session, had begun to voice their own goals and views, and the United States and other Western countries were forced to make several concessions to gain their acceptance of the ITO charter.[2]

States' policies toward market regulation during the ITO discussions were heavily influenced by the events of the interwar period, in particular, depressed prices and proliferating attempts to control international commodity markets. Most of the interwar schemes were undertaken by industrial associations rather than by governments, but in many cases national governments strongly supported producers' efforts to stem sharp declines in prices—the typical cause of commodity agreements.[3] In a few instances, such as the control schemes for tin, rubber, and wheat in the 1930s, the agreements were actually signed by governments, although industry representatives played key roles. "It was gradually becoming realised during the 1930s . . . that except possibly in industries with highly centralised ownership . . . really strong control schemes of a stable character, and their effective administration, could only be secured in practice by governments."[4] The depression of the 1930s had had a devastating effect on the prices of primary commodities, and it was generally accepted that international action would be required to ensure that this unfortunate experience was not repeated after the war.

In 1945 the U.S. Department of State published its *Proposals for Expansion of World Trade and Employment* and included provisions for the negotiation of agreements to address the problems of primary commodity trade.[5] This perspective was also reflected in the *Suggested Charter for an International Trade Organization,* produced in Washington in 1946, which contained a chapter on intergovernmental commodity agreements.[6] In contrast to the practice before the war, such agreements were henceforth to involve importing as well as exporting countries, and to apportion votes equally between the two groups. More important, Washington made it clear that it would accept commodity control only in very unstable markets and that schemes should "prevent abuses of the sort that had accompanied commodity agreements in the past."[7] Such perceived abuses consisted mainly of attempts by producers to raise prices through export controls.

Preparatory meetings commenced in London in late 1946, with the United States' *Suggested Charter* serving as the basis for discussions. The U.S. position that commodity agreements should be negotiated only in extraordinary circumstances, where free market forces were clearly unable to create a reasonable balance between production and consumption without causing severe damage to producers, was roundly attacked by several other delegations. The British, joined by France, Australia, and the few underdeveloped countries present, argued that the elimination of significant instabilty in commodity markets was a worthy goal that justified the establishment of intergovernmental agreements. John Maynard Keynes, whose thoughts had profoundly influenced the thinking of the British on many international economic questions, had written in 1928 that it was "an outstanding fault of the competitive system that there is no sufficient incentive to the individual enterprise to store surplus stocks and materials, so as to maintain continuity of output and to average, as far as possible, periods of high and low demand."[8] His solution to the problem of commodity price volatility, elaborated in more detail in 1942, called for the use of international, government-controlled buffer stocks to even out the often vicious swings of the "trade cycle." Interestingly, Keynes was generally opposed to commodity schemes that restricted output, and saw international buffer stocks as useful aids to the market, not a replacement for it.[9]

Borrowing from Keynes, the British suggested that schemes that relied solely on buffer stocks to affect prices indirectly should be excluded from the definition of *control* agreements, which controlled production or exports to fix market prices in a more direct manner. The United States, however, was opposed to differentiating between buffer stocks and other control instruments, arguing that buffer-stock operations also would ultimately prove restrictive. Thus it insisted that the same rules apply to agreements making use of buffer stocks and of other regulatory mechanisms. In exchange for getting its way in this matter, Washington was forced to accept that price stabilization per se would be a legitimate objective of commodity agreements.[10]

Many more countries sent delegations to Havana than had been involved in the preparatory deliberations, and of the 56 countries in attendance over half were from what would later be termed the Third World. Prominent among the latter were 18 Latin American countries.[11] In retrospect, what is fascinating about their positions on commodities is their obvious anticipation of arguments that later became standard fare in the development debates of the 1960s and 1970s. At Havana the underdeveloped commodity exporters, led by Cuba, El Salvador, and Colombia, sought to have the charter reflect such themes as the need to protect commodity exporters' terms of trade and the legitimacy of unilateral producer interventions. In the draft of the commodity chapter, one of the stated objectives of intergovernmental agreements was to encourage greater stability in commodity prices and the attainment of prices that were "fair to consumers and remunerative to efficient producers." Several underdeveloped countries now demanded deletion of the adjective "efficient."[12] They argued that consideration should be given to countries' dependence on primary commodity industries when setting international price policy. Cuba noted wryly that while it was difficult to define what constituted an "efficient" industry, it was boldly prepared to offer a definition of an "inefficient" one, namely, an industry in which "producers ... resorted to sub-standard working conditions and workers' pay to achieve lower prices."[13] Eyebrows were raised in the delegations from the industrial nations at this novel characterization, but the underdeveloped countries did succeed in removing the much-feared adjective from article 57.

The developing countries were less successful in their more important effort to insert into the list of objectives a provision requiring the maintenance of the buying power of commodity exports. El Salvador suggested adoption of the following definition of "remunerative prices": "The term remunerative prices shall be understood to mean prices which maintain a fair relationship with the prices which the producers of primary commodities are obliged to pay for manufactured ... goods and general consumption goods."[14] In a similar vein, Cuba wanted to define a "reasonable return" to producing countries as one "adequate to maintain the purchasing power of their inhabitants, as importers and consumers, at a level sufficient to meet the requirements of a proper standard of living."[15] What was obvious about these suggestions—although left unsaid by their sponsors— was that some form of indexation of commodity prices to industrial-import prices would likely be required to guarantee the purchasing power of commodity exports. The British, joined by France and the United States, rejected this line of thinking out of hand at Havana, a position to which they and other industrial countries continued to adhere in subsequent years.[16]

Another argument advanced by underdeveloped commodity producers was that the charter should permit unilateral producer actions to stabilize and support commodity prices. Before the war, governments and industries in commodity-producing countries had frequently acted to curtail production and control the accumulation of stocks in order to bolster depressed markets. Many developing countries wanted to continue this practice and tried to secure support for it in the charter. However, a major goal of the United States, Britain, and several other industrial countries was to abolish producer cartels. At Havana they succeeded in doing this, in that the only type of market regulation envisaged by the charter was producer-consumer schemes in which voting power would be distributed equally between the two groups.[17]

When the Havana Conference ended, most underdeveloped countries voiced displeasure with both the overall assumptions and the specific provisions of the commodity chapter of the charter (chapter 6). They particularly objected to the philosophy that commodity agreements were to be *exceptional* instruments designed to deal with unusual circumstances, preferably on a temporary basis. Article 62 of the charter stated that commodity control schemes were only to be adopted in the event that one or both of the following conditions were met:

(a) a burdensome surplus of a primary commodity has developed or is expected to develop, which, in the absence of specific governmental action, would cause serious hardship to producers among whom are small producers who account for a substantial portion of the total output, and that these conditions could not be corrected by normal market forces in time to prevent such hardship, because, characteristically in the case of the primary commodity concerned, a substantial reduction in price does not readily lead to a significant increase in consumption or to a significant decrease in production; or
(b) widespread unemployment or under-employment in connection with a primary commodity . . . has developed or is expected to develop, which, in the absence of specific governmental action, would not be corrected by normal market forces in time to prevent widespread and undue hardship to workers because, characteristically in the case of the industry concerned, a substantial reduction in price does not readily lead to a significant increase in consumption but to a reduction in employment, and because areas in which the commodity is produced in substantial quantity do not afford alternative employment opportunities for the workers involved.

Agreements were to be negotiated at commodity conferences convened for this purpose. The maximum duration of an agreement was to be five years.

The enumerated objectives of commodity agreements included the following: to achieve market stabilization at prices "fair to consumers" that "provide a reasonable return to producers . . . "; to prevent or alleviate the "serious economic difficulties which may arise when adjustments between production and consumption cannot be effected by normal market forces alone as rapidly as the circumstances require"; to facilitate the shifting of resources away from "over-expanded industries"; to promote expansion of consumption where this could be achieved to mutual advantage; and to "assure the equitable distribution of a primary commodity in short supply."[18] Conspicuous by its absence was any mention of resource transfers to producers by way of higher prices. Intergovernmental action to restructure markets in order to further the economic development of producers was anathema to the industrial powers. The underdeveloped countries were well aware of this attitude, and several of them objected strenuously to it. Perhaps the most emphatic denunciation of the norms and rules of the new Havana Charter regime came from Cuba, the host country:

It is a great error in perspective, in our opinion, to try to obtain in the drafting of the Charter a balance of forces between producers and consumers, because such a balance would be broken in the consumers' favour in any situation requiring the application of the measures envisaged in Chapter VI. Equality in voting, vagueness in the determination of the level of prices to be obtained, indications that the commodity should be acquired economically, are misleading guides from which commodity agreements may suffer in the future. What this Chapter wants is direct protection to the producer, who is the one who would be in trouble, in a very weak position, and at the consumer's mercy.[19]

Overall the underdeveloped countries were able to obtain only minor changes in the commodity provisions previously put together by the United States, Britain, and other industrial countries, and the "main outlines and substance" of chapter 6 were in fact "similar to the original United States proposals."[20] The commodity control arrangements envisaged in the Havana Charter constituted a modest exception to the general norm of noninterference with markets that was the core of the American approach to postwar trade. "The general point of view . . . was that commodity control is a necessary evil—a remedy to prevent hardship to small producers and wage-earners when normal market forces cannot be relied upon to do so, and a remedy to be applied for short periods only."[21] Nonetheless, the charter did legitimize intergovernmental intervention into commodity markets to achieve greater stability and to address the perennial problem of excessive production. Even the United States, which had grave reservations about the restrictive effects of commodity control, felt compelled to support these goals. As was astutely pointed out at the time, the role of the U.S. government in domestic agriculture made it rather difficult for American trade negotiators to claim that all forms of government intervention in commodity trade ought to be eschewed.[22]

Because of opposition in the U.S. Congress and a lack of enthusiasm in other countries, the ITO never came into existence. But this did not mean that a complete regulatory lacuna existed in the sphere of international trade. In October 1947, 23 of the participants in the ITO negotiations had paused briefly and produced a trade accord, the General Agreement on Tariffs and Trade (GATT), that incorporated the trade-barriers chapter of the draft ITO charter.[23] The GATT emerged as a permanent forum for international trade negotiations once it became clear that the ITO would not be established. A similar pattern occurred with respect to commodity market regulation. In March 1947, the developed states took the initiative in the UN Economic and Social Council (ECOSOC) of securing the passage of a resolution that explicitly endorsed the commodity trade chapter of the draft charter. It also created an Interim Coordinating Committee for International Commodity Agreements (ICCICA) to promote the implementation of the provisions relating to the convening of meetings on individual commodities until the ITO came into existence.[24] When the ITO scheme collapsed, ICCICA became a permanent body, but it was not really a forum where governments could discuss broad issues of commodity policy.

During the 1950s the institutions and rules of commodity regulation were unchanged. The ICCICA formed a number of study groups on specific commodities and in 1953 sponsored conferences that formulated ICAs for tin and sugar. More extensive negotiations on commodity problems occurred in the FAO's Committee on Commodity Problems and in the Commission on International Commodity Trade established by the UN in 1954. However, none of these bodies served as important centers for the generation of new norms on commodity trade during the 1950s.[25]

THE CREATION OF UNCTAD

The decade of the 1960s witnessed increasing attacks by the Third World on the existing institutional arrangements and norms that had governed postwar economic relations. A key development was the convening of the first United Nations Conference on Trade and Development in Geneva in March 1964. (UNCTAD was made a permanent subsidiary body of the UN General Assembly in December 1964.) The developing countries had lobbied vigorously in the early 1960s both for a special conference on trade and development and for a new organization devoted to promoting their international economic interests. The holding of the 1964 conference, and the subsequent decision to make UNCTAD a permanent institution, thus constituted a victory for the Third World, one that was to have a substantial impact on commodity politics.[26]

UNCTAD has given the developing countries a sympathetic forum in which to address a variety of economic issues, including those pertaining to commodity policy. In addition to substantive issues, a major topic of debate throughout the organization's existence has been its institutional character and the roles of various groups of countries in its decision-making process. Examination of this debate is particularly relevant for the present book, because since 1964 UNCTAD has been the most important forum dealing with international commodity policy.

The developing countries that attended UNCTAD I met before the conference and produced a Joint Declaration of the Developing Countries, which spelled out most of their demands. The issuance of this document marks the formation of the Group of 77, an institution that has had a major influence on the way in which international economic negotiations are structured. Originally consisting of 75 countries, by the time of the 1964 conference the group had grown to 77 as a result of the withdrawal of New Zealand and the addition of three more Third World states. This gave the developing world a clear majority at UNCTAD I, at which 120 states were in attendance.

Although they brought a long list of economic grievances and demands to the conference, it has been noted that for the G77 "the largest question overhanging the three-month proceedings was entirely political, namely, the institutionalization of some kind of permanent organization devoted to the broad goal of economic development."[27] Many of the developing countries—as well as the communist states—called for the creation of a new, comprehensive international trade organization that would, inter alia, subsume the GATT and provide an institutional and normative framework for discussions of commodity issues.[28] They hoped that such a body would legislate new international rules for commodity control that would be *binding* on the participants in individual commodity conferences. The developed countries indicated immediately that a new ITO (in which LDCs would have a clear majority) designed to control both the GATT and commodity issues was out of the question.

Negotiations then turned to the legal and institutional character of UNCTAD itself. The developed countries wanted it to be subordinate to ECOSOC, in which they wielded considerable influence, whereas the developing countries argued that UNCTAD ought to be responsible to the General Assembly, a universal body in which their numerical primacy gave them a decisive political edge. The G77 emerged victorious on this issue when it was decided that UNCTAD would report to the General Assembly, although as a concession to the developed countries it was also agreed that it would do so "through" ECOSOC. The developing countries succeeded as well in obtaining authority for UNCTAD to sponsor conferences to draw up binding legal instruments such as commodity agreements, a power that the developed states had hoped to retain exclusively for ECOSOC.[29]

One contentious issue dealt with at UNCTAD I related to voting in both the conference itself and its executive council, the Trade and Development Board (TDB). The developed countries sought acceptance of a system of dual majorities in both organs. Under this proposal, a resolution would require simple majorities of both the industrialized and the developing nations. In addition, they favored equal representation of developed and developing countries on the Trade and Development Board. Eventually, a two-thirds voting formula was adopted in the case of the conference, and a simple majority formula for committees and the Trade and Development Board. Within the board the Latin American and Afro-Asian states (Groups A and C) were given 9 and 22 seats, respectively, the Western developed countries (Group B) 18 seats, and the communist bloc (Group D) 6 seats. Seats on all UNCTAD committees were allocated according to this group formula. The Western nations accepted this decision-making system because it was also agreed that, as with General Assembly resolutions, the decisions of UNCTAD bodies would be solely recommendatory.

In the debate over how many standing committees to create within the new organization, developed-country delegates did not oppose the establishment of a permanent Committee on Commodities to take over the responsibilities historically vested in ICCICA. However, they successfully argued that drawing up multilateral legal instruments such as ICAs should remain the prerogative of individual commodity conferences. While such conferences might well be sponsored by UNCTAD, they would be free to determine their own decision-making procedures and substantive rules.[30]

UNCTAD came into existence on December 12, 1964, when the General Assembly passed Resolution 1995. It immediately took over the functions of ICCICA and became the center for global commodity discussions. Its new Committee on Commodities quickly developed into the main global body for developing new principles, promoting specific commodity accords, and facilitating coordination among other international organizations in the commodity field. This committee, like all UNCTAD bodies, would soon be preoccupied with LDC attempts to extract major concessions from the developed nations.

THE UNCTAD GROUP SYSTEM AND INSTITUTIONAL DEVELOPMENTS, 1964–1973

UNCTAD has evolved a new decision-making process that has spread to or been adopted by many other UN bodies.[31] The UNCTAD process involves the development of positions by, and the conduct of negotiations among, three well-organized groupings—the Group of 77, the Group B developed countries, and the East European communist states.[32] After UNCTAD I, the developed, market-economy countries in Group B, who number about 25, began to coordinate their policies through the Organization for Economic Cooperation and Development (OECD) in

Paris as well as through regular meetings in Geneva. Although the most powerful Group B countries naturally exert greater influence in decision-making than smaller states, often the strong opposition of even a single small member to a particular LDC proposal will lead the other Group B members to support its position. Because of the need to accommodate the views of the least tractable members in hammering out a Group B stance, its positions often appear to be "the minimum common denominator" of the members' views, or, as Branislav Gosovic put it, "the sum of the most negative positions on the different components of a proposal."[33] Seldom if ever do the developed countries originate a proposal within the UNCTAD setting; rather, their behavior is overwhelmingly reactive. As will be seen, significant differences exist among Group B countries on some international economic issues. At times the so-called like-minded countries—the Scandinavian states especially—display considerable public sympathy for the general thrust of proposals made by the developing countries and the UNCTAD Secretariat, and on individual policy issues a host of fracture lines may appear. Such internal splits can assist Third World efforts to obtain changes.

Since 1964 the G77 has grown to over 125 states, and it now constitutes over 75 percent of the UNCTAD membership.[34] From the birth of UNCTAD, the G77 has been organized into three subgroups—the Latin Americans, the Africans, and the Asians. The first two coordinate their policies through the Special Commission on Latin American Coordination and the Economic Commission for Africa. The Asian states tend to be much more loosely organized.[35] On all agenda items each of the three subgroups will meet, and a common G77 position will be worked out by representatives of the three groupings, the chairman of the G77, and often UNCTAD staff members. Although the G77 lacks a secretariat and a formal organizational existence, "UNCTAD personnel have for practical purposes fulfilled the function of a secretariat for the Group of 77."[36] UNCTAD staff members generate proposals and are also very active in mediating and resolving conflicts among the LDCs.[37]

A high-level ministerial meeting of the G77 occurs every three or four years, just before each UNCTAD conference, in order to articulate the positions and demands of the Third World. Since the G77's inception, it has been agreed that all members have an effective veto. The basic mode of decision-making thus requires consensus, which is achieved "when no state has taken a formal exception to the course of action that is being proposed."[38] Rarely will a single state exercise its implicit veto power, but the general rule has meant that concerted efforts must be made to accommodate the views of all members when drafting a negotiating position. As one critic has written, often conflicts within the group "have been resolved by addition: that is, the final Group package simply incorporates everyone's demands."[39] As a result, G77 positions often contain extravagant demands that are all but guaranteed to meet with summary rejection from most of Group B, and even cause dismissal of the whole G77 package. Because the negotiating process is so complex and takes so much time and energy, many G77 members at times appear to eschew even considering whether a proposal is likely to be accepted by the developed countries, from whom concessions must of course be won if the desired reforms are to be achieved. The imperative of developing a G77 position assumes more importance than reaching an accord with other groups.[40]

The last and smallest of the three groups in the UNCTAD system is Group D, the communist states of Eastern Europe. It has 9 members, including the two Soviet republics with UN membership; they coordinate their policies through the Council for Mutual Economic Assistance (CMEA). They are not normally prominent participants in UNCTAD, and generally blame the problems of Third World countries on the past and present policies of the capitalist states.[41]

Once Groups B and D and the G77 have each worked out a negotiating position on a particular issue, a "contact group" of representatives from the groups will meet in an attempt to achieve agreement. Because much of what transpires in UNCTAD consists of the G77 making demands of Group B, in some cases only these two groups will be involved in reaching an accord. Often Group B and the G77 are so far apart that agreement is impossible, and positions must be reformulated. But since "compromises threaten to unravel one or the other side's package," both groups—but especially the G77, which is more unwieldy and heterogeneous—can be very reluctant to modify their initial proposals.[42] Attempts to redraft a negotiating position may require new trade-offs that affect not only the issue under consideration but others as well. The immoderation encouraged by the group negotiating system was trenchantly criticized in a Dutch submission to UNCTAD, which observed that group positions

tend to be based on the extremes within each group. As a modified Gresham's Law, one could say: extreme positions drive out moderate ones. Maximum demands confront minimum offers. Moreover, the group positions have, once arrived at, turned out to be changeable only with the greatest difficulty. This group rigidity has played havoc with the traditional method, according to which countries most directly involved in a problem strive to work out a compromise, and, during and after the working out of a compromise, endeavour to convince their allies and friends that their compromise is reasonable.[43]

In spite of these criticisms and evident shortcomings, the group system that first appeared at UNCTAD in 1964 has remained intact. It has been the quintessential feature of deliberations in UNCTAD.

In the years following UNCTAD I commodity issues were addressed in a variety of bodies. At both the 1968 New Delhi and the 1972 Santiago Conference commodity policy was considered at length. Within UNCTAD, ongoing discussion was centered in the Committee on Commodities, which soon established under its auspices a Group on Synthetics and Substitutes to deal with that important issue. Both the United Nations Committee on Tungsten and its Lead and Zinc Study Group were formally brought under the aegis of UNCTAD in the 1960s, although they continued to function autonomously. UNCTAD also established several ad hoc bodies to study primary commodities of export interest to the developing countries, and in conjunction with the FAO created a Working Party on Forest and Timber Products. UNCTAD did not, however, bring under its supervision the many FAO commodity study groups (later retitled "intergovernmental groups") that proliferated during this time, and in fact an institutional rivalry was clearly developing between these two bodies in the commodities field. Finally, UNCTAD sponsored a number of conferences to renegotiate ICAs agreed to before 1964, and also, following unsuccessful attempts in 1966 and 1967, sponsored a conference that produced the 1972 International Cocoa Agreement.

The debate over "the institutional issue" at UNCTAD I continued during meetings of the Trade and Development Board and at the 1968 and 1972 conferences. The highly contentious proposal to create a comprehensive trade organization was reintroduced periodically by the G77, but Group B was quick to reject it. Another institutional issue involved UNCTAD's ability to help implement its recommendations. General Assembly Resolution 1995 creating UNCTAD had papered over the differences between the developing and developed states on this question by simply calling on the board to "keep under review and take appropriate action" for the implementation of all decisions. In part, the divergence between developed and developing states flowed from the fact that the former had opposed many of the principles passed at UNCTAD I; but in addition there was a broader disagreement over UNCTAD's proper role and legal authority in international trade relations. The G77 wanted countries to be required to provide detailed information on their compliance with UNCTAD decisions; wanted the annual report on implementation to examine each country's compliance with each decision; and wanted the board to examine critically the performance of each state. Group B states were adamant that UNCTAD not engage in a country-by-country examination. Group B's intransigence succeeded in that at the second TDB meeting in 1965, the board simply called on the Secretary General to prepare annually "a report on international trade and economic development with particular reference to the rates of growth and progress made in economic development of developing countries. . . . "[44] Reviews of implementation soon evolved into little more than bland discussions of recent economic progress in the Third World.[45]

As noted above, in creating UNCTAD, the General Assembly bestowed on it the conference-sponsorship function previously vested in ICCICA, and before 1974 UNCTAD sponsored several conferences intended to produce commodity agreements. Most members of existing commodity organizations did not object to UNCTAD's sponsorship, but they tended to guard rather jealously the right of ICA members to generate their own proposals and to decide when conferences would be held. This was true both of the memberships of the international commodity organizations and of the FAO study groups. The members of these bodies—especially the developed states, but many LDCs as well—successfully fought to retain their right to determine the procedural and substantive rules of their conferences and agreements.[46]

In retrospect it is evident that the Group of 77 accomplished little in its quest to enhance the role of UNCTAD or their own collective power in the formal decision-making procedures for commodity negotiations during the decade 1964–73. No progress was made in breathing real life into the idea of an international trade organization, and the G77 failed to win for UNCTAD any teeth to implement its decisions. UNCTAD's Committee on Commodities, Trade and Development Board, and Secretary General were certainly able to press for the convening of international commodity consultations, but in the end a joint decision by the producers and consumers of an individual commodity was necessary to obtain an agreement. Moreover, each commodity conference remained free to dictate its own rules, and participants were not obliged to go along with a treaty if they did not wish to. In short, not much had changed since the years before 1964.[47]

SUBSTANTIVE DEVELOPMENTS IN THE GLOBAL COMMODITY REGIME, 1964-1973

The policy discussions in UNCTAD during the same period reveal a fairly consistent pattern. The developing countries, assisted and sometimes prodded by the Secretariat, would complain about various problems such as price instability, declining price trends, or competition from synthetics, and then proceed to lay siege to one or more of the Havana Charter commodity provisions. The developed countries would typically respond by first admitting that international trade in primary commodities often posed difficulties for LDC exporters, but then suggesting that fundamental changes in the Havana Charter principles were not required to deal with the difficulties. The communist countries were normally quiet, but sometimes they would inveigh against the system of international economic exploitation that they alleged was the root cause of the problems facing Third World commodity producers. Rarer, but in some ways more interesting, were the occasional doubts they expressed about the feasibility of certain reform proposals advanced by the G77.

The records of UNCTAD commodity discussions over the decade show that a number of specific issues received consistent attention. The most important by far was what we term "price policy," i.e., the interrelated questions of commodity price instability, the real price trend of commodities exported by LDCs, and the levels and trends of their commodity export earnings. A related issue concerned the desirability of using different instruments—chiefly export or production controls and buffer stocks—to regulate commodity prices. Other issues regularly discussed included competition from synthetics, the appropriate basis for negotiating agreements (by commodity or for groups of commodities), and market access for LDC exports. Compensatory financing, another key commodity-related issue, was also discussed regularly; it is treated separately later in this chapter. Since the nature and tone of the debates that took place did not change significantly during the years under review, the discussion below of each of these issues encompasses the entire 1964–73 period.

Commodity Price Policy

Price policy has long been a major preoccupation of the developing countries in UNCTAD. As noted in chapter 1, they have felt that the instability characteristic of many commodity markets causes hardship by inducing periodic downturns in export earnings. In addition, as was also noted, the UNCTAD Secretariat and the G77 have propounded the thesis that the terms of trade have moved against LDC commodity producers, an argument that has generated considerable controversy among economists. Proposals to index primary commodity prices to prices of manufactured goods have thus joined the compendium of G77 prescriptions.

At UNCTAD I Secretary General Raul Prebisch, noting that primary commodities accounted for almost 90 percent of LDCs' total export earnings, argued strongly in favor of international measures to reduce price fluctuations and to expand the earnings of Third World producers. A central element of his argument was that commodity prices had declined relative to prices of manufactured goods. Since developing countries were overwhelmingly exporters of the former (mainly to the Western countries) and importers of the latter (mainly from the Western countries), their growth and development were being stymied by the deteriorating terms of trade of their major exports.[48] Prebisch thus recommended that ICAs be established to stabilize *and* increase the trend prices of commodities largely exported by LDCs. He also suggested that developed countries lower their support prices for domestic agricultural commodities that competed with LDC exports, improve LDC access to their markets, and provide generous compensatory financing to LDCs with commodity-earnings shortfalls.[49]

The tone of the UNCTAD I debate was set by the Secretariat official who initiated the discussions. She stressed the need to revamp significantly the principles of commodity control set forth in the Havana Charter. She also challenged the legitimacy of market price trends, noting that the commonly used standard of "'equitable and remunerative prices' . . . must be interpreted to relate to terms of import purchasing power, which enabled primary exporting countries to buy the imports which they needed."[50] Indexation and increased export earnings for developing countries were two themes consistently touched on by LDC representatives at the conference. Overall, the G77 was clearly calling for a dramatic break with the norms of the Havana Charter.

The developed countries were quick to rebut the precepts of the challenge. The Japanese delegate stated simply that "excessive emphasis on the artificial raising of prices would impose an undue burden on the major importing countries." The British representative chose a more indirect route of attack, arguing that the level of government intervention and the price standards advocated by the developing countries would in fact be inimical to their own long-term interests:

the knowledge that high prices would be maintained for a long period would stimulate the search for substitute products; to increase prices to the consumer, be it through the imposition of export quotas or the imposition of compensatory taxes, would reduce demand; if a reduction in demand was artifically imposed there was bound to be a surplus of supply and producing countries would be faced with the choice of holding large stocks off the market or cutting back production; and holding up prices by means of export quotas would penalize the efficient producing countries which could otherwise increase their export earnings; it would also adversely affect new producers for whom fair and adequate provision would barely be possible.[51]

It is interesting to record that during the debate on price policy the Soviet Union, then seeking to identify with the Third World, nonetheless appeared to endorse competitive markets—much to the disappointment of the leaders of the G77. At one point, for example, the Soviet delegate remarked that

prices should be determined on the basis of the following factors: the relationship between supply and demand; production costs and the possibility of obtaining a reasonable income for exporting countries; price changes through increased productivity, mechanization and improved agricultural methods; elasticity of demand in relation to price; and the maintenance of a reasonable relationship between prices for different commodities.[52]

In concluding, he leveled an implicit criticism against the G77 when he noted that his delegation "considered that it was wrong to finance the stabilization of markets at the expense of the consumer."[53]

The dissension made it impossible to achieve a consensus on the language to be used in the conference texts that articulated various international economic "principles." "General Principle Seven" was the major conference statement concerning commodity prices and LDC export earnings.

All countries should cooperate through suitable international arrangements, on an orderly basis, in implementing measures designed to increase and stabilize primary commodity export earnings, particularly of developing countries, at equitable and remunerative prices and to maintain a mutually acceptable relationship between the prices of manufactured goods and those of primary products.[54]

All 27 developed capitalist states at the conference either voted against or abstained on this principle because of its implicit support for indexation. The Soviet-bloc states supported it, satisfied that the "mutually acceptable" clause provided adequate protection.

With respect to commodity agreements, the conference recommended that a basic objective of ICAs be "to stimulate a dynamic and steady growth and insure reasonable predictability in the real export earnings of developing countries ... while taking into account the interests of consumers in importing countries." To this end, ICAs should promote "remunerative, equitable and stable prices for primary commodities, especially those exported by developing countries, having due regard for the import purchasing power of the commodities exported. ... "[55] Developed countries did not like the phrases "real export earnings" and "import purchasing power," and several recorded reservations; but overall they were prepared to back the recommendation because of the obliqueness of its references to indexation.

Another issue considered at UNCTAD I concerned the regulatory instruments to be used to implement an internationally accepted price policy (provided one were ever achieved). Several developed countries expressed serious reservations about the use of export and production controls, which could maintain higher commodity prices only by preventing "more efficient producers from expanding their production."[56] During the discussion of buffer stocks, the LDCs suggested that consumers in ICAs ought to contribute to financing such stocks. The only ICA up to that time that incorporated a buffer stock was the tin agreement in which producers alone had borne all the costs. Group B was noncommital, and no consensus was reached on which specific instruments should be employed by ICAs to regulate prices.

Sharp divisions between the G77 and Group B on price policy persisted throughout the decade. The developing countries reiterated their views at the Algiers ministerial meeting of the G77 held in October 1967 to prepare for an upcoming UNCTAD conference in New Delhi. The resulting Charter of Algiers stated:

The main objectives of pricing policy should be: (i) elimination of excessive price fluctuation; (ii) the highest possible earnings from the exports of primary products; [and] (iii) maintenance and increase of the purchasing power of the products exported by the developing countries in relation to their imports.[57]

At UNCTAD II in 1968, the developed countries rhetorically supported the goal of reduced price fluctuations, but as for promoting the "highest possible earnings," many Group B members professed not to understand what that term meant. The third proposal—to index commodity prices to those of manufactured imports—elicited unanimous Group B opposition. Representatives of developed countries pointed to the problems such a plan would cause because of the differences in terms of trade from country to country and the negative effects on LDC export earnings that could result from raising commodity prices above the market trend. They also voiced concern about the implications of indexation for international economic "efficiency," and even more so for the prices they would have to pay.[58]

Developing-country spokesmen chose not to dwell on the technical merits of indexation but rather emphasized what they saw as the inherent justice of the demand that they receive more for their exports. The Jamaican delegate expressed a representative view:

The terms of trade could never appreciably be altered if market forces were allowed free play. The industrialized countries were well aware of that fact, the more so since they had long realized the need for official protection of their agricultures in order to spare agricultural produce excessive competition from industrial products. In a recent year, the United States, the United Kingdom, and the countries of the European Economic Community had together spent up to 10 billion dollars on agricultural subsidies. For the sake of fairness alone, the same principles should in future be adopted throughout the world, thus helping to stabilize developing countries' export earnings from certain commodities and ending the deterioration in the terms of trade.[59]

No agreement could be reached on this issue, and it was referred to the Committee on Commodities for further attention. Nor was most of Group B prepared to accept the G77 demand for joint and equal producer-consumer financing of ICA buffer stocks.[60]

Intensive negotiations on principles continued in UNCTAD in the late 1960s and early 1970s.[61] At the G77's Lima Conference, held in late 1971 before UNCTAD III, the developing countries reiterated their support for "the principles and objectives set forth in the Algiers Charter, which retains every bit of its relevance...."[62] The general failure of UNCTAD III in 1972 was reflected in the absence of any progress on commodity price questions. Developed countries, while continuing to lend verbal support to price stabilization, remained implacably hostile to any form of indexation and were unwilling to endorse the use of export and production controls in a large number of commodity markets. Although they were more receptive to buffer stocks, most Group B countries continued to oppose the notion of obligatory joint financing. The chasm separating the G77 from Group B on price questions continued through 1973 and 1974. In ten years, UNCTAD negotiations yielded no agreements that revised the Havana Charter guidelines on this central issue.

Synthetics and Substitutes

Another commodity issue addressed at the 1964 conference and quite regularly thereafter was the impact of synthetics and substitutes on LDC commodity producers. Competition from synthetics has long clouded the market prospects for such exports as jute, cotton, hard fibers, and natural rubber. At the Geneva conference in 1964 the G77 did not ask Group B to curtail the production and development of synthetics. Instead, the conference resolution dealing with synthetics merely requested that the developed countries assist LDCs in producing and marketing their primary products and refrain from "giving special encouragement to the ... production of new synthetics which may displace other natural products."[63] At its first meeting in 1965, UNCTAD's Committee on Commodities appointed a group of 17 states to give the issue further attention; this body was later entitled the Permanent Group on Synthetics and Substitutes at the 1968 conference in New Delhi.

At the latter meeting the developing countries called on Group B to help finance research aimed at improving the competitive position of natural products and to stop subsidizing the development of synthetics.[64] Pakistan, which was especially concerned about jute and cotton, complained bitterly that the developed states "were producing synthetics to encroach upon the market of primary products of developing countries. They were thus in effect waging a war of economic aggression against such countries."[65] Some LDCs suggested that the industrialized countries should limit their production of synthetic materials and reserve a part of their domestic markets for the developing countries' natural products, but Group B showed no willingness to discuss this. Debate within the Committee on Commodities and the Permanent Group on Synthetics and Substitutes continued over the years 1968–73 and provided some useful information to producing countries on how to improve their productive processes and market their commodities. However, no substantive changes occurred in the policies of the developed states.[66]

At its Lima meeting in 1971 the G77 for the first time demanded that the developed states accept a formal commitment to protect and increase the market shares of natural products. They asked that the industrialized nations "not take measures in the context of their national policies which will encourage production of synthetics and substitutes which will compete with the natural products of developing countries," and called on Group B to "levy some measure of taxation on [synthetics] in order to raise funds for research and development programs for improving the competitive position of natural products of developing countries."[67] At the 1972 UNCTAD conference both the Western and the communist countries opposed these proposals, and the conference could pass only a tepid resolution asking states to support research projects designed to improve the competitiveness of natural products.[68]

The Basis for Negotiating Agreements

A long-standing source of dispute in the UNCTAD discussions has been the appropriate basis for negotiating agreements to regulate commodity markets. The Havana Charter specified that ICAs had to be negotiated on an individual basis and include both producers and consumers. At Geneva in 1964, some members of the UNCTAD Secretariat and a number of developing-country delegations suggested that more ICAs would be established if arrangements for several commodities were negotiated simultaneously, with some interdependence among the negotiating bodies. Group B responded with a defense of the traditional case-by-case approach and stressed the myriad differences among commodity markets. The conference resolution on this issue was a compromise. It stated that although ICAs "should usually be on a commodity-by-commodity basis," they could "also cover groups of commodities under certain circumstances."[69]

This issue also provoked extended debate at UNCTAD II and at the autumn 1968 meeting of the Committee on Commodities. Developed countries were virtually unanimous in their continued support for the commodity-by-commodity negotiating mode.[70] Before the 1972 Santiago conference the G77 again requested that the conference "adopt a set of generally accepted principles and guidelines with a view to promoting a rational international commodity policy in formulating a general agreement on commodity arrangements."[71] However, largely because of the skepticism of certain Latin American states and a few other LDCs, who were concerned that multicommodity deliberations might undermine existing ICAs, the G77 did not really press the issue at Santiago. The UNCTAD Secretariat complained of a "notable lack of success" in negotiating individual ICAs since UNCTAD II, and suggested that a multicommodity approach might usefully be pursued. But given what the deputy director of UNCTAD's commodities division termed delicately a "lack of support for a general approach" within the G77 itself, nothing could be achieved at this point.[72]

A related topic of debate that appeared on UNCTAD's agenda by the late 1960s was the legitimacy of collaboration among producers to influence markets. Chapter 1 mentioned the desire of the leading participants in the Havana Charter negotiations to prevent the development of producer cartels. Even then some LDCs had argued that they ought to be able to take unilateral action to stabilize prices of commodities of which they were major exporters. By the late 1960s, the lack of progress in forming producer-consumer ICAs convinced many developing countries—led by Algeria and the other key radical members of the nonaligned movement—to call for the creation of producer cartels among LDC commodity exporters.[73] The Algiers Charter of 1967 stated that "producing developing countries should consult and cooperate among themselves in order to defend and improve their terms of trade by effective coordination of their sales policies."[74]

Intermittent discussion of unilateral producer action took place in the Committee on Commodities in 1969 and 1970, and the developed countries finally agreed to a watered-down resolution permitting the Secretary General to organize separate meetings of producers and consumers "in exceptional circumstances," provided that all members of each group were invited to participate. In acquiescing, Group B made it palpably clear that such separate meetings had to be directed toward forming joint producer-consumer agreements, not producer associations.[75] Interestingly, the only country to record a formal reservation to this resolution was the Soviet Union, which spoke of the virtues inherent in the traditional producer-consumer negotiating format. However, perhaps embarrassed at being the only country attempting to stand in the way of what the G77 called "an important step forward," the Soviets suddenly withdrew their reservation at the next meeting of the Trade and Development Board in September 1970.[76] At UNCTAD III in 1972, in the face of stiff opposition from the United States and other Group B countries, a resolution was passed to establish a working group to prepare a draft charter on the economic rights and duties of states that would, inter alia, assert the legitimacy of producer cooperation and the unfettered sovereignty of countries over their natural resources, as requested by the G77 at Lima in 1971.[77] This decision foreshadowed the heightened interest of the Third World after 1973 in producer sovereignty and collaboration with respect to natural resources.

Market Access

A final commodity-related issue that commanded attention in UNCTAD throughout this period was market access. The ability of the Secretariat and the G77 to get the developed countries to negotiate seriously on the subject in UNCTAD has always been severely constrained by the existence of another institution with powerful legal and political authority over trade barriers, namely, the General Agreement on Tariffs and Trade. The developed countries have remained unwilling to see any of the GATT's authority devolve upon UNCTAD, where their influence is much weaker. They have opposed G77 efforts to negotiate on trade barriers within UNCTAD, and have also been reluctant to see UNCTAD try to fashion new international economic principles in this area. Although the LDCs generally have failed in their attempts to get the developed countries to discuss market access seriously outside the GATT, they have tried to address the subject in UNCTAD on many occasions.

At UNCTAD I the G77 pushed through "Special Principle Five," which called on developed countries to ensure that their domestic agricultural support policies did not prevent developing countries from "supplying a fair and reasonable proportion of the domestic consumption and the growth of such consumption. . . . "[78] Virtually all of Group B abstained during the vote on this principle. The conference also recommended a suspension of new trade barriers against any LDC exports (not just commodities), and a "substantial" reduction of developed countries' tariffs, quantitative restrictions, and internal revenue and fiscal charges imposed on LDC commodities. However, Group B made sure that the resolution was couched in language that eschewed any mention of concrete obligations, and in the period following the Geneva Conference they did nothing to implement these recommendations.[79]

At UNCTAD II the G77 repeated its call for no new trade barriers and demanded reductions in tariffs, quantitative restrictions, and revenue charges. The majority of the developed countries held that they could not accept additional commitments not to introduce barriers or to eliminate existing ones.[80] In September 1970 the Trade and Development Board adopted a resolution dealing with market access that emerged after lengthy negotiations within the Committee on Commodities. To secure the acquiescence of Group B, the language originally proposed by the G77 was diluted with several qualifying clauses and reservations, and the end result was little more than a wish list of actions that the developed countries "should" take "to the fullest extent possible" or "as far as possible."[81] The G77 again demanded no new trade barriers and the reduction of existing barriers in the Lima Declaration of 1971 and at UNCTAD III, but Group B still refused to offer anything but the hortatory commitments previously made, arguing that the upcoming GATT Multilateral Trade Negotiations would provide the appropriate forum for negotiations on market access.[82]

During the initial decade of its existence, UNCTAD succeeded in carving out a legitimate role for itself in the sphere of international commodities. It became the principal institution for discussion of the general principles and major issues of international commodity policy. On a more concrete level, it sponsored a conference in 1972 that led to the conclusion of a new ICA for cocoa as well as other conferences to renegotiate existing agreements for tin, coffee, wheat, and sugar. Yet the G77 was unable to use the institution to substantially reform—much less overthrow—the traditional Havana Charter regime.

The reluctance on the part of the developed countries—or at least most of them on most occasions—to accept the proposals of the G77 and the UNCTAD Secretariat testified to the persistence of a fundamental difference between North and South on commodity policy: while the LDCs increasingly believed that intergovernmental market regulation through ICAs and other schemes was *inherently desirable,* the developed Western countries continued to envisage commodity agreements as exceptions to the norm of free, unregulated commodity markets. Divisions between North and South on the particular issues discussed above are to a large extent traceable to this underlying difference.

THE NEW INTERNATIONAL ECONOMIC ORDER AND THE IPC, 1974–1981

Overview

The most vigorous efforts by the developing countries to change the postwar commodity regime occurred in the wake of the Arab oil embargo in 1973 and the subsequent fourfold increase in the price of petroleum. As was mentioned earlier, after OPEC's startling success in late 1973, the view quickly began to spread among the developing countries that the South now possessed a newfound "commodity power" that could be used to wring concessions from the developed states on a broad range of issues.

The next few years saw a succession of international conferences at which developing countries unveiled ambitious demands for change and sought to pry major concessions from the industrialized world.

The first key North-South confrontation came at the Sixth Special Session of the UN General Assembly on raw materials and development, held in April–May 1974. Debate was highly acrimonious. The developed countries, led by the United States, flatly refused to accede to the South's demands, including, again, the indexation of commodity prices and legitimation of producer cartels. A large majority of the industrialized nations either voted no or abstained on the two major resolutions of the session— the Declaration and the Program of Action on the Establishment of a New International Economic Order.[83] At the fall 1974 session of the General Assembly, the G77 again united to pass a general Charter of Economic Rights and Duties of States.[84] Then in February 1975 the nonaligned movement convened a Conference of Developing Countries on Raw Materials in Dakar, Senegal, to which all members of the G77 were invited. This session led to the further refinement of LDC positions on a wide array of commodity questions.

Until spring 1975 the dialogue between developing and developed countries was openly hostile, but thereafter the discussions became somewhat more constructive. The developed countries, particularly the United States, found that their intransigent position and harsh attacks on OPEC precipitated neither the expected split between the oil-exporting and developing oil-importing countries nor a retreat by the OPEC states on oil prices. For their part, many developing countries concluded that the G77's militant demands were not yielding significant results; they were also growing less optimistic about Third World resource power with the end of the 1972–74 commodity price boom. These changing attitudes led to a more harmonious diplomatic atmosphere and to a decision to hold a Seventh Special Session of the General Assembly on Development and International Economic Coorporation in September 1975. In October 1975 North and South also agreed to launch the Conference on International Economic Cooperation (CIEC). The developed countries originally wanted this conference to focus exclusively on energy, but the LDCs successfully insisted that it deal with the entire range of their NIEO demands. Twenty-seven states (18 developing and 9 developed) participated in the protracted conference, which extended from December 1975 to June 1977. The CIEC did not, however, produce much in the way of concrete agreements.

The deliberations in the General Assembly and the CIEC captured most of the headlines between 1974 and 1976, but UNCTAD was where the important commodity negotiations were actually taking place. UNCTAD's thrust began in early 1974 with a wide-ranging proposal by the new UNCTAD Secretary General, Gamani Corea of Sri Lanka, to the Preparatory Commission of the Sixth Special Session. He argued that an integrated program, encompassing multiple approaches to increased prices and producer earnings, should be developed, and that a key strategy should be to establish a large fund to finance the buffer-stock operations of existing and future ICAs.[85] The General Assembly agreed. At the end of the special session it called on UNCTAD to develop "an integrated program . . . for a comprehensive range of commodities of export interest to developing countries."[86] With this mandate, the Secretariat set about drafting a series of comprehensive proposals. The powerful influence of the UNCTAD Secretariat in the birth of the Integrated Program for Commodities was to continue throughout the various stages of its evolution.

During 1974 and 1975 the Secretariat issued a number of studies that analyzed various regulatory approaches to be included in the IPC.[87] The main proposals were the following: simultaneous negotiations on 15–20 commodities to formulate international commodity agreements; a new Common Fund to finance buffer stocks of international commodity organizations; expanded use of multilateral supply and purchase contracts between producers and consumers; the financing of diversification, processing, and research and development in LDC exporting countries; improved compensatory financing for shortfalls in LDC commodity export earnings; and better market access for LDC commodity exports. The last two subjects failed to provoke much debate, since it was soon evident that the industrialized nations would discuss them seriously only in the IMF and GATT, respectively. Nor did multilateral contracts attract a great deal of attention, despite the communist countries' claim that they were the best model for the management of international trade. The Western countries rejected the degree of government regulation of trade that such contracts would require.

The subsequent dialogue in UNCTAD thus largely focused on two proposals: simultaneous negotiations on a host of commodities of particular importance to LDCs, and the creation of a Common Fund to finance the buffer stocks of those commodities for which buffer stocks were regarded as feasible. In the end 10 of the 18 selected commodities were so regarded and were labeled the "core" commodities. Compensatory financing became central to the discussion of reform by the late 1970s, and is considered in some detail later in the chapter. The financing of diversification, processing, and research and development—often called "other measures"—also aroused considerable interest, but again was not discussed seriously until the late 1970s.

The Common Fund was advocated strongly by most members of the UNCTAD Secretariat as well as the G77 for several reasons. First, they assumed that the primary impediment to creating ICAs in the past had been a lack of adequate financing—a view not shared by most developed countries—and that the existence of a sizable fund from which concessional loans could be offered would be a catalyst to the formation of ICAs. Second, the Secretariat felt that money could be saved by creating a joint financing facility rather than separate ones for each commodity. It was posited that commodity prices rise and fall at different times, and that the proceeds from the sale of some stocks could be used to purchase others. These offsetting trends supposedly would reduce the amount of money that the various ICOs would jointly require for financing buffer stocks. Also, since the size of loans sought by the fund would be greater than those sought by individual ICOs, and the risks of such loans would be spread over a large number of commodity organizations, creditors would be prepared to offer lower interest rates. Finally, LDC and Secretariat supporters of the fund argued that the risk to governments from participating would be reduced because it would be spread over a number of ICAs rather than solely on the one or small number of which they were members.[88]

While these arguments—which had been put forward on behalf of comparable schemes by economists in the past—undoubtedly weighed heavily on the minds of Common Fund proponents, other factors also led them to favor this approach. In particular, a "euphoria about the new 'resource power' of the poor" was strong in some Third World circles, and many LDCs had exaggeraged expectations of support from OPEC states for Third World producers.[89] They hoped that their new leverage would enable them to win acceptance of the Common Fund, and that producers of "strong" commodities (e.g., minerals required by Western industries) would use their influence to assist producers of "weak" commodities (e.g., agricultural products for which substitutes could be found) when negotiating ICAs. In addition, the UNCTAD Secretariat and, to a lesser extent, the G77 membership were anxious to establish a new role for UNCTAD in international economic relations. Secretary General Corea, who assumed office in January 1974, pursued an aggressive organizational strategy, under pressure from the G77 leadership to exploit the prevailing climate. A well-financed Common Fund was attractive because it would provide the LDCs with significant financial rewards and necessitate the creation of a powerful new global body to administer it under UNCTAD's auspices. As one observer has commented: "The decision to pin down the overall goal to a specific ambitious effort possibly reflected a basic, unarticulated wisdom about survival: an awareness that without the continued stimulus of a meaningful job to be done, the organization would soon run down and its structure would atrophy."[90]

Throughout the negotiations to formulate the IPC from 1974 until UNCTAD IV in May 1976, most Group B countries sharply criticized the Common Fund scheme which, even with the exclusion of wheat and rice, was initially expected to cost at least $6 billion. They were willing to entertain the idea of negotiations on various individual commodities, but they believed that the G77's focus on price regulation for a wide range of commodities was misdirected. The United States and other Group B members suggested that ways to channel more private investment into LDC commodity industries had to be found. The United States advanced two proposals along these lines, one for an International Investment Trust unveiled at the Seventh Special Session in 1975, and the other, Secretary of State Henry Kissinger's proposed International Resources Bank sprung on surprised delegates at UNCTAD IV in May 1976. The United States and other developed countries had long worried that the flow of private investment into Third World mineral industries was inadequate. They hoped that new international investment bodies would lead to increased mineral production and thus reduce the risks faced by Western-based mining companies whose holdings had been expropriated or nationalized with increasing regularity.[91] However, the UNCTAD Secretariat and the G77 quickly rejected the idea of an investment bank, viewing it as little more than a disingenuous attempt to divert attention from the Common Fund and the other key elements of the IPC.

The first major confrontation on the Common Fund took place in the spring of 1976 at UNCTAD IV. The G77 demanded passage of a resolution authorizing the immediate commencement of negotiations on the fund. After prolonged, acrimonious discussion, Group B finally accepted a conference to discuss "*a* Common Fund," as well as negotiations on the 18 commodities.[92] The LDCs soon proclaimed that Group B was now bound to negotiate the establishment of "*the* Common Fund" as conceived by them, but this was not the case.[93] The first meetings began in late 1976, even though most of the developed countries remained adamantly opposed to the UNCTAD Secretariat/G77 version of the fund. A few Western European states were prepared to work toward a more modest, less expensive type of fund, but the United States and most of the larger Group B countries continued to favor the demise of the whole scheme.

The years 1974–77 were frenetic ones in North-South diplomacy. The developing nations put forward a host of reform proposals that prompted many negotiations, but little was accomplished. On individual commodities, various attempts at producer collaboration apart from OPEC largely failed. The CIEC terminated inconclusively in June 1977. Its only contribution to the commodity dialogue—and incidentally one of the few to flow from the entire conference—was an agreement by industrialized countries to accept a Comon Fund, albeit without a commitment to any specific characteristics. (The formal conference to consider the creation of a fund had actually started in late 1976.) This concession by the larger OECD nations was motivated mainly by a feeling that some step toward meeting the demands of the G77 was necessary to improve the overall climate of North-South relations. The United States was unhappy with the concession but bowed to the pressure of its European allies, especially the French and British.[94] The Common Fund talks finally yielded an agreement in June 1980, but it was an emasculated version of what the G77 had originally advocated, providing for virtually no subsidization of buffer stocks and very little financial assistance to LDCs for restructuring commodity industries. While the Common Fund negotiations were occurring, UNCTAD meetings on the 18 commodities were also proceeding; but these produced only one new ICA—for natural rubber.

Producer Collaboration and Indexation

At the Sixth Special Session of the General Assembly in the spring of 1974, and during the assembly meetings to draw up the Charter of Economic Rights and Duties of States in autumn of that year, the legitimacy of unilateral producer collaboration proved to be one of the most divisive subjects. The G77 submitted resolutions applauding producer groups' attempts to regulate commodity markets, and these were passed despite the negative votes and abstentions of the developed states. The G77 position was set out clearly in the economic charter: "All states have the right to associate in organizations of primary commodity producers.... Correspondingly all states have the duty to respect that right by refraining from applying economic and political measures that would limit it."[95] The developed countries, led by the United States, labored assiduously to have this article deleted but were voted down.

In 1974, Third World producers of coffee, copper, iron ore, mercury, natural rubber, bananas, and bauxite either created or strengthened existing producer associations and sought to influence the international markets for these commodities.[96] While for the most part they were not particularly successful, these initiatives helped to bolster the principle that LDC governments had the right to form cartels. Developed countries could do little to prevent such producer collaboration, and most of them soon stopped even trying. But neither could the developing countries prevent the industrial nations and their multinational corporations from taking steps to undermine producer cartels. The developed countries' continued support for the implicit Havana Charter norm against market regulation by producers also received a blow in 1975 when it was revealed that a number of Western governments and industries involved in the export of uranium—notably those of Canada, Australia, France, South Africa, and Britain—had established a secret cartel. Any protests by these major Western nations against Third World producer associations henceforth had a distinct ring of hypocrisy. At conferences sponsored by the G77 and the nonaligned movement in 1975 and 1976, the developing countries supported the formation of a Council of Producer Associations that would seek to encourage the creation of cartels, but little came of this initiative.[97] However, by this time few believed that the legitimacy of such efforts could effectively be challenged. Cartels could perhaps be thwarted by consumer power but not by appeals to international law.

As noted earlier, price policy for ICAs has always been an important issue, and for many years a significant number of developing countries have been strong advocates of indexation. Support for indexation was reflected in two UN resolutions: Declaration on the NIEO of April 1974 and the Charter of Economic Rights and Duties of States passed later that same year.[98] In December 1973 the UN General Assembly asked UNCTAD to prepare a report on indexation, which was published in July 1974.[99] Although the report suggested that indexation could have negative consequences for the global demand and exports of certain commodities, and might also raise the cost of some commodity imports to Third World states, the UNCTAD Secretariat firmly supported the principle in its first documents on the IPC, then just beginning to take shape. In July 1974 it noted that the acceptance of "an appropriate relationship with prices of essential industrial products imported by developing countries" could be an important method of assuring remunerative prices and preventing excessive short-term fluctuations.[100]

At a meeting of the Trade and Development Board in August–September 1974, most of the developed-country representatives criticized the concept, arguing that "indexation might bring about a serious misallocation of resources, since, by bringing rigidity into the pattern of relative prices for different commodities, and also into the price relationship between commodities and manufactures, it could prevent resources from being shifted to where they would be used more efficiently."[101] The meeting did, however, agree to continue examining the issue and requested that new studies be done. At about the same time the General Assembly asked for another study of indexation and instructed the UNCTAD Secretary General to convene a group of experts to undertake the project. This group met in late April 1975, but its members could not agree on whether there had been a decline in the terms of trade of commodities and, if so, how it should be rectified. A large majority of the members held that if indexation were to be employed, an indirect system would be preferable to a direct one.[102]

By late 1975 support for indexation within the G77 began to wane, especially among producers of the weaker agricultural commodities who feared its impact on world demand. But it remained part of the evolving Integrated Program because of pressure from the OPEC states and, to a lesser extent, from some producers of nonfuel mineral commodities.[103] The other members of the G77 felt that OPEC's diplomatic backing was crucial to the success of the whole IPC campaign. The UNCTAD IV resolution launching the IPC thus called for "pricing arrangements . . . which would be periodically reviewed and appropriately revised, taking into account, inter alia, movements and prices of imported manufactured goods, exchange rates, production and world inflation, and levels of production and consumption . . ."[104] Despite the inclusion of this provision, the developed countries refrained from voting against the resolution in order to allow the IPC negotiations finally to begin, although several recorded their opposition following its passage.

By the time of the preparatory meetings for the first Common Fund conference in March 1977, the G77 for all intents and purposes had dropped its insistence on indexation, thanks to both the continued vehement opposition of the developed states and the increasingly serious doubts of some G77 members.[105] A formal declaration of this shift in policy was not announced, but all the participants understood that indexation was no longer a central G77 objective. From then on most LDCs informally accepted the traditional norm of *stabilizing* prices around a long-term market trend. However, many saw stabilization (especially if accompanied by a commitment to defend a "reasonable" floor price) as a way of increasing earnings in the long term.

THE COMMON FUND: FINANCIAL SUPPORT FOR ICAs AND LDC POWER IN INTERNATIONAL ORGANIZATIONS

The head of one developed-country delegation to several Common Fund conferences remarked in an interview that at any given meeting the number of individuals with a thorough grasp of all the economic and political issues under discussion could be counted on one hand. Several other participants interviewed for this book added that, while most developing countries were woefully bereft of expertise and therefore had to rely on the UNCTAD Secretariat for assistance, many delegates from the developed world too found aspects of the fund proposal difficult to comprehend. The confusion and policy differences evident at meetings were in part due to the fact that the delegations were disparate groups composed of foreign ministry officials, finance ministry officials, and commodity experts from mining, agriculture, and trade ministries, with each group tending to understand only limited aspects of the whole debate. Given the complexity of the issues, any summary of the negotiations must necessarily ignore much interesting detail, and what follows outlines the essential features of the protracted debate.

The Common Fund negotiations can be divided into three periods. The first stretched from the unveiling of the proposal by the UNCTAD Secretariat in 1974 through to the November 1977 conference when Group B finally presented a detailed plan. From 1975 through the spring of 1977 the Scandinavians, Dutch, and French offered vague support for the Common Fund idea, but not until a series of European and broader Western meetings between March and June 1977 did the Group B countries actually commit themselves to working toward an accord. A special committee of the OECD under a U.S. chairman was formed to develop a plan, which was drawn up in time for the November 1977 conference. At this point two distinct negotiating proposals were finally on the table. The crucial second stage of the negotiations, when an agreement was reached, lasted from early 1978 through June 1980. During this period the G77 moved much further in the direction of the Group B position than Group B did toward G77's. Since the June 1980 agreement there has been a third stage of negotiations, one dominated by attempts to secure the required number of ratifications and to address various matters left unresolved in the final treaty.

Fund Negotiations, 1974–1977

The central issues in the Common Fund dialogue were, first, the sources of financing for the fund and, second, the terms of its loans to ICOs for buffer-stocking operations. The G77/UNCTAD Secretariat position, as enunciated in a series of documents from 1974 to 1977, advocated a "source" model for the fund, whereas Group B countered in late 1977 with what was called a "pool" model. The source proposal stipulated that the fund should obtain $2 billion of its funding from governments ($1 billion in subscriptions and another $1 billion to be used as collateral for borrowing by the fund), with the remaining $4 billion to come from loans secured on the commercial market. With such extensive government financing, the fund could provide loans to ICOs at concessional or below-market rates.[106]

Group B's pool proposal—which had been suggested by some developed countries before autumn 1977—assumed that the fund's financial resources should come from affiliated ICOs, loans raised on the commercial market, and "stock warrants" (i.e., certificates of ownership of commodity stocks given to the fund by ICOs in exchange for loans). Each affiliated ICO would determine its maximum financial requirements (MFR) and then deposit 75 percent of this sum (which would be raised from members) with the fund. The ICO could then borrow from the fund up to 100 percent of its MFR on the basis of both its financial contribution and its deposit of stock warrants with the fund. Under this pooling system the fund would *not* offer subsidized loans based on capital donations by all fund members. However, it "might provide some savings to commodity pacts through offsetting sales and purchases and better terms on loans (as risks to lenders would be spread over a number of commodities as collateral) and economies in negotiating larger loans than individual commodity organizations might need."[107]

One concession Group B made was to accept that the buffer-stocking operations of ICOs should henceforth be jointly and equally financed by producers and consumers, not just by producers as in the past. Thus, the ICO subscriptions to the fund would include contributions from the consuming countries. While Group B's styling of this as "a major concession" overstated its significance, it did represent a departure from their previous policies *toward those ICOs that they decided to join.*[108] The absence of any direct government contributions to the fund in the Group B plan suggests that the developed countries had accepted "their lowest common denominator on the far right"—namely, the preferred stance of Germany, the United States, Japan, and Britain.[109] As Robert Rothstein has observed, these countries "were intent on establishing a common fund that would do almost none of the things the Common Fund was meant to do."[110] The Soviets, despite their oft-stated sympathy for the plight of LDC commodity producers, supported a concept of the fund basically similar to that proposed by Group B.[111]

The G77 condemned the Group B plan, complaining that it was "so narrowly conceived that it virtually negated the kind of Common Fund envisaged in Resolution 93 (IV)."[112] It argued that a pooling scheme could not act as a catalyst for the creation of new ICAs because the loans for buffer-stocking operations would not be obtained at below-market rates, and added that Group B's plan would not provide adequate incentives for all ICOs to join the fund. The LDCs also pointed out that because financing under Group B's proposal would come mainly from ICOs rather than directly from governments, the developing countries would have to contribute a larger percentage of the fund's capital than their own plan had envisaged.[113]

While the fund debate in the latter part of the 1975–77 period centered largely on the differences between the source and pool models, several other important questions were raised. One closely related to the source versus pool debate concerned the powers of the fund to prescribe policies for individual ICOs. Another was the ability of the fund to assist LDC commodity producers *outside* the context of ICOs. Two issues arose here: could the fund seek to influence prices for commodities for which ICAs did *not* exist by buying and selling stocks? And would it be able to provide funding for developmental projects ("other measures")? Finally, there was the question of the decision-making structure of the fund. The LDCs hoped to acquire considerably more power there than they possessed in most other international economic organizations.

In the early stages of the negotiations the UNCTAD Secretariat and various leaders of the G77 sought to invest the fund with strong coordinating powers over ICOs. They specifically wanted to grant the fund the right to set commodity price objectives, establish rules for the operation of buffer stocks, and mandate supply-management measures.[114] Group B countries were not enamored of the idea that a body in which the developing countries were bound to have a dominant voice could dictate basic policy guidelines to hitherto independent organizations. Several major LDC producers in existing or projected ICOs (especially that for coffee) were likewise rather uneasy about the prospect of losing some of their influence over the management of commodity markets in which they had a major interest.[115] Given the inflexible posture of Group B on this issue, as well as the concerns of certain LDC producers, the autonomy of the ICOs was no longer in much doubt by the time of the November 1977 conference, although the desirability of providing the fund with some influence over the ICOs was still alluded to from time to time.

The proposal that the fund should provide aid to producers of commodities for which ICAs did not exist by buying and selling them was first introduced by the UNCTAD Secretariat.[116] It soon generated vigorous debate. The Asian and especially the African states, who did not export raw materials for which regulatory schemes existed or were likely to exist, became strong supporters. But, they received little sympathy from those G77 members involved in exporting "stronger" commodities. For its part, Group B claimed that acceptance of the proposal would be a prescription for economic chaos. If the fund were to buy stocks during a declining market and there were no production or export restraints, large losses would result because of storage costs and the need eventually to sell at a very low price. Group B made clear that it would accept the fund's cooperation only with those ICOs dedicated to price stabilization and based on sound economic practices.[117] This proposal was essentially abandoned by the time of the 1977 negotiations, but it was retained in UNCTAD and G77 submissions out of deference to the African states who continued to see little in the Common Fund scheme of potential benefit to themselves.[118]

From the very beginning of the discussions the financing of development projects from fund resources loomed as a critical issue, again largely because the African and South Asian LDCs anticipated few advantages from the financing of ICA buffer stocks. The Latin American and Southeast Asian LDCs, in contrast, were not enthusiastic about the inclusion of such "other measures," fearing that this would weaken the financial viability of the fund. But they knew that while they would be unlikely to benefit significantly from the "other measures"—the African and South Asian producers would lay claim to the lion's share of such funding—they "had little choice but to raise the common denominator" by agreeing to add the proposal in order to maintain G77 unity in the bargaining process.[119]

The 1975–77 period saw a standoff between Group B and the G77 on this issue. The G77 wanted funding not just for research on production and marketing but also for vertical expansion (e.g., the building of processing plants), industrial rehabilitation, and diversification into other sectors in situations of excess production. The industrialized countries opposed financing these projects because of the magnitude of the funds required and the likelihood that their own industries would be undercut. They argued that existing institutions were already supplying the necessary financial aid, and that it was in any case almost inconceivable that the fund would have significant leftover resources if its loans to ICOs for buffer-stocking were at concessional rates.[120] At the November 1977 conference Group B began to hint that it might be willing to consider a development assistance component for the fund if this were clearly separated from buffer-stock financing (i.e., the creation of two separate "accounts") and if other aspects of the fund were deemed acceptable. From this point on the Common Fund dialogue was focused on two administratively separate accounts: a first account, or "window," for buffer-stock financing, and a second account for financing development projects.

The question of the decision-making structure of the fund was a high priority for the G77 not only because they viewed it as critical to their ability to influence fund policies, but also because they wanted to reverse the practice of correlating power with states' financial contributions in international agencies such as the World Bank and the IMF. One of the South's chief objectives in seeking a New International Economic Order was to alter this situation.[121] During the early stages of negotiations on institutional matters the debate focused almost solely on the weight to be given respectively to the principle of sovereign equality and to the size of states' financial contributions in distributing votes. Group B spokesmen made it clear that "if members of Group B were to participate in a Common Fund, they would insist on a close relationship between contributions and voting rights."[122] Many of the statements of G77 members stressed the need to establish a new model for voting arrangements. Some LDCs also hoped that the fund's voting system and its powers with respect to ICOs would afford them greater influence over ICO policies. As one analyst wrote: "Since they are largely exporters, developing countries cannot have a decisive role in individual ICAs which are equally controlled by exporters and importers. But if they can control the central institution, they can influence the entire course of the IPC."[123] As on so many fund issues, the two sides established general positions in the years 1975–77, but the hard bargaining did not commence until 1978.

Fund Negotiations, 1978–1980

The period 1975–77 ended in a mood of acrimony as the G77 terminated the November 1977 conference before it was due to end. In part, the intransigence evident on both sides was a product of dissension within each group, especially the G77; neither could agree on a new negotiating position. But at three major negotiating conferences held over the next two and a half years—November 1978, March 1979, and June 1980—Group B and the G77 finally came to an agreement. The G77 made the most extensive concessions during this process, but compromises were also accepted by Group B. Interestingly, a number of major commodity producers from Latin America and Southeast Asia went along with the Common Fund treaty despite serious reservations about its benefits for the ICOs to which they belonged. But by the late 1970s there was so much pressure from the UNCTAD Secretariat and the G77 leadership to salvage something from the IPC negotiations, and to achieve progress in realizing a New International Economic Order, that public rejection of the scheme became almost impossible for G77 members.[124]

The debate over the source and pool models was firmly resolved in favor of the latter. The initial concessions by the UNCTAD Secretariat and the G77 were contained in a new proposal submitted at the November 1978 conference.[125] This accepted a reduction in the amount of government contributions to be paid to the fund from $2 billion to $500 million, and reversed the previous G77 position on ICO contributions by stating that the ICOs should deposit 25 percent of their maximum financial requirements and certificates of stock ownership with the fund. On the basis of these contributions each ICO would be entitled to borrow up to 100 percent of its MFR. This concession was welcomed by the Group B countries, who now indicated for the first time that they were willing to entertain direct government subscriptions to the fund, although they remained uneasy about the figures contained in the G77/Secretariat proposal.

Between the November 1978 and the March 1979 conferences the G77 moved further toward Group B's position. At the 1979 meeting reduced dollar figures were agreed to, and these were finally incorporated into the June 1980 treaty. The treaty stipulates that governments should collectively contribute $400 million to the "First Account" for buffer-stock financing, one half in cash and one half in collateral to be used for borrowing by the fund. Affiliated ICOs are required to deposit with the Fund cash or stock warrants equal to one-third of their MFRs and to provide guarantee capital for the other two-thirds. Particularly important is the provision that the government subscriptions cannot be loaned directly by the fund; they can only be used as collateral for its borrowings and to cover its administrative costs and short-term liquidity needs. This means that the fund's loans to ICOs *cannot* be at concessional rates and must reflect the market rates at which the fund itself has to borrow. Thus, at best the ICOs might be able to obtain loans at rates marginally below those prevailing on the commercial market as a result of the spreading of risk and the volume of fund borrowings. Only those ICOs with joint producer-consumer financing of buffer stocks are eligible to affiliate with the fund. LDC producers had long sought to gain acceptance of the norm of joint producer-consumer financing, and in the Common Fund agreement they finally succeeded.

On the question of the responsibilities of individual states and groups with respect to the $400 million required for the First Account, the following formula was accepted: each country is to contribute $1 million to the fund, with the remaining sum required for the First Account to be divided on the following basis—Group B, 68 percent; Group D, 17 percent; the Group of 77, 10 percent; and China, 5 percent.[126]

The first major concessions on the "Second Account," or the financing of development projects, also came at the November 1978 conference. The UNCTAD Secretariat now proposed that the total account be reduced from $1 billion to $300 million, with two-thirds coming from voluntary contributions. It also agreed to restrict "eligible projects" to those having to do with research and development, marketing, and limited aspects of vertical diversification, thus dropping its previous demands for the inclusion of horizontal diversification, industrial rehabilitation for countries threatened by synthetics, and ambitious efforts at vertical diversification.[127] Group B welcomed this initiative but insisted that *all* Second Account funding should come from voluntary contributions.[128] In the end the final accord stated that from the sum of the $1 million mandatory assessments, $70 million should go to the Second Account. The treaty also provided that Second Account disbursements could be in the form of concessional loans or grants, and that they had to be sponsored by international commodity bodies composed of both producers and consumers.[129] The latter provision militates against the creation of producer cartels. Overall, the Second Account offers only limited resources for restructuring commodity markets. Little funding is to be provided for capital investment, and none at all for projects to assist LDC producers to expand control of other sectors of the same industry or to move workers into new industries.

The last major issue to be resolved was the fund's decision-making structure. Much time was spent in 1978 debating what weight to give to states' financial contributions, their prominence in commodity markets, and the principle of sovereign equality. The discussions centered on the percentage of total votes to be given to the UNCTAD negotiating groups as well as the percentages required for passage on different types of votes. At the March 1979 conference the G77 called for the following distribution: G77, 50 percent; Group B, 40 percent; Group D, 8 percent; and China, 2 percent. For its part, Group B wanted equal shares of 45 percent for itself and the G77. Even this was a significant concession from past Group B policy, given that the developed states were to be responsible for 68 percent of the fund's subscriptions.[130] Eventually, after the Europeans had pressured the United States and serious divisions had appeared within the U.S. delegation, the following formula was accepted: G77, 47 percent; Group B, 42 percent; Group D, 8 percent; and China, 3 percent. Some members of the U.S. delegation opposed this formula, but a high-level Washington review of the issue backed the compromise.[131]

While the United States and the other Group B states suffered a defeat on the fund voting distribution, they made sure that the provisions concerning required majorities for different types of votes (three-quarters, two-thirds, and one-half) would still allow them to defeat important resolutions.[132] For example, three-quarters or "highly qualified" majorities are required to alter the method of payment, to revise subscriptions, to change the guarantee capital provided by ICOs, and to amend the treaty. During the negotiations the U.S. delegation was commited to winning a veto power for what it termed "the G5 bloc" (the United States, Britain, West Germany, Japan, and Canada) over virtually all significant fund decisions. At times the Scandinavian delegations and the Dutch were at such loggerheads with the larger developed states on this and other fund issues that they were viewed as "vendeurs" by many Group B countries.[133]

At the June 1980 conference that approved the Common Fund agreement, UNCTAD Secretary General Gamani Corea stressed the importance of the fund's decision-making structure, noting that it was "different from that prevailing in any other financial institution" and "stood in contrast with that of the Bretton Woods institutions, where developing countries played only a peripheral role." He concluded that "it marked a significant innovation in international institutions concerned with economic cooperation."[134] A similar comment was made by a long-time observer of international trade institutions and negotiations, who wrote that the Common Fund structure was "indeed a far cry from the Bretton Woods institutionş and may well constitute an initial breakthrough in [the] North-South dialogue."[135] This is certainly possible. Fund votes are not correlated primarily with financial contributions, and the G77 enjoys a larger number of votes than Group B. But it would be wrong to conclude that the developing countries have achieved a decisive decision-making position in the fund. The developed countries as a whole, and indeed just five of the most powerful, have an effective veto power. The North still holds the reins firmly in its hands.

A comprehensive analysis of why the Common Fund treaty was negotiated would encompass a host of factors, only a small number of which deserve emphasis here. First, the role of the UNCTAD Secretariat was critical to the generation and the revision of the fund proposals. The Secretariat served as the de facto bargaining arm of the G77. Few developing countries sent delegations with a reasonable grasp of the technical details of the fund; so the G77's overwhelming dependence on the Secretariat is easy to understand. As far as the Secretariat itself was concerned, it sought an agreement because the organization's reputation, if not its very future, had been staked on the outcome of the IPC and its centerpiece, the Common Fund. If the long and tortuous negotiations on the fund yielded nothing, both the organization and its leadership could have been seriously discredited in the eyes of the developing world. Eventually the UNCTAD Secretariat chose to accept an emasculated version of what it had originally put forward in order to salvage something, and it was very active in seeking to convince the LDCs to accept this scaled-down fund.

Second, the Common Fund came to assume a symbolic importance for the G77, or at least its diplomatic leadership in Geneva, during the late 1970s. As optimism about the dawn of a more egalitarian global economic order began to fade in the late 1970s, the fund was viewed as one of the few possible accomplishments of the NIEO campaign. One reason why the G77 focused (and was inflexible) on the fund voting formula was that this seemed to be the last area where a significant victory over Group B could be realized in the quest to promote the NIEO. The G77 was basically defeated on the question of the obligation of the developed countries to raise prices and earnings of LDC commodity exports when a pooling as opposed to a source model for the fund was accepted. The outcome of the negotiations on decision-making allowed the G77 leadership to maintain that a breakthrough of sorts had been achieved.

Third, the developed countries, particularly the Western Europeans, were sufficiently worried about the potential Third World reaction to the complete failure of its lobbying for NIEO proposals that they felt it essential to make some concessions. In the late stages of the CIEC in the spring of 1977, they concluded that one such concession would be the grudging acceptance of "a Common Fund." The G77 had warned that the fund's defeat "could severely endanger any chance for North-South détente,"[136] and many feared a growing alienation between the First and Third Worlds if some progress in the North-South dialogue were not quickly recorded. The developed countries did not believe that the South could impose meaningful sanctions on the West, and they were also properly dubious of the extent to which the statements of Geneva-based LDC diplomats actually reflected the views and expectations of their governmental superiors.[137] But at the same time, there was a fear among Group B members that the absence of any progress could have negative long-run consequences for their overall relations with the developing nations. It is necessary to repeat, however, that most Northern countries were prepared to commit only relatively small sums of money to the Common Fund, and would not countenance major changes in the structure of international commodity markets. The realization by 1978 that very few new ICAs were likely to emerge from the IPC negotiations, and that many existing ICOs might choose not to affiliate with the fund, also made Group B more willing to accept the Common Fund.

A final factor was the pressure that proponents of an accord put on reluctant members of their own groupings. Within Group B, the U.S. decision in the spring of 1977 to negotiate a Common Fund was largely due to pressure from its European allies; the same was true of U.S. acceptance of the fund voting arrangements in March 1979. During the Group B talks in the OECD Committee on the Common Fund (created in the summer of 1977) the French became "a swing factor" between the "softliners" (the Scandinavians and the Dutch) and the "hardliners" (the United States, West Germany, and to a lesser extent Britain), and their influence was often decisive. They usually sided with the larger and more conservative states, but occasionally they wavered and had a moderating influence on the policies of other major Western countries. As for the Group 77, its leaders often put very effective pressure on dissidents to keep silent. Several of the Asian newly industrializing countries (NICs) were cool to the fund because they feared it would increase the prices of their commodity imports; the same was true of some relatively well-to-do and resource-rich Latin American countries such as Brazil and Argentina. Brazil, for instance, made it known that it opposed any impingements by the fund on the autonomy of the commodity organizations, and it worked to lessen the likelihood that the treaty would come into force by arguing for stringent ratification requirements. However, even Brazil never *publicly* rejected the fund. Like other LDCs harboring various doubts about the proposal, Brazil chose not to risk explicit criticism and ostracism by the G77.[138]

Post-1980 Developments Concerning the Fund Treaty

As so often occurs with international treaties, the struggle to secure the entry-into-force of the Common Fund accord has been almost as long and arduous as the process of negotiating it. The treaty states that entry-into-force requires acceptances by 90 states that collectively account for at least 66.66 percent of the financial subscriptions. The original target date for reaching these figures was March 1982, but the deadline has had to be extended several times. After the 1980 conference ratifications increased gradually, finally reaching 90 states in January 1986. However, these ratifications accounted for only 57.87 percent of the subscriptions. Among the more than 50 UN members who had not accepted it were a good number of developing countries, including some important Latin American commodity exporters. But, more important for the treaty, the nonratifiers included the United States and the Soviet bloc, which account for 15.71 and 10.21 percent, respectively, of fund subscriptions.[139] Finally, at UNCTAD VII in July 1987 the Soviet Union, in a gesture of goodwill toward the Third World, announced it would ratify the treaty—thus assuring its entry into force.

Throughout the lengthy discussions aimed at implementing the fund treaty, it has been evident that some members of the G77 have been either hostile or indifferent. Several of these states are members of existing international commodity organizations, and are skeptical of the wisdom of having their organizations affiliate with the fund because of the financial costs involved and the uncertain benefits. In the 1981–82 period, Malaysia refused to accept it, apparently surmising that the tin and rubber organizations could do at least as well raising loans without the fund. It was also worried that both ICOs would be more hesitant to increase their floor prices if this meant increasing their "maximum financial requirements," and thus their financial contributions to the fund. However, in late 1983, in the wake of very depressed global commodity prices, Malaysia ratified the agreement and several LDC members of other ICOs also became more favorably disposed toward it than they had been over the previous two years.[140]

Many African members of the G77 have been noticeably unenthusiastic, believing that the scheme would be of little direct benefit to them. In 1981–82 several African countries claimed that their failure to accept the agreement was due to "technical problems," and the UNCTAD Secretariat dispatched officials to African capitals to explain the agreement to doubtful governments. By mid-1984, in large part thanks to a decision by the OPEC states to pay the required $1 million subscriptions for each of the 35 least developed LDCs (most of which are African), approximately 30 African countries had ratified the fund accord. Throughout the early 1980s, the constant prodding of the UNCTAD Secretariat was a significant factor behind the decisions of a number of G77 members to accept the agreement.[141]

Virtually all the Western European states and Japan have ratified the treaty because they have not wanted to be seen as undermining one of the few accords to emerge from the NIEO dialogue. The United States has always held a more negative view, and this intensified under the Reagan administration. As for the Soviet Union and its allies, their refusal to accept the treaty for many years was evidently based on a strong reluctance to fund international financial organizations. The Soviets probably realized in 1987 that they could score political gains against the United States in the Third World by accepting the treaty, since Washington seemed dead set against the fund. Also, with the demise of the tin agreement and the general disfavor into which market regulation had fallen, they probably thought that the fund's first account would be rather inactive—if not dormant.

In concluding this discussion of the Common Fund, it is important to consider what significance the fund will have when it comes into existence. The short answer is—not much. The principal gains for Third World states will likely consist of modest financial assistance from the second account. It will have little impact on the formation of new commodity accords because its loans will be at very close to market rates. Also, there are only two operating ICAs with buffer stocks (natural rubber and cocoa), and it is uncertain whether their members—especially consumers, but also some producers—will want to affiliate with the fund. Even if several new ICAs with jointly funded stocks were created, the fund would yield few benefits because of the interest rates it would charge. On the more positive side, the fund agreement does establish the principle that buffer stocks should be jointly financed. Moreover, its voting system creates a precedent for the design of future international economic organizations. But overall the Common Fund reflects the norms of the Havana Charter regime on the conditions justifying the creation of ICAs, the price objectives of ICAs, and the bestowal of veto power in ICOs on important members. Its provisions for equal cost sharing and a more "democratic" distribution of votes constitute quite marginal changes to the traditional regime.

COMPENSATORY FINANCING NEGOTIATIONS

Although international commodity negotiations since World War II have focused mainly on proposals designed to regulate market prices, efforts have also been made to address the issue of export earnings directly by providing LDC exporters with funds when their earnings decline. These negotiations on "compensatory financing" have taken place in the IMF and, to a lesser extent, in UNCTAD. In addition, the European Community has developed a related scheme as part of its Lomé agreements with the African, Caribbean, and Pacific (ACP) countries.

Many developing countries, while seeking to achieve improved global compensatory financing arrangements, have continued to direct most of their attention toward ICAs and other proposals to regulate supplies and prices directly. They have argued that simply providing LDCs with a form of export earnings insurance or a loan to be repaid with interest fails to attack the underlying problems: price instability and, especially, declining real price trends. As one analyst sympathetic to this position has put it: "Earnings stabilization . . . is viewed as merely financial assistance to mitigate swings in prices around the same unsatisfactory trend."[142] Developed countries, however, have tended to view compensatory financing as a more attractive way to deal with the problems of LDC commodity exporters than schemes that directly affect commodity prices and supplies. Compensatory financing does not require either direct intervention into markets or accurate calculations of future global demand and supply.

Since its establishment in 1944, one of the IMF's chief functions has been to provide *short-term* financial assistance to member countries experiencing balance-of-payments deficits. IMF loans generally are not intended to deal with long-term or structural problems, although many LDCs have lobbied to have the fund play a greater role in this area. Interest rates charged by the IMF normally have been considerably below commercial rates. The amount of loans or financial assistance available to member countries depends on their "quotas," which in turn are determined by their capital "subscriptions" to the fund. Quotas and subscriptions vary with the size and importance of countries in the international economy. The votes of IMF members also depend largely on their quotas, with the Western industrialized countries accounting for more than 60 percent of fund votes.[143]

Originally, IMF members were allowed to borrow 25 percent of their quotas without having to meet any conditions; if they wanted to borrow beyond this point, the fund would impose increasingly stringent economic conditions. Since the late 1940s, however, the fund's Board of Governors has frequently increased the amount that countries may borrow under the IMF's regular borrowing arrangements. In addition, the fund has created several other accounts from which members may borrow in certain conditions. The Compensatory Financing Facility (CFF) is one such additional account.[144] It has not been designed to address such problems as declining real price trends, nor is it specifically intended to assist countries facing problems caused by reduced commodity export earnings. Nonetheless, the CFF has provided considerable assistance to Third World countries heavily dependent on primary commodity exports.

As early as 1953 a United Nations group of experts suggested that the IMF should offer assistance not only for temporary balance-of-payments deficits but also specifically for shortfalls in commodity export earnings. But the issue did not really receive serious international attention until the early 1960s, when strong pressure from the developing countries prompted the IMF to consider ways to expand the opportunities for borrowing to deal with payments deficits brought about mainly by falling commodity export earnings. Two key issues arose in this connection: the possible expansion of members' borrowing rights, and the nature of the conditions that might be attached to additional IMF loans. (Members were then permitted to borrow up to 200 percent of their quotas.) During the discussions, representatives from most developing countries argued in support of an *automatic* right to borrow without conditions.

From November 1962 until February 1963 intensive negotiations took place within the fund on the shape of a new Compensatory Financing Facility. Agreement was eventually reached on a facility that would grant IMF members somewhat greater borrowing rights and slightly more relaxed conditions. In the face of declines in the trend of their *merchandise export earnings*, members would be allowed to borrow an additional amount equivalent to 25 percent of their quotas. However, such earnings shortfalls had to result in deficits in a country's balance of payments, had to be short term, and had to be attributable to circumstances beyond the control of the country (e.g., falling international prices). Moreover, countries borrowing under this new facility had to pledge to collaborate with the IMF in finding solutions to the problems—a stipulation that would allow the fund to require changes in their economic policies. The IMF Board—dominated by the United States and the Western European nations—explicitly rejected any "blank check" approach. In addition, the fund effected a clear separation of drawing rights under the CFF from ordinary IMF drawing rights when it waived the provision that the fund could not extend a loan to a country in excess of 200 percent of its quota (see table 2.1).[145]

At UNCTAD I in 1964, Secretary General Raul Prebisch stated that compensatory financing schemes should maintain the total purchasing power of the export earnings of developing countries.[146] This idea was taken up by the LDCs at the conference. The G77 argued that compensatory financing should be in the form of outright grants as opposed to loans.[147] The developed countries replied that countries faced with declining export earnings should be assisted by development aid programs, not compensatory financing.[148] Over Group B's opposition, the developing states forced through a special principle that supported their position:

Whenever international measures to stabilize prices of primary products in relation to the prices of manufactured goods are inadequate, arrangements should be made on an equitable and universal basis, and without prejudice to the general level of financial aid to developing countries, *to correct and compensate for the deterioration in the terms of trade* and short-term decline in the export earnings of countries exporting primary commodities, with a view to facilitating the implementation of economic development plans and programs [emphasis added].[149]

Much of the debate on compensatory financing at UNCTAD I focused on reforming the freshly minted IMF facility. While the developed countries rejected both automatic drawing rights and any change in the formula for calculating export earnings shortfalls, they did permit certain recommendations to be passed "without dissent." One such recommendation suggested that a country should be able to draw up to 50 percent as opposed to just 25 percent of its quota; a second stated that CFF drawings should be completely independent of ordinary drawings from the fund (i.e., CFF drawings should not lead to more stringent conditions being required of states making ordinary drawings); and a third suggested that possible methods of refinancing CFF loans for countries with persistent earnings shortfalls should be explored.[150]

TABLE 2.1

Changes in IMF Compensatory Financing Facility

	1963	1966	1975	1979, 1981
Trade included in computation	Merchandise trade			Services trade added (1981: increase in cost of cereal imports becomes basis of loan requests)
Amount that can be borrowed (% of IMF quota)	25%	50% (maximum of 25% in 12 months)	75% (maximum of 50% in 12 months)	100% (restrictions removed) (1981: 125%, but maximum of 100% for either export receipts or increases in cost of cereal imports)
Amount that can be borrowed (% of total export earnings)	4–5% (1963–66)	5–9% (1967–75)	5–6% (1976–78)	6–9% (1979–81)
Conditions to be met by borrowers	Must collaborate with IMF in rectifying situation	If borrowing above 25% of quota, member must follow policies "reasonably conducive to the development of its exports"		Stricter tests of collaboration with IMF for borrowings above 50% of quota
Amount that was borrowed	SDR $7 million (1963–65)	SDR 1131 million (1966–75)	SDR 4048 million (1976–July 1979)	SDR 2516 million (August 1979–1981)

Sources: Louis M. Goreux, *Compensatory Financing Facility* (Washington, D.C.: IMF, 1980), pp. 38 and 51–57; and data for 1980–81 provided by IMF.

Discussions soon began in the IMF on changing the CFF in ways suggested by UNCTAD, and in 1966 the facility was in fact revised. It is of interest that the official IMF history of this period structures its discussion of this 1966 revision around the specific proposals put forward in the 1964 UNCTAD resolution. It was decided that members would now be able to borrow up to 50 percent of their IMF quota from the CFF. Two qualifications were attached, however, and these were soon subject to criticism by the LDCs. First, a state's increase of its borrowings in any twelve-month period could not exceed 25 percent of its quota; and second, any drawing beyond 25 percent would be granted only if the member had been following policies "reasonably conducive to the development of its exports." In a second important 1966 revision, drawings from the facility were completely separated from borrowings from other IMF facilities. This meant that members drawing on the CFF would not be required to meet more stringent criteria if they made subsequent drawings from other IMF facilities, or if they previously had made drawings from the IMF.[151]

The next two years saw a significant increase in members' use of the facility, partly because of a downward trend in commodity prices. However, despite their greater use of the CFF, the developing countries remained critical of certain aspects of it. At the Algiers meeting of the G77 in 1967 and at UNCTAD II in 1968 they demanded that IMF members be allowed to draw up to 50 percent of their quotas without having any conditions imposed on them and that special refinancing provisions be developed through a liberalization of the requirement that loans be repaid within three to five years.[152] The developed-country representatives and the IMF staff took the position that, in light of the short period of time since the revision of the CFF, new changes should not be made until IMF members had had more experience with the facility. The developing countries apparently accepted this suggestion, and thus did not press for a specific conference resolution on the subject.

The CFF proved valuable for a large number of developing countries in the late 1960s. Beginning in 1971, demands on the facility suddenly declined with the general rise in international commodity prices. At the G77 ministerial meeting in 1971 compensatory financing was not even addressed by the participants; the same was true of UNCTAD III in 1972. But with the end of the boom in commodity prices by late 1974 and the sharp increase in oil prices, balance-of-payments problems again became vital to many developing countries. Thus in 1974 and 1975, in connection with its IPC proposal, the UNCTAD Secretariat suggested a variety of changes to liberalize existing arrangements.[153] At the Seventh Special Session in the autumn of 1975, the United States and other Group B countries adopted a fairly conciliatory posture toward LDC demands on compensatory financing and other issues, and indicated their willingness to liberalize the CFF.[154]

The terms of the CFF were then altered in December 1975, but this did not entail basic changes in guidelines. IMF members were now allowed to draw up to 75 percent of their quotas (versus 50 percent in the past), and up to 50 percent within a twelve-month period (versus 25 percent).[155] But no sooner had the CFF been revised than it was again subject to review, first by the G77 meeting in Manila in early 1976 and then by UNCTAD IV in Nairobi in May of the same year. The G77 called for the elimination of the requirement of a balance-of-payments deficit (i.e., for compensation for earnings shortfalls regardless of the balance-of-payments situation); the calculation of shortfalls in terms of the *real value* of exports (indexing); and the easing of repayment terms and expansion of grants, especially for the poorest countries.[156] Given both the developed countries' disinclination to consider any further changes immediately and the developing countries' preoccupation with elements of the IPC other than compensatory financing (i.e., ICAs and the Common Fund), little discussion of the subject occurred at UNCTAD IV.[157] At that time IMF members were in fact drawing on the CFF in record amounts as a result of the global recession and the previous revisions of the facility's rules. In 1976 alone IMF members drew more than twice as much as over the entire period 1966–75.[158]

The STABEX Model

The discussion of compensatory financing during the latter 1970s and the early 1980s was influenced by an agreement reached between the European Community and a large group of African, Caribbean, and Pacific countries—most former colonies—in 1975. Known as STABEX (the Stabilization Fund for Export Earnings), this agreement was a major component of the first Lomé Convention signed in February 1975, and covered the export earnings of eligible LDC signatories for 12 key commodity groups.[159] Under STABEX, the community agreed to compensate LDC producers for shortfalls in their earnings from exports to the community of the specified commodities. Unlike the CFF, it offered compensation for shortfalls in respect of *individual* commodities or commodity groups, and its disbursements were in the form of interest-free loans or grants (the latter being available only for the least developed Third World signatories). Because of these features, STABEX has been viewed by the G77 and the UNCTAD Secretariat as superior to the CFF, and they have pressed for the establishment of a global arrangement modeled after STABEX.

During the course of the first Lomé Convention, several other minor agricultural commodities were included in STABEX; and when the second convention was accepted in 1979, still more were added and a separate scheme, MINEX, was developed for a number of mineral commodities.[160] In certain respects, STABEX and MINEX are somewhat less generous than they may first appear. With few exceptions, the commodities covered by STABEX and MINEX are not produced in Europe in significant amounts, and virtually all processed commodities are excluded; this has largely eliminated the potential problem of competition with European commercial interests.[161] The total funding set aside for the scheme under Lome I comprised only 10 percent of the European Development Fund, or 375 European Units of Accounts (EUA); this was then increased under Lome II for the period 1980–85. Although this was sufficient to satisfy all requests for assistance during the life of the first convention, in the early 1980s many claims could not be honored as the world recession sharply reduced Third World commodity export earnings.[162] In addition, the number and amount of requests for STABEX grants and loans have been limited by a variety of qualifying criteria and rules.[163]

Despite these and other limitations, overall the developing countries, as was noted earlier, have favored STABEX over the IMF's compensatory arrangements, for the reasons mentioned before and because it does not require the recipient states to spend the funds in any prescribed way.[164] A measure of the attractiveness of STABEX from the perspective of poor LDC exporters is that during the period when the first Lomé Convention was in effect (1975–79), no less than 67 percent of the value of STABEX transfers went to countries that were not required to make reimbursements.[165] The motivation of the European Community in establishing compensatory financing more generous than the CFF is partly a continuing desire to strengthen and safeguard long-standing political and economic relations. The community has also been concerned with encouraging investments in Third World resource industries in order to assure stable, long-term sources of supply. Finally, the European signatories to the Lomé Conventions have shared the overall view of the developed industrial countries that compensatory financing is preferable to commodity agreements that seek to directly regulate prices and supplies.[166]

Negotiations in the Late 1970s and Early 1980s

By the time of the G77 ministerial conference in early 1979 and UNCTAD V in the summer of the same year, the developing countries' interest in reforming the CFF was growing. Few LDCs by now harbored many illusions about the prospects for the creation of a large number of new ICAs or about the likely gains from a Common Fund. Compensatory financing schemes, while offering more modest rewards, were viewed as increasingly attractive—especially by many non-oil-exporting LDCs beset with serious balance-of-payments problems. At its conference in Arusha, Tanzania, in early 1979 the G77 called for several changes. The subsequent UNCTAD V resolution concerning the CFF simply asked that the IMF take into account the views expressed in the Arusha Program when revising the facility.[167]

When the IMF next discussed the CFF in July 1979, the board agreed to meet some of the demands of the developing countries. It increased the amount each member could draw to 100 percent of its quota and eliminated all restrictions on how much could be drawn in a twelve-month period. It also agreed to include services as well as merchandise trade in the calculation of shortfalls. However, contrary to the G77's position, the board decided to impose *stricter* conditions on loan recipients when loans exceeded 50 percent of their quotas.[168] Developed countries and IMF officials, increasingly concerned about the ability of LDC borrowers to pay their debts, demanded greater influence over their economic policies. The IMF board also rejected G77 demands that the fund extend the traditional repayment period beyond five years, index shortfalls to the cost of imports, and establish a CFF interest rate below the regular IMF rate. Two key existing principles—that the CFF should be directed solely at assisting countries with short term declines in export earnings that caused balance-of-payments problems, and that it should not serve as a vehicle for large-scale resource transfers—were thus basically left intact.

This is not meant to deprecate the importance of the CFF, particularly from the mid-1970s. Indeed, the amounts developing countries drew from the CFF averaged around 25 percent of what they borrowed from all IMF facilities. Fund officials were also quite flexible, at least until 1984, in determining the amounts that developing countries could draw and in outlining the conditions that they had to meet. Despite some past and present dissatisfaction, the CFF has provided developing countries with a sizable volume of loans at concessional rates and assisted them in adjusting to export earnings shortfalls.[169]

UNCTAD V in 1979 passed another resolution on compensatory financing that asked the Secretariat to prepare a report in cooperation with the IMF on the creation of a new, "autonomous" global facility.[170] The resolution included two provisions that provoked strongly adverse reactions from most developed nations and caused them to vote against or abstain on the resolution. First, it stipulated that the new facility should guarantee LDCs a certain level of purchasing power from their commodity exports through some form of indexing. Second, it stated that the new facility should "compensate for shortfalls in earnings of each commodity." LDC supporters of this proposal had in mind "a global STABEX." The G77 and the UNCTAD Secretariat had been encouraged to press for such a facility by recent statements from Sweden and West Germany supporting new initiatives on compensatory financing.[171] During the UNCTAD V debate, however, almost all Group B states (including West Germany) opposed the two key proposals, arguing that compensatory financing should not be used to solve long-term, structural problems best addressed through domestic policies and development financing.

The first Secretariat report on compensatory financing following UNCTAD V was issued in June 1980. This report simply compared different methods of calculating earnings shortfalls, and indicated how the gross aggregate shortfalls formula would benefit the LDCs.[172] UNCTAD's major study was not produced until October 1981. UNCTAD's proposal covered all 18 IPC commodities plus rice, maize, lead, zinc, and tobacco. It suggested that compensation should be based on gross aggregate shortfalls in *real* export earnings and that the loan interest rate should be fixed at 8 percent, with no interest on loans to the least developed LDCs.[173] The Secretariat projected that under its formula the LDCs would have needed $34.7 billion, and that states would have been required to contribute $21.3 billion in paid-in capital, over the period 1969–78. For the years 1981–90 it estimated that these figures would rise to $140 billion and $61 billion, respectively. Reaction to the report from the industrialized countries ranged from astonishment to derision. Not only did they object to its basic philosophy, but they harshly criticized the report's feasibility and its underlying economic analysis. In fact, elements of the UNCTAD Secretariat shared these views, and they were influential in having the Secretariat later issue (in December 1981) a truncated proposal requiring only $10 billion in paid-in capital over five years.[174]

The UNCTAD scheme, whether in its original or its abbreviated version, was doomed before the Committee on Commodities met to consider it in February 1982. Although the Scandinavians and France offered vague support, most Group B states adamantly opposed it. The United States took the stand that the matter should not even be discussed in the committee, since compensatory financing was a balance-of-payments question, not a commodity one, and Washington vigorously defended the CFF. A Department of State report issued shortly after the meeting claimed that the UNCTAD Secretariat's criticism of the CFF was based on a "statistical sleight-of-hand." It noted that of the 59 CFF borrowers since 1979, 44 had covered more than one-half of their export earnings shortfalls, and 23 of these had succeeded in meeting their entire shortfalls, from the IMF facility.[175]

The UNCTAD Secretariat continued to refine its proposal in 1982 and 1983. As the world recession took hold, the prices of many key Third World commodities fell sharply. The Secretariat argued that the decline in the real prices of commodity exports lent urgency to the search for improved compensatory financing. It proposed a two-stage process of reform. During the first stage, the IMF scheme would be enlarged and the rules governing eligibility, repayment terms, and the determination of shortfalls would be liberalized. Stage two would see the establishment of a new international facility with a capital subscription of $10 billion and authorization to borrow another $10 billion. Access would be based on export earnings shortfalls for eligible commodities calculated on the basis of a ten-year trend in real earnings. Drawings would be interest-free for the least developed countries.[176]

At the January 1983 meeting of the Committee on Commodities the Secretariat and a number of LDCs stressed the inadequacy of CFF resources and pressed for the adoption of the earlier UNCTAD proposals. But the opposition of the United States, Canada, and several other members of Group B, backed by the Soviet bloc, ensured that no progress would be made in establishing new arrangements outside the IMF. The Western states argued that reform of the CFF provisions was preferable to the creation of an entirely new facility, and emphasized that the structural problems afflicting many LDC commodity industries could not be effectively dealt with through a short-term expedient.[177] At UNCTAD VI in the summer of 1983 the developing countries succeeded in having a resolution passed that called on the IMF to "complete expeditiously" its review of the CFF, and requested the Secretary General of UNCTAD to convene an expert group to assess the need for new global compensatory financing. This resolution was passed by a vote of 90–1–10, with the United States being the lone opponent. Interestingly, 7 of the 10 countries abstaining were Soviet-bloc states (the others being Canada, Australia, and New Zealand). Evidently Group D was concerned that the creation of new financing arrangements might require them to contribute significant amounts of capital.[178]

An illustration of the gap that often exists between UNCTAD and bodies such as the IMF is the decision of the latter's board several months after the 1983 UNCTAD conference to revise the CFF. It reduced the percentage of a country's quota it could borrow from the facility by around 15 percent and increased the stringency of the conditions it would have to meet in order to obtain loans. The primary concern of the industrialized states was that the fund acquire more influence over borrowing states' economic policies in order to ameliorate "the debt crisis." This change in policy led to a drastic drop in drawings from the CFF and to greater reliance on other IMF facilities in 1984. It also evoked periodic criticism from developing-country members of the fund, but to no avail.[179]

The expert group set up in conformity with the UNCTAD VI resolution examined the adequacy of existing arrangements through late 1983 and 1984. Its report, released in December 1984, was unique when compared with past UNCTAD studies. It argued strongly that supply variations were generally the most significant cause of export earnings instability, particularly at the country level. In other words, it attributed the problems of LDC producers more to developments in their own countries than to economic trends in the developed world. It then went on to propose a new type of facility, one where loans or grants for shortfalls in earnings in particular commodity sectors would be used to promote supply stability. The expert group suggested that this facility be under the Common Fund (if established) or the World Bank.[180] Certain difficult issues, such as conflicts among producing states and the monitoring of recipient states' use of funds, were given little attention.

Developed-country reaction to the report was mixed. Most members of Groups B and D gave the report a vague type of blessing, and thus implicitly agreed that international negotiations should be held to hammer out the details of a new facility. The United States, however, refused to accept the report's recommendations, and has steadfastly supported the IMF and the World Bank, both of whose programs were criticized by the report as inadequate in light of the needs and problems of LDC commodity-exporting countries. Canada was the only other developed state that clearly lined up behind the United States on this matter. Canada stated that, while it would accept the forwarding of the report to the World Bank and the IMF, it could not agree to the suggestion that international negotiations should take place to establish an additional compensatory financing facility. Among other things, Canada and the United States were concerned that a new facility designed to provide loans for supply adjustment in Third World commodity industries would undermine the influence of the IMF and the World Bank and might actually contribute to problems of oversupply by encouraging LDCs to bring new capacity on stream. But their concerns about a structural adjustment facility were not shared to the same extent by other developed countries, who were willing to discuss the proposal. The Soviets rejected the idea on the ground that the source of the problem lay in the policies of the capitalist states. No important changes in negotiating positions occurred in 1985 and 1986. At a new UNCTAD group of experts meeting in July 1986 traditional divisions reappeared, with the group concluding that yet more information was required for them to make recommendations.[181]

The developed countries, including those who backed negotiations on a new structural adjustment facility, still favor international compensatory financing plans based on the CFF model. Not only does the CFF tie assistance to the prior existence of a balance-of-payments deficit, but the IMF operates on the principle that loans are contingent on the recipients' willingness to adopt policies that the developed countries believe to be in their general interest. It is clear that the industrialized nations see compensatory financing as an attractive alternative to direct price regulation, but they are likely to inject substantial sums into such schemes only if they control the rules and perceive demonstrable benefits for themselves. STABEX has modest resources, and in its present form it is politically acceptable to the European Community because it requires only limited financial outlays. A "globalization" of STABEX would probably fail to elicit a large commitment of funds from the developed world because STABEX is basically viewed as a resource transfer device—and not always a very just one at that. Most developed states believe that better means are available to direct resources to the most needy or "the most favored."

Despite adverse developed-country reactions to some of the above proposals, compensatory financing is likely to remain their preferred approach as they respond to future Third World demands for international action to address the problems of commodity exporters. In comparison to ICAs, compensatory financing is simpler to construct, does not require interventions into markets, and need not be too costly. On the other hand, developing countries have gained substantial benefits as a result of the establishment and liberalization of compensatory financing schemes, and they will continue to press for additional changes. Recent Third World efforts to develop a kind of globalized STABEX independent of the IMF indicate how their thinking appears to be evolving.

CONCLUSION

The general normative guidelines discussed above will be analyzed again at some length in Chapter 6. At this point a brief recapitulation is in order. First, the principal substantive Havana Charter norms relate to the creation and character of international commodity agreements. ICAs are only to be created in very unstable markets; they are to aim at price stabilization, and not a significant raising of the market price trend. Developed nations are not expected to assume a disproportionate share of the costs, or to use ICAs to transfer substantial resources to developing producer countries. Second, while the norms relevant to ICAs largely respect the free market, this is not as evident in other aspects of the commodity issue area. Violations of the Havana Charter's implicit stricture against cartels have frequently occurred. And states have rarely felt any constraints not to subsidize or protect their own producers. In fact, no serious attempts have been made to legislate a norm forbidding subsidies, although on occasion the G77 has tried to get developed states to refrain from assisting their producers of those commodities that the developing world also grows or mines. Assistance to and protection of commodity producers, especially in agriculture, are almost sacrosanct policies of the modern welfare state. Third, the regime holds that compensatory financing should be limited to providing loans to countries with shortfalls in export earnings. It should not be used to compensate states for "losses" incurred because of downturns in the market or to transfer large-scale financial aid to producers.

Last, there are the several normative regime guidelines with respect to decision-making. Global bodies are not empowered to legislate legally *binding* international commodity agreements; states individually have to accept ICAs in order for them to be binding. Within international commodity organizations votes should be distributed equally between producers and consumers. State practice over the postwar decades has established that within each group votes should be distributed mainly on the basis of shares of exports and imports, and that important decisions should require a two-thirds majority of votes from each group—thus giving small groups of key producers and consumers effective veto power (see chapters 3 and 4 for more information on decision-making structures).

3

THE TIN AND NATURAL
RUBBER AGREEMENTS

Since the Second World War six intergovernmental, producer-consumer commodity agreements have been negotiated to regulate the markets for wheat, tin, natural rubber, sugar, coffee, and cocoa. For all but wheat, developing countries have been both the major exporters and the primary advocates of international control. Because the largest wheat exporters are developed industrialized countries, the International Wheat Agreement is not discussed in this book, although its history is in many ways quite similar to that of other ICAs. The first postwar tin and sugar agreements were reached in the early 1950s, the coffee agreement in the early 1960s, and the cocoa agreement in 1972. Natural rubber is the only commodity for which a new agreement was concluded in the wake of the IPC in the late 1970s. In this chapter the tin and natural rubber negotiations and agreements are surveyed, with the following chapter devoted to the ICAs for sugar, coffee, and cocoa.

The tin and natural rubber markets, and the international agreements that have (at times) influenced those markets, have several similarities as well as a number of important differences. Both commodities are produced and exported by a small number of LDCs, and yield large export earnings for these countries—a yearly average of $2.3 billion for tin and $3.3 billion for rubber between 1980 and 1982.[1] Both are classed as industrial raw materials. Fluctuations in demand in the industrialized world thus have a major impact on their international market prices and trends. Another similarity is that commodity markets in both cases have been regulated at least in part through international buffer stocks.

The dissimilarities also deserve brief mention. In both cases a few Southeast Asian producers have dominated the global market, but producing countries outside this area have been more important in the case of tin than that of rubber. In addition, escalating production costs, brought about in part by declining ore grades, have been a constant feature of the postwar tin market. In the case of natural rubber, the existence of competitively priced and often substitutable synthetics has had an enormous impact on the market and on producer policies. Despite these differences the small number of producers of both commodities has helped to facilitate the reaching of both formal and informal international agreements to regulate the markets.

TIN

The Market

Most of the world's tin concentrate (casserite) is mined by exploiting deposits in river beds, particularly in Southeast Asia. About one-quarter is produced through underground mining, with Bolivia by far the major producer in this respect. Once mined, concentrates are smelted into tin metal. Most of the world's tin smelters today are located in producing countries. Tin can easily be alloyed with other metals, and its main uses are in the manufacture of tinplate, solder, white metal and pewter, and chemicals.[2] Since 1935 world consumption has grown by less than 1 percent per year. The slow growth is attributable to technological advances that have allowed manufacturers to use less tin in tinplate and to the intervention of substitutes for products made from tin.[3]

In recent decades, developing countries have accounted for more than 90 percent of net global tin exports; and the industrialized nations have been the dominant importers (tables 3.1 and 3.2). In 1982 Malaysia was the largest exporter, followed by two other Southeast Asian countries, Indonesia and Thailand. Then came Bolivia, whose market share has declined since 1970. However, Bolivia has always been more reliant on tin for export earnings than the others (table 3.3). Dramatic changes in exports occurred between 1982 and 1985 as a result of the three Southeast Asian producers' application of International Tin Council export controls, and the absence of such controls over Brazil and Bolivia. Brazil actually increased its share of global production from 3 to 13 percent—marginally higher than Thailand and Bolivia, and just below Indonesia. Among the producers Bolivia has the

TABLE 3.1

Tin: Net Exports by Main Countries[a]

Countries	% of World Exports					
	1960	1965	1970	1975	1980	1982
Australia	0.0	0.5	3.3	4.4	5.3	5.9
Bolivia	13.1	17.9	19.5	16.9	12.9	14.8
Brazil	—	—	—	1.1	1.1	3.2
China	15.3	5.2	3.8	8.3	2.3	3.1
Indonesia	17.9	10.5	12.5	11.9	17.6	21.5
Malaysia	37.0	49.7	54.9	37.4	36.3	26.4
Thailand	8.5	11.7	—	10.7	19.9	19.0
Zaire	5.6	0.9	4.1	3.3	1.5	1.4
Other	2.5	3.6	1.9	5.8	3.1	4.6
	Exports by Weight (Metric Tons)					
World	150,564	135,443	142,419	156,246	168,130	136,975

[a]Net exports are calculated as the sum of exports of tin-in-concentrates (weighed by tin content), plus exports of tin metal, minus the sum of imports of tin-in-concentrates and tin metal. Smuggled tin, which has been in the range of 10,000–20,000 tons/year recently, does not appear in the above figures.
Sources: International Tin Council, Trade in Tin, 1960–1974 (London: ITC, 1976) and Tin Statistics, 1972–1982 (London: ITC, 1983).

TABLE 3.2
Net Imports of Tin by Main Countries and Groupings, 1980[a]

Countries	Percentage of Total
Industrial Market Economies	
United States	26.4
Japan	19.2
West Germany	9.9
France	6.3
Italy	3.9
Netherlands	3.5
United Kingdom	3.1
Canada	1.9
Belgium/Luxembourg	1.3
Other	1.8
All industrial	77.2
Centrally Planned Economies	
USSR	9.6
Czechoslovakia	2.9
Poland	2.1
Hungary	1.0
Other	—
All centrally planned	15.6
Developing	7.2
World total	100.0

[a]Net imports are calculated as the sum of imports of tin-in-concentrates plus imports of tin metal, minus the sum of exports of tin-in-concentrates and tin metal.
Source: William L. Baldwin, *The World Tin Market: Political Pricing and Economic Competition* (Durham, N.C.: Duke University Press, 1983), p. 48.

highest costs of production. Smaller cost differences exist among the other producers.[4] The ownership pattern of the tin industry in the major exporting countries varies considerably. Since the mid-1950s the industry has been mainly government owned in Bolivia and Indonesia; in Thailand, a mixture of local private, foreign and government ownership has existed; and in Malaysia local private interests and the government have increased their control in recent decades, although there are still some foreign-owned mining operations.[5]

International trade in tin was centered on two markets, the Kuala Lumpur Tin Market (KLTM) (formerly in Penang), and the London Metal exchange (LME), until the beginning of "the tin crisis" in October 1985. Now tin is traded on the KLTM and through contracts between sellers and

TABLE 3.3

Percentage of Export Earnings of Developing Countries from Tin[a]

Countries	1976–78	1980–82
Bolivia	49.5	33.1
Malaysia	10.7	6.4
Thailand	7.0	6.2
Rwanda	6.9	13.7
Burma	3.3	5.4
Namibia	3.1	1.3
Zaire	2.4	1.4
Indonesia	2.2	1.8

[a]These percentages were quite a bit higher for some producers in the 1950s and 1960s. William L. Baldwin, *The World Tin Market: Political Pricing and Economic Competition* (Durham, N.C.: Duke University Press, 1983), pp. 42–43; International Tin Council, *The International Implications of United States Disposal of Stockpiled Tin* (London: ITC, 1973), pp. 11–13; John Thoburn, "Policies for Tin Exporters," *Resources Policy* (June 1981), 7:75–79.

Source: World Bank, *Commodity Trade and Price Trends* (1980), table 11 and (1985), table 9. Only countries whose exports of tin accounted for at least 2 percent of their export earnings are listed.

buyers. The market is, to say the least, unsettled.[6] Until the implementation of the first International Tin Agreement in the mid-1950s the tin market had been quite unstable; thereafter it was reasonably stable in relation to other commodities over the period 1955–81 (table 1.4, chart 3.1). During these years current and constant prices moved up, albeit unevenly. The current price dropped significantly between 1981 and 1985, and then with the collapse of the International Tin Agreement in October 1985 it was halved in a matter of months.[7]

The price of tin and the fluctuations in its price are traceable to several factors. The overall movement upward in real prices from the 1940s through 1980 was due to the ability of the small group of producing countries to control exports, to the paucity of new supplies, and to steady increases in production costs.[8] The collaboration among producers broke down in the 1980s. The instability in tin prices flows from the fact that demand and supply are both relatively price inelastic in the short run. Demand does not respond quickly to price changes because tin constitutes only a small fraction of the cost of the final products that incorporate it, and it is a highly preferred material for certain industrial uses (e.g., tinplate and solder). Supply fails to adjust rapidly to price changes because of the time lag in introducing new capital equipment, the high cost of shutting down existing mining operations, and producing countries' desire to maintain or

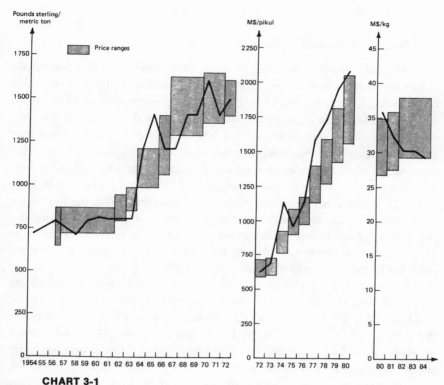

CHART 3-1

International Tin Prices and International Tin Agreements' Price Ranges;
1954 to 1984*

*Up to 1969 price ranges were denominated in £/long ton; from 1970 to 1972 price ranges were
denominated in £/ton; from 1972 to 1980 price ranges were denominated in M$/pikul; from 1981 to present price ranges are denominated in M$/kg.
Source: UN Doc. TD/B/C.1/270 (1985), p. 18.

expand existing levels of activity and employment in the mining sector.
These market characteristics mean that variations in demand and supply
can have a significant impact on price. Changes in demand caused by
economic cycles in the industrial world have been the principal source of
price instability. However, while slackening demand was partly responsible for the dramatic fall in price in the 1980s, the main cause was the increased output of producing states that were not members of the International Tin Agreement.[9]

Market Regulation Before 1953

Several attempts were made to regulate international trade in tin before the negotiation of the first postwar International Tin Agreement (ITA) in 1953. In February 1921 the colonial governments in Malaya and the Netherlands East Indies (now Indonesia) agreed to establish the Bandoeng Pool. They purchased almost 20,000 tons of tin in the next year (about 15 percent of the world production), and held this until the price rose. Although the price continued to fall in 1921, the pool "probably prevented a price slump even more drastic . . . "[10] Demand picked up in 1922 and 1923, and the accumulated stocks were sold gradually, the final sales occurring in 1925. Not only did the pool make a profit, but from the perspective of producers an important point had been proved: "In the eyes of its proponents, the pool had proved conclusively that a degree of control over stocks meant a degree of control over price."[11]

The onset of the depression in 1929 stimulated additional control efforts by producers. The first producer-only intergovernmental tin agreement was reached in 1931; additional agreements were later negotiated to cover the periods 1934–36 and 1937–41. The goal was simple: to encourage recovery of world tin prices by holding stocks and, more importantly, by curtailing exports. Some success in stemming the price fall was achieved, and consumption began to revive in 1934–35. Export controls contributed to a strengthening of prices, and use was made of a buffer stock to check sharp price rises on several occasions. The beginning of the war and its spread by 1942 to Southeast Asia brought to an end effective regulation of the international tin market.[12]

Immediately after the war, several governments began to consider the prospects for postwar tin control. At a March 1946 meeting of the International Tin Committee, the Netherlands suggested that the prewar producers' arrangement be continued, a position backed by Bolivia and Belgium (on behalf of the Belgian Congo). But Britain, still politically in control of over half the world's production, made it clear that a tin control agreement restricted to producers was out of the question; consumers too would have to be involved, as was later mandated by the 1947 ECOSOC statement of principles on commodity regulation and the commodity chapter of the Havana Charter. Thus, an international tin conference in October 1946—attended by all major exporters and importers—agreed to establish a study group to consider the problems of the industry and the prospects for producer-consumer collaboration.[13]

The first meeting of the International Tin Study Group (ITSG) took place in April 1947 in Brussels. Although consensus existed among most participants on the approach to be taken in a producer-consumer tin agreement and on the appropriate regulatory instruments to be employed, the United States blocked an early accord. In the late 1940s and early 1950s the U.S. government, aware of the country's dependence on certain imported minerals and metals, embarked upon a program to build up a vast stockpile of "strategic" commodities, including tin. Washington was not anxious to see an ICA for tin until it had met its own requirements and enlarged its stockpile.[14] Another effort was made to negotiate a tin agreement in 1950, but the recent outbreak of hostilities in Korea and the consequent increase in tin prices soon ended the discussions.[15]

The First International Tin Agreement, 1953

By the summer of 1953 tin prices had fallen to pre–Korean War levels, and this, plus fears of a reduction in U.S. purchases for its stockpile, caused the tin producers to seek a control arrangement. A UN Tin Conference was thus convened in November 1953. Contributing to the success of the negotiations was the widespread recognition of the historic instability of the tin market and the fact that some companies in major consuming countries were heavily involved in the tin-mining industries of Southeast Asia and Africa (Bolivia having nationalized its industry in 1952). In addition, Britain and Belgium were quite sympathetic to a tin agreement because of their colonial responsibilities and their familiarity with the difficulties faced by tin miners. Thus, the clear division between importers and exporters so characteristic of most commodity bargaining was blurred. This unquestionably facilitated the successful conclusion of an ICA for tin.[16]

There was little debate over the techniques to be employed to regulate the market. Given the long history of using export quotas and buffer stocks of one sort or another, it was evident from the start that these would be the tools of regulation. The United States insisted that export controls be instituted only when the tin price had dipped below an agreed floor and at least 10,000 tons of tin metal had been accumulated in the buffer stock. While the other participants accepted the second condition, it was decided that export restrictions could be imposed irrespective of the price level if the International Tin Council established to administer the accord saw fit to impose them (articles 21 and 22).[17] The producing countries then engaged in predictable wrangling to obtain the largest possible percentage share of the total export market to mitigate the impact of future restrictions. Slightly larger shares were granted to Indonesia and Bolivia than their average 1950–52 production would have dictated (table 3.4). Provision was also made for adjusting shares of producers at frequent intervals in order to accommodate actual production trends. The criteria for readjustment of shares (basically, output over the previous 1–2 years) were maintained in subsequent agreements.[18]

On the question of the buffer stock, Bolivia argued that any stock financed solely by producers should be kept small. A large stock would be likely to depress prices and cause serious harm to countries dependent on tin exports. However, the importing states demurred, and in spite of their unwillingness to contribute to the cost of the stock, the other producers supported their demand for a fairly large stock of 25,000 tons (article 7), with producers required to contribute in metal or cash in accordance with their export percentages. Under pressure from the United States, producers agreed that the price range would be divided into three sectors. When the price was in the middle sector, the buffer-stock manager could neither buy nor sell tin. When the price entered the bottom sector, he could buy, and when it hit the floor of that sector, he had to buy. When the price entered the top sector, he could sell, and when it reached the ceiling, he had

TABLE 3.4

Producers' Percentages of Global Export Quotas Under the International Tin Agreements[a]

	% Shares of Global Quotas					
Countries	1953	1960	1965	1970	1975	1981
Australia				2.82	4.37	5.95
Brazil						1.23
Bolivia	21.50	18.00	18.18	16.98	18.06	15.61
Indonesia	21.50	19.50	12.28	9.14	13.71	18.62
Malaysia	36.61	38.00	45.08	45.83	43.60	35.15
Nigeria	5.38	6.25	6.55	6.36	4.17	1.43
Rwanda			1.02			0.92
Thailand	6.29	9.00	12.01	14.36	12.55	19.28
Zaire (ex-Congo)	8.72	9.25	4.88	4.51	3.54	0.81

[a]Rwanda did not join the 1965 and 1981 agreements, and Bolivia did not join the 1981 agreement. Their shares were redistributed. These figures were revised during the course of the agreements.
Sources: The figures are found in annex A of the following documents: United Nations, *Treaty Series* (1956), 256:31; United Nations, *Treaty Series* (1961), 403:3; United Nations, *Treaty Series* (1968), 616:317; U.N. Doc. TD/TIN/4/7 (1970); U.N. Doc. TD/TIN/5/10 (1975); U.N. Doc. TD/TIN/6/14 (1981).

to sell. The crucial issue was therefore the price range itself. After lengthy debate, a range of £640–£880 per ton was accepted.[19]

As required by the Havana Charter principles, producers and consumers were each to have 1,000 votes. Producers basically were assigned votes in proportion to their production over the 1950–52 period. Most decisions required a simple majority of both consuming and producing signatories—a so-called simple distributed majority (article 4). Interestingly, decisions involving the major regulatory powers of the Tin Council—imposition of export controls in particular—did not require a two-thirds distributed majority, in contrast to the situation in the International Sugar Organization and several other commodity organizations.

By mid-1954 all the major producers had ratified the ITA except Indonesia, which was unhappy with its share of both producers' votes and the total export figure.[20] On the consumers' side, hostility to the "tin cartel" within Congress and the American business community precluded U.S. membership, despite a favorable attitude in the State Department, which wanted to assist Malaya—then involved in combatting a communist insurgency. Washington encouraged other interested parties to participate in the ITA but could not do so itself.[21] Other major tin-importing countries not participating in the first postwar agreement included Japan, West Germany, and the East European states. By the time Indonesia ratified the ITA in 1956 and thus made it operative, over 90 percent of noncommunist tin production was covered, but less than 40 percent of consumption. In light of the nonmembership of the United States and several other countries, the most powerful consuming members of the Tin Council were Britain, France, Canada, and the Netherlands, in that order.[22]

The price of tin was hovering around £750/ton, near the middle of the ITA range, as the first producer-consumer tin accord began to operate in July 1956. But it was not to remain there long, as political tension associated with the crisis in the Middle East in late 1956 soon pushed the price upward. Under normal practice the buffer-stock manager would have intervened once the price accelerated through the top sector of the ITA range, but in this case he could not. The problem was both a simple and a recurring one for the Tin Council: it had no tin in the buffer stock, owing to the permissible and understandable decision of producing members who had earlier contributed to the stock in the form of cash, pegged at the floor price level of £640, rather than in physical tin metal, then priced around £750. Critics dutifully recorded the first failure of the new commodity agreement.[23]

In January 1957 the price fell back into the upper sector of the ITA range. As the year progressed, an excess of production over consumption requirements developed, in large part because of increasing sales of tin from the USSR, a nonmember, to Western Europe. The Soviets had agreed to import substantial volumes of tin from China in the mid-1950s, and much of this could not be consumed domestically. Combined with the cessation of U.S. strategic stockpile purchases and other market trends, these Soviet exports pushed prices down sharply. In December 1957 the Tin Council decided, for the first time, to impose export reductions of 40 percent to support the price.[24] Despite these strong export control measures and continuing buffer-stock purchases, the tin price continued to rest near the ITA floor. Russian sales continued to increase, and in September 1958 prices fell below the floor. The Soviets agreed to reduce their sales, and ITA consuming states decided to restrict tin imports from the Soviet bloc. The price then began to creep upward almost immediately, moving back into the ITA range by October. The crisis was over.[25]

The Second ITA, 1960

The first agreement was due to expire in June 1961, and so the Tin Council requested the UN Secretary General to convene a conference to renegotiate the ITA. The conference met in New York in May–June 1960, and a second five-year tin agreement resulted.[26] With the Americans not involved in the negotiations, the producers succeeded in having the buffer stock cut by 5,000 tons to 20,000 tons and in revising the restriction on the use of export controls prior to the accumulation of 10,000 tons in the buffer stock. This was scaled down to 5,000 tons under the second ITA. The producers failed, however, to obtain an increase in the price range then prevailing (£730–£880) because of the slack market over the previous two years. A significant voting change was also accepted, so that most of the important decisions previously requiring a simple distributed majority would now require a two-thirds distributed majority.[27]

Some producing country delegates, particularly those from Thailand and Malaya, expressed alarm over the severity of the export restrictions instituted in 1958–59.[28] Because these countries enjoyed comparatively low production costs, they were less concerned about falling tin prices than producers, such as Bolivia, that could not cover their production costs unless a fairly high world price was maintained. However, there was never any likelihood that the unhappy producers would refuse to sign the agreement, in part because the formula designed for distributing export quotas accomodated their increased production capacities. Perhaps more surprising, the consuming countries seemed quite sanguine about the operation of the first ITA—in spite of its failure to forestall a price rise during the Suez conflict and the long period of drastic export restrictions in the late 1950s.[29] The continued involvement of European business interests in the tin-producing countries, and the noninvolvement of the United States in the 1960 negotiations, facilitated the successful conclusion, after relatively little debate, of a second International Tin Agreement.

As the first tin agreement drew to a close in mid-1961, the market price was giving indications of a buoyancy not experienced for some years. It rose above the ceiling of £880/ton, and reached £950 by August; this prompted calls by producers for a revised price range.[30] In January 1962 the consuming countries reluctantly agreed to a new range of £790–£960. The price drifted down into the middle sector by June 1962 as the United States made loud noises about soon disposing of its excess tin. Tin producers argued vigorously that no U.S. sales should be made until the price reached the ITA ceiling. They complained that sales from the U.S. stockpile at prices below the ITA ceiling would prevent new production from coming on stream and might eliminate part of the existing marginal output.[31] The United States refused to accept restrictions on sales from its General Services Administration (GSA) stockpile, but it sold a relatively small volume of tin during most of 1962 while the price was in the bottom half of the ITA range.[32]

In 1963 a tin shortage generated a more confident mood in the market, and the price edged into the upper sector by September. Despite buffer-stock sales, by November the price had risen above the ceiling, and the second International Tin Agreement (1961–66) soon ceased to exert any influence on the market. U.S. tin sales of 29,000 tons in 1964 and over 24,000 tons in 1965 prevented the world tin shortage from developing into a serious crisis and certainly forestalled an even sharper price increase, but Washington did *not* try to force the price to fall significantly. The United States was evidently content to provide sufficient tin to roughly meet the annual shortage estimated by the Tin Council.

The Third ITA, 1965

Delegations from most of the world's important tin-trading countries assembled in New York in March 1965 for the purpose of negotiating a third ITA.[33] The discussions took place in the wake of the formation of UNCTAD the previous year, and the developing-country participants were anxious to reformulate the agreement according to the principles enunciated by the Group of 77. As was generally the case at such meetings, the producers pushed for an increase in the price range, (then at £1,000–£1,200), pointing to the fact that market prices had remained above the ceiling since late 1963. The consuming countries, for their part, were unanimous in portraying the market of the last two years as inflated, and they refused to accept any rise in the range. Largely because of the consumer position on prices, Malaysia and Bolivia actually refused at first to accede to the third agreement. However, fearful of the strong possibility that the recent high prices would soon bring forth additional production and a bearish market, they finally agreed to sign the accord and accept, at least for the moment, the existing floor and ceiling levels.[34]

Producer dissatisfaction with the method of financing the buffer stock was not new, but at the 1965 conference it emerged as an important issue for the first time. The representative of Malaysia underlined the unfairness of forcing poor Third World producers to fund the stock in its entirety, even though *in principle* it worked to the benefit of consumers as well.[35] The consuming governments were not disposed to finance a buffer stock that had been unable to protect the ceiling price throughout the life of the second agreement. They also knew that in any case the U.S. GSA stockpile, which was much larger than the ITA buffer stock, was likely to perform the key role in moderating prices, as it had done since 1963. The result of the drawn-out debate over the buffer stock was the continuation of a 20,000 ton stock to which producers alone would contribute.

The tin shortage was coming to an end at the beginning of the third ITA as a result of increased production in response to the high prices of recent years.[36] It was soon clear that the tin market was at the start of another cyclical downswing. By August 1966 the market price had dropped to the midpoint of the range, which had been raised a few months before. Concern about the future course of American tin disposal policy heightened as rapidly as the market slackened. The GSA sold slightly more than 16,000 tons of tin in 1966, but over 270,000 were still in the stockpile. To producers this appeared ominous, since the stockpile "objective" specified by Congress was about 165,000 tons, leaving for sale a theoretical "surplus" of over 100,000 tons, well over half a year's (noncommunist) consumption.[37] Negotiation of some type of arrangement with Washington was imperative in order to dissipate the cloud over the tin market caused by the uncertainty surrounding U.S. tin sales. With the State Department taking the lead on behalf of the United States, an agreement was worked out in October 1966. Under the terms of this so-called "October Agreement," the Americans promised to control GSA tin sales so as not to undermine the activities of the ITA buffer-stock manager, which in general meant there would be no U.S. sales so long as the market price was in the lower sector. Provision was also made for ongoing consultation between the United States and the ITC.[38]

The October Agreement was an important victory for the tin producers, who had long labored to gain leverage over American tin disposals. Washington's reasons for finally agreeing to tie its tin policy to that of the Tin Council were essentially political:

The political factors [in U.S. eyes] had . . . swung in favour of the producers. The U.S.A. was involved in the internal struggle for the control of the raw materials of Congo-Zaire; there had started a parallel struggle in Indonesia after the overthrow of the Left there under Sukarno; Bolivia seemed wide open to subversion. Above all, there was the war in Vietnam for which the Thai airfields were valuable.[39]

GSA sales of tin dropped sharply in the next two years, totaling 7,400 tons in 1967 and only 3,600 tons in 1968; thereafter, there were *no* sales until 1973.[40]

Throughout the last months of 1966 and for the most of next year the market price hovered between the lower and middle sectors, and the buffer-stock manager, inactive for the past three years, began to make small purchases.[41] After devaluation of the pound sterling in late November 1967, the ITA range was adjusted upward to reflect the currency change, the new range being set at £1,280–£1,630/ton. Prices continued to fall, and in September 1968 the Tin Council agreed to impose export controls. The degree of restriction (only 4 percent) was much milder than during the 1957–60 period, since the size of the surplus was quite limited and U.S. GSA sales had recently been terminated.[42] Export controls were continued for over a year, until December 1969, during which time the market price generally remained in the middle sector of the range. Almost from the inception of export controls the underlying supply/demand situation began to change. Growing purchases of tin by Soviet-bloc countries, the end of GSA sales, and continuing high consumption actually led to a statistical world tin *shortage* for 1969 on the order of 5,000 tons.[43] Thus the maintenance of export restrictions throughout 1969 was not only unnecessary but in fact contrary to the policies of the buffer-stock manager, who *sold* no less than 7,000 tons of tin during the year. Resort to export regulation during this period attested to the tendency of the council, influenced strongly by producers, to rely on export controls as the main weapon against excess supply.[44] The anomaly of continuing export controls during an increasingly tight market lapsed into an absurd situation as the tin price rose through the upper sector in November 1969 and quickly exceeded the ITA ceiling. The council then ended export controls and promptly "requested" the tin-producing members to increase output and exports in the face of a new tin shortage. The whole episode "reflected little credit on the stabilising policy of the Council."[45]

The price hovered near the ITA ceiling during the first few months of 1970. Despite this, the United States did not intervene in the market, although it could quite properly have done so under the 1966 October Agreement. One reason for the inactivity of the GSA stemmed from the raising of the stockpile objective for tin by Congress.[46] A second and perhaps more important restraint on U.S. policy was concern about political instability in tin-producing countries, particularly Bolivia. On several occasions in 1969–70 the State Department vetoed GSA plans for tin sales.[47] Although the tin price had increased significantly and had exceeded the ITA ceiling several times, from the consumers' perspective the third agreement had performed much better than the second, which was inoperative during most of its life owing to high prices. That the market price had generally been kept within the ITA range seemed to producers to prove the inherent worth of the buffer-stock mechanism for both importers and exporters.

The Fourth ITA, 1970

Tin-exporting countries had long complained that only producers had financed ITA buffer-stock operations. Their insistence that consumers assume an equal share came to the fore with a vengeance at the 1970 conference. Producers now concurred with the oft-stated view of consuming countries that the existing size of the buffer stock (20,000 tons of tin metal) was inadequate to defend the ceiling price. The Indonesian delegate noted that in the future,

such a situation could be prevented by the strengthening of the buffer stock resources, which would require increased contributions in kind or in cash. It was obvious that the producers, who were already shouldering the whole burden of [providing] those resources, were unable to provide supplementary funds.[48]

During discussion of this issue the U.S delegates argued that the obvious inability of the buffer stock to protect the ceiling both during the second agreement and more recently meant that producers were in fact the sole beneficiaries of its operations. Consumers, therefore, should not be expected to support this regulatory instrument financially. This view was endorsed by Canada, Japan, Britain, and West Germany.[49]

In fact, the consuming countries were aware that, in the event of a sustained shortage of tin and a consequent price escalation, an ITA buffer stock even twice the size of the one already existing probably could not defend the ceiling. In addition, in such a situation producers would argue for an upward price-range revision long before the buffer-stock manager had exhausted his metal supplies to moderate the market price. The truth was that the agreement was *inherently* less able to defend the ceiling than the floor, for the simple reason that while it had two weapons to support the price (buffer-stock purchases and export controls), it had only one to moderate the price (buffer-stock sales). And if the producers ever chose to contribute their share to the buffer stock in the form of cash—pegged at the agreed floor—rather than tin, even this tool would be useless in a rising market. Also contributing to the reluctance of importing countries to help finance the buffer stock was the existence of the United States stockpile. Although inactive since mid-1968, the stockpile remained a potent factor in the world tin market and contained volumes of tin far in excess of what the ITA could ever hope to muster—with or without consumer assistance.

The fourth tin agreement[50] saw two important additions to the consumers' membership: West Germany and the USSR. Some 60 percent of world consumption (exclusive of China) was now covered by the agreement. Had the United States chosen to accede to the fourth ITA, more than 85 percent of consumption would have been accounted for by signatories. But once again Washington's unwillingness to permit any formal multilateral control of its policy with respect to a "strategic" commodity precluded membership, despite the generally favorable disposition of the State Department.[51]

Shortly after the 1970 conference the producers began to press for a revision of the range to accommodate their escalating costs.[52] With surprisingly little debate consumers agreed to a new floor of £1,350/ton, close to what the producers had requested. The latter were fearful that the future membership of the USSR and West Germany once the fourth agreement came into force (July 1971) would toughen the resolve of consuming countries.[53] For most of the first year of the new agreement the market price remained in the lower sector, and by the close of 1972 the buffer stock held over 12,000 tons of tin metal accumulated to support the market.[54] An important landmark in the history of postwar tin control occurred in 1972 when France and the Netherlands agreed to make *voluntary* contributions of cash to the buffer stock (£1,214,000 and £671,000, respectively). Although this was trivial in comparison with the total contribution of the producers (£27 million), the principle of consumer financial responsibility was strengthened.[55] In July 1972 the chronic instability of sterling finally led to a decision to switch to the Malaysian dollar as the reference price. The continuing dominance of the Penang market and of the Malaysian smelters justified selection of Malay currency, although tin transactions, of course continued to be conducted using various currencies. The unit of measurement also changed, to the picul (1 picul = 1.33 lb. of tin), and the new range thus became M$583–M$718/picul.[56]

The period 1973–74 witnessed extreme volatility in tin and other commodity markets as the world monetary crisis and the commodity price boom unfolded on the world stage. As tin prices rose, the Tin Council began selling heavily from the buffer stock, which disposed of over 9,000 tons in the last half of the year. Prices continued to increase, however, and in October 1973 the council agreed to revise the range upwards to M$635–M$760/picul. But within a month the new ceiling was breached, and the buffer stock soon had little metal. Prices were given additional impetus by the Middle East war and the phenomenal increase in petroleum prices which increased fears of resource scarcity. By the end of the year the tin price on the London and New York markets was twice the lowest level set at the start of the year. In May 1974 the council agreed to a new price range of M$850–M$1,050, but market prices remained above the ITA range until the autumn of 1974, even though large-scale GSA sales occurred.[57] In January 1975 the council again revised the range upward to M$900–M$1,100/picul, but by now demand and prices were softening as the worldwide recession took hold. A combination of purchases by the buffer-stock manager and the imposition of export controls by the council kept the price within the range over the remainder of the year.[58]

The Fifth ITA, 1975

In May–June 1975 tin-exporting and importing countries met in Geneva to negotiate a new pact to cover the 1976–81 period.[59] The announced intention of the United States to seek membership ensured that the negotiations would revolve around U.S. positions and priorities. While in some respects fearful of U.S. participation because it would strengthen the hands of the consumer "hawks" (especially West Germany) on the council, the producers were nonetheless anxious to have Washington on board both to increase the legitimacy of the ITA and, hopefully, to gain a degree of multilateral control over U.S. stockpile disposals. Like other developed states at this time, the United States perceived a need to offer some positive alternatives to the NIEO proposals emanating from the Group of 77 and the nonaligned countries. Participation in the ITA was consistent with past U.S. backing for producer-consumer accords. More important, key officials within the U.S. government saw it as a low cost way to earn political points with the LDCs and reduce hostility in U.S.–Third World economic relations. As a Treasury Department official noted after the conference, for the United States joining the ITA was "a political solution to a political problem."[60]

During the negotiations the most contentious issue was financing the buffer stock. Tin producers continued to insist that consumers contribute on an equal basis. The United States, backed by West Germany, refused to consider mandatory consumer financing of the buffer stock, suggesting that a better approach was for those importing nations anxious to share in the costs to do so voluntarily. In fact, Canada, Britain, Belgium, France, and the Netherlands offered in advance to provide funds.[61] On the question of the price range, the producers sought a further rise even though the range had been increased in January 1975 and the market was turning distinctly bearish. It has been reported that they feared that U.S. membership would make it much more difficult to secure the consumer votes (or acquiescence) needed to alter the price range—a fear that subsequently proved to be quite well founded.[62] The United States tersely noted that Bolivia's pleadings about high production costs were suspect because the onerous taxes and royalties imposed on the tin industry in that country somehow found their way into its calculation of costs.[63] This U.S.–Bolivian dispute over the price range would prove to be the primary axis of conflict during the life of the fifth agreement.

The toughening of consumers' resolve with the accession of the United States was demonstrated at the first meeting of the council under the fifth ITA in July 1976 when they unanimously rejected producers' request for yet another price revision—two upward revisions to M\$1,000–M\$1,200 having been adopted in the first half of 1976.[64] (The new ITA had been brought into force provisionally by those states that had signed it.) This

·refusal made the agreement effectively inoperable, since the market price was above the ceiling and the buffer-stock manager lacked metal (producers had again contributed in cash). Bolivia, the highest-cost producer and the country most dependent on tin for export earnings, was incensed and demonstrated its displeasure by announcing it would not ratify the agreement, so that definitive entry-into-force could not occur. In December 1976 the council did raise the ITA range to M$1,075–M$1,325, but this fell significantly short of the demands of Bolivia and Malaysia. In January 1977 the market price went through the new ceiling amid reports that a 20,000–30,000 ton shortage was expected for the year, partly because of stagnating production and the improved competitiveness of tinplate vis-à-vis plastic packaging as a result of rising oil prices.[65]

By March 1977 the market price of tin reached a new daily record, M$1,660.[66] And Bolivia continued its refusal to accede to the new agreement, demanding that the ITA floor price be indexed "to the cost of plant and equipment and other economic factors in industrialized countries."[67] The Malaysian Minister of Primary Industries, on behalf of the four main exporters, took this suggestion to Washington where, predictably, it received "a flat rejection from the U.S. Administration, which has repeatedly said it does not want to know about indexation in any form."[68] The European Community members gave a similar response. However, consuming members did agree in early March to the principle of periodic review of the price range. The council then established an Economic and Price Review Panel (EPRP), a permanent body charged with examining data on production costs and world inflation in order to facilitate regular, twice-yearly reviews by the full Tin Council of the floor and ceiling prices. This compromise was apparently enough for the Bolivians, who promptly announced that they would ratify the ITA before the June 30 deadline.[69]

In light of market prices well over M$1,500 and an anticipated tin supply shortage, the council agreed, after the initial report of the EPRP, to revise the ITA range to M$1,200–M$1,500 (from M$1,075–M$1,325). Debate on the extent of the revision was heated, with the main axis of conflict again pitting the Bolivians against the Americans. Bolivia, arguing that its production costs were about M$1,300/picul, demanded that the ITA floor be set at this level. But other producers felt that "they could not indirectly subsidize inefficient operations," while the United States and other consumers criticized Bolivian taxation and mining practices.[70] In exchange for not thwarting an upward revision of the ITA range, the United States insisted that there be changes in the tax regimes governing the industry in producing countries and that producers pledge not to seek export controls over the next two or three years. Most producers reportedly agreed to the latter demand and made conciliatory noises regarding taxes.[71]

An important event in the life of the fifth ITA was a 1977 pledge by the United States to contribute "voluntarily" 5,000 tons of tin metal to the buffer stock (which was completely bereft of metal for virtually its entire life owing to high market prices). Secretary of State Cyrus Vance announced the contribution at a meeting of the Conference on International Economic Cooperation in the spring of 1977, at a time when Washington was very concerned that it not be seen as completely intransigent in the North-South dialogue. Producers welcomed this announcement—all except Bolivia, quite comfortable in the role of outcast, which felt that *any* release of GSA tin, for whatever purpose, would dampen the market.[72] This change in American policy, bringing it in line with most other Western countries, set the stage for U.S. support for the principle of joint financing in the Common Fund negotiations.

In late 1977 and early 1978 bitter wrangling over the price range again occurred on the Tin Council and on the EPRP. At the July 1978 meeting of the Tin Council, producers, noting the continuing high market price (over M$1,700/picul), argued for a new range of M$1,500–M$1,900, up from the M$1,200–M$1,500 then prevailing. Consumers announced that they would reluctantly support an increase to M$1,350–M$1,700, and this was accepted.[73] But the United States, Britain, West Germany, Japan, and the USSR demanded in exchange that producers consent to a twelve-month moratorium on further increases, and the producers (except Bolivia) agreed. The new range failed to capture the market, as a new all-time daily record price of M$2,085 was recorded in November 1978.[74] The very rapid escalation of prices for tin throughout the late 1970s reflected such factors as the declining quality of ore grades in Bolivia and Malaysia, world economic recovery after the mid-1970s recession, insufficient increases in output (in part thanks to falling Bolivian production after 1977), and the absence of tin sales from the U.S. stockpile.

By July 1979 the "unwritten" agreement for a one-year moratorium on price-range hikes had expired, and the council meeting again saw harsh debate. As usual Bolivia sought the largest jump, but it eventually agreed to a joint producer request for a new range of M$1,850–M$2,400. Indonesia and Thailand were actually prepared to accept a smaller increase, since their production costs were lower than either Bolivia's or, increasingly, Malaysia's. Importing countries rejected these figures but eventually ac-

·cepted a new range of M$1,500–M$1,950/picul. For the first time in a long while, the ITA range captured the market, though only briefly.[75] In March 1980, just before the opening round of negotiations to formulate a new ITA, the Tin Council agreed to hike the range by another 10 percent, to M$1,650–M$2,145.[76]

The Sixth ITA, 1981

Negotiations to conclude a sixth tin pact[77] proved to be longer and more difficult than had those on earlier ITAs. Four separate bargaining sessions were required over 1980–81 to draft an agreement that, in the end, had the backing of neither the United States, the largest importer, nor Bolivia, a key producer. Although the late 1970s were lucrative years for tin exporters, they were unhappy with the way in which the fifth agreement had operated, and especially with the fact that the price range had lagged behind the market. The economic provisions of the tin agreement had been basically nonoperational, and producers were determined that this would not happen with the sixth ITA.

Before the formal negotiations began, the producing states met in Thailand in February 1980 and agreed to press for certain provisions. First, they supported the continuation of export control provisions and a buffer stock of 20,000–30,000 tons (to be equally financed by producers and consumers). Second, they resolved to demand a rule requiring *regular* revisions of the price range, based on "objective" criteria regarding production costs and world inflation, so that consumers would not be able to thwart upward revisions.[78]

Meanwhile, consumers were also formulating positions to take into the talks. Most importing countries wanted an agreement broadly similar to previous ITAs, but the United States took a very different stance. It put forth proposals identical to those it adopted during the 1977–79 natural rubber negotiations: reliance on a large buffer stock as the sole instrument of market regulation; no export or production controls, since they tend to freeze market shares and subsequently impede increases in output; and equal contributions by consumers and producers to a large buffer stock. The U.S. argument against export restrictions appears to have been a product of economic doctrine and a well-developed consensus within the administration that such controls were inherently detrimental to consumer interests. Buffer stocks, on the other hand, were viewed favorably by U.S. government agencies responsible for international commodity policy because, unlike export controls, they have the potential to moderate high as well as low prices—provided they are sufficiently large.[79]

Negotiations to renew the ITA began in Geneva in April 1980 under UNCTAD's auspices. The United States called for the abandonment of export controls and an increase in the buffer stock to 70,000 tons, with consumers to share equally in providing funds for this much larger stock. This package was rejected by the producers, who refused even to consider abandoning export controls, and who also argued that a buffer stock of the size demanded by Washington would, in conjunction with the huge American stockpile, act as a permanent market depressant. The European Community offered a compromise by proposing a 35,000 ton buffer stock with provision for a contingency reserve of another 20,000. This position was rejected by both the United States and the exporting countries, and the talks collapsed in mid-May.[80]

In the last half of 1980, tin prices began to decline, falling almost to the buffer-stock intervention level (M$1,815) by early December when the tin conference reconvened.[81] By this time Washington was prepared, albeit reluctantly, to include export restrictions and to be flexible on the size of the buffer stock. Conference Chairman Peter Lai presented a compromise proposal that called for a 30,000 ton, government-funded buffer stock, supplemented by another 20,000 tons to be financed by loans and government guarantees, and for the use of export controls once 35,000 tons of metal had been accumulated. This package was accepted by all delegations except the United States and Bolivia. The former announced that a 55,000 ton, government-financed buffer stock was as low as it could go, and that it would not accept export controls unless 40,000 tons of metal were in the stock. Bolivia, for its part, felt that only 15,000 tons of metal should have to be accumulated before the imposition of export restrictions. It also refused to sign any agreement that did not substantially strengthen the control of the Tin Council over noncommercial stockpiles of tin, a position that had previously been adopted by the producers collectively, but that the others were now prepared to abandon. With the two recalcitrants unable to agree to the Lai proposals, the talks came to an end in mid-December. Because of the difficulty of reaching agreement on a new ITA, in January 1981 the Tin Council decided to extend the fifth pact for an additional year, i.e., to June 1982.[82]

A fourth and, as it turned out, final attempt to agree to a new ITA occurred in June 1981. Once again the proposals previously drawn up by Peter Lai served as the basis for negotiations and were in large part integrated into the sixth agreement. The new ITA provided for a buffer stock of 30,000 tons, equally funded by exporters and importers, with another 20,000 tons "to be financed from borrowing, using as security stock warrants and, if necessary, government guarantees" (article 21). On the crucial question of export controls, producers agreed, as a concession to the United States, that 35,000 tons of metal would have to be accumulated before restrictions could be instituted by a two-thirds distributed majority (a simple distributed majority if 40,000 tons were in the buffer stock; article 32). In other respects the sixth ITA was basically identical to its predecessors. However, the new buffer-stock and export-control provisions were major changes.

Following the June 1981 conference some doubt existed as to whether the sixth ITA would come into force, as a result of dissatisfaction with various provisions among both producers and consumers. But eventually, only the United States and Bolivia failed to accept it. Bolivian opposition stemmed from the restrictions on export quotas, the size of the buffer stock, and the absence of ITA controls over sales from noncommercial stockpiles (mainly the U.S. strategic stockpile). In the case of the United States, it had been somewhat at odds with the majority of ITA members in the early conference sessions on the size of the buffer stock, the tonnage needed to initiate export controls, and the size of the required voting majorities. With the coming to power of the Reagan administation in January 1981 the gap widened on all these points, the new administration being generally less hospitable to intergovernmental market intervention than the previous one. When the United States finally announced that it would not join the sixth ITA, many Tin Council members were angered because of the changes that had been made in the agreement to accommodate U.S. preferences.[83]

In the year following the conference and the entry into force of the sixth ITA on July 1, 1982, the major development affecting the tin market was the purchase by a "mystery buyer" of significant volumes of tin between July 1981 and February 1982, which in turn drove prices upward. The mystery buyer was widely believed to represent Malaysian interests angered by consumer opposition to a large increase in the price range throughout 1981. (A modest increase of 6.85 percent was, however, accepted in October. With a change in the Malaysian currency, the official range then became M$29.15–M$37.88/kilogram.) During this period the United States sold significant volumes of tin from its stockpile to moderate the price climb. The market weakened following the cessation of purchases by the mystery buyer in February 1982. The council then instituted a 10 percent cut in export quotas in April when the price momentarily dropped below the ITA floor. The mystery-buyer episode caused consternation among consumers, and Britain and West Germany let it be known that they would withdraw from the agreement if this type of activity occurred again.[84]

The sixth ITA entered into force only provisionally in July 1982, since the consuming-state members did not account for 80 percent of world consumption (article 55). The absence of several important states reduced the expected resources at the disposal of the buffer-stock manager, but through creative interpretation of certain ITA provisions he was able to justify additional borrowings. Owing to the depressed market at the time, the council tightened export controls from 10 to 36 percent, and in August secured agreement from the United States (at the time a nonmember) not to disrupt ITA price-support activities.[85] In the ensuing year the price remained near the bottom of the range despite buffer-stock purchases and export controls, prompting Malaysia to press for producer action outside the council.

Producers met to discuss the creation of a tin producers' body in the fall of 1982, and the Association of Tin Producing Countries (ATPC) was formally constituted in June 1983. Malaysia, which was cutting back production on its own, wanted to include provisions for the possible use of export controls and a buffer stock, but Indonesia and Thailand opposed this strategy. The latter two states did, however, agree reluctantly to a "secret" memorandum of understanding which stated that the ATPC would consider market intervention if the ITA failed to protect their interests. With slightly lower costs of production, and with tin occupying a less prominent position in their economies, they were not as inclined toward strong producer intervention. Australia's decision to join ATPC, and a shift of Malaysian policy away from joint producer action in the autumn of 1983, made it less likely that the new organization would stray beyond the objectives of promoting the consumption and marketing of tin.[86]

Throughout 1983 and 1984 the tin market was weak owing to slack demand and increased global production. It was only because of the ITC's imposition of export cutbacks of 40 percent and purchases by the buffer-stock manager that prices were kept above the floor of M$29.15. To hold excess tin off the market, the buffer-stock manager not only drew on the buffer stock fund but also (as allowed by the ITA) borrowed money to purchase physical tin on the Kuala Lumpur Tin Market and to engage in forward selling and buying on the futures market at the London Metal Exchange. The money was borrowed from banks (which demanded tin warrants as collateral) for the purchase of physical tin, and also from brokers for purchases on the LME. The buffer-stock manager's financial position was strengthened at this time by the depreciation of the British pound against the Malaysian dollar (the latter being tied to the U.S. dollar). This development buoyed the price of tin in British pounds on the LME, and meant that he often made a profit on the sale of tin at the end of a forward contract. This tended to offset the interest charges on the money he was borrowing. However, during this period the buffer-stock manager pointed out to members that he did not have adequate resources to continue buying ad infinitum to protect the floor price.[87]

In 1985 the position of the manager, and of the ITC itself, grew increasingly precarious as the council's financial resources and borrowing capacity steadily disappeared. This situation was due in large measure to the appreciation of the British pound against the Malaysian dollar. Because of this the manager lost money when he sold tin at the end of a forward contract. In April and May 1985 he obtained permission to purchase tin below the floor price on the Kuala Lumpur market so as to reduce the losses he was suffering on the LME. Finally, on October 23, 1985 he called the LME and said that he no longer had the financial resources needed to meet his forward purchase commitments. It later emerged that the ITC owed almost £900 million—about a third to 14 banks, and the rest to 14 LME brokers. Through its buffer stocks and forward contracts the ITC also controlled almost 80,000 tons of tin. On October 24 the LME terminated tin transactions, and a long and arduous diplomatic effort to resolve "the tin crisis" commenced.[88]

The roots of the crisis were quickly recognized by both participants and observers. First, supply had been exceeding demand for a number of years despite ITC export controls. This was caused by increased production and exports by nonmembers such as Bolivia, China, and especially Brazil, and also by large-scale smuggling of tin in Southeast Asia to Singapore smelters.[89] Second, the banks had offered "special deals" for purchases of physical tin and brokers had given loans for forward buying with little in the way of margins or down payments required. Evidently they did not worry about their loans because of what turned out to be a misguided notion that the 22 ITC members would stand behind the ITC's debts. Third, the buffer-stock manager's operations were shrouded in considerable secrecy, and many member states did not really grasp the nature and extent of the problem until it was too late. The manager's physical purchases were publicized, but his operations on the futures market were not until three months afterward—and even then certain information was not conveyed to members. There were good reasons for the secrecy, but there were also some serious problems with this system.[90]

Immediately following the termination of tin trading on the LME and the Kuala Lumpur Tin Market intense negotiations began among ITC members, the banks, and the LME brokers. The banks and brokers were of course anxious that ITC members assume the debts accrued. However, except for Britain, which was deeply concerned about the viability of its banks and the future of the LME, states resisted acceptance of this responsibility. This position was bolstered by legal advice that they were not liable.[91] After almost two months of fruitless negotiations officials from one bank and one broker devised a proposal in late December that became the focal point of negotiations through early March 1986. This proposal called for the creation of a new company (first called Newco, and then Tinco) that would purchase the liabilities of the ITC and thus the tin that the buffer-stock manager had contracted to buy. It would then sell off this tin over a three-year period so as to moderate the fall in prices when trading recommenced. Initially the plan envisaged that governments would contribute £200 million, the brokers £50 million, and the banks another £20 million. Later the division was £115 million, £80 million, and £20 million. During the negotiations the Kuala Lumpur Tin Market was reopened in early February, but it was allowed to sell only very limited quantities.[92]

The European Community allies of Britain (particularly France, West Germany, and the Netherlands) were not enamored of this plan to rescue the banks, the LME brokers, and possibly the ITC itself. They especially did not want to do anything that implied acceptance of legal liability. However, Britain prevailed on them to go along with the plan on condition that it would contribute a larger share. In the end the Tinco plan was undermined in March 1986 by the opposition of Indonesia and Thailand. They cited various deficiencies in the proposal, and Indonesia claimed that it could not afford its contribution at a time of depressed oil prices. More fundamental reasons may have been reluctance on their part to give assistance to banks and brokers and a belief that they could expand their shares of the export market, given their low costs of production. Indonesia in fact soon announced plans to increase production.[93]

In the aftermath of the failure of the rescue plan the banks were free to sell the 45,000 tons of tin they controlled as collateral for loans. One bank and two brokers also began legal proceedings against the ITC, and in an out-of-court settlement they obtained the remaining approximately 17,000 tons controlled by the ITC. By April 1986 tin was trading at less than half its price in October 1985.[94] Given little change in this price level through 1986 and early 1987, it is quite possible that some producing states came to regret their rejection of the Tinco scheme.

In April 1987 the sixth ITA was extended without economic regulatory provisions from July 1987 to June 1989 because ITC members wanted to continue the council's information-gathering function. Some also felt that the ITC's continued existence would assist them in future legal suits. ITC members are faced with possible legal actions by various banks and brokers, although it is unclear whether the latter will be able to pierce the hard shell of state sovereign immunity and recoup their losses. Regardless of what happens on the legal front, the consumer members of the ITC are thoroughly alienated from the regulatory scheme for tin. Apart from their view that export controls and forward buying by a buffer-stock manager are recipes for disaster (especially when all producers are not members of an ICA), they are unhappy with the decision by some producers to reject the rescue plan. It may be a long time before they are again receptive to the idea of an international commodity agreement for tin.

NATURAL RUBBER

The Market

Natural rubber is obtained from trees that grow within a band about 20 degrees north and south of the equator. Once a seedling is planted, a period of six years is typically required before it will yield latex, which is then processed into different types of rubber. Synthetic rubber, invented during World War II, has gained an increasing share of the world elastomer market, accounting for about 65 percent of global consumption by 1986. The substitutability of synthetic for natural rubber is a matter for debate, but each is generally regarded as preferred or necessary for 25 percent of the market. Natural rubber is particularly preferred when a high resistance to heat is needed (for example, for airplane tires).[95]

The three major producers are all Southeast Asian states and most of their exports are purchased by the developed countries (tables 3.5 and 3.6). Malaysia has been and remains the dominant exporter, with its share of the market climbing slightly from 42 to 44 percent between 1965 and 1982. Over the same period Indonesia's share declined from 32 to 26 percent, while Thailand's rose from 10 to 18 percent. The economic and political im-

TABLE 3.5

Natural Rubber: Exports by Main Countries

Countries	% of World Exports				
	1965	1970	1975	1980	1982
Indonesia	32.2	28.4	27.0	29.9 '	26.2
Kampuchea	2.1	0.5	0.3	—	—
Liberia	2.2	3.0	2.8	2.3	2.2
Malaysia	41.8	46.8	48.8	45.4	44.3
Nigeria	3.1	2.1	1.8	0.4	0.9
Sri Lanka	5.6	5.5	5.5	3.7	4.3
Thailand	9.6	10.0	11.4	14.0	17.9
Vietnam	2.8	0.8	0.3	1.1	1.0
Others	0.6	2.9	2.0	3.2	3.2
	Exports by Weight (Thousand Metric Tons)				
World	2,200	2,785	2,920	3,265	3,060

Source: World Rubber Statistics Handbook, Vol. 2: *1965–1980* (London: International Rubber Study Group, 1984), table 7; *Rubber Statistical Bulletin* (March 1984), vol. 38, table 7.

TABLE 3.6

Natural Rubber: Imports by Main Countries and Groupings

Countries	% of World Imports				
	1965	1970	1975	1980	1982
EC-9	28.1	26.4	22.1	21.2	21.3
Other Western European	6.1	6.3	6.8	6.5	6.7
U.S.	19.0	19.0	21.4	17.8	20.3
Canada	2.1	1.9	2.2	2.3	2.3
Australia	1.8	1.4	1.6	1.3	1.2
Japan	9.5	10.4	10.0	14.1	13.5
Eastern Europe	28.1	26.4	22.1	21.2	12.3
Others	15.0	16.1	20.1	23.2	22.4
	Imports by Weight (Thousand Metric Tons)				
World	2,190	2,815	2,980	3,240	3,060

Source: World Rubber Statistics Handbook, Volume 2: 1965–1980 (London: International Rubber Study Group, 1984), table 8; *Rubber Statistical Bulletin* (March 1984), vol. 38, table 8.

TABLE 3.7

Percentage of Export Earnings of Developing Countries from Natural Rubber

Countries	1976–78	1980–82
Malaysia	20.5	11.8
Sri Lanka	15.7	13.0
Liberia	13.0	15.8
Thailand	8.9	7.4
Indonesia	5.9	3.8
Burma	2.3	2.5
Zaire	2.1	1.2

Source: World Bank, *Commodity Trade and Price Trends* (1980), table 11 and (1985), table 9. Only countries whose exports of natural rubber accounted for at least 2 percent of their export earnings are listed.

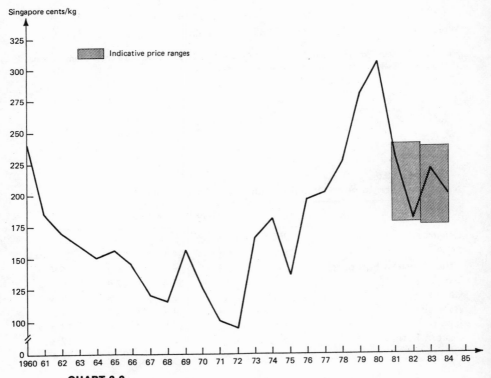

CHART 3-2

International Rubber Prices and International Rubber Agreements' Price Ranges; 1960 to 1984

Note: Prices are for Singapore, No. 1 RSS in bales.
Source: UN Doc. TD/B/C.1/270 (1985), p. 22.

portance of the rubber industries in the producing countries (table 3.7) is magnified by the fact that 80 percent of the rubber-producing area in the major producing countries is cultivated by smallholders. In Malaysia, 3 million people are employed in the rubber industry, and it directly or indirectly supports a quarter of the country's population.[96]

Natural rubber is traded on organized markets, the most important being in London, Singapore, and Kuala Lumpur. Its price has been moderately unstable, with an annual variation in constant dollars of 16.3 percent from 1955 to 1981 (table 1.4, chart 3.2). During the 1980s the market has been quite stable, but prices have been low.[97] In the short run, fluctuations in rubber prices are caused mainly by changes in demand, which in turn are rooted in business cycles in the industrial world. Producers can respond to changing demand to some extent by altering their tapping and stocking policies, but they are constrained by a six-year lag before newly planted trees yield rubber. "In the longer term, however, natural rubber prices are largely determined by the trend in synthetic rubber prices. Synthetic rubber prices set the ceiling and the floor . . . within which natural rubber prices are expected to fluctuate."[98] In the 1970s the price of synthetic rubber rose substantially because of the 1973–74 and 1979 increases in the price of oil, an important ingredient in its manufacture. This caused a dramatic rise in the price of natural rubber. The stagnation and then downturn in oil prices in the early and mid-1980s has had the opposite effect.[99]

Early Negotiations and Market Control Schemes

Attempts to regulate the rubber market first began in the interwar period. Following the collapse of the postwar economic boom in 1921 the British, on behalf of their colonies Malaya and Ceylon, instituted a compulsory control scheme in 1922. The production cutbacks required by the plan did raise the price, but the refusal of the Dutch (on behalf of the Netherlands East Indies) to adopt comparable restraints, coupled with the expansion of production elsewhere, led to cancellation of the plan in 1928. The worldwide depression of the early 1930s renewed interest in a supply-management arrangement, and in 1933 the British and Dutch concluded the International Rubber Regulation Scheme, which was based on export quotas and the curtailment of new plantings. Over the next five years this scheme had a positive effect on the price level, and it was renewed in 1938. The Japanese occupation of Southeast Asia in 1942 spurred the most significant development in the history of the rubber industry—the manufacture of synthetic rubber. By the end of the war the United States, which had previously met all its rubber needs through imports, was able to supply synthetics amounting to no less than one-third of world rubber consumption.[100]

In 1944 the International Rubber Study Group (IRSG) was established to provide a forum in which synthetic and natural rubber producing countries could meet and discuss issues of mutual interest. From the late 1940s through the early 1970s the major concerns of natural rubber-producing countries were the control of the production of synthetics and the assurance of a remunerative price for natural rubber exports. The leading consuming and synthetic-producing countries, however, refused to consider any controls over synthetic rubber production.[101] As a result, producing countries decided to establish their own organization in 1970—the Association of Natural Rubber Producing Countries (ANRPC). The initial ANRPC deliberations were unproductive. No consensus existed on what course of action to take. However, several developments soon occurred that accomplished what international negotiations had failed to do. The commodity price boom of 1972–74 and the OPEC oil price increase in 1973–74 sent the price of natural rubber skyrocketing, more than doubling between 1972 and the first half of 1974.[102]

While the immediate consequence of the rise in oil prices was to boost the price of natural rubber, it soon had an indirect negative impact when it led to a recession in the industrial world and to a resulting decline in the demand for rubber. The effects were especially severe in Malaysia, where large-scale riots of farmers and student sympathizers occurred. In December 1974 Malaysia acted unilaterally to stem the price fall. The government withdrew 104,000 tons from the market and introduced new restrictions on tapping. The price drop was arrested after the Malaysian actions, and "The evidence suggests that the immediate increase in the level of prices was largely due directly to the scheme's operations."[103]

Economic conditions improved in 1976, and the consumption of both natural and synthetic rubbers (as well as their prices) increased modestly.[104] In the meantime, Malaysia, anxious to prevent another market crisis and to spread the burden of supporting the price in future depressed markets, won the consent of other producers to explore a price stabilization program within the ANRPC. The resulting Jakarta Natural Rubber Agreement, concluded in November 1976, included provisions for the establishment of a 100,000 ton buffer stock and for the possible introduction of "supply rationalization" measures in pursuit of price stabilization. The floor price was to be determined "after taking into account *inter alia* costs of production, particularly for rubber smallholders who account for the bulk of rubber production," while the ceiling level would be determined after considering "the relative cost of synthetics vis-a-vis natural rubber. . . . "[105] The accord also left open the door to possible membership ,by consuming states.[106] The Jakarta scheme never actually became operative, thanks to buoyant demand and prices in 1977 and 1978; yet the conclusion of the accord was not without significance, for it showed consuming countries that the producers were prepared to take responsible actions to stabilize the market. Far from viewing the Jakarta agreement as an undesirable cartel, the consuming states generally sympathized with the producers' approach.[107]

The 1979 International Natural Rubber Agreement

Natural rubber was one of the ten "core" commodities incorporated in the IPC in 1976. From the beginning of the talks on rubber, the developed importing countries, and particularly the United States, indicated that they were prepared to consider seriously the establishment of a joint producer-consumer regulatory scheme. This initial predisposition of consumers to back an ICA was, of course, in contrast to their attitude on most other commodities. Before the convening of a full-fledged intergovernmental conference a series of preparatory meetings was held in 1977 and 1978. In the draft submitted by the ANRPC to the first preparatory meeting, the producers called for a jointly financed 350,000–400,000 ton buffer stock; strong supply "rationalization" measures to be implemented if the floor price was threatened; and assistance from international financial organizations for producing countries pursuing supply management (for example, to fund temporary national stocks). Producers argued that promotion of a "remunerative" price would benefit consumers because it would encourage needed investment in the industry and ensure a stable rubber supply.[108]

Consumers, while agreeing that there was much of value in the Jakarta stabilization plan, were cautious about proceeding rapidly toward an ICA and stressed the need for additional technical and exploratory work. The Western consuming nations did not have a common stance at that stage, and indeed this was true throughout the negotiations, a fact that made for rather slow progress. The Soviet-bloc countries expressed unreserved support for the proposals of the producers, and proclaimed that "because of the monopoly of international trade by imperialists, price fluctuates widely and has a deleterious effect on the terms of trade of producing countries."[109]

After the second preparatory meeting a task force was formed to examine the issues in more detail. Shortly thereafter the United States produced a lengthy econometric study on a number of price-control strategies.[110] Washington argued that a large buffer stock, on the order of 700,000 tons, was needed, and it adamantly opposed export-control provisions. In its eyes the history of the International Tin Agreements had shown that a small buffer stock could not protect a ceiling price and that export controls encouraged inefficient production and a higher price trend. The United States also opposed a guaranteed floor price and wanted to designate a general price range with a "reference price" at its midpoint, which would be adjustable in line with underlying market trends and have a large "nonintervention" zone. Again, this U.S. policy was based on its assessment of the shortcomings of "the tin model." American negotiators felt that "political" factors had been paramount in the continual upward revisions of the ITA price range. Once the concept of a fixed floor price was accepted, they argued, it was politically impossible to lower that floor, and the prospect of the exhaustion of funds to purchase tin for the buffer stock was met by calls for export controls. Britain and West Germany had some sympathy for the U.S. position on this matter.[111]

Producers were unhappy with an adjustable price range, since it would rule out the establishment of a firm, guaranteed minimum price. They also strongly favored export controls. The Malaysian, Thai, and Indonesian governments were determined to provide protection for their politically important smallholders. Indeed, establishment of a guaranteed floor price was the primary benefit that these governments saw from a commodity agreement. The European Community states voiced reservations about the financial requirements necessitated by a very large buffer stock and thus criticized the 700,000 ton figure proposed by the United States. The Europeans were prepared both to see export controls incorporated into an agreement and to support a fixed floor price. The EC's differences with the United States were in part attributable to its stronger dislike of government financial contributions, but also flowed from a somewhat weaker attachment to free market doctrines.[112]

A decision was taken in February 1978 to convene a conference in November and December of that year. Work done before the conference resulted in some narrowing of differences, but several key points of divergence remained. Washington's demands precluded a joint consumer position; and in some respects, the other consuming countries—both Western and communist—were much closer to the producers' perspecive than to that of the United States. During the first stage of the conference in late 1978 the United States continued to oppose both a fixed price floor and export controls, although it did scale back its earlier buffer-stock demand by 100,000 tons. The producers then made a major concession by agreeing to exclude export controls from the proposed pact, and also indicated a willingness to expand the size of the buffer stock to 500,000 tons. But they refused to abandon their goal of a guaranteed minimum price.[113]

Upset with Washington's intractable stance, the producers decided to cut a deal with the European Community. This deal called for a 300,000 ton buffer stock, the inclusion of export-control provisions, and the retention of the concept of a guaranteed floor price. The EC-producer coalition then tried to pressure Canada and Japan to back this agreement, perhaps hoping that isolation of the United States would lead to a more flexible American posture. (The communist countries were also thought likely to back this EC-producer scheme.) But Canada and Japan were hesitant about supporting the plan, fearing that it would antagonize the United States. They also argued that without U.S. participation an ICA for rubber would be of little use. Canada thus launched an attack on this backroom deal, prompting the embarrassed EC delegation to abandon the arrangement. At this point the conference broke up and delegations returned to their capitals to prepare for the next round.[114]

Although United States policy had been the primary reason for the collapse of the December 1978 negotiations, the Carter administration was nonetheless strongly committed to an ICA for natural rubber, believing that a display of goodwill and flexibility was crucial to overall U.S.–Third World relations. Before the formal resumption of talks, U.S. officials visited the capitals of the major producers as well as Tokyo and Brussels. These discussions bore fruit when the 49-nation conference resumed in late March 1979. First, Washington accepted the producers' earlier proposed range of M$1.50 to M$2.70/kg. This had not previously been a particularly contentious issue, and other consumers had already given their support; but formal U.S. agreement on the price range was still welcomed. Second, the United States now accepted the notion of a floor price *which would be defended to the limit of the buffer stock's resources.* But Washington insisted that the zones of intervention in which the buffer-stock manager could buy and sell be adjustable to reflect underlying market trends at least partially and that export controls be eschewed. Producers reluctantly accepted these stipulations, since they felt that the natural rubber price would remain strong for the foreseeable future (at the time it was near the agreed ceiling of M$2.70). A third important American concession was to lower the buffer stock target to 550,000 tons, close to the producers' position of 500,000 tons.[115]

The International Natural Rubber Agreement (INRA),[116] which was formulated following the above changes in American and producer policies, included some rather complex regulations concerning the price range and buffer-stock operations. A price range of 150–270 Malaysian/Singapore (MS) cents was set for the first 30 months of the agreement. (A combination of Malaysian and Singapore currencies was used because of the importance of the Kuala Lumpur and Singapore markets.) A "reference price" of 210 MS cents was set at the midpoint of the range (although it could be altered upward or downward). Upper and lower "intervention prices" were established at levels 15 percent above and below the reference price (241.5 and 178.5 MS cents), and above and below these points the buffer-stock manager *could* begin to sell or buy rubber. Upper and lower "trigger action prices" were set at points 20 percent above and below the reference price (252 and 168 MS cents), and when the price went above or below these points, the manager *had to* begin to sell or buy. The reference price was to be reviewed every 18 months and revised downward (or upward) by 5 percent if the average market price over the previous six months was below the lower intervention price (or above the upper intervention price), or by 3 percent if net buffer-stock purchases (or sales) since the last price-range assessment totaled 300,000 tons. Unlike the reference price, the floor and ceiling prices of the range (called the "indicative prices") were not subject to automatic adjustment, but were to be reviewed every 30 months or when members with at least 200 votes so requested. Many producers were unhappy both with the wide band in the price range where the buffer-stock manager could not intervene (178.5- 241.5 MS cents) and with the absence of export controls, but they accepted those provisions in order to secure U.S. commitment to the floor price and to the agreement as a whole.[117]

The question of financing the 550,000 ton buffer stock generated conflict during the final stage of the negotiations. Some Western European consumer states were initially reluctant to accept joint producer-consumer financing, but they soon gave way in the light of producers' insistence on the principle and the growing acceptance of it among most developed countries. As a concession to the EC, the agreement divided the buffer stock into a "normal" stock of 400,000 tons and a "contingency" stock of 150,000 tons, the latter presumably to be used only if the normal stock (or the equivalent funds) proved insufficient to stabilize the market. However, since signatories "commit themselves to finance the total . . . international Buffer Stock of 550,000 tons," there do not appear to be significant differences between the normal and contingency stocks (article 28).

Although the United States and Canada voiced some interest in incorporating supply-commitment provisions so that producers would be obligated to sell rubber at the ceiling price if the ceiling were breached, the agreement contained no rules of this kind. This appears to be one of the few contentious negotiating issues on which the exporters got their way. A related issue of concern to the consuming countries was the assurance of adequate rubber supplies—including both increased plantings and a commitment by the producing countries not to cut back production and exports. The producers were reluctant to give explicit commitments, but they did accept the following language in article 43: "Exporting members to the fullest extent possible undertake to pursue policies and programmes which ensure continuous availability to consumers of natural rubber supplies." U.S. Assistant Secretary of State Abraham Katz noted that this article "implies, at a minimum, that these members should not restrict production or exports through government actions."[118] A perhaps more perspicacious observation was offered by a Firestone official during U.S. congressional hearings on the INRA: "In Article 43 there are words, but no real commitments in my mind."[119]

Several factors contributed to broad support among producers and consumers for the 1979 INRA. Producers' willingness to back a stabilization agreement with a "reasonable" price range (the market price was above the ceiling in 1979) and a large nonintervention band was mostly due to the existence of synthetic rubber substitutes. They knew that attempts to raise prices through supply control would inevitably encourage greater use of synthetics. The best they could expect was market stabilization, and the producers decided it was desirable to get consuming states to bear part of the financial burden of a buffer stock. Other factors encouraging producer accord on the INRA were the close regional economic and political ties among the key states (especially in the context of the Association of Southeast Asian Nations, ASEAN), their roughly comparable production costs, and the overwhelming dominance of smallholders. The Malaysian government, in particular, was frightened of unrest among rubber growers that could recur in a depressed market, and it badly wanted some insurance against this.[120]

The reasons why the developed states agreed to the INRA are more complex. One important consideration was the perceived relationship between price stabilization and a steadily increasing flow of supplies of natural rubber. With stable prices it was expected that farmers would be more willing to invest in increased plantings, and that producing governments would be prepared to encourage exports by lowering export taxes and eschewing supply cutbacks. Producers did accept vague commitments on taxes and supply controls (article 43), and these commitments were highlighted by U.S. government officials seeking to persuade Congress to approve the treaty.[121]

The principal reasons for consuming states' support of the INRA, however, were really political. First, they thought it prudent to make some concessions to the Third World during the North-South dialogue in the late 1970s. Natural rubber was one of the few IPC commodities for which the North believed a price-stabilizing ICA might be both acceptable and workable. And the INRA was the only *new* ICA to emerge from the prolonged UNCTAD commodities negotiations starting in 1976. Second, the major Southeast Asian rubber producers all enjoyed good political relations with the West. Providing some economic assistance to these countries was widely seen as consistent with overall Western strategic interests. Relevant to this point is Deputy Secretary of State Richard Cooper's comment during the congressional hearings on INRA: "At present ASEAN represents an important collective unit through which the United States can supplement our bilateral strategic and political interests in the region. In the aftermath of our departure from Vietnam and in view of the present instabilities in the area, strengthening and improving our ties with ASEAN has assumed great importance."[122] The British had strong political motivations for seeking to assist Malaysia, while the other European states and Japan were also predisposed to promote good relations with these producing countries by accepting a stabilization accord.[123]

The INRA was to come into force on October 1, 1980 for a five-year period. Definitive entry-into-force required the accession of countries accounting for 80 percent of both world imports and world exports; provisional entry-into-force required the accession of countries accounting for only 65 percent of imports and exports. The latter was accomplished by late October 1980 after U.S. ratification. In late 1980 the market price for natural rubber began to fall from its levels of the previous three years—levels generally above the ceiling of the new pact's price range (i.e., above 270 MS cents/kg). By mid-1981 the price was still above the buffer-stock accumulation range of 150–179 MS cents, precluding purchases by the manager.

Pressured by its smallholders, who were unhappy with the price fall, the Malaysian government acted to encourage stocking by traders and by the industry in Malaysia. However, the government reportedly would not intervene itself for fear of offending the spirit of the new agreement.[124] Subsequently, the onset of a world economic recession in the latter half of 1981 and the fall in the cost of synthetic rubbers due to softening oil prices further depressed the market, and prices reached the lower-intervention, or "may buy" level of 179 MS cents in November 1981. The buffer-stock manager of the International Natural Rubber Organization commenced purchases at this time and kept the price close to this level until January 1983, when the market strengthened.

In this 15-month period of a depressed market, serious strains were evident between producing and consuming members of the INRA. At the time of the first 18-month review of the price range in May 1982, the consumers called for the automatic 5 percent reduction of the reference price that the agreement stipulated should occur when the average indicator price for the preceding six months was below the lower intervention level. After long and acrimonious discussion it was agreed to reduce the price by just 1 percent. But within several weeks the producer organization, ANRPC, pressured by Malaysia, called on members to stockpile 350,000 tons (later reduced to 250,000)—a decision that evoked heated condemnations from rubber consumers. Another major confrontation was barely averted in late 1982 when the buffer stock reached 280,000 tons—20,000 tons short of the level that according to the INRA would have necessitated a 3 percent decrease in the reference price.[125]

In early 1983 the market for natural rubber strengthened because of increased demand and stocking by consumers. The price rose to close to the upper intervention level of 239 MS cents. It stayed above 200 MS cents for most of 1983 and 1984, and was just below that level when the INRA members met in April 1985 to discuss renewal of the agreement. The producers demanded an increase in the price range, while the consumers countered that the existing one was quite adequate. With the failure of this negotiating session the INRO council agreed in June 1985 to extend the agreement for two years until October 1987 and to proceed with additional conferences to formulate a new INRA.[126]

The gradual weakening in the market in 1985 led to the growth of the buffer stock to 300,000 tons—and hence to demands by consumers that the reference price be decreased by 3 percent. The producers objected, but eventually they acquiesced at the August council meeting, concerned about alienating consumers.[127] The price remained relatively low in the last half of 1985 and the first half of 1986 (around 185 MS cents). But it began to rise by the time of the May 1986 conference to formulate a new agreement.

Malaysia led the producers in demanding a 30 percent increase in the price range. It also raised the idea of introducing export quotas. The Malaysian government was anxious to secure assistance for its rubber smallholders before the May 1987 election. The consumers were unreceptive to the proposed price range given market trends and the size of the buffer stock (equivalent to 8 percent of annual world production). Nor would they consider export controls. The European Community and Japan were particularly hostile to any attempt to distort market trends after their experience with the collapse of the tin agreement. The session failed to bridge these differences, but the parties did agree to continue their negotiations.[128]

In March 1987, approximately six months before the end of the first INRA, producers and consumers finally agreed to a new rubber pact. Even though the market price had risen gradually over 1986 and early 1987 to near the middle of the price range, the producers secured none of the major changes they were seeking. The second INRA differs very little from the first and, in fact, contains one important proposal of the Western importing countries—the shortening of the time between price reviews by the council from 18 to 15 months. The producing nations retreated from their previous demands because they feared the depressing effect of the liquidation of the 360,000 ton buffer stock, and because they appreciated the modest price-support influence of the agreement. The consuming countries were not happy with the cost of the buffer stock, but they accepted the new INRA because it so closely reflected their model of a price-stabilizing ICA. Interestingly, the European Community adopted a stronger free-market stance in these negotiations than either the United States or Japan. On the political side the Western states did not want to risk alienating the Southeast Asian producers by terminating the accord. Their political sensitivity to the region is perhaps not so acute as during the period of Vietnam's invasions of Laos and Kampuchea, but the prosperity and goodwill of the three Southeast Asian producing states are still high priorities for the Western powers.[129]

CONCLUSION

The International Tin Agreement is the oldest, and the International Natural Rubber Agreement the newest, of the five postwar global commodity agreements analyzed in this book. However, the ITA has collapsed amid much bitterness among governments and private participants in the market, while the INRA is still operating with reasonable success. Several factors appear to have influenced the successes and failures of these two ICAs.

First, there are a relatively small number of tin and rubber producers, most of whom have close cultural and political ties and roughly comparable costs of production. Malaysia, Indonesia, and Thailand, all members of ASEAN, have displayed similar foreign policy orientations and coordinated their policies toward the tin and natural rubber agreements. Malaysia, as the largest producer, has often assumed a leadership role. The two countries most responsible for undermining the sixth ITA, Brazil and Bolivia, were from Latin America. Brazil enjoys low production costs and has dramatically increased its tin output; Bolivia suffers from high production costs and refused to cut back its tin exports.

Second, the producers of both commodities recognized that it would be difficult to operate a cartel successfully because of the availability of substitutes, the existence of the U.S. strategic stockpile, and certain differences within the producer group. They sought occasionally to act on their own, but without much success. Malaysia was usually the leader of such efforts but found it difficult to convince other producers to follow.

Third, the major Western consuming countries have had close political and economic ties with the producing states and have been willing to make small economic sacrifices to maintain amicable relations. Moreover, particularly in the 1970s they wanted to accept some of the Group of 77's proposals for a New International Economic Order in order to lessen hostility between the North and South. Price-stabilization arrangements for individual commodities were relatively inexpensive ways to exhibit concern for Third World development. It is true that the United States joined only the 1975 ITA, but throughout the agreement's history it conducted its stockpile sales so as not to undermine the activities of the International Tin Council.[130] The United States was less amenable to accepting provisions or actions that would boost prices, but it was prepared to assist in stabilizing markets.

Finally, a variety of characteristics influenced the acceptance and operation of the two ICAs. The inclusion of a formula in the ITA for adjusting export quotas in accord with shifts in productive capacity certainly encouraged most producers' continued loyalty to that accord. Related to this point is the importance of all major producers' adherence to a price-control scheme. During the first five ITAs all the significant exporters were members, but with the sixth agreement not only did Bolivia fail to renew its membership, but Brazil and China increased their market shares and remained outside the International Tin Council. Their refusal to accept the council's export controls (coupled with some smuggling of tin out of the Southeast Asian producing states) undermined the tin agreement. As for the INRA, which relies solely on a buffer stock, the inclusion of all producers is not as vital, although members could grow increasingly resentful of exporters who stayed outside and still benefited from buffer-stock operations that they had not helped to finance. In the case of INRA this is not a problem, since all the key producers have accepted the agreement. A principal reason for their adherence has been the willingness of the developed, consuming states to provide half the finances needed for the stock. Without such joint consumer-producer financing, the viability of a pure buffer-stock arrangement would be threatened.

4

THE SUGAR, COFFEE, AND COCOA AGREEMENTS

Sugar, coffee, and cocoa are among the most important Third World tropical agricultural exports. Over the period 1980–82, Third World exports of coffee averaged some $9.3 billion per year, while in the case of cocoa developing countries earned about $2.2 billion from sales to the world market. Sugar exports from the Third World averaged $8.8 billion per year, with sales from developed exporters worth another $4.5 billion.[1] A substantial number of developing countries depend on each of these commodities for a major share of their export earnings, and millions of people in Africa, Asia, and Latin America owe their livelihoods to the harvesting of these primary commodities. Sugar differs from the other two commodities in two significant respects. First, it is grown in large quantities by many developed industrial countries, and two of the biggest exporters are actually developed areas (the European Community and Australia). Second, a large and increasing share of global sugar imports (40 percent in 1982) has been accounted for by developing countries.

Attempts by producers, and occasionally consumers, to regulate the markets for these commodities were common in the first four decades of this century. This is not surprising, since they all suffered from marked price instability. The first postwar ICA for one of these commodities was the sugar agreement, which was negotiated in 1953. In the case of coffee the United States took the lead, and a global agreement was established in 1962. This agreement had the effect of preventing a widely anticipated collapse of the coffee market. Reaching an agreement on cocoa proved to be far more difficult, partly because of the relative indifference of American policymakers to the problems of the mainly African cocoa exporting countries. Not until 1972 was a producer-consumer cocoa pact established, and even then the United States decided not to become a member.

The history of negotiations aimed at creating control agreements for sugar, coffee, and cocoa provides an opportunity to examine in some detail several factors that typically influence the outcome of international commodity bargaining. The battle among exporters for market shares, and for large quotas when export controls are under consideration, is a central theme in the negotiations on all three of these commodities. The need for the cooperation of importing countries to make agreements effective has been a major factor behind the efforts of producing countries to negotiate ICAs. The problem of designing workable agreements when there are a large number of commodity exporters has often bedeviled attempts to fashion ICAs for the tropical agricultural commodities. When important exporters remain outside a commodity agreement, or when they are members but are in violation of its rules, the likelihood that an ICA can regulate a market successfully diminishes greatly. The difficulties posed for ICAs when developed countries are exporters are starkly revealed in the case of sugar. Finally, the importance of broader foreign policy considerations in shaping the policies of developed countries toward ICAs is a theme that runs through the history of all three commodities.

SUGAR

The Market

Sugar is derived from two plants, sugar cane, and sugar beet. Cane is a tropical or subtropical plant and is by far the most important source of sugar production in developing countries, while beet is a temperate-zone plant. Unlike most of the commodities examined in this book, a relatively small share of world sugar production (about 25 percent) is traded internationally, and close to half of this trade is conducted outside the "free market" under various preferential price and quota arrangements. The major existing preferential agreements are between the EEC and the African, Caribbean, and Pacific (ACP) states that are parties to the Lomé Convention, between the United States and about 35 producing states, and between the USSR and the East European bloc and Cuba.[2]

While developing countries have accounted for about 50 percent of world sugar production, their share of global exports has been much higher. Between 1955 and 1975, their export share was in the 75–78 percent range, but by 1982 it had dropped to 65 percent owing to the emergence of the European Community as a large exporter. The Latin American countries have always accounted for close to two-thirds of total LDC exports, with Cuba and Brazil being the biggest exporters within this grouping. Among the developed countries, the most important exporters are the European Community and Australia (table 4.1). A large number of exporters are highly reliant on export earnings from sugar (table 4.3).

Turning to sugar imports, the share of developing countries in the world total rose from 26 percent in 1955 to 41 percent in 1982. The Soviet bloc's share has also increased, from 9 to 28 percent, as a result of their large purchases from Cuba in the early 1960s. The decline in the import share of the developed market economies has been due to their adoption of a policy of greater self-sufficiency and the increasing popularity of alternative sweeteners in North America (table 4.2). Virtually all the developed countries have domestic sugar industries that survive thanks to the imposition of duties or quotas on sugar imports and the provision of subsidies to domestic producers.[3]

Sugar prices have been considerably more unstable than those of the other commodities reviewed in this book. The average annual change in constant dollars from 1955 to 1981 was 42 percent (chart 4.1 and table 1.4). As one official of the International Sugar Organization wrote: "Every five to seven years there is a shortage of sugar (or a phantom shortage as in 1979–80) and sugar prices lurch to unsustainable levels, which only succeed in encouraging overproduction and dampening off demand, leading to another five to seven years of low prices."[4] Several factors help to explain the chronic instability of the global "free market" for sugar. First, since only about 12 percent of world production is sold on the free market, relatively small variations in supply and in national protectionist policies can send shockwaves through the market. In addition, swings in the market are exacerbated by the facts that it usually takes sugar cane producers two to three years to respond to price signals and that producer coordination is difficult because of the vast number of sugar-growing countries. The fluctuations in supply that provoke the boom-bust cycle are attributable to producers' responses to price signals and to the impact of weather and disease. Changes in the policies of major importers toward greater self-sufficiency have also had a disruptive influence on world prices and trade patterns.[5]

Market Regulation Between 1919 and 1953

During the 1920s plentiful global supplies depressed sugar prices and prompted unilateral Cuban efforts to restrict production after 1926. This

TABLE 4.1

Sugar: Exports by Main Countries and Groupings

Countries				% of World Exports			
	1955	1960	1965	1970	1975	1980	1982
Developed Market	17.6	14.1	14.6	14.9	31.1	31.1	32.3
EC-10	12.6	8.5	7.9	8.2	9.6	18.4	20.1
Australia	4.5	4.8	6.7	6.3	9.2	8.1	8.2
Centrally planned	7.5	7.5	10.4	9.4	2.0	2.7	3.0
Developing countries	75.0	78.4	74.9	75.6	76.6	66.2	64.7
Africa	7.1	6.1	8.3	9.1	8.0	8.9	8.4
Mauritius	3.3	1.7	2.9	2.6	2.3	2.4	2.0
South Africa	1.7	1.5	1.9	3.6	2.6	2.9	2.8
Asia	13.6	13.3	17.0	11.7	15.7	12.9	15.8
Philippines	6.4	5.5	5.4	5.6	4.5	6.4	4.1
Taiwan	3.5	5.3	4.2	1.9	—	—	—
Thailand	—	0.0	0.4	0.3	5.2	1.7	7.0
Latin America	53.5	58.0	48.1	53.0	51.8	44.0	42.1
Brazil	4.1	4.5	3.9	5.1	8.1	9.6	8.7
Cuba	38.1	32.2	27.0	31.1	26.4	22.6	24.9
Dominican Repub.	4.0	6.4	2.7	3.5	4.4	2.9	2.7
	Exports by Weight (Thousand Metric Tons)						
World	14,373	17,188	19,341	22,180	21,717	27,340	31,040

Sources: Food and Agriculture Organization, *Trade Yearbook* (various years). Only the major exporters in the three groups of states are included.

TABLE 4.2

Sugar: Imports by Main Countries and Groupings

Countries	1955	1960	1965	1970	1975	1980	1982
				% of World Imports			
Developed countries	65.5	65.2	57.1	58.8	57.1	38.1	31.3
U.S.	24.8	25.6	18.8	21.6	15.8	13.7	8.8
EC-10	22.9	22.3	18.4	15.0	17.4	8.6	7.4
Japan	7.4	7.5	9.0	11.7	11.2	8.3	7.3
Centrally planned	8.5	12.2	16.0	19.4	18.2	21.5	28.0
Developing countries	26.0	22.7	26.9	21.8	24.7	40.4	40.7
Africa	6.9	6.7	8.1	6.2	7.8	9.3	10.3
Asia	15.7	14.4	17.4	14.6	16.7	25.3	24.7
Latin America	3.2	1.5	1.5	0.6	0.8	5.7	5.5
			Imports by Weight (Thousand Metric Tons)				
	14,435	16,715	18,803	11,032	22,069	27,222	29,451

Sources: Food and Agriculture Organization, *Trade Yearbook* (various years). Only the major importers in the three groups of states are included.

TABLE 4.3

Percentage of Export Earnings of Developing Countries from Sugar

Countries	1976–78	1980–82
Reunion	82.9	—
Mauritius	69.7	63.2
Cuba	—	76.4
Fiji	52.6	51.5
Belize	50.3	54.5
Swaziland	43.2	35.5
Guadeloupe	31.0	—
Guyana	30.7	27.8
Dominican Republic	29.5	36.5
Barbados	20.4	33.5
Philippines	12.4	9.7
Malawi	10.4	19.0
Jamaica	9.0	5.5
Thailand	8.5	5.4
Guatemala	8.4	4.6
Panama	8.2	13.5
Mozambique	6.4	19.3
Nicaragua	5.9	7.1
Peru	4.9	1.0
Bolivia	4.5	2.9
El Salvador	3.0	2.1
Brazil	3.2	4.7
India	3.2	1.3
Zimbabwe	2.9	5.4
Madagascar	2.4	2.6
Costa Rica	2.3	3.4
Honduras	0.8	4.6

Source: World Bank, *Commodity Trade and Price Trends* (1978) table 11 and (1985) table 9. Only countries whose exports accounted for at least 3 percent of their export earnings are included. A figure for Cuba for 1976–78 is not in the World Bank publication.

had an appreciable effect in maintaining the world price above what otherwise would have prevailed, but the onset of the Great Depression soon sent prices tumbling.[6] Cuba convinced several other producers—but not the United States, Britain, or their dependencies—to join a producers' regulatory scheme (the Chadbourne Plan) designed to liquidate accumulated

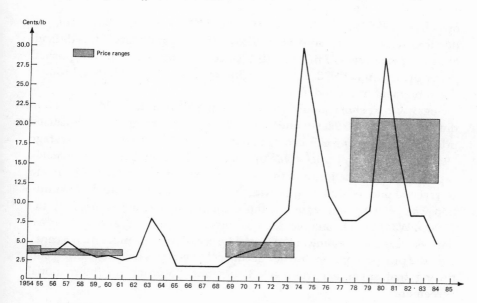

Chart 4.1

International Sugar Prices and International Sugar Agreements' Price Ranges, 1954–1984

Note: Prices are for f.o.b. Caribbean ports, bulk basis.
Source: UN Doc. TD/B/C.1/270 (1985), p. 27.

stocks and support the price. But this plan failed to stem the price decline, even though the participating countries almost halved their production between 1930 and 1933, because only 25 percent of world production was covered by the arrangement.[7]

In May 1937 the first producer-consumer International Sugar Agreement (ISA) was concluded by the major importing and exporting governments, including the United States and Britain for themselves and on behalf of their overseas territories. Exporters were assigned quotas for the free market, and agreed to reduce their stocks to 25 percent of their quotas. The Americans and British, concerned about the political implications of economic dislocation in some of the producing areas, were persuaded to satisfy stated portions of their consumption needs by buying from exporting members.[8] Although no price range was specified, a "reasonable price" objective was sought, defined vaguely as one "not to exceed the cost of production, including a reasonable profit, of efficient producers."[9] It is difficult to assess the success of this first ISA, since the anticipation of war pushed prices up after mid-1938, and the beginning of World War II then brought the agreement to an end.[10]

Sugar was in short supply when the war ended, and world production did not attain its 1939 level until 1948. Removal of wartime controls caused prices to rise to over 5 U.S. cents per pound in 1947, three times the average 1934–38 free market price. This upward spiral precipitated the inevitable expansion of production, and the world price predictably declined, only to be rescued once again by a new war, this one in Korea. Although consumption was growing impressively, the increased production caused by the Korean War boom soon reversed the buoyant price trend, and by 1953 exporters were complaining about a world price of scarcely more than 3 cents, with the prospect of even further declines.[11] Given this context, it is not surprising that sugar exporters felt it essential to reach an international agreement.

The 1953 International Sugar Agreement

With the backing of most participants in the sugar trade, a Sugar Conference was convened in London in October 1953 and soon produced a new International Sugar Agreement (ISA).[12] The agreement had three major economic mechanisms to support its basic objective—price stabilization. Most important were the provisions relating to the allocation and adjustment of export quotas. Exporting members were given "basic export tonnages" or percentages of projected sales on the free market (table 4.4). Their actual quotas, as set by the Sugar Council, would mirror their basic export tonnages when the market price was in the upper part of the range (3.25–4.25 cents). But if prices fell, national quotas could be reduced by the Sugar Council to 80 percent of basic export tonnages (90 percent in the case of the smallest producers). When the price exceeded the ceiling, quotas were to be lifted.[13] Cuba's primacy among the exporting signatories was evidenced by its huge basic export tonnage of 50.7 percent. This entitlement actually comprised only about half of Cuba's total sugar exports for 1954, the remainder being sold to the United States, all of whose imports were purchased through preferential arrangements with a host of producers.[14]

TABLE 4.4

Basic Export Tonnages Under the International Sugar Agreements

Countries	% of Total			
	1953	*1958*	*1968*	*1977*
Argentina				2.8
Australia			14.2	14.7
Brazil		8.8	6.5	14.7
Colombia			2.1	
Cuba	50.7	38.8	27.9	15.7
Czechoslovakia	6.2	4.4	3.5	1.1
Denmark		1.2		
Dominican Republic	13.3	10.5		6.9
Fiji			2.0	0.8
Guatemala				1.8
Haiti	1.0	0.7		
India			3.2	5.1
Mauritius			2.2	1.1
Mexico	1.7	1.2		0.5
Peru		7.9		2.2
Philippines	0.6	0.4		8.8
Poland	5.0	3.5	4.8	1.8
South Africa			8.1	5.5
Taiwan	13.5	10.5	8.2	
Thailand				7.5
USSR	4.5	3.2		

Sources: United Nations, *Treaty Series* (1957), 258:153; United Nations, *Treaty Series* (1961), 385:137; United Nations, *Treaty Series* (1969), 654:3; and UN Doc. TD/SUGAR/9/10 (1977).

A second key element of the 1953 agreement related to the accumulation and disposal of stocks, with producers prohibited by article 17 from stocking more than 20 percent of their production. This provision was included to prevent the accumulation of huge stocks of sugar that would then "overhang" the market and depress prices. Exporting signatories were also required to maintain *minimum* stocks of not less than 10 percent of their basic export tonnages so that sudden increases in free market demand could be met without thrusting the price above the ceiling (article 13). The third pertinent economic provision of the 1953 ISA was an obligation on the part of importing signatories not to purchase from nonmember exporters as a group during any quota year more sugar than they had imported from such countries during one of three previous years, 1951, 1952, or 1953 (article 7). The obvious intention of this rule was to prevent nonmember exporters from benefiting from the quota limitations accepted by ISA exporters.[15]

The Sugar Council set up to administer the agreement was divided into groups of exporters and importers for purposes of decision-making, each possessing an equal number of votes (1,000) as stipulated in the Havana Charter. Routine council decisions required a majority of the votes cast by each group (i.e., a distributed majority). On more important matters (e.g., the determination of quota adjustments), a "special vote" was required, defined as a two-thirds distributed majority (article 36). A system of weighted voting, based largely on countries' importance in the global sugar trade, was adopted. The United States and the United Kingdom accounted for almost half of the importers' votes, while Cuba had slightly less than a quarter of those granted to exporters (articles 33 and 34).

The question of *why* the exporting and importing states were able to put aside their inevitable intra- and intergroup differences and reach the necessary degree of consensus must be addressed. The wrangling among exporters that attends every effort to negotiate a commodity control arrangement was not absent in the case of sugar.[16] But the traditional battle for export quotas and market shares was muted by two salient facts. The first was Cuba's unquestioned dominance. As the world's largest sugar producer since World War I, Cuba dwarfed all other exporters. In addition, its quota agreement with the United Stated allowed it to sell over half its exports in the American market at a price 50–100 percent above the prevailing world price. It thus enjoyed considerable influence in bargaining over quota distributions. As one long-time participant in sugar negotiations commented: "In reality, Cuba's predominace was greater than these figures reveal; for its 1952 production showed that it could make or break the world market—and break it at relatively less cost to itself than to others."[17] Also helping to prevent more severe conflicts was the absence or limited involvement of several other major traders. The Philippines, for example, an exporter of almost one million tons annually during the mid-1950s, depended on the U.S. market—where it enjoyed a preferential arrangement—for virtually all its exports, and thus was not inclined to quibble over its tiny share of the free market.[18] Similarly, Australia, South Africa, and Mauritius were not vitally concerned with the ISA deliberations, since most of their exports were covered by the Commonwealth Sugar Agreement, under which they normally enjoyed higher prices than were obtainable in the world market. (The first two did become ISA members, however.)[19]

Had these various sugar-exporting countries been more dependent on the free market, it is probable that the determination of export quotas in 1953 would have been a measurably less gentlemanly affair.

During the bargaining, the developed-country importers from the free market (the most important being Britain, West Germany, Japan, and Canada) hoped to obtain a moderately low price range, but, like the United States, they also wanted a stable market that would provide reasonable profits to efficient producers. The two dominant players among the industrialized nations were Britain and the United States. The former was concerned about the well-being of Commonwealth exporters (many of which also sold sugar on the free market) and had officials from these areas on its delegation. For its part, the United States, anxious to assist Cuba and several other Latin America sugar producers, decided for largely political reasons to support the agreement. Even though the United States did not import sugar from the free market—all its imports coming under preferential arrangement—it was a major force at the conference, influencing its Western allies as well as the Latin American producers. However, the developed states would not let the ISA become a vehicle to transfer large sums to the producing countries.[20] In their desire to keep the price range at a relatively low level, the importing states had a useful ally in Cuba, which had comparatively low production costs and hoped that moderate prices would discourage other exporters from expanding their output.[21]

In 1954, the ISA's first year of operation, the agreement won fairly broad international backing, with its members accounting for 84 percent of exports to, and 54 percent of imports from, the free market.[22] The council was able to achieve reasonable success in stabilizing prices in 1954–55. In May 1956 a conference was held in Geneva to review the ISA. Cuba launched a major campaign to forestall the anticipated efforts of other exporters to reduce its huge basic export tonnage. It was successful in this endeavor, retaining over 50 percent of the total free market.[23] It was also agreed in 1956 that the price range would be lowered temporarily to 3.15–4 cents per pound, a move that apparently satisfied consuming countries sufficiently to keep them on board. But events conspired to threaten the support of the consuming nations for the sugar scheme as the Suez crisis in late 1956 led to increased transportation costs and stockpiling in response to the political insecurity. This sent prices soaring well above the ceiling (peaking at 6.8 cents in April 1957), where they remained throughout 1957, in spite of the council's decision in January of that year to suspend all quotas and to permit purchases from nonmembers.[24] An increase in production in response to this market trend, combined with the cessation of consumer stockpiling undertaken during the recent political disturbances, resulted in falling prices in 1958. The 1957 events were thus shown to be but a temporary consequence of unforeseeable political tensions.

Overall, the 1953 ISA must be judged a success in that free market prices stayed in the range for 56 out of 60 months. This stability was significantly attributable to Cuba's policy of maintaining several million tons of stocks and releasing them judiciously to prevent sharp price fluctuations. In a sense, Cuba "acted as the world's buffer stock."[25] As one analyst has noted, Cuba's stabilization strategy in the 1950s "was in Cuba's long-term interest, and it was fortunate that the interests of the largest producer benefited the entire world sugar economy."[26]

The 1958 ISA

The ISA was up for renewal in the autumn of 1958, and the key changes made to the agreement concerned the accession of Brazil and Peru, the major free market exporters outside the first accord. Some 95 percent of free market exports were now covered. With Brazil and Peru each obtaining basic tonnages of around 9 percent, Cuba's share had to drop, which it did from over 50 percent to 38.7 percent.[27] On the importers' side, broad foreign policy and political objectives remained central to the continued support of Britain and the United States for the agreement.[28] Japan was the importing member least happy with the first ISA, and in 1958 it sought to force exporters to hold larger stocks in light of the inadequacy of such stocks during the turmoil of 1957. In response to this complaint, the 1958 sugar agreement raised from 10 to 12.5 percent of basic export tonnages the size of stocks exporters were required to hold.[29] Other than this fine tuning, the 1958 ISA was essentially indistinguishable from its 1953 predecessor.[30]

The following year, 1959, witnessed a sharp increase in world production. The council's slashing of export quotas to their permissible minimum levels failed to stem a decline that had pushed the free market price down to 2.5 cents by July. The average price for the year as a whole was considerably below the ISA floor. In 1960 a development occurred that was to have an enormous long-term impact on the ISA. The United States decided to cut and then to abolish Cuba's quota in the U.S. market because it opposed the foreign and domestic policies of the new Castro government. At the time, Cuba supplied over 30 percent of total U.S. consumption.[31] Fortunately for the new regime, however, Soviet-bloc countries and the People's Republic of China soon began massive purchases of Cuban sugar that over the period of 1961–65 absorbed almost 70 percent of Cuba's sugar exports. Moreover, these communist countries were prepared, as the United States had been earlier, to offer Cuba a price considerably in excess of that prevailing on the free market.[32] The United States began programs designed to increase the output of its domestic sugar industry and proceeded to redistribute the Cuban quota to other, chiefly Latin American, countries. It pursued this latter policy partly because sugar supplies were available from these sources, and partly too because support for "friendly" countries in the Western Hemisphere was a central element in Washington's anticommunist foreign policy toward the region.[33]

Although these developments created "a drastic discontinuity in the market structure" governing international sugar trade, the pattern of low sugar prices established after 1957 continued unchanged for a time because of good crops in most of the producing countries.[34] In the autumn of 1961 it was once again necessary to renegotiate the ISA export quotas. Cuba adopted a hard line, insisting that it be given about a third of the free market, despite its generous sales contracts with the communist bloc. Other producers predictably rejected Cuba's demands. Without anything vaguely resembling a consensus on export quotas, the economic provisions of the ISA were abandoned on December 31, 1961.[35]

The 1968 ISA

The breakdown of the sugar agreement in 1961 was followed by a period of unusually high sugar prices beginning in late 1962. Poor harvests in 1961–62—particularly in Cuba, where the withdrawal of American capital and technical personnel and agrarian reform combined to slash production by almost 40 percent between 1961 and 1963—pushed average free market prices to more than 8 cents U.S. per pound in 1963; and they remained at almost 6 cents over the subsequent year. These heady price levels encouraged expanded production in many countries. In addition, Latin American and Caribbean producers moved to increase their crops to take advantage of Washington's reallocation of the massive Cuban share of the American market.[36] A 25 percent increase in world sugar production was recorded over the years 1963–65, and the free market price fell precipitously in 1965, averaging scarcely 2 cents for the year. Other important reasons for the low price in the mid- and late-1960s were the Soviet-bloc states' reexports of Cuban sugar to the free market, and the increasing self-sufficiency in sugar of the developed market economies.[37]

It was in this environment that an International Sugar Conference met in Geneva in September 1965. Developing exporter countries brought with them some of the ideas and objectives that had characterized the first session of UNCTAD one year before, and indeed the conference itself was the first commodity negotiation sponsored by the new body. Serious divisions soon appeared among the Third World producers on the allocation of export quotas.[38] But conflict among exporters was by no means the only, nor even the primary, reason for the failure of the negotiations. The very low prices then characterizing the world sugar market induced consuming countries to demand similarly low prices under any revised ISA, with the figure of 2.5 cents per pound suggested as a floor. Cuba, still the biggest producer and exporter of sugar, refused to sign any agreement with such a low price floor. Cuba's bargaining position was considerably strengthened by the agreements it had negotiated with the Soviet Union and China, in 1963 and early 1965, respectively, under which they paid roughly 6 cents per pound for over two-thirds of Cuban sugar exports.[39] Cuba could thus afford to ride out the depressed world market in hopes of more buoyant conditions.

Failure to negotiate a new sugar accord redounded to the detriment of exporters during the next several years as the world sugar price declined to very low historical levels. Over 1966–68 the average world price was 1.8 cents per pound, less than production costs in most countries.[40] In March 1966 the major exporters met in Geneva in an effort to improve market prospects. Most accepted an undertaking not to sell sugar at less than 2.5 cents per pound, well above the world price, but supplies were so plentiful that some members sold below the agreed price. The group soon decided to terminate the plan. Cuba's refusal to adhere to the 2.5 cent minimum was the main reason for its failure.[41]

In July 1967 the Secretary General of UNCTAD, Dr. Raul Prebisch, visited Havana, Washington, Brussels (for the EC), and Moscow to sound out these key actors on the possibility of negotiating a new sugar agreement. He soon obtained their support for another world conference. From the perspective of Third World producers, the "prolonged price depression had badly hurt many sugar producers, making them much more appreciative of the need for a new agreement."[42] Thus another International Sugar Conference was convened under UNCTAD's auspices in April 1968. As in earlier conferences, imports of sugar by the United States under its Sugar

Act, and by Britain under the Commonwealth arrangement, were excluded from consideration, and producers' sales to these markets would thus not be charged against their ISA quotas. However, participants were less willing to include all Cuba's sugar sales to Soviet–bloc countries in the category of "special" exports to be ignored in determining ISA basic export tonnages, since a large portion of Cuba's exports to these countries was in fact resold.[43] At a second negotiating session in July 1968, Secretary General Prebisch succeeded in fashioning a delicate compromise on the crucial issue of Cuban reexports. The Soviet Union agreed to limit its exports to the free market to 1.1 million tons in 1969 and 1.25 million tons in 1970 and 1971, while Cuba agreed that its exports to Poland, Hungary, and Czechoslovakia would count against its basic ISA quota to the extent they exceeded 250,000 tons annually.[44]

On the question of prices, exporters reportedly "insisted" on a minimum floor price of 3.5 cents per pound, while Canada and Japan, two of the biggest free market importers, refused to sign any agreement with a floor above 3.25 cents, the minimum provided by the 1958 ISA.[45] The exporters, only too aware of the devastatingly low prices that had prevailed for over three years, reluctantly yielded and accepted a 3.25 cent floor price. Also contributing to the success of the 1968 negotiations was the quick concurrence of participants to the introduction of differential treatment in favor of LDCs in structuring quota provisions. Developing exporters were granted quotas at least equal to their best performance during 1960–67, whereas quotas for developed countries were lower than their best performance.[46] Other provisions assisting LDC exporters related to redistribution of shortfalls (article 47) and the establishment of a "hardship" quota for small exporters (article 44).[47] Like the earlier sugar agreements, the 1968 ISA also contained measures providing for stocks, and here too differential treatment was accorded to developing exporters. All exporters were required to maintain minimum stocks on call by the Sugar Council, but for developed countries the amount was 10 percent of basic quota while for developing exporters the figure was 15 percent (article 53). More important, exporters agreed, apparently in order to secure Canada's accession to the ISA, to a "supply commitment clause" under which once the price reached 6.5 cents per pound they would guarantee supplies of "specific quantities" of sugar to "traditional" customers at this price.[48]

Overall the sugar negotiations produced an agreement of considerable benefit to sugar exporters, particularly LDCs, in light of the extremely depressed state of the free market at the time. A minimum price significantly higher than the market price was accepted; exporters received assurances from importing members that no sugar would be purchased from non-member exporters if sugar prices fell below the floor; and LDCs were granted more favorable treatment in the design of the rules relating to quotas and stocks. That UNCTAD's influence helped to ensure an agreement reasonably favorable to developing countries is clear.[49] However, the decision of the European Community not to join the agreement as part of its Common Agricultural Policy commitment to increase production and exports posed a serious threat to the ISA's ability to regulate the free market effectively. During the negotiations the EC was offered an export quota of 300,000 tons, but this proved totally unacceptable given the community's ambitious plans to become a huge net exporter.[50] And indeed in the years subsequent to the negotiations, the community did precisely this: between 1969 and 1974, its net exports increased threefold, from 497,000 tons to 1,516,000 tons. Moreover, EC sugar exports were very heavily subsidized and were in effect dumped on the world market, depressing prices.[51] The other major nonsignatory, the United States, felt that the 1968 agreement was far too generous to Cuba, which had the largest export quota, and to the Soviet Union, which was permitted to reexport large volumes of Cuban sugar. Because the United States was no longer concerned with the welfare of the Cuban industry and had provided quotas and a generous price for many Third World producers under the Sugar Act, it had little interest in the success of the ISA.

In the years after the 1968 ISA (which was to operate from 1968 to 1974), world free market prices experienced unprecedented buoyancy. As a result, the sugar agreement was under great strain and, like its predecessor, eventually collapsed. The market price reached the ISA floor of 3.25 cents in February 1969 and surpassed the 4 cent level in October–November 1970. By November 1971 it had reached 5 cents, and a year later it was well above the ISA ceiling, in the range of 9 cents per pound.[52] Observers of the sugar market have suggested that a primary reason for the sharp rise was the way in which the ISA allocated export quotas. What appears to have happened is this: although the agreement made a fairly accurate estimate of demand, the decision to give some 40 comparatively small exporters the bulk of the basic export tonnages came back to haunt consuming countries as these LDCs generally failed, often spectacularly, to produce enough sugar to fill their generous entitlements. Thus, the "bias in favour of developing exporters" in the sugar scheme "greatly weakened the 1968 agreement."[53]

By January 1972, with the world price well above the ceiling, the agreement began to operate by virtue of the "supply commitment" clause.[54] A number of exporters were unable to meet their supply obligations or to provide the required volumes of stockpiled sugar when requested to do so. However, many exporters did sell substantial quantities of sugar to traditional importers, particularly Japan and Canada, at or below the supply commitment price.[55] The higher average world prices (7.3 cents for 1972 and 9.5 cents for 1973) were viewed as "delayed justice" by the long-suffering exporters, but for importers the failure of the agreement to "stabilize" prices within the prescribed range (3.25–5.25 cents) led to a different, and less sanguine, conclusion.

In May 1973 negotiations to renew the ISA commenced under UNCTAD's auspices in Geneva. At the time the sugar agreement was effectively moribund, with the free market price over 12 cents per pound, all ISA stocks released, and quotas suspended. Exporters were ecstatic at the skyrocketing price after several years of hardship. But they also recognized that these high prices would very soon lead to increased production and downward pressure on price. They requested a range of 6–9 cents per pound and a supply commitment price of 11 cents. Importers countered with an offer of 4.5–7.0 cents and a supply commitment price of just over 7.5 cents. The chairman put forth a compromise of 5.4–7.9 cents, and 8.9 cents for the supply commitment obligation. The "hardliners" among the consumers and producers—Canada and Cuba, respectively—refused to accept this suggestion.[56] Consumers also demanded that larger minimum stocks be held by exporters under any new agreement, since the stockholding obligations of the previous ISA had been shown to be totally inadequate. This the exporters strongly opposed. The 1973 conference thus collapsed, and the economic provisions of the ISA were terminated—victims of the bullish market for sugar then prevailing.[57]

Following the abortive 1973 talks, prices rose astronomically, averaging almost 30 cents per pound in 1974 and 20.4 cents the next year. A major reason was that the efforts of the developed countries to increase their domestic production after the initial price rise in the early 1970s had failed. Poor crops in the Western and communist countries led to seriously reduced yields.[58] Intermittent negotiations to renew the agreement were held between 1973 and 1976, but with continuing high prices the producers saw little incentive to regulate the market. In the meantime the United States, which had been unable in spite of the strict import and production controls prescribed by the Sugar Act to protect its market from the world price escalation, allowed the Sugar Act to expire in mid-1974. The domestic coalition of growers, refiners, and processors that had backed the act collapsed in disarray because of the turbulent market conditions. There was also a strong feeling in some government and congressional circles that the unseemly politicking for export quotas on the part of various foreign governments should be ended.[59] Rather than individual country quotas, the United States now set a "global quota" (which totaled 7 million tons in 1975) to regulate imports. The new procedure for sales to the United States was "first-come, first-served," although Cuba and other Soviet bloc exporters were still denied access to the American market.[60]

In 1975 the expanded European Community negotiated a sugar protocol in connection with the Lomé Convention between itself and 46 African, Caribbean, and Pacific developing countries. Because of the volatile world market, inadequate supplies, and recent astronomical prices, France and the other original EC members agreed to continue the Commonwealth Sugar Agreement (CSA) under which Britain imported most of its sugar from Commonwealth states, rather than require it to buy its sugar from EC producers.[61] The CSA exporters, excluding Australia, obtained a commitment that the prices paid to them under the Lomé accord would be "linked" to those paid to EC beet growers and subject to annual renegotiation. Although the community was now obligated to import some 1.3 million tons of sugar annually from its ACP partners, its plans to become a massive net exporter were maintained. Under the 1974 EC sugar policy, domestic beet producers were guaranteed a price (then below, but normally expected to be much above, the world price) and a market for a quantity of sugar sufficient to satisfy 100 percent of domestic consumption. Production in excess of this amount up to 45 percent of domestic consumption was also guaranteed a market at a lower price and was eligible for export subsidies. Any sugar produced beyond this level was to receive no guarantees and had to be disposed of outside the community at the growers' own risk.[62]

The community's decision to expand exports and sharply increase domestic production helped to turn the market situation around after 1975. These EC policies, combined with greater production elsewhere and the increasing use of alternative sweetners such as high fructose corn syrup, created an excess of production over consumption beginning in 1976. This in turn caused prices to fall almost as dramatically as they had risen earlier. The average 1974–76 world price of 20.5 cents per pound declined to slightly above 8 cents in 1977.[63] Given these developments, the growing interest of exporters in negotiating a new sugar agreement came as no surprise to those involved in the sugar trade.

The 1977 ISA

In this declining market, a conference to formulate a new ISA was convened under the auspices of UNCTAD in May 1977. Between the first session and the second in September, sugar prices continued to fall, from about 11 cents to 8 cents/lb.[64] The exporters, by now most anxious to negotiate an accord, were much more predisposed to compromise. The one major exception was the European Community. As in 1968, the community wanted to avoid any restriction on its future exports. It did express some willingness to support a pure buffer-stock arrangement, but all the other major participants rejected this idea out of hand—preferring the traditional system of export quotas and national stocks. While the Western European countries were criticized by many Third World exporters, they were seldom strongly attacked by the LDC producing states about whom the EC was most concerned, namely the ACP countries. These countries benefited from having sugar quotas in the lucrative community market.[65]

Within the importers' group at the conference, countries such as Japan, the USSR, and Canada adopted positions very similar to those they had taken in the past. While prepared to sign an agreement that stabilized prices, they insisted on a price range close to the market trend and did not want to assume any major costs. One importer, however, took quite a different stance than it had advocated in the past: the United States. It had two chief concerns. First, it wanted an agreement which would make unnecessary an expensive price-support program for domestic producers and possibly also its system of import duties and fees. This required an ISA that would at least keep the price *above* a floor of 11 cents. Second, the United States wanted to assure a decent price for those producers in the Third World (especially in Latin America) that until 1974 had possessed quotas in the American market and whose prosperity and goodwill Washington hoped to promote. This was probably the most important consideration, although there are differences on this question among American and other participants in the 1977 talks.[66]

As in the past, the three central issues at the conference were the price range, the quota system, and national stocks. The Latin American producers initially pushed vigorously for a floor price of 15 cents, but the opposition of the consumers and a few other exporters (Australia and Thailand), coupled with a continued decline in prices, convinced them to back a 13–23 cent range by the beginning of the September session. Most of the consumers supported a 6–8 cent floor, although the United States favored 11 cents. The U.S. Congress had just passed the United States Farm Bill, which stipulated that import controls and higher tariffs should be instituted unless the Secretary of Agriculture found that the international sugar scheme could maintain a world minimum price, and hence the price at which foreign producers could sell in the U.S. market, of about 11 cents. Conference participants eventually settled on a range of 11–21 cents.[67]

The most contentious issue at the conference was the quota system. Under that system all producers are given basic export tonnages (BETs), the aggregate total of which should theoretically come close to the annual "global quota" set by the Sugar Council. The global quota is the estimated amount of sugar that the larger members of the ISA can sell to the free market at prices within the range; it is equal to the estimated demand of the free market *minus* the exports of nonmembers *plus* the exports of the smallest producing members (referred to as annex II states). "Country quotas" are those volumes that individual countries are allowed to export in a particular year; they are set in terms of certain percentages of the BETS. For the system to succeed in stabilizing the market, the total sum of country quotas must approximate the global quota.

At both sessions of the 1977 conference the bargaining over the size of national BETs and over the total of all BETs led to serious conflicts among the approximately thirty larger exporters (states exporting more than 70,000 tons). At the center of the discussions were Cuba, Brazil, Australia, and the Conference President, E. Jones-Parry, although the United States was active in trying to bring about a consensus. In the end, Cuba was allocated 16 percent of total BETs (15.9 million tons), while Brazil and Australia obtained 15 percent each (table 4.4). Many smaller exporters as well as Australia were extremely upset with the size of their quota allocations.[68] An additional quota issue that caused controversy concerned the maximum size of cuts in BETs to establish individual country quotas. The participants eventually agreed that for most ISA members, the maximum reduction would be 17.5 percent (that is, quotas could be no lower than 82.5 percent of countries' BETs); for countries such as Australia, Thailand, and the Dominican Republic, which shipped at least 60 percent of their sugar to the free market, the reduction figure would be 15 percent (and quotas 85 percent of BETs). Most producers were adamant that the reductions not be larger, since they feared the prospect of having to absorb major cuts in their production and in employment in the sugar industry.[69] The conference also agreed that the BETs could be renegotiated for the last two years of the new ISA, and that if there were no consensus on this issue, the BETs would be altered according to a formula set out in the agreement. What was evidently not understood at the time was that the formula would have a strongly inflationary effect on the size of BETs, and thus on country quotas, if it were strictly applied—as it was in 1981 and 1982.[70]

The final major issue confronting the 1977 conference, related to the obligation of members to stock sugar for release in periods of rising prices. The United States, always anxious to design ICAs so as to protect the ceiling as well as the floor of a range, proposed that stocks be 4 million tons rather than the approximately 1.3 million tons written into the 1968 ISA. Developing–country exporters objected, arguing that such stocks were expensive to store and would have a depressing effect on the market. The two sides compromised and accepted 2.5 million tons, including certain "special stocks" whose storage costs could be financed by loans from a fund raised by a levy imposed on every ton of sugar traded. Unlike the 1968 ISA, no distinction was made between the stocking obligations of developing and developed exporting states.[71]

Overall, the participants in the 1977 conference were far from overjoyed with the new ISA. Neither the quota provisions nor the stocking provisions satisfied the objectives of the producers or the consumers. However, most governments were optimistic that the new agreement would be able to bring the price up into the range from its prevailing level of 8 cents. This view was based partly on the policy of the United States, which for both domestic economic and foreign policy reasons supported a higher world price. Other factors suggested that a more pessimistic appraisal was called for, especially the weakness of the quota system (i.e., the size of the BETs and the limited cuts that could be made in them) and the refusal of the EC to join. As it turned out, the pessimistic view proved more correct.

Throughout 1978 and most of 1979, world prices remained below the ISA floor of 11 cents, even after quotas were slashed by the permissible amount. The total of country quotas remained above the global quota for both years because the BETs were too high, the maximum reduction was too low, and the EC continued to expand its exports. Partly because of this, the United States instituted higher tariffs on imported sugar in order to protect the domestic price guaranteed to United States producers (now 14–16 cent/lb.), with the level of the tariff increasing in 1978 and again in 1979.[72] It is difficult to argue that developing exporters benefited much from the ISA in its first two years, although the free market price (which varied from about 7 to 9 cents/lb.) probably would have fallen in the absence of the ISA–mandated export reductions. On the other hand, producers would have been under no obligation to acquire stocks had it not been for the 1977 sugar agreement.

Near the end of 1979 there began one of those surges in the sugar market that seems to occur every 5 to 7 years. In November, prices climbed through the 11 percent floor; in January 1980 they hit 15 cents, at which point quotas were suspended.[73] In the spring prices went through the ceiling, and by September they had reached a high of 43 cents. In response, the Sugar Council raised the price range to 13–23 cents. A number of factors caused the temporary price surge in 1980–81: some countries had curtailed production in the light of poor prices in the late 1970s; several producers experienced bad weather, which was expected to reduce production; and Brazil diverted a significant quantity of sugar into the production of fuel alcohol. In addition, some exporting members of the ISA had failed to acquire the stocks that they were obligated to hold. This was in part caused by the delay until 1980 in the application of the levy system, which was to yield the funds to assist producers with the costs of storing stocks. This in turn was due to a postponement in the ratification process for the 1977 ISA in the United States because of the legislative battle over the domestic price–support program for American producers.[74] There was a general expectation of a long period of inadequate supplies because of the above developments, but the shortages did not persist. Instead, a situation of excess supplies recurred and the price began to fall dramatically in 1981.[75]

The serious downturn in the market that came in the fall of 1981 prompted demands for action by the Sugar Council. However, the council found itself less able than it had been in the late 1970s to stem the price decline. Under the 1977 ISA, the BETs of all producers were to be altered by a particular formula for the last two years of the accord (1981–82) in the event that the members were unable to agree on new figures among themselves. The application of this formula increased exporting countries' BETs far in excess of what had been expected in 1977. This meant that the total volume of country quotas—even with the maximum 15–17.5 percent reductions in BETs–could not be brought even close to the global quota for three years. Thus, after hovering just below the floor in the last half of 1981, the price dropped steadily to around 6–7 cents by mid-1982.

In November 1981 the council decided to extend the ISA for two years beyond the end of 1982, and in the spring of 1982 it agreed to keep BETs for this two-year extension at their 1982 levels. Attempts were made during 1982 to secure an agreement between ISA members and the EC (now accounting for over a quarter of exports to the free market) to reduce exports, but to no avail.[76] In the spring of 1982 the United States decided that it could no longer maintain an adequate price for domestic producers with its existing system of import duties and fees. It also concluded that the ISA was not assisting U.S. sugar-producing allies in the Third World. Washington therefore reinstituted the national quota system it had abandoned in 1974. Under this system, over thirty countries were assured a price of around 17 cents/lb. for given volumes of sugar sold in the U.S. market, although the total volume imported by the United States between 1977 and 1983 was halved.[77] With the departure of the United States from the free market and the continued depressed price, the Sugar Council decided in late 1982 to initiate negotiations for a new ISA. Over its five-year life the 1977 ISA had been able to keep the price within the range for only 13 months; prices were below the floor for almost 36 months, and above the ceiling for about 11 months. The need for some basic changes was recognized by all the sugar-trading nations. Integration of the EC into the scheme was clearly the most urgent objective.

The 1982–1984 Negotiations

Negotiations in pursuit of a fifth ISA began in December 1982 and eventually ended with a conference in June 1984. The talks took place in the context of a very depressed sugar market. In contrast to the 1977 negotiations, on this occasion the European Community was a central and active participant. The community was now not only a net exporter but also the largest exporter to the global free market. A new agreement without it would be virtually meaningless. On the other hand, the most important participant in 1977, the United States, played only a minor role this time. With its quota system in place, the United States was helping those developing-country producers of particular concern to it. Moreover, given the changes in trading patterns within the free market, the United States no longer viewed the ISA as a useful vehicle for helping the poorer developing nations. Only about a quarter of sugar exports to the free market were sold by this latter group of Third World states, whereas almost half came from developed countries (the EC, Australia, and South Africa) and the rest from Brazil, Argentina, and Cuba.[78]

From the very beginning of the negotiations the debate centered on a new proposal advanced by the European Community. The community suggested that export quotas be abolished for the big exporters and that they be required instead to stock sugar when the price fell. Behind this position was the insistence of the European producers, especially the French, that they not be forced to cut production. According to the plan, the ten major producers that accounted for over 75 percent of exports would be given "reference export availabilities" (REAs) of set tonnages. As the price fell to the first trigger point, these exporters would have to stock all production above this amount ("surplus stocks"); and if prices fell below a second trigger point, they would be required to stock certain percentages of their REAs ("security stocks"). Two of the four largest producers, Brazil and Cuba, strongly opposed this proposal because of its cost and their fear that it would not address the perennial overproduction problem. According to one long-time student of the ISA, most of the other participants in the talks considered the community proposal unworkable and "a deliberate camouflage" to allow it to escape from having to reject future pleas to reduce exports.[79] Australia, however, endorsed the plan, seeing it as the only basis for integrating the community into the ISA. By late 1983 almost all participants indicated a reluctant willingness to negotiate on the basis of the EC stocking scheme.

This agreement on the basic mechanism still left other issues to be resolved. Most important was the aggregate size of the REAs and the allocations of particular REAs to the ten major producers. It was judged that, in order to maintain the price in the existing range, the REAs should total approximately 17 million tons; but adding the demands of the key producers collectively produced a figure close to 24 million tons. Another conflict concerned the extent to which Cuban exports to the Soviet bloc should be counted toward its free market quota. Australia in particular insisted that they should be included, arguing that the exclusion of Cuban exports would grant Cuba an unlimited ability to increase sales. Differences also emerged over the size of stocks that producers would have to hold. The community, the United States, and Brazil advocated a relatively high figure, while Japan, Australia, and several other exporters sought a low one. The price range was not a major problem, as most states were willing to support a range close to the one prescribed in the old agreement.[80]

The negotiations culminated with the convening of a conference in June 1984, by which time the price was hovering around 5 cents/lb. The central issue was the size of the REAs. Several attempts were made to achieve a consensus among the major exporters. The conference president, Jorge Zorreguieta of Argentina, suggested that the total of REAs should be 21 million tons (a figure most importers thought too high), with the "big ten" receiving 17.3, the European Community 4.9, Brazil and Australia 2.6 each, and Cuba 2.2. Brazil and "the six" (the Philippines, the Dominican Republic, South Africa, Argentina, India, and Thailand) accepted their shares with some reluctance. However, Australia and Cuba quickly rejected their allocations as well as those of other producers, while the community wanted a firm assurance that its figure would not be lowered for the five-year life of the accord. At this point the talks collapsed. The chairman and most of the delegates pointed to the conflicts among the producers over market shares as the nub of the problem, although there were other outstanding issues.[81] With the failure to develop a new ISA after a year and a half of discussions, the signatories to the 1977 agreement decided simply to extend it, without economic provisions, for 1985–86.[82]

Because a number of major sugar-importing countries have granted certain producers preferential quotas, while others have strong interests as sugar exporters in their own right, the developed countries as a whole were not strong supporters of a new sugar agreement designed to stabilize the free market and to assist Third World countries reliant on this important commodity. The political and foreign policy gains to be made through the conclusion of a sugar agreement did not carry enough weight to induce them to accept significant sacrifices. From 1985 through early 1987, free market sugar prices were at very low levels, ranging between 3 and 8 cents/lb. The fate of the ISA over the longer run is difficult to foretell. The system of preferential arrangements has in a sense served as a functional equivalent of a global regulatory agreement. Moreover, because a few developed countries are major exporters, while some developing-country suppliers are regarded as either politically unfriendly (e.g., Cuba in the view of the United States) or else sufficiently wealthy not to need the protection of the ISA (e.g., Brazil and Taiwan), key importing countries apparently have concluded that full-fledged regulation is not necessary. Also clouding the ISA's future prospects are several other factors, notably the unwillingness of the European Community to alter its export policy or to support an ISA control mechanism based on export quotas, and the continuing problem of Soviet-bloc reexports of Cuban sugar.[83]

COFFEE

The Market

Coffee beans are grown on trees in tropical regions between 25 degrees north and 30 degrees south. There are two main types, arabicas and robustas, with the latter now constituting about 25 percent of the market, up from 10 percent in the early postwar period.[84] Arabicas are produced mainly in the Western Hemisphere, while robustas are grown in Africa and Asia. Arabicas have a milder flavor and are more expensive; they are categorized into three types: Colombian milds, other milds (grown in all Latin American countries except Brazil and Colombia), and unwashed Arabicas (largely produced in Brazil). Coffee is comparatively easy to store, and can be held for more than three years with little erosion of quality if proper precautions are taken.[85]

The positions of the various coffee-growing countries in the world market have changed considerably since the mid-1950s. The Latin American and Caribbean producers' share of global exports has declined steadily (table 4.5). The African countries have modestly increased their proportion of world coffee exports, while the Asian producers have enjoyed a significant rise. Although their dominance has diminished in recent decades, Brazil and Colombia remained by far the most important coffee producers throughout the period under review; in 1982 they still accounted for close to 40 percent of global exports. On the demand side of the market, the Western industrial countries have consistently purchased about 90 percent of the coffee traded (table 4.6). Per capita coffee consumption has been declining in North America and growing only very slowly in Western Europe for several years, suggesting that major existing markets offer only limited growth prospects.[86] Demand is generally insensitive to price changes (i.e., it is price inelastic) because coffee drinking, as many know, is quite habit-forming. On occasion, as in 1977, very high prices can lead to declines in consumption.[87]

Coffee has been and remains one of the most critical commodity exports for developing countries. In many years it has ranked higher in export earnings than any other commodity except petroleum, earning on average $9.3 billion/year in the period 1980–82 (table 1.3). Coffee is of great importance to a large number of LDCs. In the years 1980–82, five LDCs earned between 50 and 90 percent of their export earnings from coffee; eleven between 20 and 40 percent; and seven between 10 and 19 percent (table 4.7). Coffee prices have been quite unstable in recent decades. The average price change per annum in constant U.S. dollars between 1955 and 1981 was 18 percent; only sugar and cocoa experienced significantly more instability (table 1.4).

Changes in coffee prices are largely attributable to variations in supply. There are several reasons for supply fluctuations. Frequent changes in

TABLE 4.5

Coffee: Exports by Main Countries and Groupings

Countries	% of World Exports						
	1955	1960	1965	1970	1975	1980	1982
Industrial (including centrally planned)	1.2	2.2	2.0	2.1	4.1	4.9	2.0
Developing	98.8	97.8	98.0	98.0	96.0	95.1	98.0
Latin America	75.4	70.0	60.7	60.0	57.6	59.9	57.7
Brazil	39.5	38.2	29.1	29.3	21.9	20.1	23.0
Colombia	16.9	13.5	12.1	—	13.7	18.4	13.8
Costa Rica		1.8	1.7	2.1	2.2	1.9	2.5
El Salvador		3.4	3.6	3.4	3.9	3.9	3.0
Guatemala		3.1	3.4	2.9	3.8	3.4	2.1
Mexico		3.2	2.9	—	4.0	3.5	3.3
Africa	20.8	24.2	30.5	31.1	30.8	24.1	27.3
Angola	2.8	3.3	5.7	5.5	4.6	1.1	1.2
Cameroon	0.7	1.2	1.7	1.9	2.6	2.5	2.0
Ethiopia	2.0	2.0	3.2	—	1.6	2.5	2.1
Ivory Coast		5.6	6.7	5.9	7.2	5.4	7.0
Kenya	0.9	1.1	1.4	1.6	1.9	2.1	2.5
Madagascar	2.3	1.5	1.8	1.6	1.8	1.5	1.4
Uganda	3.6	4.5	5.7	5.8	5.4	3.2	4.5
Zaire	2.1	2.2	0.8	1.8	1.7	1.7	1.8
Asia and Oceania	2.7	3.6	6.8	7.4	7.7	11.1	13.0
Indonesia	1.1	1.6	3.8	2.9	3.6	6.4	5.9
Exports by Weight (Thousand Tons)							
World	2,081	2,645	2,984	3,287	3,566	3,729	3,863

Source: Food and Agriculture Organization, *Trade Yearbook* (various years). Only the larger exporters in the group of developing states are included.

TABLE 4.6

Coffee: Imports by Main Countries and Groupings

Countries	1955	1960	1965	1970	1975	1980	1982
				% of World Imports			
Industrial	92.2	90.1	90.2	87.9	88.8	88.4	87.0
North America	59.2	53.7	47.3	38.7	36.2	31.3	29.4
United States	56.9	51.4	44.7	36.3	33.8	29.1	27.1
Western European	33.0	36.4	41.3	45.7	47.8	50.8	51.1
Centrally planned	0.8	2.3	3.6	5.3	5.6	6.0	5.9
Developing	7.0	7.7	6.1	5.7	5.7	5.6	7.1
			Imports by Weight (Thousand Tons)				
World	2,072	2,577	2,866	3,272	3,655	3,799	3,908

Source: Food and Agriculture Organization, *Trade Yearbook* (various years). Only the largest importing regions and states in the groups of industrial states are included.

TABLE 4.7

Percentage of Export Earnings of Developing Countries from Coffee

Countries	1976–78	1980–82
Burundi	89.5	88.7
Uganda	89.0	93.3
Ethiopia	71.9	62.1
Rwanda	69.4	52.9
Colombia	65.2	37.3
Equatorial Guinea	47.3	38.8
Madagascar	44.1	38.8
El Salvador	43.3	67.6
Guatemala	40.3	24.0
Tanzania	37.2	28.9
Kenya	35.9	23.6
Costa Rica	33.3	26.1
Honduras	32.7	23.9
Haiti	31.4	29.7
Cameroon	30.3	18.6
Ivory Coast	30.3	20.2
Nicaragua	26.6	31.1
Zaire	25.0	7.9
Angola	23.6	10.5
Papua New Guinea	18.9	14.7
Brazil	18.4	9.4
Dominican Republic	16.9	8.6
Ecuador	16.2	5.3
Sierre Leone	15.1	13.5
Togo	11.2	8.4
Peru	10.0	3.3
Mexico	9.3	2.0
Yemen Arab Republic	8.4	0.2
Liberia	5.0	4.7
Paraguay	4.4	0.4
Indonesia	4.3	1.9
Benin	3.4	13.4
Congo	3.1	0.5
Panama	1.9	3.5
Central African Republic		9.7

Source: World Bank, *Commodity Trade and Price Trends* (1980), table 11 and (1985), table 9. Only countries whose exports of coffee accounted for at least 3 percent of their export earnings are listed.

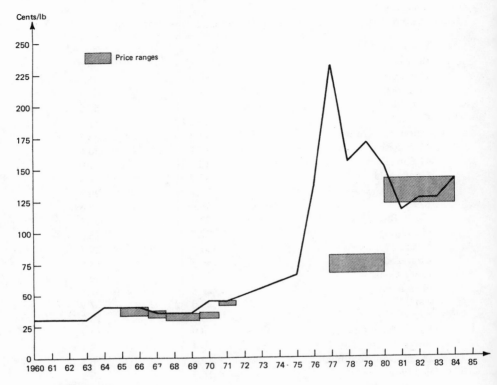

Chart 4.2

International Coffee Prices and International Coffee Agreements' Price Ranges, 1960–1984

Note: Prices are for the International Coffee Organization's "composite indicator price 1976."
Source: UN Doc. TD/B/C.1/270 (1985), p. 24.

climatic conditions, especially the onset of frosts, have often had a major impact. These have affected Brazil in particular, where severe frosts occurred in 1963, 1969, 1972, 1975, and 1981. Another source of supply instability is to be found in producers' reactions to prices—excessive increases in plantings when prices are high, and a failure to scale back production when they are low. When prices rise, there is often pervasive optimism that the tight market will continue. Producers fail to take into account the policies of, or to coordinate decisions with, other producers. The effects of such producer responses are magnified by the fact that the gestation period of coffee trees is 3 to 4 years. In periods of low prices, producers typically do not want to destroy trees that have taken years to come into full production; and in any case they are often assured a relatively stable price for their coffee beans by government purchasing policies and thus have little incentive to cut back production. As one economist who has studied government involvement in the industry concluded: "the amount of coffee grown was not primarily influenced by change in demand . . . but principally by certain policies of the governments of one or all producing countries toward their coffee producers."[88] Governments understandably want to protect their coffee farmers against the effects of depressed prices, but this can contribute to the "bust" trends that afflict the market.[89]

Coffee trading is centered in New York, which has both a "spot" market and a futures or terminal market. The former is not really a market at all: it is a name applied to all the transactions to buy and sell actual physical coffee.[90] The commodity is also traded on other markets, such as London and Bremen, Germany. Virtually all Brazilian and Colombian coffee is sold under contracts with roasters in the United States and other consuming countries, so the price quotations for these coffees on the New York market are quite artificial.[91] The coffee processing industry is a highly concentrated one, with the largest four firms in the United States accounting for over 60 percent of the market. A significant degree of concentration characterizes the Western European industry as well. The soluble or instant coffee industry, which is important in the United States, is even more concentrated, with one firm, General Foods, accounting for more than half the market in the early 1970s.[92]

Attempts to Regulate the Market Before 1962

From the beginning of the twentieth century until the start of World War II, efforts to limit coffee output mainly consisted of periodic stocking and planting restrictions on the part of Brazil, which then controlled at least two-thirds of world production. Brazil tried on several occasions to persuade other producers to share the burden of price support, but to no avail.[93] The war evidently induced a more cooperative attitude on the part of the other Latin American producers, and also of the United States, by far the largest importer of coffee. The signing of the Inter-American Coffee Agreement in November 1940—"a measure of Pan-American solidarity among allies"[94]—introduced market regulation by way of annual export and import quotas, although the agreement had no price provisions per se. Following the attack on Pearl Harbor, the import prices paid by the United States were fixed at roughly double the levels existing when the accord was first signed. The quotas were dropped after 1945, and the agreement itself was terminated in 1948.[95]

The combination of high postwar demand, exhausted Brazilian stocks, and limited growth in non-Brazilian supplies led to a rapid escalation of coffee prices in the early postwar period, with peak levels being reached in 1954.[96] These high prices stimulated new plantings, particularly in Africa, whose producers now began to increase their share of the market. But given the time lag between planting and production, it was not until the late 1950s that this new production came on stream.[97] Thus began the chronic problem of overproduction that was to plague the coffee market until the early 1970s.

Falling prices in the late 1950s prompted several producers to take action. In 1955 Brazil and Colombia sought to coordinate a stock retention program, but the volume of coffee withdrawn was insufficient to bolster the price, and the scheme soon ended. In early 1957 the members of the Coffee Federation of the Americas (including most of the smaller Latin American producers) tried unsuccessfully to maintain prices by stocking coffee.[98] Then, in October 1957 Brazil, Colombia, and five other Latin American producers reached an accord known as the "Agreement of Mexico," designed to support prices by means of stock retention and quarterly export quotas. Prices recovered somewhat in early 1958, but the scheme failed to curb exports effectively or to reduce overproduction. Prices had resumed their downward trend by late 1958.[99]

A critical development in 1958 was the shift on the part of the United States from opposition to support for international action to solve coffee market problems. This policy change was largely motivated by growing fears that depressed economic conditions in Latin America would facilitate Soviet penetration of the region. In June 1958 the United States took the initiative in establishing, under the FAO's auspices, the Coffee Study Group (CSG) to examine the possibilities for international collaboration. The first agreement produced by the CSG was the Latin American Coffee Agreement, signed following the failure of negotiations with the African colonial governments (Britain, France, and Portugal). Britain did not want to disrupt its purchase contracts with the East African coffee boards, while France and Portugal were concerned that the agreement might impede expansion of production in West Africa and Angola.[100] The 15 Latin American signatories agreed to national stock retention and export quotas, and Brazil also agreed to maintain its traditional price-defense policies. However, prices continued to decline, and this led to a more cooperative attitude on the part of the African colonial governments. As a consequence, it proved possible to negotiate a broader International Coffee Agreement within the Coffee Study Group in September 1959, with France and Portugal (on behalf of their African colonies) joining the Latin Americans in an attempt to raise prices through reduced exports. U.S. pressure to support the agreement was influential in persuading certain African countries to participate, partly because they feared exclusion of their coffees from the American market under a purely Western Hemisphere arrangement.[101]

The 1959 accord proved to be reasonably effective. After sharp declines in 1958–59, prices generally stabilized in 1960.[102] But while the agreement was having some success, several problems remained: production was still too high in many countries, and stocks were increasing steadily; the global quotas adopted were still too large given consumption requirements; and, because of ineffective policing, some countries violated their assigned export quotas. At this point the United States and a number of other countries concluded that consumer participation was essential for the effective policing of a market regulatory accord. This set the stage for the negotiations over the 1962 producer-consumer International Coffee Agreement.[103]

The 1962 International Coffee Agreement

When the United Nations Coffee Conference convened in New York in July 1962, it had the benefit of a draft agreement previously worked out within the Coffee Study Group. The basic provisions envisaged in the draft included: the establishment of a price range (open to yearly readjustment); the annual determination of a global quota; the setting of basic quotas for all producing members; and provisions for the reduction of export entitlements if the price began to fall within or below the range. Other rules dealt with exports to nonmembers, enforcement of export restrictions, and decision-making. On all these issues there were conflicts between producers and consumers as well as divisions within each group.

Producers and consumers were unable to reach consensus on the price range, with the former seeking a higher floor than the latter were willing to accept. As a result, the only specific provision relating to price in the 1962 International Coffee Agreement (ICFA) stated simply that coffee prices should "not decline below the level of such prices in 1962."[104] (The International Coffee Agreement is commonly assigned the acronym ICA. We use ICFA to distinguish it from the acronym for international commodity agreement.)

The principal conflict between producers at the conference was over the setting of export quotas. The main adversaries were Brazil and Colombia (the "oligopolists") on the one hand, and the Africans (the "revisionists") on the other.[105] The former had seen their market positions suffer because of recently expanded African production, and thus wanted quotas to be based on historical production trends. The latter insisted that quotas reflect *potential* production. The two groups also differed on whether future export cuts should be made across the board (the Latin American preference), or according to demand for different types of coffee—the so-called "selectivity" principle (the African preference). The Africans' position was influenced not only by their rising market share but also by the cost of storing coffee. In the end the Brazil-Colombia view was accepted, largely because of their market power and a U.S. threat to exclude nonmembers from its market. But in addition the African producers, like the Latin Americans, favored an agreement to provide a floor under their export earnings.[106]

Each producing country was assigned a basic quota determined by its average exportable production over either the two coffee years 1961/62–1962/63 or the four coffee years 1959/60–1962/63. This formula tended to benefit Brazil and Colombia, which obtained 39 and 13 percent, respectively, of the total basic export quotas (table 4.8). Countries with expanding production were accommodated by certain other provisions: basic quotas were to be reviewed after three years (two years before the end of the five-year agreement) "in order to adjust them to general market conditions" (article 28); and exports to "new markets" (annex B countries) whose per capita consumption of coffee was low would not be charged against ICFA quotas (article 40). The United States and other countries realized that this latter provision was an invitation to violate the accord by reexporting through annex B countries, but they accepted it to win the backing of many African and smaller Latin American producers.[107]

The ICFA enforcement system hinged on the issuance of certificates to all producing members allowing them to export set volumes, and on the obligation of all importing members to refuse shipments without certificates (article 44). Japan and several Western European countries did not really support strict enforcement, but the United States was able to persuade them to adopt a reasonably tough system in order to make the agreement work. However, a weakness was permitted when it was agreed that

TABLE 4.8

States' and Regional Groupings' Percentage Shares of Total Basic Quotas Under the International Coffee Agreements

Countries	1962	1968	1982
Latin America	69.68	69.55	68.07
Brazil	39.09	38.02	30.83
Colombia	13.09	38.02	16.28
Costa Rica	2.06	2.00	2.16
Ecuador	1.12	1.36	2.17
El Salvador	3.11	3.45	4.48
Guatemala	2.92	3.27	3.47
Honduras	0.62	0.77	1.49
Mexico	3.28	3.20	3.65
Nicaragua	0.91	1.00	1.28
Peru		1.34	1.31
Venezuela	1.26	0.59	
Africa	26.33	27.18	24.98
Burundi	1.09	0.42	
Cameroon	1.66	1.82	2.66
Congo (Dem. Rep.)		1.82	
Ethiopia	2.55	2.71	2.62
Ivory Coast	5.05	5.58	7.52
Kenya	1.12	1.56	2.48
Malagasy Republic	1.80	1.65	1.42
Portugal	4.83	5.04	
Tanzania	0.95	1.27	1.36
Uganda	4.10	4.32	4.44
Zaire	2.48		2.12
Asia	3.33	3.23	6.95
India	0.78	0.76	1.24
Indonesia	2.55	2.47	4.55
Papua New Guinea			1.16

Sources: United Nations, *Treaty Series* (1962), 469:169 (annex A); United Nations, *Treaty Series* (1968) 647:3 (annex A); International Coffee Organization, *International Coffee Agreement 1983* (London, October 1982), annex 3. Only countries with at least 1 percent of total basic quotas in one of the agreements are listed. Very small producers are not given percentage shares of total basic quotas, but maximum export figures. In the case of the 1976 ICFA, there were no specific figures for basic quotas but rather a formula for establishing them if needed. The ICO council did establish basic quotas in 1980, 1981, and 1982; these figures are in ICO documents.

any limitations on imports from nonmembers would require a decision of the council of the International Coffee Organization (ICO). This opened the door for producing members to exceed their quotas by shipping coffee to nonmembers, who would then reexport it to consuming members.[108] The decision-making arrangements in the International, Coffee Organization were similar to those of other commodity organizations in that 1,000 votes each were given to producers and consumers, and key decisions of the council required a two-thirds distributed majority. Eighty-five percent of the votes were distributed on the basis of members' export and import shares; but no country could have more than 400 votes—thus limiting the voting power of the United States and Brazil.[109]

The International Coffee Agreement was clearly designed to transfer resources to developing-country producers. Its creation derived in large measure from the policies of the United States. American decision-makers at this time were deeply concerned about the spread of Castroism and Soviet influence in Latin America. They sought various means to raise the standard of living in the region and to reduce the appeal of communist and radical movements. The ICFA was an important part of this strategy, since many Latin American countries relied on coffee for significant shares of their export earnings. The U.S. coffee industry had doubts about the economic implications of the agreement but reluctantly decided to accept Washington's policy.[110] U.S. concerns were cogently summarized by Senator Jacob Javits during Senate hearings on the agreement: "unless this agreement and similar agreements are ratified, Castroism will spread like the plague throughout Latin America."[111] Other Western consumers to some extent shared U.S. anxiety about Latin America. France and Britain also favored the accord because it would assist their former colonial territories in Africa.[112]

The first ICFA entered into force in 1963. During its first year of operation coffee prices fluctuated around a rising trend, although after a sharp increase in 1963–64 they dropped back to their 1962 level in real terms.[113] Ironically, the first major problem that the ICO Council faced was slowing a price increase precipitated by a drought in Brazil in mid-1963. The council accepted an increase of 2.25 percent in quotas to moderate the rising market, but only after concessions had been offered to some producers still dissatisfied with their quotas. Most producers recognized that a policy of encouraging moderation in prices had to be pursued if consumers' commitment to the agreement was to be maintained. Following a downward turn in the price trend in 1964, the two sides were able to agree on what had eluded them in 1962—a consensus on a price range (38–44 cents/lb for all coffees). A semiautomatic quota-adjustment mechanism was also accepted.[114]

In 1965 and 1966 major disputes arose over both the enforcement system and a renewed demand by some producers, especially the Africans, for "selectivity" in distributing shortfalls (i.e., quota underfulfillments). The chief proponents of strengthening the enforcement system were Brazil, Colombia, and the United States, all upset by the reexport of coffee from "new market" countries and nonmembers to the major consuming nations of Europe and North America. They accused African producers and a few Latin American countries of evading their quota limits and of undermining the agreement. These producing countries countered that loopholes were necessary to market their growing crops, and argued that "selectivity" would enable them to respond to increasing demand for their types of beans. The trade-off that finally resulted included both a stronger enforcement system (the U.S.-proposed "stamp plan"), and a partial selectivity system. With these revisions to the ICFA in 1966, the agreement began to function more effectively.[115]

The 1968 ICFA

With the first ICFA due to expire at the end of 1968, efforts were made to negotiate a new accord in late 1967 and early 1968.[116] Both producing and consuming states viewed the previous experience with market regulation favorably. The producers believed the ICFA had prevented a collapse of the market, boosted prices somewhat, and increased their export earnings.[117] The consuming states judged that the resource transfers had promoted political stability in, and improved their political relations with, coffee-exporting countries.[118] Nonetheless, several conflicts did emerge during the negotiations on a second ICFA.[119]

The key issues concerned the allocation of quotas (which encompassed the selectivity issue), the tightening of the enforcement system, the introduction of production controls, the creation of a diversification fund to encourage growers to move out of coffee production, and a U.S.-Brazilian dispute over Brazil's exports of soluble coffee. On quota allocations, the Africans—backed by most importers—succeeded in achieving modest quota increases. With respect to selectivity, a decision to set different price ranges and to adjust quotas for different types of coffee was approved after some rather sharp interproducer exchanges (article 37). As anticipated, these provisions had the effect of raising the sales and prices for African robustas.[120] The Brazilians and Colombians were able to achieve tougher enforcement procedures and, more important, won acceptance of the idea of production targets and the creation of a Diversification Fund (to be financed by levies on coffee exports). On these issues they were supported by the United States, which shared their desire to attack the structural bases of a weak market. The 1968 ICFA required that production goals be determined each year by individual exporting members and then approved by the council's executive board. Members would not be granted quota increases until the board had approved their production plans (article 48). Financing for the Diversification Fund was to be provided by a 60 cents/bag levy on coffee exports (article 54, annex A).[121] The most contentious question for the United States related to Brazilian soluble-coffee exports. The United States charged that soluble exports to its market had grown both because Brazil exempted such exports from the taxes it imposed on "green"coffee exports and because it made available to its soluble manufacturers low-grade "grinders" not sold internationally. After much discussion Brazil, realizing that continued U.S. support of the ICFA was essential, relented and agreed to a provision prohibiting "discriminatory treatment in favor of processed coffee as compared to green coffee" (article 44).[122]

One year after the conclusion of the second ICFA a significant rise in prices took place following reports of weather damage to the Brazilian crop. Automatic and negotiated quota increases proved insufficient to stem the increases. In the spring of 1970, the consuming countries demanded an end to the ceilings put on selective quota adjustments. The African and Central American "revisionists" supported this position, while Brazil and Colombia opposed it. The latter were able to block the action until the August 1970 council meeting, which witnessed "a decisive consumer assertion of countervailing power."[123] The ceiling on selective quota adjustments was removed, and a complex new quota formula was introduced that increased the annual global quota. Thereafter, prices declined to the levels prevailing before the reports of weather damage.[124]

Another crisis developed after the devaluation of the U.S. dollar by 10 percent in December 1971. Since coffee prices were denominated in U.S. dollars, the producers asked for a 4 cent increase in the floor and ceiling prices at a meeting of the executive board of the council in February 1972. The consuming nations quickly rejected this. The United States and Canada also vetoed a 2 cent increase, arguing that producers were already earning good returns from their exports. This prompted a majority of Latin

American and African producing states to organize their own price-control arrangement outside the ICFA through a forum called the Geneva Group. The Geneva Group's stock retention and buffer-stock provisions were never really tested because just as they were about to be put into effect, news broke of a serious frost in Brazil, which soon sent prices climbing by 25 percent. With this development the Geneva Group's stock retention obligations were terminated.[125]

At both the August and the December 1972 council meetings much hostility between producers and consumers was evident. This led to the collapse of the second ICFA one year before it was legally due to expire. Consumers resented the unilateral attempt by producers to manipulate the market. They also rejected the producers' view that export restrictions should be retained and the price range increased. Overall, the consumers had "generally concluded that the ICFA was a producer-biased agreement, with no supply protection for importers, and no price protection if the quota release mechanism were blocked." They therefore decided that their only option "was to suspend the basic control mechanisms of the ICFA.[126]

In 1973 and 1974 several attempts were made to revive the ICFA. Despite the buoyant coffee prices then prevailing, some producers sought a new accord because they feared a collapse of the market. But they could not persuade the producer group as a whole.[127] During this period the larger producing states engaged in market regulation on their own, as they had done in 1972. In August 1973 they organized a stock retention and buffer-stock plan called "Café Mundial," but it unraveled in early 1975 when the four largest producers (Brazil, Colombia, Angola, and the Ivory Coast) failed to convince smaller exporters to cooperate. Many of the latter were extremely dependent on coffee for export earnings. The situation changed radically when Brazil suffered the worst frost of its coffee-producing history in July 1975. Prices shot up 50 percent in just a few days, and had climbed 335 percent by early 1977.[128] Against this backdrop of skyrocketing prices coffee producers and consumers met to discuss the revival of the ICFA in late 1975.

The 1975 ICFA

Given that producers' interest in commodity control usually varies inversely with prices, it is perhaps surprising that a new coffee pact was successfully negotiated in the last half of 1975.[129] The coffee exporters knew, however, that despite the strong prices they were then enjoying, quota restrictions might be necessary in the future as production increased in response to the high prices and as Brazil's output recovered from the 1975 crop disaster.[130] The consumers entered the negotiations with many reservations about past ICFA arrangements—especially the reporting and distribution of shortfalls, the criteria for allocating quotas, and the continuation of quotas after prices had begun to rise. They also objected to the various producer attempts to regulate the market unilaterally. Consumers were not prepared to accept a new ICFA unless changes were made. However, the United States, France, and to a lesser extent other Western countries remained sympathetic to the idea of a safety net for Latin American and African producers' export earnings, and hoped to promote greater economic and political stability in these regions. In addition, they wanted to lend some support to existing ICAs in the face of UNCTAD's recent attempts to expand its powers vis-à-vis such arrangements through the Common Fund scheme described in chapter 2.[131]

On the issue of quota shortfalls, the developed countries, upset by previous delays in reporting and redistributing unfilled quotas, succeeded in obtaining tougher rules governing shortfalls, but without penalties for violations (article 40). They were also able to secure new provisions providing for the *automatic* introduction and termination of quotas at certain price levels—thus precluding the continuation of quotas in a tight market (article 33). The most important gain by the consumers concerned the formula for setting national basic quotas. The agreement stated that 70 percent of a country's quota would be dependent on its exports over a previous four-year period, and 30 percent on its volume of stocks. This formula was supported by several producers anxious to expand their production. The inclusion of stocks in determining the 30 percent portion was seen as encouraging the stocking of coffee that could then be sold off in a rising market.[132] To some extent this provision was a kind of surrogate for a buffer-stock scheme in that it provided reasonable assurances of stock sales to moderate price escalations. In fact, there was a long discussion of a buffer-stock proposal at the conference, but the idea was rejected because of costs, administrative complications, and the fears of many producers that it would depress the market.[133] It is noteworthy, but not surprising, that during the negotiations no concern was expressed about the perennial overproduction problem, an issue that had loomed so large in 1968. The Diversification Fund disappeared from the ICFA, and the single article alluding to production controls imposed no obligations on exporting countries (article 50).

The new agreement legally entered into force for a six-year period in October 1976. There was little expectation that it would have much immediate relevance to the market, given recent price trends, and this proved to be the case. Coffee prices rose from around $1.00 to $2.00/lb in 1976, above the $0.78 figure at which the 1976 ICFA specified that quotas should be introduced. In the spring of 1977 prices peaked at $3.40 and then began to fall.[134] While prices were high, hostility toward the producers, especially Brazil, was evident within the consuming countries, and some quite effective consumer boycotts of coffee were launched.[135] By mid-1978 prices had declined to about $1.50, and this prompted calls for international action by the producers. ICO meetings held in August and September failed to yield agreement on raising the price range and reactivating the economic provisions of the ICFA. Consumer countries were wary of reintroducing quotas given their memory of the lack of producer cooperation in 1976 and 1977.[136]

After the failure of the 1978 meetings to reintroduce quotas, a number of Latin American producers formed a body known as the Bogota Group. The original members were Colombia, Brazil, Venezuela, and Mexico; they were soon joined by El Salvador and Honduras, bringing their share of world exports to some 55 percent. The new group established a fund to purchase coffee on the major exchanges, and this soon raised prices. A frost in Brazil in July 1979 put further upward pressure on prices, which rose from around $1.30 to $2.00 between early 1979 and the autumn of the same year.[137] Prices remained high through June 1980, at which point they began to fall because of increased production and stocks. The consuming members of the ICFA made it clear that any reactivation of the agreement was dependent on the termination of unilateral producer ventures; and this trade-off was accepted in October 1980.[138] After considerable wrangling the producers and consumers agreed on a range of $1.15–$1.55/lb and to cuts in quotas when the price dropped below $1.35. The United States exercised significant influence during these deliberations. The U.S. Congress had yet to pass implementing legislation authorizing participation in the 1976 ICFA, and coffee-producing countries were understandably worried about the possible nonadherence of the world's largest importer.[139]

Despite four quota cuts between the October 1980 council meeting and the summer of 1981, the price continued to waver around the floor of $1.15 until another frost struck Brazil. The September meeting of the ICO Council set a new price range of $1.20–$1.40 and a new global quota of 56 million bags. The allocation of national quotas caused great resentment among some African, Asian, and even Latin American producing countries, with the Ethiopian delegate claiming that the agreement was merely "an extension of the biggest coffee producers like Brazil" and that "small exporters have no voice whatever."[140] Yet virtually all producers realized that the cost of opting out of the agreement was too high.

The 1982 ICFA

With the agreement set to expire in September 1983, talks to formulate a new ICFA began in early 1982.[141] Between then and September 1982, the key issue once again was the distribution of quotas. As usual, Brazil and Colombia were at the center of the bargaining. The consumer states generally supported Colombia's quest for a bigger quota, since they forecast a greater demand for Colombian beans. Brazil and Colombia eventually reached a compromise on quotas at the expense of Indonesia, Uganda, Ethiopia, and a few other small producers, while the consumers succeeded in getting an agreement that basic quotas would be renegotiated after two years. The price range and global quota were kept at their previous levels because of projections of continued surpluses and stagnating demand.[142]

Washington's willingness to support this fourth ICFA is noteworthy given the Reagan administration's expressed hostility toward intergovernmental market regulation. Once again it appears that political and foreign policy considerations carried the day. Moreover, for the first time the U.S. National Coffee Association came out in favor of the agreement, having been somewhat critical in the early 1960s and neutral in the late 1960s and mid-1970s. The association, concerned about a recurrence of the market instability of the late 1970s that led to a drop in coffee consumption, now supported efforts to promote price stability.[143]

The decision to keep Indonesia's quota at a modest level is an interesting example of the politics of the ICFA. Indonesia sharply expanded its production in the 1970s when prices were high, but it was warned by Brazil and Colombia that the producer group would not allow it to convert this increase into ICFA basic quotas when the market softened. This is exactly what happened in the 1980s. Indonesia was then forced to sell most its coffee to nonmembers on the so-called "parallel market," where prices were around one-half of what ICFA members paid. (In fact, Hungary, Israel, and Hong Kong renounced membership in the ICFA in 1982 in order to obtain this cheaper coffee.) What happened to Indonesia illustrates the extent to which the ICFA operates as a kind of consumer-sanctioned producer cartel.

Within limits, the major producers and groups of producers are allowed to decide on market shares and to control both the entry of new producers and the expansion plans of existing ones.[144]

In the year following the September 1982 conference—during which time the price remained within the range—the major issues confronting the council concerned producers' underfulfillment of quotas, growing shipments of coffee to nonmembers, and illegal transshipments to members. The council agreed to take a number of measures to control such violations. The September 1983 and 1984 council meetings ratified the previously accepted $1.20–$1.40 price range; and the global quota figure of 56.2 million bags was very close to what had prevailed during the last two years. In 1984 the ICO average market price actually went a bit above the ceiling, and additional releases were authorized.[145]

Before the September–October 1985 council meeting, the price was just below the $1.20 floor. At the session producers and consumers agreed to retain the $1.20–$1.40 range, but serious differences arose over the appropriate size of the global export quota. The producers pressed for 55 million bags, the consumers for 60 million. The final compromise was 58 million bags. However, the United States voted against the resolution specifying this figure because it did not prohibit shipments by exporting members to nonmembers when the former had not fulfilled their export quotas. Despite its dissatisfaction with the outcome, the United States continued to back the accord for political reasons.[146]

Soon after the October 1985 council meeting a significant change occurred in the coffee market as it became clear that a drought in Brazil would severely slash its production capability. By December the price was above the ceiling, and by April 1986 it had reached $2.40. It dropped back close to the ceiling in the summer as supplies grew more plentiful than first expected. Under the rules of the agreement, this price spiral led to the termination of export controls in February 1986 and to a return to the free market for the first time in five years.[147]

When export quotas were suspended, the consumers stressed that they would not agree to reintroduce them when prices fell unless the producers agreed to a new distribution of quotas, one that more closely reflected changes in productive capacity. The Western countries reiterated this position at the September 1986 council meeting when the price was still well above the ceiling. To the surprise of most states, the price began to decline precipitously in the fall and was below the floor of $1.20 by the February 1987 council meeting. The Western states, good as their word, refused to approve quotas under the old system. Many producing states, including most of the Africans, preferred the old distribution but were willing to negotiate. Brazil, on the other hand, refused to countenance any reduction of its 31 percent share and stymied any progress—much to the consternation of the Central Americans, Indonesia, and even Colombia. During the spring and summer of 1987 the price remained depressed around $1.00/lb. In October a compromise was finally reached whereby the traditional quota distribution will be kept for a year, and then the consumers' plan will be implemented during the following year. The producers, and Brazil in particular, realized that a continuation of their intransigence would cost them a substantial sum of money.[148]

The International Coffee Agreements have bestowed considerable benefits on coffee producers since the early 1960s. A very good indication of this is that the producing members have generally accounted for around 99 percent of world exports. Despite consumers' present insistence that the operation of the agreement be more sensitive to changes in trends in productive capacity, the major Western countries remain committed to the ICFA for political reasons. Their present concern about the coffee export earnings of the producing states and the overall workability of the agreement is very high given the serious debt problems of so many of the producing nations.

COCOA

The Market

Like coffee, cocoa is grown almost exclusively in tropical areas by developing countries. The trees that yield cocoa beans require three to five years' growth before harvesting. Unlike coffee, cocoa is quite homogeneous. There are only two basic types of cocoa beans, "flavor" (or "fine") beans, grown largely in parts of Latin America, and "ordinary" beans, grown in all producing areas, which constitute 85–90 percent of processed cocoa. The former usually command a small market premium.[149] The storage life of cocoa beans varies according to area—less than a year in tropical climates, but three years or more in temperate areas.[150] Producers generally export cocoa in raw form (i.e., cocoa beans), but there has been a trend, especially in Brazil and the Ivory Coast, toward greater domestic processing and exporting of intermediate products (cocoa liquor, powder, and cake). It remains the case, however, that the countries that grow cocoa account for only a small share of world production of the end products. End products include beverages, chocolate confections, pharmaceuticals, and cosmetics.[151]

In analyzing export patterns, a distinction must be drawn between beans and cocoa products; the latter include butter, powder, cake, and paste. In the case of beans, the most significant export trends have been the declining market shares of Ghana and Nigeria and the growing importance of the Ivory Coast, Brazil, and Cameroon (table 4.9). Also noteworthy is Malaysia's recent emergence as an exporter. A decline has occurred in Ghana's and Nigeria's share of world exports of cocoa products (table 4.10). Ghana's falling exports of beans and cocoa products are due mainly to managerial problems, the deterioration of its economic infrastructure, and the relatively low percentage of the world price that the government actually passes along to cocoa farmers. The decline in the industry has had major effects on the Ghanian economy because of the country's high reliance on cocoa export earnings (table 4.11). In Nigeria's case, the problem is traceable in part to lessened interest in the cocoa industry following the increase in petroleum export earnings in the mid-1970s.[152] Turning to imports, the shares of the various importing countries have remained quite stable (table 4.12). A relatively small group of multinational corporations in the Western countries account for the bulk of these countries' raw cocoa purchases as well as for the processing of cocoa and the manufacture of chocolate and other cocoa products. Included among their number are such well-known names as Nestlé (Swiss), Cadbury-Schweppes and Rowntree (British), and Hershey, Mars, and General Foods (American).[153]

Cocoa prices have been very unstable throughout most of the postwar period. According to World Bank figures, the average annual price change in constant dollars between 1955 and 1981 was 25 percent; only sugar prices have been more unstable (chart 4.3 and table 1.4).[154] The roots of cocoa's price instability lie in the relative price inelasticity of both demand and supply in the short run. Responsiveness to world price changes is often affected by governments' control of the prices that farmers receive, although there are significant differences among producer countries in this area.[155] As a result of the inelasticity of demand, changes in supply have a decisive effect on prices. In the short run, these changes can result from climatic conditions, diseases, and pests; in the longer run, from national decisions to increase or decrease production. Periods of relatively high prices will typically encourage the harvesting of a larger proportion of the beans and better care of the crop, and will also spur farmers to plant new

TABLE 4.9

Percentage Shares of Five-Year Averages of Gross Exports of Cocoa Beans, 1961 to 1979/80, and Annual Percentage Shares for 1979/80 and 1981/82

Countries	1961–65	1966–70	1971–75	1975/76, 1979/80	1979–80	1981–82
Brazil	7.3	10.1	10.6	12.8	14.0	11.2
Cameroon	6.4	6.8	6.9	6.7	8.4	9.0
Dominican Republic	2.0	2.5	2.3	2.5	2.3	3.1
Ecuador	3.2	3.9	4.1	1.8	1.6	4.1
Ghana	39.5	32.5	30.3	24.7	20.2	15.8
Ivory Coast	10.0	11.5	13.9	21.1	24.2	33.0
Malaysia	0.1	0.2	0.4	1.9	3.0	4.5
Nigeria	19.8	19.0	18.2	16.9	14.3	10.1
Papua New Guinea	1.4	2.1	1.6	2.8	3.1	2.4
Other	10.3	11.4	10.7	8.8	8.9	6.8
Exports by Weight (Thousand Tons)						
World	1,083	1,074	1,146	1,014	968	1,139

Source: International Cocoa Organization Document PCA/3/6 (1984) pp. 22–23. Only countries accounting for at least 2 percent of world exports over time period are included.

TABLE 4.10

Percentage Shares of Five-Year Averages of Net Exports of Cocoa Products by Producing Countries, 1961 to 1979/80, and Annual Percentage Shares for 1979/80 and 1981/82

Countries	1961–65	1966–70	1971–75	1975/76–1979/80	1979/80	1981/82
Brazil	30.3	18.1	30.7	36.1	42.3	44.8
Cameroon	18.2	12.2	10.0	8.6	5.8	7.0
Ecuador	0.1	1.9	5.0	19.0	22.6	9.5
Ghana	47.4	39.3	26.5	14.0	8.8	5.1
Ivory Coast	4.0	18.4	16.9	16.3	13.2	24.6
Nigeria	—	10.2	10.9	5.4	6.0	6.8
Malaysia	—	—	—	0.6	1.3	2.3
Exports by Weight (Beans Equivalent) (Thousand Tons)	67.1	149.7	226.0	305.3	338.4	269.5

Source: International Cocoa Organization Doc. PCN/3/6 (1984), p. 24.

TABLE 4.11
Percentage of Export Earnings of Developing Countries from Cocoa Beans
(Annual Average)

Six Major Producers	1976–78	1980–82
Ghana	63.2	46.3
Ivory Coast	22.5	25.6
Cameroon	21.4	13.7
Nigeria	4.6	0.9
Ecuador	3.6	1.9
Brazil	3.2	1.2
Other producers		
Equatorial Guinea	42.7	42.9
Togo	19.5	11.7
Sierra Leone	12.2	9.9
Benin	10.4	26.9
Papua New Guinea	10.3	6.1
Dominican Republic	10.2	5.1
Vanuatu	6.3	3.5
Haiti	2.3	1.9
Liberia	1.6	n.a.

Sources: World Bank, *Commodity Trade and Price Trends* (1980), table 11 and (1985), table 9. Only countries whose exports of cocoa accounted for at least 2 percent of their export earnings are listed.

trees. However, the higher prices that precipitated the plantings may no longer exist three to five years later when the new trees begin to yield. Even if prices remain high, the additional output will probably depress them. This lagged price-supply relationship normally means that periods of boom and bust will alternate in the context of an unregulated market.[156]

Negotiations in the 1950s and 1960s

No intergovernmental cocoa control schemes were in effect before World War II, although exporting companies operating in the colonies of Africa and the West Indies cooperated on occasion to influence market developments.[157] In the decade after the war prices showed considerable instability, and shot up dramatically between 1953 and 1954.[158] Numerous small chocolate manufacturers in Belgium and Switzerland went bankrupt because they lacked the large stocks normally kept on hand by bigger firms. This prompted the Belgian and Swiss governments, supported by France, to call for an international stabilization agreement. The Cocoa Study Group

TABLE 4.12

Percentage Shares of Five-Year Averages of Total World Net Imports of Cocoa Beans, 1961 to 1979/80, and Annual Shares for 1979/80 and 1981/82

Countries	1961–65	1966–70	1971–75	1975/76, 1979/80	1979/80	1981/82
Industrial						
EC	44.7	42.5	40.5	45.1	48.4	49.7
United States	28.7	24.1	21.6	18.2	13.8	15.3
Japan	2.4	3.1	2.9	2.5	2.5	3.1
Other	10.0	10.8	10.6	10.4	10.9	9.5
Centrally planned	10.3	15.2	20.3	19.8	19.4	16.9
Developing	3.9	4.3	3.8	3.6	4.0	4.1
			Imports by Weight (Thousand Tons)			
World	1,058	1,090	1,174	1,020	960	1,146

Source: International Cocoa Organization Doc. PCA/3/6 (1984), pp. 25–26.

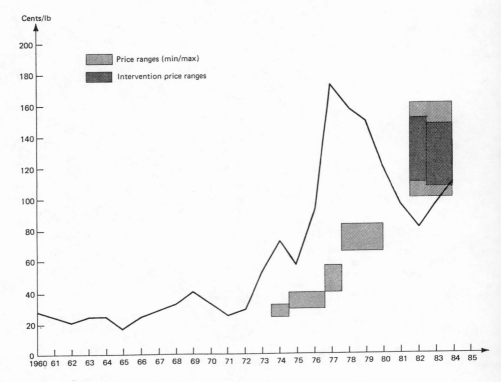

Chart 4-3
International Cocoa Prices and International Cocoa Agreements' Price Ranges,
1960–1984
Note: Prices are for the daily average (New York/London). The price ranges correspond to crop years.
Source: UN Doc. TD/B/C.1/270 (1985), p. 26.

was established under the auspices of the FAO in June 1956. Thus began
the protracted search for a control scheme for cocoa, a quest that one observer called "a minor epic in the diplomatic history" of the postwar
world.[159]

Although at first importing countries were the keenest proponents of a
stabilization agreement, producers quickly became the principal supporters because of declining prices and the failure of their own attempts at export control.[160] The largest consumers (the United States, Britain, West Germany, and the Netherlands) did not oppose market regulation outright, but
they were under pressure from manufacturers and traders hostile to the

idea. They also had doubts about the efficacy of a price-stabilization scheme. The continuing delay in obtaining an accord was harshly condemned by producers. In October 1961 they warned that they might soon unilaterally intervene to stabilize the market. A few months later, the five major producers (Ghana, Nigeria, Ivory Coast, Cameroon, and Brazil) announced the formation of the Cocoa Producers' Alliance (CPA), which was formally constituted in May 1962. But the CPA undertook no major action at this time, since consuming countries had recently agreed to attend a UN Cocoa Conference scheduled for September 1963.[161]

When delegates from 33 exporting and importing countries assembled in Geneva in September 1963 to negotiate a first international agreement for cocoa, considerable optimism prevailed. Members of the Cocoa Study Group had already achieved significant consensus on the general outlines of an accord. Prices would be stabilized by means of an export quota scheme similar to the one used for sugar, with quotas adjusted according to changes in market price. A special fund, financed by levies on cocoa exports, would be created to promote consumption and to assist producers forced to hold large stocks.[162] As the Geneva talks proceeded, it became clear that the optimism was misplaced. While producing and consuming countries had been able to agree in advance on the broad outlines, they had not resolved the contentious problem of the price range, and continuing disagreement over this matter was the basic cause of the failure of the first cocoa conference. The producers insisted on a range higher than most consuming countries would accept. In their final joint statement to the conference, the producers argued that a cocoa agreement was of no use to them unless "it is designed to stabilize and *gradually expand* the foreign exchange earnings of exporters, and . . . is able to reestablish their terms of trade at a more reasonable level than they have been in the recent past" (emphasis added).[163] The United States took the hardest line of any consuming nation at this first conference. This suggested that Washington did not feel an urgent need to assist the mainly West African cocoa producers, which contrasted with the approach adopted toward the Latin American coffee exporters in the early 1960s. Of the other importing countries, only France appeared to have a strong interest in devising an agreement intended to increase the producers' economic returns.

After this abortive negotiating session, cocoa prices continued to decline, reaching a post-1945 low of 17 cents/lb in March 1965. Using the CPA as a forum, the producers decided to take unilateral action. A Cocoa Producers' Stabilization Agreement was drawn up through the CPA. The producers adopted a minimum "indicative price," initially set at 25 cents/lb, and agreed to slash exports if the market price fell below this level. Withdrawals of supplies from the market occurred in October and November 1964, and some accumulated stocks were destroyed. The scheme, however, was a complete failure. The Ivory Coast and Cameroon, partly because of their lack of storage facilities, exceeded their assigned quotas by a considerable margin. Shortly after the CPA scheme went into effect, the Ivory Coast announced an ambitious plan to expand cocoa production by three to four times its then-current level—hardly a timely indication of support for export controls. Ghana was politically committed to the producer stabilization plan, but because it was adhering to its obligations under that plan it soon began to suffer a severe balance-of-payments crisis. By February 1965 Ghana—along with Nigeria and Brazil, which had also withheld supplies—began to dump its stocks on the market, and the price fell "at a rate which had not been thought possible."[164]

Following this failure, diplomatic action returned to forums in which both producers and consumers were members. UNCTAD Secretary General Raul Prebisch took the initiative in pressing for a resumption of serious negotiations. In June 1965, in one of its first acts, UNCTAD's Trade and Development Board established a Working Party on Cocoa Prices and Quotas. It met on a number of occasions in 1965–66 and prepared a draft regulatory agreement, which provided a basis for the Second UN Cocoa Conference, held in New York in late May 1966.[165] This meeting also ended in failure, once again because of discord over the appropriate price range. The United States was again the most important obstacle. Unlike other consuming nations, it refused to accept a floor price above 18 cents/lb, while producers would not sign an agreement that did not specify 20 cents as the price floor. According to one study, "American industry opposition to an agreement was clearly decisive in the outcome of the negotiations."[166]

It was becoming increasingly clear that the primary dispute was, as the Ghanaians put it, "not so much between producers and consumers as between the United States delegation and all other delegations."[167] Most Western European countries were prepared to see a higher market price because of their sensitivity to the complaints of recently independent African countries heavily reliant on cocoa. Because of continuing pressure from producers and the UNCTAD Secretariat, intense diplomatic preparations were made for another UN conference in the months immediately following the collapse of the 1966 negotiations. The United States and Ghana, respectively the largest consumer and largest producer, held bilateral discussions in May–June 1967 aimed at ironing out their differences. These bilateral talks led to an agreement on the major elements of a future accord, including a price range of 20–29 cents/lb.

As the third UN Cocoa Conference got under way in Geneva in December 1967, the participants again assumed that an accord would be successfully negotiated, again wrongly. The third attempt ended, as had the previous two, in failure. Several reasons have been adduced to explain this unexpected result. First, Brazil would only accept the 20 cents/lb minimum if it did *not* include freight and insurance charges, a position unacceptable to the United States, the Netherlands, and some other consuming-country delegations. Second, Brazil also insisted, in vain, that the EEC's tariff preference on cocoa beans imported from its African associates be eliminated, or at least that a commitment be made to phase it out.[168] Finally, the fact that cocoa prices had begun to increase since late 1965 after several years of hovering at very low levels meant that some producers were momentarily less interested in obtaining an agreement—an explanation offered by no less an expert than Secretary General Prebisch.[169] This price trend caused some producing countries, notably the Ivory Coast, to conclude that the 20–29 cent range was too low, and that the absence of market regulation would not be harmful to exporters since supplies were likely to be tight for several years.[170]

Following the collapse of the 1967 talks, various consultative meetings were held leading up to another full-dress conference in 1972. Widespread agreement already existed on many points, but on the minimum and maximum prices a consensus still proved elusive. Despite the high cocoa prices prevailing during much of this period (generally 30–40 cents in 1968 and 1969), the United States continued to insist that prices in the area of 20–22 cents were remunerative to efficient producers. Conflicts also existed among producers on quota allocation.[171] Between 1970 and 1972 prices dropped back below 30 cents on several occasions and this revived producers' interest in a regulatory arrangement.

The 1972 International Cocoa Agreement

The 1972 UN Cocoa Conference, held under UNCTAD's auspices, got under way in early March, but after only four days the participants decided to suspend proceedings until after the forthcoming UNCTAD III. The negotiations resumed in September and resulted in the conclusion of the first International Cocoa Agreement (ICCA).[172] Before the September negotiating session, most countries had hammered out a compromise range for the minimum price of 21–24 cents, but Washington "consistently objected to establishing this range as a basis from which to negotiate a minimum price, arguing that the healthy current price for cocoa . . . and the ability of the cocoa market to dispose of most of its stock annually since 1965 indicated that a minimum of more than 20 cents would encourage overproduction."[173] Producers insisted on a minimum of 24 cents, but they eventually accepted a range of 23–32 cents/lb in exchange for the participation of all the consuming states except the United States and West Germany.[174] The fact that prices were not only low in comparison with most of the post-1967 period (about 26 cents/lb. in the autumn of 1972) but were also thought likely to decline even further exercised considerable influence over the thinking of the producers. Had the market price been closer to that which prevailed in the late 1960s, they would certainly have held out for higher minimum and maximum prices; and had they known that prices would rise astronomically in 1973–74, they might well have preferred to have no agreement at all.[175]

Two control mechanisms to regulate the market were incorporated into the 1972 agreement—export quotas and a buffer stock. As with sugar and coffee, the cocoa agreement provided for the setting of a yearly global quota, with the size of each producer's export quota to be based on its "basic" quota or share of the global quota (article 30). (For the national shares in the 1972 ICCA, see table 4.13). Variations in the market, or "indicator," price would trigger automatic changes in members' export quotas. The maximum automatic reduction was 10 percent of basic quotas, which would apply if the price was less than 24 cents/lb but greater than the minimum of 23 cents. The council set up to administer the agreement could also institute further quota cuts once the price fell to the floor. Prices higher than 29 cents would automatically suspend quotas (article 34). The initial basic quotas were based on members' highest annual production figures since 1964–65—a provision that seemed to ensure a built-in bias toward overproduction, as the U.S. delegation pointed out, but that satisfied the exporters' desire for large quotas.[176]

The 250,000 ton buffer stock was designed not only to complement the export quota mechanism but also to provide exporters with some assurance that their surplus cocoa would be purchased. In the event that quotas were reduced, the buffer-stock manager had to buy surplus cocoa beans at a minimum of 10 cents/lb (article 40). The buffer–stock fund was to be financed by the imposition of an export levy of 1 cent/lb, but the council

TABLE 4.13

Basic Export Quotas under the Cocoa Agreements

Countries	% Share of Global Quota	
	1972	*1975*
Ghana	36.7	32.5
Nigeria	19.5	19.6
Ivory Coast	14.2	15.5
Brazil	12.7	15.0
Cameroon	8.0	8.9
Dominican Republic	3.0	2.9
Equatorial Guinea	2.4	1.6
Togo	1.8	1.8
Mexico	1.7	2.2

Source: UN Docs. TD/COCOA.3/8 (1972), annex D; and TD/COCOA.4/8 (1975), annex F. The 1980 and 1986 agreements do not have export quota provisions.

could also borrow funds if the levy proved insufficient (articles 37, 38). Further protection for cocoa-producing countries was provided by the inclusion of article 54, which limited the amount of cocoa that member importing countries could purchase from nonmember exporters to the average of such imports over the 1970–72 period, and which also required a reduction in this volume if the market price fell below the floor. The cocoa accord also gave consumers a role in enforcing the quota provisions: consumers had to require certificates for all imports (article 48).

The 1972 Cocoa Agreement closely resembled other ICAs in its voting rules. Importing and exporting members each had 1,000 votes; the first 100 were divided equally among members of each group, and the remaining 900 were apportioned according to basic quotas in the case of exporters and import levels over 1969–71 in the case of importers. Most decisions required a simple distributed majority, but on some important matters (e.g., revision of price range, setting annual export quotas), a two-thirds distributed majority was needed (article 10).

The successful negotiation of the 1972 agreement was in some respects the logical and expected outcome of more than 15 years of international discussions. Previous conferences had come close to reaching agreement, with the opposition of the United States being the primary impediment. By 1972, producing countries were adamant that American intransigence not be permitted to prevent agreement. Indeed, most delegations from both sides fully expected the United States to oppose certain elements of whatever scheme was agreed to by the other countries.[177] In seeking to understand U.S. policy toward cocoa regulation, it is essential to recognize, as has been mentioned before, that Washington's preoccupation with political and economic developments in Africa has normally not been as strong as its concern for similar developments in Latin America. The fact that African countries are the major cocoa exporters, whereas the Latin Americans are more prominent in the coffee market, meant that broader political considerations played a smaller role in U.S. policy toward cocoa. This fact worked against U.S. ratification of the accord. For the Western Europeans, the situation was just the reverse.[178]

Also contributing to the conclusion of the 1972 cocoa agreement was the fact that the UNCTAD Secretariat viewed an accord as an "essential symbol" of the organization's success. The Secretariat sought to ensure that discord among producers would not occur, and itself drafted the compromise on the price range that saved the conference. The Secretariat stressed to consuming delegations the need to go ahead despite the absence of the largest consumer and argued that the negotiation of a cocoa accord was "an acid test of international cooperation."[179] This strategy apparently had some influence on the positions of Canada, Japan, and other importing countries. A final reason for success may have been the threat of exporting countries to act unilaterally if the talks collapsed. Although cocoa prices had recently been fairly depressed, many consuming countries felt they could obtain some protection from very high prices through the ICCA's economic provisions, especially the buffer stock.

The agreement came into force at the end of June 1973, following the accession of all the major exporting countries and all the key importers except the United States. However, its economic provisions never became operative owing to the fact that cocoa prices remained well above the ceiling throughout the duration of the first agreement. Both production shortfalls due to weather and to economic management problems and the effects of the 1972–74 "commodity boom" were felt in the cocoa market as the average New York spot price shot from 29 cents/lb in 1972 to 71 cents in 1974. Prices continued to escalate during most of the rest of the 1970s. In retrospect, the low prices of the early and mid-1960s appear to have been not the norm but an exception caused by the rapid growth of production and exports in the Ivory Coast, Nigeria, and Cameroon in particular.[180]

By September 1975, as negotiations to renew the agreement began under UNCTAD's auspices in Geneva, the buffer-stock fund had accumulated more than $50 million through the imposition of the 1 cent/lb levy. Since the market price was far above the agreed range, no cocoa beans could be purchased by the buffer-stock manager, and thus he was entirely incapable of moderating the escalation of prices.[181] For the exporting countries who had consistently sought a cocoa agreement, the heady prices they were now obtaining helped to assuage any anguish they might have felt over the desuetude into which the agreement's economic provisions had fallen.

The 1975 ICCA

Efforts to renew the 1972 cocoa agreement took place against the backdrop of the negotiations to formulate UNCTAD's ambitious Integrated Program for Commodities and the general G77 quest for a New International Economic Order. The UNCTAD Secretariat identified cocoa as one of the "core" commodities for which buffer-stock-type agreements were to be negotiated. UNCTAD Secretary General Gamani Corea, noting that the primary task facing the conference was the selection of a new price range more aligned with recent market trends, suggested that a much higher range was imperative in order to further "developmental objectives."[182] Producers, using the recently expanded CPA as a forum,[183] echoed the Secretary General in calling for a higher price range. However, they were still conscious of the vicissitudes of the market and of the desirability of obtaining a firm floor price. The producers wanted the minimum price to be determined on the basis of the average daily price over the preceding three years, and asked for a range of 41–59 cents/lb. The consumers were unanimously opposed to a range this high, arguing that the preceding three years were not a "normal" period.[184]

The United States participated actively in the 1975 negotiations[185] even though it had refused to sign the 1972 accord. It presented a proposal to the conference that would have resulted in less market intervention and greater flexibility. The American plan included a buffer stock as the only price-defense mechanism (export quotas would be eliminated), a lower price range than that favored by most participants, and a wide range (20 cents), with the buffer stock operating only in the top and bottom 5 cents of that range. This would leave a wide, intervention-free range for the operation of market forces.[186]

The price issue was resolved by way of a classic compromise: the new range, 39–55 cents/lb, was roughly midway between what the European Community and the producers had put forth. The larger gap between floor and ceiling was a concession to U.S. demands. Other modifications were also made to curry favor with Washington. The new agreement placed less emphasis on export quotas and relied more heavily on the buffer stock to regulate price; a wider band of nonintervention was included; and the maximum automatic quota reduction was 4 percent (article 34) as against 10 percent in the 1972 ICCA. However, despite these changes the United States, under strong pressure from its confectionery industry, opposed the agreement, mainly because of the export controls.[187]

The successful conclusion of a second cocoa agreement was threatened for a time by the opposition of the Ivory Coast to the price range specified and especially to its own share of the basic quota (15.5 percent), both of which it considered inadequate. It was particularly unhappy that its rapidly growing production and ambitious plans to expand output were not given proper weight in determining the basic quotas, which were based on average production over the crop years 1969/70 to 1973/74. For example, Nigeria's basic quota (19.6 percent) was considerably larger than that of the Ivory Coast, even though both countries had produced almost the same quantity of cocoa in 1973–74 and the Ivory Coast had actually produced more in the 1974/75 crop year. Nor was the sharply downward trend in Ghana's production reflected in a formula based on past production, and this also worked to the advantage of the Ivoreans. Despite these misgivings the Ivory Coast had formally ratified the agreement when the old one expired in September 1976.[188]

The economic provisions of the 1975 ICCA never came into operation, because cocoa prices continued to hover above the ceiling. In the ongoing negotiations on the price range in the Cocoa Council, producing countries consistently called for a higher range, while the consuming countries, although generally willing to see some increase, refused to accept the steep rise sought by the producers. Among the consuming members, France and Belgium were the most sympathetic to producers' demands, with Britain, West Germany, and Canada the leading "hardliners."[189] All the consuming nations were disturbed by the spiraling market prices of the late 1970s: the average price was up to $1.72/lb in 1977, almost double the year before, and stayed a little below this figure in 1978 and 1979.[190] In October 1977, the council had agreed to raise the price range from $0.39–$0.55 to $0.65–$0.81/lb in an effort to reflect market developments.[191]

The 1980 ICCA

In the midst of the bullish market of the late 1970s, the United States indicated in November 1977 that it would participate in the renegotiation of the ICCA if the 1975 agreement were allowed to lapse in September 1979 (the 1975 agreement ran for three years with the possibility of a two–year extension).[192] In February 1978, Washington stated that the United States would join a renegotiated ICCA only if it were based solely on a buffer stock and if its price range could be adjusted in accordance with market trends. At the first part of the negotiating conference held in January–February 1979, producing countries inveighed against the U.S. idea of an adjustable price range, arguing that it would stabilize prices in a downward direction when market conditions became depressed. They also insisted that export controls be maintained, although Brazil and the Ivory Coast, with growing market shares, were less adamant on this issue than either Ghana or Nigeria. Buoyant market conditions in 1977–78 prompted the cocoa producers initially to request a price range of $1.86–$2.26, with a small nonintervention zone from $2.01–2.11. The developed countries rejected this outright, and the talks quickly came to an end.[193]

By the next negotiating session in August 1979, it was clear that cocoa prices were moving downward. The most important consequence was that the cocoa producers significantly modified their price demands. When the conference chairman, Ambassador Anthony Hill of Jamaica, proposed a range of $1.05–$1.75/lb, with a nonintervention zone from $1.12–$1.68, producer delegations did not object, even though these levels were far below what they had demanded only a few months earlier. Consuming countries generally felt that the $1.12 lower intervention price (LIP) was excessive, prompting Hill to suggest a revised range of $1.03–$1.67 with no intervention between $1.10 and $1.60. This proved acceptable to the EC and most other consumers, but the United States argued that, in light of projections suggesting a growing world surplus of cocoa, an LIP (at which the buffer stock would begin buying cocoa) in excess of $1.00 was unwise. Cameroon, Nigeria, and the Ivory Coast, on the other hand, considered a $1.10 LIP too low. Therefore no agreement was reached.[194]

Negotiations resumed in Geneva in November 1979. Although the price was definitely on the way down, it remained considerably above the ceiling of the prevailing price range. At this session agreement was reached on a 250,000 ton buffer stock that could, by a special vote of the Cocoa Council, be raised to 350,000 tons. The producing countries continued to insist on export controls as at least a secondary regulatory mechanism, a position still unacceptable to the United States (but not to other consuming countries). Producers also rejected once again the U.S. demand for an adjustable price range based on variations in the size of the buffer stock. Although West Germany and Britain showed some interest in this idea, the other consuming countries were prepared to support a fixed floor price. Producers remained firm in their rejection of the $1.10 lower intervention price accepted by most consumers in August. They called for a range of $1.20–$1.66, the then-prevailing market price of $1.45 being roughly in the middle of this proposed range. Consumers advanced $1.00–$1.46, which was actually less than most of them had been willing to accept a few months earlier. Both sides, in fact, were scaling their price-range proposals downward as a result of a weakening market. With continuing dissension on so many important issues, the talks again terminated without a new agreement, although the existing one was extended until March 31, 1980.[195]

The prospect of the collapse of the ICCA and a further price decline soon galvanized the producers. They decided to take unilateral action to regulate the market by forming the Abidjan Group, which included most members of the Cocoa Producers' Alliance, in December 1979. Led by Brazil and the Ivory Coast, the most outspoken proponents of a high price range during the recent unsuccessful ICCA negotiations, the Abidjan Group agreed that members would refrain from selling cocoa for less than $1.50/lb. Since the average price in December 1979 was about $1.45, this meant that producing countries would have to remove some cocoa from the market in future months in order to protect their agreed minimum price. However, some exporting countries (especially Ghana and Brazil) undercut the $1.50 minimum and increased their exports. The Ivory Coast and Nigeria, on the other hand, did scale back their cocoa sales. As the price declined, producing countries agreed in early 1980 to try to enforce a lower minimum of $1.20. But even this reduced target was violated on several occasions, including by the Ivory Coast in June 1980.[196] While the behavior of certain producers can certainly be said to have thwarted the producer scheme, a more fundamental reason for its failure was the emergence of large cocoa surpluses, which in turn were the predictable consequence of the very high prices of the post-1972 period.

This experiment in unilateral market stabilization highlighted the fragility of producer unity, especially in conditions of oversupply. Ghana, Cameroon, and several small African producers were extremely reluctant to stockpile cocoa because of inadequate storage facilities and fears about quality deterioration. When Brazil indicated it might be willing to purchase and semiprocess some of the stockpiled African beans, Brazilian cocoa growers successfully mobilized to prevent the implementation of this plan, arguing that demand for domestic beans for processing would be adversely affected. In addition, producers could not reach agreement on whether to use the $230 million buffer-stock fund accumulated under the second ICCA, to which they were entitled under the terms of the agreement. These funds could have been used to support the cocoa price, but Ghana and several smaller exporters strongly opposed such use. They evidently feared that spending the fund would not stem the projected price decline. Nor did the other producers seem keen on the idea. The UNCTAD Secretariat, well aware that it would be much more difficult to negotiate a third ICCA with consuming countries if the producers seized the $230 million, exerted strong pressure on the Ivory Coast and other exporters to leave the money untouched.[197]

A final and at least nominally successful negotiating session to conclude a third ICCA[198] was held in Geneva in November 1980, by which time the market price had fallen to around $1.00/lb. Although similar in some respects to the previous ICCAs, this third cocoa agreement (with a price range of $1.00–$1.60) had some new elements. The goal of price stabilization was to be pursued by way of buffer-stock operations only; no explicit mention of export controls is found in the 1980 ICCA. Thus the United States was victorious on this issue. On the other major U.S. demand, an adjustable price range, Washington also achieved at least partial success. Article 27 of the agreement provided for a nonintervention zone of $1.10–$1.50, leaving a wide band within which market forces would be permitted to operate unfettered. More important, these intervention levels could be adjusted according to the volume of buffer-stock sales and purchases. But the compromises made to secure a U.S. adherence came to naught, as Washington judged the price and the provisions for its adjustment to be inadequate. Canada shared many of Washington's reservations and also refused to join. The other consuming countries (led by France) decided to accept the new accord in order to provide some modest assistance to the African producers.[199] Within the producer camp the largest exporter, the Ivory Coast, also decided to reject the accord. It objected to the floor price, the provisions to reduce it in case of large buffer-stock purchases, and the exclusion of export controls.

From the November 1980 conference through 1981, the price continued to fall from around $1.00 to $0.75. In June the decision was made that the accord would provisionally enter into force on August 1, 1981, and the market price immediately moved up to the bottom of the price range in anticipation of purchases by the buffer-stock manager.[200] At the end of September the buffer-stock manager began to buy cocoa, and in less than two weeks he had spent more than half of the $230 million inherited from the previous ICCA in an unsuccessful attempt to force the cocoa price to the lower intervention level ($1.10). Producers immediately requested that the council approve commercial borrowings, as permitted by article 32 of the agreement, but France and West Germany refused to consider such a step so early in the agreement's life.[201] Later in the year, the approval of consuming members for commercial borrowing was obtained, and in addition the buffer-stock financing levy of 1 cent/lb was raised to 2 cents in order to increase the manager's resources. A Brazilian-led banking consortium indicated in February 1982 that it was willing to lend $75 million, but the council could not agree on whether it should take advantage of the offer. By early 1982 the $230 million in the buffer stock had been expended and 100,000 tons of beans accumulated in a totally futile attempt to defend the floor of the price range. The price was then about $0.80/lb. as the global recession and an estimated surplus for the 1981/82 crop year of more than 80,000 tons exerted relentless downward pressure and rendered the 1980 ICCA ineffectual.[202]

The second half of 1982 remained bleak for cocoa producers—and for the ICCA itself. Prices remained well below the ICCA floor, and producers and consumers could not agree on how to use the loans that they had authorized to support the market. The consumers, especially the Western Europeans, wanted to lower the price range. Many of the producers advocated a deferred payment scheme for buying up surplus stocks from members and nonmembers of the ICCA. Some producers called for action by the Cocoa Producers' Alliance to reverse the market trend, but a successful, coordinated producer program of supply management was most unlikely. Too many countries were opposed to reducing actual or projected production to permit a serious attack on the market slump.[203]

The 1986 ICCA

During 1983 widespread dissatisfaction developed with the operation of the ICCA. In July the council decided to ban all buffer-stock operations, thereby preventing use of the funds that had been building up since the last cocoa purchases in early 1982. It also agreed that a conference should be convened to formulate a new agreement.[204] Five sessions were held between May 1984 and July 1986, and the final conference, much to the surprise of many observers, succeeded in concluding a fourth agreement.[205]

The central matter of contention was the price range, although there were also heated disputes over the roles of a buffer stock, export quotas, and a withholding scheme (discussed below). The producers were anxious to secure a price range close to that in the existing agreement (around $1.00–$1.60) and a commitment to define a set floor price, whereas the consumers sought one about 30–40 cents lower as well as automatic adjustments in the range in response to market developments. The consumers justified their support for lower floor and ceiling prices by pointing to the appreciation of the American dollar and long-term supply and demand trends. As might be expected, the producers had different market projections. In the early stages of the negotiations they were also able to point to the upward price movements (an average of $1.09 in the 1983–84 year), which were due to poor weather conditions in several producing states. The price then began to fall back, however, to an average daily price of $1.00 in the 1984–85 year and to $0.88 at the time of the final conference in July 1986; producers consequently modified their position somewhat.[206]

On the question of price-control mechanisms, the producers strongly supported the reintroduction of export quotas. They also favored the continuation of a buffer stock and were willing to entertain the idea of a withholding scheme. The latter, suggested by both the secretariat of the International Cocoa Organization and the EC, was a proposal that all producing members be required to store or withhold certain amounts of cocoa at their own expense when prices fell into the lowest portion of the range. EC spokesmen argued that a withholding scheme had significant advantages over export quotas in that it would not protect high-cost producers or create a parallel market, such as existed for coffee.

The consumer group was dominated by the EC both because of its large share of global imports and because of the American decision not to participate actively in the talks. Within the community France was willing to accept export quotas and a set floor price and to compromise on the midpoint in the price range. But most, especially Britain, the Netherlands, and West Germany, were quite adamant in holding to their original positions. Also, the USSR was not particularly forthcoming in its stance toward the producers. It was prepared to accept export quotas, but it favored a low price range and a smaller buffer stock.

The tough bargaining occurred in 1986; the old agreement would expire in September. The first conference in February broke up after the walk-out of the largest and most "hardline" producer, the Ivory Coast. It was dissatisfied with the position of the major consumers and calculated that its action might affect their bargaining stance. But in the interim between the February conference and a new one in July, it was the producers, not the consumers, that made the major concessions. In fact, they accepted virtually the entire package of proposals supported by the conservative consumers such as Britain and West Germany.[207] The price range was set at $0.85–$1.20 with a wide nonintervention band of $0.88–$1.17 (converted from Special Drawing Rights, SDRs, in which prices were now denominated) (article 27). The SDR, whose value is determined by the exchange rates of five major currencies according to an IMF formula, was chosen in order to avoid tying prices to fluctuations in the American dollar. Price-control mechanisms were limited to a buffer stock of 250,000 tons (100,00 tons already being in it) and a withholding scheme (articles 39–43). Under the withholding scheme producers must store cocoa under the supervision of the International Cocoa Organization according to a set formula when the market price has been at or below the lower intervention level for 15 days, and when the buffer-stock manager is not buying on the market (articles 30 and 40). Also, there are provisions for the automatic adjustment of the price range depending on the market price and the volume of buffer stock purchases (article 27).

There are a variety of reasons why the producers accepted such major concessions. With the market price then at $0.88, they wanted some protection against a precipitous decline. They also were convinced, especially through discussions with French and EC officials, that they could not expect compromise from several key consumers. In addition, they were worried about the effects of dumping 100,000 tons of cocoa from the buffer stock onto the market if the ICCA were not extended.

On the consumer side a judgment was made that they could not turn their backs on an agreement so close to their "market" model of what an ICA should be. There was also a feeling that an effort should be made to reflect concern for Third World producers, especially with the seventh UNCTAD conference coming up in 1987. This view was strongest among the French and EC representatives but it was not confined to them. The French, of course, maintained their interest in assisting the Ivory Coast and Cameroon, and they also helped to persuade the Ivory Coast to accept the new accord.

Despite the fourth ICCA's market orientation, the United States had not accepted it by the time of its provisional entry-into-force in January 1987 and the commencement of buffer-stock operations in April 1987. While there are minimal economic costs for the United States (especially if all key producers join and impose a 2 cents/lb levy), it will probably refuse to sign because of a lack of political incentives and the economic ideology of the

Reagan administration. One prominent trade publication has summarized American views as follows:

[Cocoa beans] are grown in only a handful of countries, some of which are already receiving strong support elsewhere, e.g., Brazil (coffee) and the Dominican Republic (sugar). Ecuador is a member of OPEC and therefore, under existing law, of low priority for assistance, and the African countries are considered the economic responsibility of the EEC. So the arguments for full U.S. participation have to be economic.[208]

The one important producer that has not signed the 1986 ICCA, Malaysia, could pose a greater problem for the viability of the agreement. In recent years its production has been expanding rapidly. It can escape the levy by shipping to nonmembers, and as a nonmember it will be able to avoid any stock-withdrawal requirements. Consequently, it will be able to expand its market share and benefit from the higher price caused by the withdrawals of producer members. Considerable pressure will be exerted on Malaysia to accede to the fourth agreement, but given its past policy, the probability of its joining is not great.

The first two ICCAs had almost no influence on the cocoa market because of tight supplies and high prices. The same was true for the third agreement, but for opposite reasons—oversupply and declining prices. Of course, the third ICCA did not have export quotas. The viability of the 1986 accord will probably rest on the success of the withholding scheme, where producing states can probably evade complete compliance, and on the percentage of production controlled by nonmembers. If Malaysia and small producers do not join, this will increase the incentives of members to try to avoid obligations to store cocoa. The effectiveness of the agreement will also depend on the willingness of producers to allow the ICCA to respond to market developments. In the summer of 1987 they blocked a downward adjustment in the price range in line with ICCA provisions, and the consumers retaliated by refusing to allow purchases for the buffer stock.[209] A continuation of this strategy by producers will lead to the effective collapse of the agreement. The fate of this market-oriented ICA is very much in the hands of the producers.

CONCLUSION

Two overriding considerations have led Third World producers of sugar, coffee, and cocoa to press for producer-consumer control schemes during much of the postwar period. First, historically prices for these commodities have been notably unstable, often with prolonged periods of declining prices. Moreover, in the case of tropical agricultural commodity markets that are inherently unstable owing to such factors as short-run inelasticities, a large number of producing countries, and the impact of weather and diseases, producers recognize that strong prices and bullish markets are inevitably the precursors of more depressed market conditions in the future. Thus many producers have been willing to consider ICAs even when market conditions are favorable.

Second, developing–country exporters of sugar, coffee, and cocoa have been unable to achieve their objectives through unilateral producer action. Although exporters have sought on occasion to regulate these markets through producer schemes, such efforts have been almost wholly unsuccessful; and this has convinced most Third World producing countries that ICAs involving consuming countries are the most feasible strategy. For example, consuming states are needed to assist in enforcing export quota schemes and financing buffer stocks; and their cooperation is also required to restrict imports from producing countries that operate outside a commodity agreement. Above all, the producers have sought to win the support of the developed nations for the idea of guaranteed minimum export prices, and it is only through producer-consumer ICAs that such a commitment can be obtained.

Interproducer conflicts have been serious in the negotiations on all three agricultural commodities, and at times have led to the demise of the accords. The roots of the conflicts lie in the large numbers of producers (especially for sugar and coffee), differences in their costs of production, and varied expansion programs. Depressed markets have convinced them to adopt compromises on market shares, although at times only by accepting excessive global quotas. In the cases of sugar and coffee the existence of a dominant producer (Cuba and Brazil, respectively) was tremendously important: these producers could credibly threaten to flood the market if concessions were not made. The influence of dominant producers has declined over time, but they are still central to the bargaining process. For example, in early 1987 Brazil blocked an accord on a new distribution of quotas. One analyst remarked that Brazil was the only country in the coffee market "with the capacity to supply 40 percent of consumer needs, and the only country with the physical capacity to store its whole production if necessary."[210] In the case of cocoa the inexorable decline of the industry in Ghana and Nigeria as well as the buoyant market for most of the 1970s eliminated serious conflicts. The exclusion of export quotas from the 1980 and 1986 agreements did the same during the 1980s. The demise of the sugar negotiations in 1961 and then in 1984 was largely due to inter-producer differences, but the reasons varied. In 1961 it was Cuba's exclusion from the U.S. market, while in 1984 it was the emergence of a key developed-country exporter, the European Community, which did not want to subordinate domestic interests to international ones.

For the developed, consuming countries the central motivations for supporting ICAs for the three commodities have been political, although they have also had some interest in stable prices and supplies. In the case of coffee, the desire of the United States and France to assist the Latin American and African producers, respectively, has been crucial. The cocoa agreement has been strongly backed by France because of its close ties with the Ivory Coast and Cameroon. The International Sugar Agreement had significant consumer support in its early years. The United States was concerned about the situation of Latin American producers, and Britain was pledged to assist Commonwealth sugar exporters. Over time this situation has changed. The Cuban-U.S. break reduced the latter's interest in the accord. In addition, the U.S. preferential quotas (except for the years 1975–81) were seen as an effective alternative way to help Third World friends. Soviet–bloc preferences for Cuban sugar and EC preferences for the sugar exports of the ACP countries have played a comparable role. On top of this, the emergence of developed countries (the EC and Australia) as major exporters and of developing nations as important importers has reduced the North's political incentive to support prices. ICAs are very difficult to conclude when there are both Third World and industrialized exporters. When the roles of the North and South as exporters and importers overlap significantly, the political bases of support are generally too weak to maintain a commodity regulatory scheme.

5

UNSUCCESSFUL ATTEMPTS TO NEGOTIATE INTERNATIONAL COMMODITY AGREEMENTS

Most of the early postwar negotiations to establish ICAs occurred under the auspices of the United Nations and the Food and Agricultural Organization. After UNCTAD was formed in 1964, the discussion of commodity issues largely shifted to its bodies and conferences, although the FAO continued to play a modest role. The majority of these commodity negotiations ended in failure. This chapter will focus on 13 commodities for which ICAs were *not* created but which were included in UNCTAD's Integrated Program for Commodities in 1976.

A few commodities for which ICAs have been considered are not included in this chapter because developing-country producers do not account for a high percentage of world exports. For example, rice and wool were discussed in the FAO, and UN/UNCTAD study groups on tungsten, lead, and zinc have examined market regulation schemes over the past three decades. Rice, wool, and wheat (for which an ICA existed until 1971) were included in early proposals for the IPC because the Third World has an interest in them as a net importer. Eventually they were left out because the IPC was generally confined to commodities of which the LDCs are the main exporters.[1]

The negotiations on the commodities analyzed in this chapter often took place concurrently during particular periods (1973–74 and 1976–82). In 1972 UNCTAD III called for "intensive intergovernmental negotiations" on 14 commodities.[2] However, as has happened so often in the past, no significant progress in creating ICAs occurred. In retrospect, an UNCTAD Secretariat report concluded that the individual commodity-by-commodity approach could not "be relied upon to produce sufficiently swift and effective results."[3] Thus, when the IPC was launched in 1976, the Secretariat and the G77 hoped that negotiations on the 18 commodities could be linked. Discussions on ten "core" commodities would be interrelated by their potential reliance on the Common Fund for buffer-stock financing. In addition, the UNCTAD Secretariat and the G77 leadership anticipated that it would be possible to obtain trade-offs between the negotiations on "strong" and on "weak" commodities. Strong commodities consisted of certain minerals on which the industrialized world depended heavily; weak commodities were mainly agricultural products for which demand was more elastic and substitutes easily available.[4] This strategy assumed both that demand for the strong commodities was relatively inelastic with supplies or substitutes in the developed world scarce, and that their producers would be willing to sacrifice potential gains in order to assist LDCs producing weak commodities. These assumptions proved to be inaccurate. Only tenuous linkages were made among the talks on the different commodities.

The chapter first analyzes negotiations on five mineral commodities and then turns to the eight agricultural commodities. The treatment of three of the latter—tropical timber, oils and oilseeds, and bovine meat—has been kept very short because they are inherently unsuited to ICAs. Tropical timber and oils and oilseeds have so many interchangeable varieties that international regulation of markets is virtually inconceivable. The chief obstacle with regard to bovine meat was that only a very small percentage is exported by developing countries.

MINERAL COMMODITIES

Copper

The Market. Copper is a versatile commodity with a wide range of uses. It is employed in electrical generation and telecommunications, as well as in industry as a heat conductor and in construction as piping. A number of substitutes exist for copper, including aluminum for electrical generation and fiber optics for telecommunications, but at present these substitutes are not cost-competitive for most uses.[5] Assuming that consumption remains constant, the World Bank estimates that existing reserves will last for about 60 years. Scrap recycling could increase the future supply.[6] Dispersion of global reserves would appear to militate against long-term supply-restriction policies by individual producers. The United States and Chile each account for 20 percent of total reserves, while the Soviet Union, Canada, Peru, Zambia, and Zaire all possess between 5 and 10 percent.[7]

Copper exports, which represent some 50 percent of world production, increased on average by 5.3 percent per year between 1961 and 1980, although the rate of increase dropped after the mid-1970s. Developing-country exporters gained slightly from this increase, raising their collective export share from 60 percent in 1961 to 65 percent in 1982. Of the five main Third World exporters, three experienced significant changes in market shares between 1961 and 1982. Zambia's export share dropped from 18 to 12 percent, while that of the Philippines rose from 2 to 5 percent and that of Chile from 18 to 22 percent. Zaire's fell from 10 to 9 percent, and Peru's from 7 to 6 percent. Among developed countries, Canada is the most prominent exporter—with a share of about 10 percent. The United States' export share dropped dramatically from 13 to 4 percent, but it is still the largest producer of copper in the world (table 5.1; for import patterns, see table 5.2). In some cases shifting trade patterns have resulted from differences in production costs among producers. Production costs are generally lower in the Third World, with Papua New Guinea and Chile having the lowest.[8]

Because of the LDC exporters' marked dependence on copper (table 5.3), volatile price fluctuations from year to year can impose a tremendous burden on them. Between 1955 and 1981 copper prices in constant dollars varied on average by 19 percent per year (table 1.4). Periods of high prices included 1964–66, 1968–69, 1972–74, and 1979–80. Prices have been very low since 1981.[9] Instability of the copper market is attributable to a number of factors. First, prices are quite sensitive to the business cycle in the industrialized world, which helps to explain the depressed market of the mid-1970s and early 1980s. Second, there is a time lag of up to ten years between the decision to exploit a deposit and the beginning of production, during which demand may fall from what was expected.[10] Third, ownership of copper-producing companies in the developing world has been transferred in large part to local governments that are reluctant to cut back on production when demand decreases because of the impact on foreign exchange earnings and employment. For example, despite poor global market conditions in the early 1980s, some producers were reluctant to reduce production or cancel expansion plans.[11] Fourth, the price is determined on the London Metal Exchange, although only a small percentage of transactions is actually conducted there. Copper prices are not based, like

TABLE 5.1

Copper: Exports by Main Countries and Groupings[a]

Countries	% of World Exports				
	1961	1970	1975	1980	1982
Industrial	38.2	34.7	32.4	32.7	27.3
Canada	9.2	10.9	13.6	12.3	8.8
United States	13.0	6.8	3.6	2.6	4.1
EC-10	12.4	12.1	9.4	9.2	7.6
Centrally planned	2.2	4.3	6.9	3.2	7.4
Developing	59.6	61.0	60.1	64.1	65.3
Philippines	1.6	3.8	4.6	6.0	5.0
Zambia	18.4	17.6	13.6	12.1	10.9
Zaire	9.7	9.5	10.6	9.1	9.3
Chile	17.8	17.1	16.9	17.7	21.9
Peru	6.5	5.5	3.2	7.0	6.2
	Exports by Weight (Thousand Tons)				
World	3,043	3,910	4,658	5,053	5,525

[a]The figures include copper ore, blister, and refined.
Source: Data provided by World Bank, Commodity Studies and Projections Division. Only the larger exporters in the three groups of states are included.

TABLE 5.2

Copper: Imports by Main Countries and Groupings[a]

Countries	% of World Imports				
	1961	1970	1975	1980	1982
Industrial	87.7	89.6	86.8	83.3	83.6
United States	13.7	9.5	6.3	10.1	10.4
EC-9	59.3	54.1	51.4	44.7	42.1
Japan	7.3	18.1	21.1	21.4	26.1
Centrally planned	7.2	4.8	5.7	4.6	4.4
Developing	5.1	5.7	7.4	12.2	12.1
	Imports by Weight (Thousand Tons)				
World	3,006	3,849	4,456	5,271	5,176

[a]The figures include copper ore, blister, and refined.
Source: Data provided by World Bank, Commodity Studies and Projections Division. Only the larger importers in the group of industrial states are included.

TABLE 5.3
Percentage of Export Earnings of Developing Countries from Copper

Countries	1976–78	1980–82
Zambia	92.3	91.7
Namibia	73.3	27.2
Zaire	61.4	37.8
Chile	54.1	45.5
Papua New Guinea	28.3	29.9
Botswana	28.2	5.5
Peru	22.0	16.5
Philippines	8.4	7.7
Mauritania	3.7	0.3
Zimbabwe	—	2.2

Source: World Bank, *Commodity Trade and Price Trends* (1980), table 11 and (1985), table 9. Only countries whose exports of copper accounted for at least 2 percent of their export earnings are listed.

those of some other metals, on long-term contracts or on transfer pricing within individual multinational corporations.[12] This lessens the prospects for stability. Finally, instability can also be caused by strikes in producing countries, speculation, and currency movements.[13] Given these various factors, it is not surprising that copper prices have been the most unstable of all the metals.

Negotiations. From the latter part of the nineteenth century to the mid-1960s intermittent attempts were made by companies in the copper industry to stabilize prices, but these had little impact on the market. The first effort by governments to deal with market instability occurred in the late 1960s. In 1967, following a precipitous drop in prices the preceding year, the four major developing-country exporters (Zambia, Zaire, Peru, and Chile) established the Council of Copper Exporting Countries (usually known as CIPEC). In its early years the organization concerned itself almost solely with the exchange of information and the promotion of national control of the copper industry. This was primarily because the two Latin American members, which possessed larger reserves and had lower production costs, were opposed to market regulation, fearing that it would prevent them from expanding their output and market shares. In the early 1970s Chile voiced some interest in joint cutbacks, since its production was declining owing to a variety of domestic problems, but the reluctance of other producers to reduce output and earnings, coupled with the existence of a bullish market, prevented any serious negotiations.[14]

When copper prices again fell drastically in late 1974, certain producers manifested less opposition to price regulation. In November 1974 CIPEC members agreed to a 10 percent production cutback; in April 1975 they accepted a further 5 percent reduction. Despite these agreements, Chile unilaterally increased its copper output, and it soon became apparent that this attempt at market regulation had failed. With lower production costs, vast reserves, and a strong desire to maintain export earnings and employment levels, Chile had little incentive to implement the CIPEC policy. On the prospect of producer collaboration, Sir Roland Prain apty concluded in 1975 that "It would appear . . . that only if production costs were virtually the same in all the CIPEC countries would there be much chance of an effective *entente cordiale* and the ability to make rapid decisions as required."[15]

Since 1975 CIPEC has not really been at the center of producers' attempts to promote market regulation, although Indonesia has become a full member and Australia, Papua New Guinea, Mauritania, and Yugoslavia have become "associates."[16] With the demise of the CIPEC plan, several Third World producers decided to promote the creation of an ICA. Given the policy differences among them and the fact that CIPEC only controlled about 30 percent of world production, they recognized that the cooperation of the developed countries was necessary if they were to achieve effective market management. Many producers also hoped that with the ongoing negotiations in pursuit of a New International Economic Order, the industrialized world might consent to an international arrangement that would buoy copper prices. At the request of seven CIPEC members, the Secretary General of UNCTAD convened a meeting of producers and consumers in March 1976. Most of the developing countries pressed for price regulation, but the developed countries expressed interest in establishing an institution concerned only with facilitating information exchange.[17] The meeting adjourned with a view to convening again at a later date. The launching of the IPC in May 1976 then led to a change in the format of the producer-consumer dialogue.

At the intitial IPC meeting on copper in November 1976 a majority of developing-country producers voiced strong support for the creation of a buffer stock and supply-management measures. However, the developed consuming and exporting countries were concerned about the high cost of a buffer stock (estimated at $3 billion by academic and UNCTAD studies in

1975–76) and about the feasibility and legality (under their own laws) of production and export controls.[18] During 1976 and 1977 the two sides were at loggerheads. Most developed countries opposed a scheme that relied largely on a costly buffer stock, although a few of them—the Scandinavian countries, the Netherlands, Belgium, and France—were willing to accept an ICA based on export controls. Developed producing nations such as Canada, Australia, and the United States opposed production or export controls, fearing that the burden of any production cutbacks in a depressed market would fall on them disproportionately. Among LDC producers Chile was the least enthusiastic about supply management. Its ambitious plans to increase output, which drew strong criticism from Peru, were incompatible with any export quotas. But the G77 successfully prevailed upon Chile not to voice its opposition at the IPC meetings. Zambia was willing to support any plan that proimised higher prices, and the same was basically true of Zaire. The most vocal proponent of the official G77 position was Peru. The main reason for its stance was a desire to obtain international constraints on Chile's plans to increase production. However, it is unclear whether the industry in Peru would have gone along with production or export controls.[19]

With this impasse in the negotiations on price regulation, the talks focused on the creation of a producer-consumer consultative body in 1978. But after lengthy meetings the two sides failed to reach an accord. The G77, under Peruvian leadership, interpreted the proposal for a consultative body as an attempt to divert attention from price regulation. There were also divergent views on the structure and purposes of a consultative organization. In the course of the meeting, the Zambian delegate, who saw some value in a consultative body, attacked his G77 compatriots, commenting acidly that the negotiations had failed because of some representatives' "gift of eloquence, on which people could not feed."[20]

In 1979 the United States shocked the other developed countries by suggesting that the committee consider the establishment of a large buffer stock without supply controls. This U.S. proposal, which was controversial within Washington policy circles, reflected a desire to make a "constructive" démarche in the North-South negotiations. It was also based on the findings of government research studies favoring pure buffer-stock arrangements for ICAs.[21] Peru violently attacked the U.S. plan, arguing that it would only depress prices, to the detriment of exporters. The representative from Canada, the largest developed-country exporter, feared that the proposal would have "particularly disastrous consequences."[22] The Europeans and Japanese also opposed the American buffer-stock plan because of the size of the contributions they believed they would be required to make. In the end, the United States abandoned its own proposal in the face of the determined opposition of other countries and the dawning realization that it would have to pay a significant portion of the projected cost of $3 billion.[23] Following this meeting, a CIPEC publication trenchantly observed: "A skeptic attending the interminable negotiations on copper under UNCTAD has said that there are only two days in a five or six year cycle on which there is a hope of achieving an agreement between producers and consumers on measures to stabilize the price; one when the price is at the mid-point of its rise and the second when it is halfway through its fall."[24]

After another unproductive IPC meeting in 1980, an UNCTAD report noted that most states "had still not decided the key issue of whether an international stabilization agreement was feasible and if so, the kind of measures that should be included."[25] This rather pessimistic appraisal was echoed in a major 1979 study of the world copper industry by Raymond Mikesell.[26] On the possible effects of an ICA geared to price stabilization, Mikesell observed that agreements for commodities such as copper, whose price instability stems from variations in demand rather than supply, often lead to decreases in producer revenues. He suggested that a better method of stabilizing export revenue would be compensatory financing. He also doubted the ability of a buffer-stock scheme to defend a price ceiling, noting that its existence might encourage investment in excess mine capacity. Turning to the policies of LDC producers, Mikesell argued that they base their output decisions on social opportunity costs, not monetary costs, since "In the case of government enterprise, not only are taxes on the enterprise a part of the revenues from the standpoint of the government, but the social opportunity cost of labor is substantially less than its monetary cost to a private international mining firm."[27] There are also major technical and political problems involved in setting price ranges, establishing the size of a buffer stock, and operating the stock.[28]

Mikesell likewise was skeptical of the prospects for collaboration among CIPEC members. Past experience indicates they would have a difficult time agreeing on and maintaining a given price range. Moreover, CIPEC-mandated output cutbacks would probably not increase producer revenues, because CIPEC members provide only about 23 percent of the total copper and 32 percent of the refined copper consumed in the noncommunist world. In fact, even if all LDC producers joined CIPEC, they would still not control enough of world production to guarantee higher revenues. They could only succeed in increasing export receipts if developed-country producers such as the United States and Canada imposed production controls, which is highly improbable. It is thus evident that Third World exporters have insufficient leverage in the copper market to control prices.[29]

Recent experience has borne out Mikesell's conclusions. The devastating recession of the early 1980s saw copper prices decline drastically to their lowest levels in real terms since the early 1930s. Despite this, CIPEC has undertaken no collective action to stem the price fall. Indeed, in 1982 Chile actually *increased* its output by 14 percent over 1981. Even more than other LDC exporters, it "continued to pump out metal, despite low prices, in a desperate effort to bring in much-needed foreign exchange."[30] CIPEC did meet in July and August 1982 to consider market-intervention schemes, but it could not agree on a firm proposal—except that an accord should not require any reductions in output![31] Earlier hopes that a Third World copper cartel could be developed have been shattered. The Peruvian Minister of Mines reflected this sobering realization when he observed in late 1982 that "CIPEC has not the resources to attempt to influence market prices."[32] Copper market regulation, whether among producers or between producers and consumers, thus has been undermined by the structure of the market, the availability of substitutes, and serious differences in interests within and between producer and consumer groups.

An interesting development in copper diplomacy occurred in 1985 and 1986 when the United States suggested in the OECD and UNCTAD that an international study group be established. The proposal originated from pressure by the American copper industry, which wanted its government to take some action to limit copper imports or encourage cutbacks in production by lower-cost foreign producers. The United States initially met considerable opposition from most states. The LDC exporters feared that the study group would be used to pressure them to limit exports and to extract valuable industrial information. The developed importers were suspicious that the proposed group might be used to raise prices and thought that there was no need for an information-gathering body since several already existed. However, by late 1987 Third World opposition had dissipated, and some of the industrial nations were more receptive. An initial negotiating session to consider the proposal was set for mid-1988.[33]

Iron Ore

The Market. Iron ore is one of the most abundant minerals found in the earth's crust. Significant reserves of it can be found in almost all regions of the globe.[34] Since iron ore has no known substitutes, total demand tends to be price inelastic. However, this does not seem to have improved the lot of iron-ore producers, mainly because of the relative abundance of the commodity worldwide. Even if it were possible to restrict the entry of new suppliers, producers would face a number of other obstacles to the exploitation of price inelasticity. The creation of buffer stocks or the use of export controls would necessitate expending large sums of money to maintain stocks. Iron ore was excluded from the "core" IPC commodities largely because of the expense of stockpiling.[35]

The absence of a single, open marketing system for iron ore also limits the ability of producers to promote market regulation. Some 60 percent of the iron ore entering international trade is sold on the basis of long-term contracts. These typically have a lifespan of between 5 and 20 years (and an average of 10 years). Originally they specified price and tonnage for the length of the contract, but since the late 1970s they have provided for a measure of flexibility with respect to both prices and volume on an annual basis.[36] The purpose behind long-term contracts is to provide a secure supply for consumers and to ensure that a sufficient market exists to permit mines to operate near full capacity.[37] The remaining 30–40 percent of iron ore entering world trade is sold on the basis of short-term contracts or intracompany transfers. Intracompany transfers were developed as a means for consumers to guarantee supplies through the development of their own "captive" mines, but "with the nationalization of mines in Venezuela, Peru, and Mauritania, and the growth of non-captive sources of supply elsewhere in Latin American, Africa and Australia, the proportion of total trade which may be described as captive has declined rapidly in recent years."[38]

Before World War II, the steel industry in the industrialized countries was able to obtain iron ore from domestic and regional sources. Later, the progressive exhaustion of high-grade ores in Western Europe and the United States led to the development of new deposits in the southern hemisphere.[39] Between 1961 and 1982 developing countries increased their share of global exports from 43 to 49 percent. Brazil accounted for almost half of this total, with India, Liberia, and Venezuela commanding market shares of between 2 and 8 percent. Among the developed-country exporters Australia's share rose dramatically in the past two decades; by 1982 it accounted for 23 percent of global exports (table 5.4; for import patterns see table 5.5). Only two of the smaller exporters depend on iron ore exports for large shares of their export earnings (table 5.6).

The major problem facing all exporting countries has been the steady decline of real prices. The commodity boom of 1973–74 caused a recovery, but this proved to be short lived.[40] While real prices have declined steadily

TABLE 5.4
Iron Ore: Exports by Main Countries and Groupings

Countries	% of World Exports				
	1961	*1970*	*1975*	*1980*	*1982*
Industrial	46.1	42.2	42.7	42.3	40.6
Canada	10.1	12.2	9.4	10.5	8.6
France	17.3	5.8	4.2	2.8	1.8
Australia	0.3	12.8	11.5	22.5	23.0
Centrally planned	10.9	11.2	11.5	10.8	10.1
USSR	10.9	11.2	11.5	10.8	10.1
Developing	43.0	46.6	45.8	46.9	49.3
India	6.6	6.6	5.9	6.0	7.7
Liberia	1.9	7.3	4.9	5.4	5.2
Brazil	4.1	8.7	19.1	21.1	23.0
Venezuela	9.7	6.6	5.2	2.9	2.1

	Exports by Weight (Thousand Tons)				
	149,549	321,710	379,864	370,261	315,700

Source: Data provided by World Bank, Commodity Studies and Projections Division. Only the larger producers in the three groups of states are included.

TABLE 5.5
Iron Ore: Imports by Main Countries and Groupings

Countries	% of World Imports				
	1961	*1970*	*1975*	*1980*	*1982*
Industrial	85.5	86.7	83.5	78.2	73.3
United States	17.5	14.3	12.8	6.8	4.7
EC-9	50.0	38.7	32.9	33.1	28.8
Japan	14.0	32.0	35.4	35.5	36.3
Centrally planned	13.9	11.9	13.7	15.6	16.1
Developing	0.7	1.5	2.8	6.1	10.6

	Imports by Weight (Thousand Tons)				
World	150,108	318,756	372,756	376,930	316,671

Source: Data provided by World Bank, Commodity Studies and Projections Division. Only the larger importers in the group of industrial states are included.

TABLE 5.6

Percentage of Export Earnings of Developing Countries from Iron Ore

Countries	1976–78	1980–82
Mauritania	81.1	70.0
Liberia	63.1	59.0
Swaziland	10.9	0.2
Brazil	8.4	7.8
Peru	4.5	2.9
India	4.4	5.0
Chile	3.6	3.5
Venezuela	2.0	0.8

Source: World Bank, *Commodity Trade and Price Trends* (1980), table 11 and (1985), table 9. Only countries whose exports of iron ore accounted for at least 2 percent of their export earnings are listed.

over the long term, prices have not fluctuated wildly. Only two other commodities (bauxite and bananas) listed in table 1.4 have experienced smaller annual average price changes. The relative stability of iron ore prices is partly due to the method of price-setting through contracts and intracompany transfers.[41] But since long-term contracts now can adjust prices at more frequent intervals, greater fluctuations may occur. Nonetheless, short-term price stability and a declining real-price trend are likely to continue to characterize the market for the foreseeable future.

The main reason for declining real prices since the 1970s has been an excess supply of iron ore caused by a significant drop in demand for steel and the opening of new mines by low-cost producers—notably Brazil and Australia.[42] Some exporters also argue that consumers and multinational corporations (MNCs) have deliberately manipulated the system to keep prices low. Most contracts specify that consumers have a tonnage option, perhaps of ± 10 percent. If the contract calls for 1,000 tons and the consumer consistently takes 900 tons, an excess of supply continues, and this helps force prices down.[43] Manipulation of the pricing system by consumers is made easier by the high degree of concentration in the steel industry, where a few companies have a great deal of power. "By exerting their monopsonistic power steel companies and merchant ore companies can influence prices charged by independents and if need be price their own supplies differently."[44] The ownership of mines by steel companies, while less important now than before, also increases the market power of the steel industry.[45]

Negotiations. Faced with steadily declining real prices and powerful MNCs, developing-country exporters began to search for ways of improving their earnings in the late 1960s. In 1968 exporters met in Caracas to discuss market problems—low prices and excess supply—and to propose solutions.[46] Discussion continued in 1969, but no concrete proposals were forthcoming. In 1970, UNCTAD entered the picture by sponsoring a meeting of consumers and producers in accordance with a 1968 conference resolution. In 1970 and 1972 developing-country exporters pressed for indexation of iron ore to steel prices.[47] While some industrialized consuming states recognized the problems faced by many producers, most seemed content to benefit from more efficient extraction technologies and the growing output of the lower-cost producers. To the demand that iron ore prices be indexed, one developed-country representative responded:

The proposal to link iron ore prices with those of steel was both impractical and economically unsound; even if a satisfactory conceptual basis for such a link could be found, the result would be to stimulate iron ore production, curb the growth of consumption, and simultaneously introduce a self-renewing inflationary factor into the world economy.[48]

The 1972 meeting merely agreed to commission a study on the relationship between steel and iron ore prices. But when the report was completed in 1974,[49] prices were on the rise, prompting many producers to lose interest in the study.

The failure of the UNCTAD meetings, coupled with OPEC's example and the realization that the price increases during the "commodity boom" were temporary, soon led the developing countries to seek the creation of a producers' association. Nineteen countries met in 1974 to consider a proposal, formulated by Algeria, India, and Venezuela, to establish an OPEC-style producers' organization. The three largest exporters—Australia, Brazil, and Canada—refused to accept unilateral market regulation by producers and stressed the need for consumer participation.[50] The proposal was then rewritten to accommodate certain views held by these states, since their cooperation was thought essential.

In 1975, the Association of Iron Ore Exporting Countries (usually known by its French acronym APEF), including eight developing (Algeria, Chile, India, Mauritania, Peru, Sierra Leone, Tunisia, and Venezuela) and two developed countries (Australia and Sweden), was formed.[51] APEF was *not* given a mandate for market regulation, being conceived as purely "a center for the diffusion of the economic and technical information capable of helping member countries make investments in the local iron ore industry or negotiate export contracts more succesfully."[52] Still, a number of important exporters refused to become members because they saw APEF as a possible step toward joint producer intervention in the iron ore market. Canada would not sign the agreement because consuming states were not allowed to join; Brazil signed but never ratified the agreement for fear that it would be pressed to compromise its ambitious plans to expand iron-ore exports;[53] Liberia withheld acceptance of the agreement for a time but did join eventually; and the Soviet Union rejected the idea outright. The absence of such important exporters effectively nullified any chance that unilateral market regulation might be attempted by producers.

Following the creation of APEF, negotiations continued in UNCTAD. Iron ore was brought into the IPC because developing-country exporters accounted for close to half of world exports and because India, worried about preserving the market for its ore, pressed for iron's inclusion. Between late 1977 and the end of 1978 two committee and two experts' meetings were held in UNCTAD, but negotiators on both sides appeared to be simply "going through the motions."[54] A report by the UNCTAD Secretariat stated that the experts were "unable, for lack of any relevant proposals by governments, to direct consideration to the question of appropriate measures and techniques."[55] One former UNCTAD official stated that "it was not even possible to secure any agreement that 'problems' exist in the iron ore market which would form the basis for discussion."[56] What appears to have happened is that smaller developing producers did not think it worth the effort to present proposals to raise the price and/or their own market shares given that Brazil and the developed producers and consumers were certain to oppose them. In 1984, after several years of decreasing trade and falling prices,[57] discussions were held at UNCTAD to form a producer-consumer study group to provide for greater market transparency. Several producing and consuming states were receptive to the idea, but the opposition of the United States and Brazil did not bode well for the study group. They seemed fearful of any venture that might create pressures for intergovernmental regulation. No progress occurred in UNCTAD in the next several years. Then, in 1986 APEF suggested that it be reconstituted into a producer-consumer organization. The United States and some other developed countries rejected the idea, and therefore it is unlikely to be approved.[58]

To many observers the lack of progress in negotiations on iron ore was hardly surprising. Considering the abundance of iron ore, the developed countries' control of over half of world exports, the conflicts over market shares among developed and developing producers, and the prevalence of long-term contracts, there was never much chance of success. It is noteworthy that the largest Third World exporter, Brazil, has always been averse to a producer cartel or an ICA. This policy is likely to be maintained with the completion of its large Carajas iron ore project. With both Brazil and Australia determined to increase their market shares, the smaller- and higher-cost producers, while continuing to have an interest in regulation, would be wise not to expect any real progress.

Manganese Ore

The Market. Manganese is essential in steelmaking, with over 90 percent of world production consumed by the steel industry. In recent years technological innovations have reduced the amount of manganese used per ton of steel manufactured. Manganese ore—which varies considerably in grade or manganese content—may either be used directly in the steelmaking process or else first be converted into a manganese ferro-alloy.[59] Known land-based resources of managanese are large but irregularly distributed. The largest known high-grade deposits are located in the Soviet Union and South Africa, which together account for 85 percent of known global reserves. Gabon's deposits are also important, even though they are small in comparison to Soviet or South African sources, because the ore is extremely high-grade. One source not included in the above figure is manganese contained in nodules on the deep seabed. Exploitation of these deposits, although most unlikely for several decades, would swiftly take away any advantage enjoyed by existing land-based producers.[60]

Manganese ore exports doubled during the years 1961–75, but then dropped in the late 1970s and early 1980s.[61] This decrease was due to the recession in the economies of the industrialized importers, a decline in the amount of manganese needed in steelmaking, and an increase in the production of manganese ferro-alloys and steel in the exporting countries (e.g., India and Brazil). In the period 1960–82 the pattern of exports changed considerably. The share of the developing countries fell from 67 percent to 42 percent, despite the fact that Gabon's exports rose from zero to 20 percent of the world market. Major gains were made by several developed states: Australia rose from 1 to 13 percent and South Africa from 13 to 31 percent. Despite the USSR's substantial reserves, its share of world exports has dropped over the past two decades. Most of its production is consumed domestically (table 5.7). With respect to manganese ore imports, the drastic decline in the U.S. share (table 5.8) is mainly attributable to its increasing importation of ferromanganese.[62]

The annual average change in manganese ore prices (in constant dollars) from 1955 to 1981 was 10.3 percent; among unprocessed minerals only bauxite and iron ore had smaller average fluctuations (table 1.4). The relative stability is a result of the structure of the international market. Approximately 90 percent of the ore traded internationally is sold through annual or long-term contracts and "tied sales" (i.e., sales from mines in which the importer has a financial interest).[63] While price instability has not been a major concern of manganese ore producers, the same cannot be said of the price trend,[64] which has been downward because of lower extraction costs, strong competition among producers, and declining demand.[65] However, for no producer do revenues from manganese ore sales constitute a significant percentage of export earnings (table 5.9).

TABLE 5.7
Manganese Ore: Exports by Major Countries and Groupings (Manganese Content)

Countries	% of World Exports				
	1960	1970	1975	1978	1982
Industrial	15.4	26.9	39.8	39.7	44.2
Australia	0.9	7.1	11.5	11.2	12.9
South Africa	13.3	19.4	26.6	26.4	31.1
Centrally planned	17.4	13.0	12.3	13.8	14.2
USSR	16.5	12.7	12.1	13.8	14.2
Developing	67.2	60.1	47.9	46.5	41.6
Brazil	14.7	16.8	13.4	10.4	10.4
Gabon	0.0	19.4	21.0	22.5	19.9
Ghana	10.1	3.8	2.8	3.0	0.2
India	20.9	13.1	5.3	5.0	5.6
Morocco	6.7	1.8	1.5	2.5	n.a.
Zaire	5.5	3.1	1.0	0.7	n.a.
	Exports by Weight (Thousand Tons)				
World	2,649	4,244	5,250	3,873	3,375

Source: Data for 1960–78 from UN Doc. TD/B/IPC/MANGANESE/7/add. 1 (1980), table IIa; data for 1982 from World Bank, Commodity Studies and Projections Division. Only the larger producers in the three groups of states are included.

TABLE 5.8
Manganese Ore: Imports by Major Countries and Groupings (Manganese Content)

Countries	% of World Imports				
	1960	*1970*	*1975*	*1978*	*1982*
Industrial	87.8	90.1	84.3	77.1	71.9
EC-9	34.7	33.5	24.0	27.8	26.7
Japan	3.8	23.9	29.4	20.7	25.4
United States	40.2	19.2	14.1	7.6	3.7
Centrally planned	12.0	9.1	12.9	17.9	18.0
Developing	0.2	0.7	2.8	5.0	10.1
	Imports by Weight (Thousand Tons)				
World	2,742	4,000	4,918	3,752	3,407

Source: Data for 1960–78 from UN Doc. TD/B/IPC/MANGANESE/7/add. 1 (1980), table IVa; data for 1982 from World Bank, Commodity Studies and Projections Division. Only the larger importers in the group of industrial states are included.

Negotiations. Manganese was first discussed in UNCTAD in 1970 and 1971 within the Committee on Commodities. Negotiators who met in February 1972 at a special session devoted solely to manganese ore were able to agree that a steady decline in real prices had occurred. Developed- and developing-state participants, however, differed on whether a "problem" existed requiring international action, and they failed to reach a consensus on future negotiations. At a 1974 UNCTAD meeting some developing countries called for the formulation of a draft ICA, but most negotiators—consumers and producers alike—felt that this was premature. LDC exporters remained apprehensive about declining real prices (despite the dramatic upswing in prices since 1973) and advocated the indexation of manganese ore prices to those of steel-based products. Other exporters

TABLE 5.9
Percentage of Export Earnings of Developing Countries from Manganese Ore

Countries	1976–78	1980–82
Gabon	8.4	4.4
Vanuatu	3.7	—
Ghana	1.4	0.8

Source: World Bank, *Commodity Trade and Price Trends* (1980), table 11 and (1985), table 9. Only countries whose exports of manganese ore accounted for at least 1 percent of their export earnings are listed.

pressed for a discussion of trade barriers and of possible oversupply of manganese through seabed exploitation. On all these proposals the consumers were basically unyielding, arguing that trade barriers should be discussed in the GATT and seabed mining at the UN Conference on the Law of the Sea, and that indexation would not be beneficial to anyone.[66]

The major proponent of including manganese in the IPC was Gabon, which was concerned that its higher production costs could lead to a falling market share and export revenues. It was also very worried about South Africa's aggressive marketing activities. Manganese was not included in the "core" commodities because the predominance of contract sales rendered a buffer stock impracticable. An initial IPC meeting on manganese was held in 1977, but it was noteworthy only for the paucity of interest displayed by most participants. The meeting essentially saw Gabon, a few *nonproducing* LDCs, the UNCTAD Secretariat, and France (which had investments in the Gabonese industry) argue for some type of ICA with export-control measures, with all the other producers and consumers showing a distinct lack of interest in any such scheme. Brazil, the second-largest LDC exporter, clearly distanced itself from Gabon when it refused to sign a joint producers' statement.[67]

A second meeting was held in 1980 largely because of Gabon's lobbying efforts. Gabon first tried without success to get the developing producers as well as other LDCs in attendance to support a united approach toward market regulation. The developed countries noted that they had not been presented with any proposals, and the discussion that ensued basically focused on general market developments.[68] Following some Secretariat studies and commentaries by governments on market problems a meeting of experts was convened at UNCTAD in 1982. On behalf of all the producing countries Gabon presented a list of problems facing producers, including deteriorating prices and declining demand. It hinted that intergovernmental action was needed. The U.S. representative immediately retorted that "his Government had concluded that market intervention measures were not feasible or required because of the absence of a terminal market, the lack of price volatility, the heterogeneity of ores, and the high cost of stockpiling ores. . . . " Gabon then was forced to admit that "producers had not proposed in their statement the taking of any specific international measures"—thus signaling the futility of the whole enterprise.[69]

As was mentioned earlier, several characteristics of the manganese market seriously impede efforts to conclude a regulatory agreement. Of even greater importance are the general opposition of the industrialized nations to intervention in relatively stable markets and the intense competition among producers. The dramatic shifts in market shares in recent decades illustrate how competitive the market has been. Gabon has, in fact, been one of the major beneficiaries of this trend, and other producers are not predisposed to protect its position. This is true not just of developed producers such as Australia, South Africa, and the USSR, which would be pressed to accept reductions in their exports in an ICA, but also of Brazil, which is planning to increase its production substantially. Also undermining the prospects for producer collaboration in an ICA or a cartel is the fact that "the political complexion of the four [major producing] countries and their economic and strategic interests could not be more diverse."[70]

Bauxite

The Market. Bauxite, an oxide-type ore containing hydrated alumina, is used in the smelting of aluminum, but it must first be processed into alumina before the smelting can occur. Exploitation of nonbauxite sources of alumina could affect long-term demand, but the high alumina content and low impurities of bauxite give it an advantage (i.e., less energy is required in processing). Alternate sources are cost-effective only when bauxite prices are extremely high.[71] An important feature of the bauxite/alumina/aluminum market is the high degree of concentration among six vertically integrated multinational corporations: the Aluminum Company of America (ALCOA), Alcan Aluminum, Reynolds Metals, Kaiser Aluminum and Chemical Corporation, the Pechiney Ugine Kuhlman Group (PUK), and Alusuisse. These firms have come to dominate the industry as a result of such factors as the sizable investments required for bauxite mining, economies of scale, the need for an efficient infrastructure in the ore-producing nations, high transport costs, and the necessity for capital- and energy-intensive refining and smelting processes. Fifty smaller firms also compete at various levels of production. One or more of the "big six" MNCs are present in most of the major bauxite-producing countries except Guyana, Yugoslavia, and Indonesia, where the industry has been totally nationalized. In 1980 the six large MNCs still controlled 45 percent of bauxite mining, 63 percent of alumina production, and 53 percent of aluminum capacity outside the communist bloc. Because of the vertical integration characteristic of the industry, bauxite and alumina are traded mostly internally or by intrasystem transfer between the parent company, its subsidiaries, and affiliated enterprises. In 1976 this was the case with almost 90 percent of the bauxite and nearly 83 percent of the alumina traded.[72]

Third World producers' share of global exports fell from 81 to 64 percent between 1961 and 1982, the decline being attributable to the growth of alumina processing within these countries and to the emergence of Australia as the largest exporter (26 percent of global exports). Leaders among the LDC exporters in 1982 were Guinea (24 percent) and Jamaica (13 percent). Since 1961 the share of the four Caribbean producers has declined dramatically from 68 to 18 percent (table 5.10; for import patterns, see table 5.11). The developing countries also sell about a third of world alumina exports. As for known bauxite reserves, 71 percent are located in developing countries, with 26 percent in Guinea and 10 percent in Brazil.[73] For most of the important developing producing states bauxite sales are crucial to their economies (table 5.12).

When discussing bauxite prices, it is essential to note that no single global price exists. Varying ore grades, transportation costs, and the bargaining between governments and corporations all influence the price

TABLE 5.10

Bauxite: Exports by Main Countries and Groupings

Countries	% of World Exports				
	1961	*1970*	*1975*	*1980*	*1982*
Industrial	15.2	26.2	33.5	28.1	33.8
Australia	0.2	13.8	24.2	22.2	25.5
Yugoslavia	5.8	7.3	3.9	2.0	4.3
Greece	6.5	4.4	4.8	3.7	3.5
Centrally planned	4.3	2.4	1.8	2.3	2.7
Developing	80.5	71.4	64.7	69.5	63.6
Indonesia	2.6	3.3	3.0	3.3	2.3
Guinea	2.2	2.9	22.1	27.3	24.4
Jamaica	31.3	27.8	16.6	16.2	13.4
Surinam	21.1	12.3	6.8	3.8	1.6
Guyana	10.1	11.0	6.5	4.3	2.3
Dominican Rep.	5.4	4.6	2.8	1.4	0.5
	Exports by Weight (Thousand Tons)				
World	16,140	27,816	32,939	37,462	30,180

Source: Data provided by World Bank, Commodity Studies and Projections Division. Only the larger exporters in the three groups of states are included.

TABLE 5.11

Bauxite: Imports by Main Countries and Groupings

Countries	% of World Imports				
	1961	*1970*	*1975*	*1980*	*1982*
Industrial	92.1	89.0	83.6	86.2	84.4
United States	59.5	50.2	37.1	38.5	37.7
Canada	9.9	9.2	7.4	9.5	8.6
EC-9	14.9	15.8	24.7	18.8	23.1
Japan	7.3	13.2	14.0	15.4	11.5
Centrally planned	7.0	9.0	15.0	12.2	14.5
USSR	2.9	5.6	10.6	8.5	10.5
Developing	1.0	2.0	1.3	1.6	1.0
	Imports by Weight (Thousand Tons)				
World	15,866	27,567	32,765	37,050	29,796

Source: Data provided by World Bank, Commodity Studies and Projections Division. Only the larger importers in the three groups of states are included.

levels. The price is often actually a transfer price between divisions of a single company or between affiliated companies. This transfer price constitutes the basis for governmental taxes in most producing countries. The average bauxite price has been very stable over the years in both current and constant dollars, although a marked increase occurred in the mid-1970s and a downward trend was evident in the early 1980s.[74] In producer-dominated markets such as that for bauxite—in contrast to competitive

TABLE 5.12

Percentage of Export Earnings of Developing Countries from Bauxite

Countries	*1976–78*	*1980–82*
Guinea	69.5	36.7
Guyana	33.7	28.4
Jamaica	21.4	18.1
Surinam	18.3	9.0
Haiti	10.4	7.1
Sierra Leone	4.0	3.4
Dominican Republic	2.8	1.3

Source: World Bank, *Commodity Trade and Price Trends* (1980), table 11 and (1985), table 9. Only countries whose exports of bauxite accounted for at least 1 percent of their export earnings are listed.

markets such as that for copper—prices are set by intracompany, intercompany, or government-company bargaining. In these markets "firms generally attempt to set prices to reflect long run cost and demand conditions, and to dampen or eliminate price fluctuations due to purely cyclical changes in demand. As a result, producing firms often increase their stocks and cut back production during down swings in the business cycle."[75] This type of pricing system has not been opposed by governments in the industrialized world. Indeed, "there is plenty of evidence that [OECD] governments are not only aware of oligopolistic behavior in the market, but that these governments positively support these activities and cooperation between firms, which are seen as a guarantee of stable prices, adequate investment flows, and minimal disturbance to the economies of the industrialized countries."[76]

Negotiations. Efforts to implement intergovernmental management of the bauxite market have tended to involve the producers only. Movement toward the formation of a producers' association in the bauxite industry began in the late 1960s, but it took the OPEC oil price hike of 1973–74 to bring about the first firm signs of cooperation. Jamaica, once the most important bauxite-producing country, had long been the major proponent of greater consultation among producers. In the wake of OPEC's success, seven bauxite-producing countries (Jamaica, Guyana, Surinam, Guinea, Sierra Leone, Yugoslavia, and Australia) met in Conakry, Guinea in February 1974 and agreed to establish the International Bauxite Association (IBA). This group was later joined by the Dominican Republic, Haiti, Ghana, Indonesia, and India; by 1975 IBA members accounted for 72 percent of world bauxite production. The purposes of the IBA included promoting greater national control of the industry and boosting producers' earnings from bauxite exports.[77]

Believing that an "understanding of general objectives" had been achieved, Jamaica quickly followed up the 1974 accord by imposing a standard royalty and production levy on exports and by partially nationalizing its bauxite mines. These actions raised the taxes on bauxite and alumina exports by over 700 percent. However, since bauxite constitutes only 10 percent of the cost of aluminum ingots, there was no major impact on the price of aluminum.[78] Although the Jamaican move was neither part of an IBA program nor backed by a firm commitment from the other members to do the same, subsequent months did see most of the remaining key producers (but not Australia, the largest producer) institute similar taxation and nationalization schemes.[79]

The most important collective efforts of the IBA have been in the area of pricing policy. At its second meeting in November 1974, the need for an established floor price for bauxite was emphasized, although Australia opposed such a plan.[80] Discussion of minimum price-setting continued at subsequent IBA gatherings, until agreement on a recommended base price was finally reached in December 1978. This represented the first common policy formulated by the IBA membership and moved the association beyond its previous status as simply an information-exchange and market-analysis group. Nevertheless, IBA pricing decisions have not had much impact. They are not binding on producers and have generally reflected prevailing market prices.[81] At its November 1982 meeting IBA members tried but failed to reach an accord on a recommended price.[82] In the words of an IBA official, "the role of the producer countries in general and the IBA in particular in the areas of production, pricing and choice of export markets is extremely limited."[83]

Nonetheless, the mere presence of the producers' association does influence some activities in the bauxite market. This was never more apparent than during the December 1980 IBA meeting in Jamaica, when for the first time the proceedings were attended by representatives of four MNCs. While talk of price regulation was avoided because of the sensitivity of American firms to possible prosecution under U.S. antitrust law, it is clear that the aluminum giants were becoming increasingly attuned to the deliberations of the IBA.[84] The MNCs most certainly realized their stake in cooperating with the IBA in order to avoid further nationalization programs. Their presence at the Jamaica meeting indicates that they were not ignoring the IBA's explicit desire to form a "partnership" with the companies.[85]

Although IBA members control the bulk of world bauxite exports, and other market factors are also conducive to collective producer action, several obstacles confront the bauxite-producing LDCs. The wide distribution of reserves and new sources of bauxite is one important obstacle. Many producing states have viewed Brazil's refusal to join the IBA as undermining any possibility of market regulation, given that country's plans to develop its huge reserves. Brazilian attempts to entice MNCs with offers of low aluminum production costs and inexpensive hydroelectric power have worried the IBA membership.[86] Furthermore, there is no guarantee that Australia, anxious to increase its market share and also possessing a significant proportion of world reserves, will not leave the association at some later date. While in the IBA, Australia is unlikely to support the pursuit of higher prices at the expense of its OECD allies. In fact, Australia's main goal is to obtain larger shares of world alumina and aluminum production and to persuade the major industrialized nations to lower trade barriers imposed against these products. In exchange, it is willing to oppose pressure to turn the IBA into a producer cartel.[87]

A potent threat to future collaboration arises from competition among, and the different policies pursued by, IBA members. Since 1974 they have followed divergent strategies in seeking to improve their national well-being, and in so doing they have undermined the potential for collective action. In the wake of their nationalization and taxation programs, producers such as Jamaica, Guyana, and Surinam witnessed an exodus of MNC investment dollars to the more favorable business climates of Australia and Guinea in particular. These conflicts of interest surfaced when the 1981–82 international economic recession precipitated a decline in bauxite demand. In the late 1970s, Jamaica undertook separate negotiations with MNCs and indicated its willingness to cut taxes in order to secure greater investment and to recoup some of the market share it had lost in previous years.[88] Talks with the major consumer states have also been pursued, and some relief was gained for the troubled Jamaican economy when the United States agreed in 1981 to purchase a large amount of bauxite for its strategic mineral stockpile. This acquisition signified Washington's desire to prevent "a real collapse of the Jamaican economy in a region of the world where political stability and the spread of left-wing ideology is of much concern to Washington," but the very scope of this extra-IBA Jamaican activity provides further evidence of the producer group's limited power in the face of financial and ideological differences.[89] Alan Litvak and Christopher Maule have aptly summarized the IBA's situation: "The recent moves by Jamaica attest to the need to take unilateral action in the face of severe domestic conditions. The cohesiveness and discipline of the group appears strong where it does not matter (i.e., as an information exchange), and weak where it does (i.e., in setting prices)."[90] Thus the IBA's potential to influence the international market is less than promising.

Collaboration between bauxite producing and consuming governments has been even more limited. No producer-consumer discussions occurred before 1976, and bauxite was included in the IPC that year mainly because LDCs accounted for over two-thirds of world exports and half of world production. At the time, Jamaica was quite sympathetic to the general thrust of the IPC and was concerned about its own decreasing share of world exports. However, when the UNCTAD Secretariat began to discuss the possibility of convening producer-consumer negotiations in 1977, all the other exporters stated that they would have to be shown clearly that some benefits might result before they would agree to participate. Given the vertical integration of the industry, the relative stability of the market, and the producers' ability to secure higher returns from the companies, many exporters were hostile to the intergovernmental approaches favored by the IPC advocates.[91] As C. Fred Bergsten has remarked, the producers "clearly prefer to negotiate with the companies at this point, a further indication of the symbiotic relationship between the two groups."[92]

Following consultations between IBA members and the multinational corporations in 1980 and the emergence of a sluggish market, the producing states became more receptive to the convening of a producer-consumer meeting by UNCTAD. In December 1982 the first such meeting was held. Both the UNCTAD and the IBA secretariats submitted reports with comments on the market and suggestions for possible international action. Only the UNCTAD report addressed the issue of market regulation directly. It proposed a harmonization of producers' tax policies (a strategy that would not require consumer consent) and new bilateral supply and purchase commitments. On the former proposal the report noted that taxation "has been shown to be a feasible and effective form of 'pricing policy' for bauxite in countries whose bauxite industries are largely controlled by foreign interests. Such policies need to be harmonized for maximum effectiveness. . . . "[93] The implication was that producing states could maximize their earnings if they refrained from competing for corporate investment. The idea was not taken up in the meeting because it was well recognized that the producers were not about to foreswear their ability to compete with each other. As the IBA report commented: "Every national system for achieving direct returns from bauxite mining operations conducted in various jurisdictions is unique to that country. . . . Included among the revenue structures currently employed in the bauxite industry are: production levies, corporate taxation, dividends or contributions via equity ownership and royalties."[94] IBA members had discussed harmonization frequently with little success, and the IBA Secretariat was under no illusion as to a possible accord. Nor were the consuming states likely to be too receptive to such a proposal. The other UNCTAD Secretariat suggestion concerned long-term supply-purchase contracts at the intergovernmental or commercial level. In fact, the vertical integration of the industry and the various joint government-industry ventures implicitly involve such commitments.

The UNCTAD meeting did not touch on the actual regulation of prices and earnings despite the various suggestions in this area in the Secretariat report.[95] Rather, it dealt with issues such as information sharing, technology transfer to producing states, loans by international financial institutions, and cooperation among producers in the energy field. Underlying many of the producers' specific concerns was their desire to assume a larger role in alumina processing. The industrialized nations, however, wanted to focus solely on the primary product, bauxite ore. The Secretary General of the IBA later remarked: "We took to the consumers what we considered to be a reasonable case from the producers, and we went to Geneva to talk about bauxite and alumina ... the consumers wanted to talk about bauxite alone."[96]

On the basis of producer and producer-consumer discussions from the mid-1970s to the early 1980s, there is little prospect of achieving intergovernmental market management for bauxite, or an agreement that would transfer a greater share of alumina processing to LDC producers. The degree of vertical integration in the industry, the absence of significant price instability, serious competition among developing producers for market shares, and the existence of a major developed producer with huge reserves (Australia) all militate against a consensus. As in the past, individual producers will probably be able to obtain greater benefits through bargaining with the corporations, nationalization, and joint ventures.

Phosphate Rock

The Market. Almost 90 percent of mined phosphate rock is used in the production of fertilizers, with the remaining 10 percent used in a variety of industrial products.[97] Proven reserves total approximately 25 billion tons, of which Morocco possesses 65 percent; the United States, South Africa, and the Soviet Union have 12, 11 and 3 percent of the global total, respectively.[98] The developing countries' share of world exports in 1980 was 64 percent, the leading LDC exporters being Morocco (32 percent of the world total), Jordan (7), Togo (6), Nauru (4), the Christmas Islands (3), and Tunisia (3). The export share of the developed market economies was 28 percent—almost all of it coming from the United States (table 5.13; for import patterns, see table 5.14). Among developing-country producers, Morocco, Jordan, and Togo enjoy relatively low costs of production, while

TABLE 5.13

Phosphate Rock: Exports by Main Countries and Groupings

	% of World Exports			
Countries	*1961*	*1970*	*1975*	*1980*
Industrial	20.4	27.8	23.3	27.6
United States	20.4	27.8	23.1	27.5
Centrally planned	11.8	15.3	14.2	8.7
USSR	10.8	14.7	11.9	8.7
Developing	67.8	56.8	62.4	63.7
Jordan	1.9	1.7	1.5	6.9
Morocco	37.2	29.4	28.4	31.5
Tunisia	8.4	5.5	3.7	2.8
Togo	0.3	3.9	2.5	5.5
Nauru	7.1	5.4	3.3	4.0
Christmas Is.	3.8	2.5	3.0	3.1
	Exports by Weight (Thousand Tons)			
World	20,515	38,455	46,120	52,277

Source: Data provided by World Bank, Commodity Studies and Projections Division. Only the larger exporters in the three groups of states are included.

TABLE 5.14

Phosphate Rock: Imports by Main Countries and Groupings

	% of World Imports			
Countries	*1961*	*1970*	*1975*	*1980*
Industrial	78.9	71.8	65.9	66.3
Canada	4.7	5.8	6.8	7.3
EC-10	40.1	38.0	29.2	32.1
Japan	9.8	8.1	6.3	4.9
Oceania	11.5	8.6	7.1	7.4
Centrally planned	12.6	16.6	20.7	18.8
Developing	8.5	11.5	13.3	14.8
	Imports by Weight (Thousand Tons)			
World	21,078	38,595	43,715	52,272

Source: Data provided by World Bank, Commodity Studies and Projections Division. Only the larger importers in the group of industrial states are included.

Senegal, Tunisia, and most of the other small producers have higher costs.[99] For most of these producing states phosphate rock exports are important to their economies (table 5.15).

The price of phosphate rock in current U.S. dollars increased substantially from 1960 to 1981 but then declined sharply. In 1980 constant U.S. dollars, the price actually fell from $47 in 1961 to $40 in 1983. Except for a dramatic fourfold jump in 1974 and several other more minor increases, the price trend in both current and constant dollars has normally been slightly downward.[100] Prices have also been quite unstable, with an average annual change in constant dollars of 17.4 percent between 1955 and 1981 (table 1.4). Instability is caused by the considerable time lag that exists between a decision to increase production and the actual commencement of expanded production.[101] After 3 to 5 years demand may have abated, and increased production by a number of producers may have led to oversupply. Fluctuations in demand for fertilizers have contributed to a cycle of overinvestment and underinvestment in phosphate rock production, and this in turn has caused imbalances in supply and demand and thus variations in price.[102]

Sales of phosphate rock and processed phosphate products (e.g., phosphoric acid) are made between producer oganizations and foreign corporations. They are normally based on annual contracts, the terms of which are often secret. The two most important commercial bodies are Morocco's Office Cherifien des Phosphates (OCP), and the Phosphate Rock Export Association (Phosrock) in the United States. Most phosphate rock enters

TABLE 5.15
Percentage of Export Earnings of Developing Countries from Phosphate Rock

Countries	1976–78	1980–82
Togo	50.7	43.6
Morocco	37.9	30.5
Jordan	23.4	23.3
Nauru and Christmas Is.	18.3	73.9[a]
Senegal	12.6	12.6
Tunisia	5.8	2.3
Syria	2.0	1.6

[a]Also includes Cook Islands, Western Samoa, and Kiribati.
Source: World Bank, *Commodity Trade and Price Trends* (1980), table 11 and (1985), table 9. Only countries whose exports of phosphate rock accounted for at least 2 percent of their export earnings are listed.

developed countries duty-free. But phosphate products, which developing producers do not export in great volume, are subject to tariffs.[103]

Negotiations. UNCTAD consultations on phosphate rock began in January 1972, with the initial meeting directed at generating additional market information. Little discussion of market regulation took place, with the participants simply agreeing that the exchange of information should be improved and that the possibility of increased processing of phosphate rock by LDCs deserved study.[104] The next consultations were held in April–May 1974, at a time of escalating prices. The UNCTAD Secretariat suggested that stabilization schemes be formulated to take account of the interests of developing states that *import* phosphates. It argued that any ICA should have provisions to aid LDCs that depend heavily on phosphate rock and fertilizer imports.[105] The thrust of these proposals differed from the Secretariat's approach to other commodities in that they recognized the existence of a major difference in interests between importing and exporting LDCs and advocated assistance for Third World importers. Morocco and the United States—together responsible for over 50 percent of world phosphate rock exports—loudly disputed the need for market regulation. Morocco considered the fourfold price increase in 1974 to be a "normalization" of the price to offset inflation, while the United States did not want an ICA and felt that inadequate supply was the chief problem. Other industrialized countries were at least willing to discuss price regulation, and several developing exporters and importers were also favorably disposed—albeit for different reasons. Because of the plethora of conflicting views, the gathering simply agreed to call on the Secretariat to undertake further studies.[106]

A number of smaller producers and some LDCs concerned about the price of fertilizer successfully lobbied for the inclusion of phosphate rock in the IPC. (However, Morocco, the largest exporter, did not.) The first IPC meeting was convened in December 1977. The UNCTAD Secretariat presented several proposals, the major one calling for a price stabilization or indexing agreement that would take into consideration the interest of Third World importers.[107] The views expressed at the meeting were varied and on the whole quite vague; according to an UNCTAD report, "little substantive discussion took place."[108] Most developing-country producers were predisposed to an ICA designed to improve their economic returns and stabilize prices. Morocco, however, failed even to send a delegation, and its absence was correctly interpreted as opposition. The major developed producer, the United States, did not explicitly reject the Secretariat's proposals but argued against artificially raising prices and stated that it "did not wish to interfere with the operation of what was an efficient and competitive private industry."[109] Among the importers, some developing countries wanted protection against precipitous price increases, while the industrialized countries differed in their attitudes.[110]

It was agreed that the value of any subsequent meeting would depend on Morocco's presence, and the G77 thus pressured it to attend. When the second meeting convened in June 1978, Morocco was still not there, and the session soon adjourned. Moroccan officials "argued publicly that the UNCTAD Secretariat documentation was not available in French well enough in advance of the meetings and privately expressed the view that [Morocco] did not see that any additional measures which might result would increase its already-improved trade position."[111] According to participants in the meetings, Morocco feared that the smaller exporters would seek protection for their market shares. Given its huge reserves and relatively low costs of production, this would not be in Morocco's commercial interests.[112] Since 1978 UNCTAD members have regularly expressed doubts about the value of convening further meetings because of the dismal results of the early ones.[113]

Quite apart from the problems posed by the absence of an open market and the costs of storage, the divisions among producers and consumers—both developed and developing—are such that successful negotiations are most unlikely. The only supporters of an ICA seem to be a group of small exporters. The exporting "superpowers," Morocco and the United States, remain firmly opposed to international regulation.

Conclusion

Despite considerable optimism about the prospects for creating ICAs for "strong" mineral commodities when the IPC was launched in 1976, the negotiations surveyed above proved to be basically fruitless. In fact, aside from copper, the discussions on regulatory agreements seemed to be largely pro forma. The developed importing countries were unsympathetic to ICAs for commodities such as iron ore, manganese, and bauxite, for which prices had been quite stable; nor were they anxious to disrupt interfirm and intrafirm arrangements that had hitherto promoted stability and reliable supplies. They also vociferously opposed agreements that would boost price trends, thereby increasing the costs for importers, consumers, and in some cases governments. The projected costs of buffer stocks for these minerals would have been high for both importing and exporting states. The developed exporting countries were less than enthusiastic about accords that might impose direct costs on their governments and restrictions on their foreign sales. They feared that in situations of oversupply they would be pressured to accept bigger cutbacks than the developing producers. For these five minerals, such fears probably were justified, since developed states account for over half of world exports of iron ore and manganese and for about one-third of exports of copper, bauxite, and phosphate rock. With the exception of copper, there was also the problem of a lack of an open exchange, without which the operation of an ICA would be difficult.

Resistance to the creation of ICAs did not come solely from industrialized countries. Frequently the developing producer states were divided on the issue. Generally, the largest exporters with the biggest reserves and lowest costs of production were more skeptical toward market regulation. In the case of copper, this was true of Chile (and sometimes Peru); for phosphate rock it was certainly true of Morocco; and in the case of manganese ore and iron ore Brazil was opposed to any agreements. Negotiations on an ICA for bauxite never really moved forward, but Guinea (the largest exporter) and Brazil (with major reserves) were demonstrably unreceptive to schemes that might hinder their expansion plans. In short, the developing producers adopted policies based essentially on their own competitive positions and perceived commercial interests in particular markets.

AGRICULTURAL COMMODITIES

Tea

The Market. An evergreen tree that thrives in the wet regions of the tropics and subtropics, tea is grown in three major varieties—China, Assam, and Cambodia—and many hybrids. Classification is done according to the processing procedure used, while grading is based on leaf size. This results in three classes of tea—black tea (fermented after plucking), green tea (unfermented), and oolong (semifermented). Over 90 percent of exports consist of black tea (most green tea exports come from China); and all international negotiations regarding market regulation have also concerned black tea.[114] Teas can be stored, but they begin to deteriorate in quality after six months. Thus, teas stored in a buffer stock would need to be rotated in order to minimize losses in quality and value.[115]

The developing countries have accounted for over 90 percent of global exports since 1961. (The limited foreign tea sales of the developed countries are actually reexports.) Asia's share of global exports fell between 1961 and 1982 from 85 to 68 percent—with India dropping from 35 to 21 percent and Sri Lanka from 32 to 20 percent. China's recent export share (13 percent) includes approximately equal amounts of green and black tea. The export share of African producers has risen from 8 to 19 percent, with Kenya's increasing from 2 to 9 percent[116] (table 5.16). The one producing state for whom tea exports have provided a substantial percentage of export earnings is Sri Lanka, but exports have also been moderately important for several African countries (table 5.17). Turning to tea imports, a significant change has been the rise in the developing countries' share from 29 to 39 percent (table 5.18). Tea is one of the few commodities included in this book of which the developing countries are large importers.

Teas are sold mainly at auctions, the most important being in London, Calcutta, Colombo, and Mombassa. Prices vary considerably according to

TABLE 5.16

Tea: Exports by Main Countries and Groupings

	% of World Exports				
Countries	*1961*	*1970*	*1975*	*1980*	*1982*
Industrial	4.2	6.1	6.0	5.3	5.6
Centrally planned	1.3	1.6	2.7	3.0	1.8
Developing	94.4	92.3	91.2	91.8	92.6
Asia	85.0	73.5	71.5	69.4	68.1
India	34.5	26.6	26.4	23.8	21.3
Sri Lanka	32.3	27.7	25.6	19.5	20.0
China	8.2	8.1	9.8	13.6	12.8
Indonesia	5.4	4.9	5.6	7.8	7.1
Bangladesh	2.7	3.9	3.0	2.6	2.7
Africa	8.2	14.5	16.3	17.1	19.4
Kenya	2.0	5.6	6.6	8.0	8.8
Malawi	1.9	2.4	3.0	3.3	4.1
	Exports by Weight (Thousand Tons)				
World	594	751	828	947	905

Source: Food and Agriculture Organization, *Trade Yearbook* (various years). Only the larger exporters in the groups of developing states are included.

TABLE 5.17
Percentage of Export Earnings of Developing Countries from Tea

Countries	1976–78	1980–82
Sri Lanka	49.1	32.6
Malawi	20.6	14.0
Kenya	14.6	13.1
Rwanda	10.2	11.9
India	7.2	6.0
Bangladesh	6.4	5.1
Mozambique	6.3	13.8
Tanzania	3.9	4.1
Uganda	3.3	0.2
Burundi	2.6	2.9
Mauritius	2.2	1.5

Source: World Bank, *Commodity Trade and Price Trends* (1980), table 11 and (1985), table 9. Only countries whose exports of tea accounted for at least 2 percent of their export earnings are listed.

TABLE 5.18
Tea: Imports by Main Countries and Groupings

	% of World Imports				
Countries	1961	1970	1975	1980	1982
Industrial	67.2	60.2	54.0	48.7	49.6
United States	8.5	8.4	9.0	9.2	9.1
EC-10	48.4	41.5	34.7	31.0	30.5
United Kingdom	42.6	34.2	27.1	23.0	22.9
Centrally planned	3.9	6.1	11.6	11.7	11.3
Developing	28.9	33.7	34.5	39.5	39.1
Asia	12.3	15.6	18.0	23.4	24.2
Pakistan	2.7	4.0	6.3	6.7	7.6
Africa	14.0	15.5	14.2	13.5	14.9
Egypt	3.9	4.0	3.0	2.6	4.4
	Imports by Weight (Thousand Tons)				
World	591	742	804	917	909

Source: Food and Agriculture Organization, *Trade Yearbook* (various years). Only the larger importers in the three groups of states are included.

class and quality. On average, current prices declined gradually from the mid-1950s through 1973. The 1974–77 period witnessed sharp increases, but prices fell again from 1978 to 1981. In 1982 they began to rise, jumping rapidly in 1983 and 1984. However, in *real terms* prices fell by over 60 percent between 1955 and 1973, and in 1983 they were only about 10 percent higher than in 1973.[117] Short-term price instability has been caused by the commodity boom of 1973–74, speculation, inflation, climatic conditions, competition for market shares, and the growth of domestic consumption in producing states. In the future, price changes will be influenced particularly by India's domestic consumption and export policy, the rise of "new" producers (e.g., Brazil), and the impact of high tea prices on demand in low-income countries.[118]

Negotiations. The first attempt at market regulation in the post-war era occurred in the mid-1950s and involved only producers. The export-quota scheme soon collapsed because of disagreements over market shares and a substantial increase in prices in 1953–54.[119] In the mid-1960s a downward price trend brought on by increased supplies prompted acute concern among South Asian producers. India and Sri Lanka called for international talks on the tea market, and producer-consumer discussions took place in the FAO in 1965. Attention at that session and at another one in 1967 chiefly focused on the exchange of market information, but the continued price decline soon convinced a number of producers to step up pressure for negotiations on market regulation. In 1969 their effort bore fruit with the creation of the FAO Consultative Committee on Tea (retitled the Intergovernmental Group in 1972), an Ad Hoc Working Party on International Arrangements for the Stabilization of Tea Prices, and a Sub-Group of Exporters to facilitate a consensus on a plan of action. India and Sri Lanka were the principal proponents of these decisions, since their exports were stagnating in volume and declining in price. African exports, by contrast, had been growing and were not affected as seriously by the depressed prices.[120]

In July 1969 fourteen exporters met in Mauritius and reached a consensus on an informal, non-binding "gentlemen's agreement" involving an indicative price range and export quotas. Annual quotas were to be set for three consecutive years to aid in planning, and were to be determined on a yearly basis with the assistance of a group of conciliators charged with handling the inevitable disputes. A buffer-stock program was rejected because prices had not been unstable, because a stocking system might depress prices, and because significant technical obstacles existed. Although the informal arrangement initially gained the support of importers on the FAO Consultative Committee in December 1969, it soon broke down because of recurring disputes over quota allocations.[121] Officials from the FAO and UNCTAD visited the producing states to try to obtain agreement on quotas, but Kenya—and particularly the Kenya Tea Board, which represents smallholders—refused to accept any restrictions on output or expansion.[122] Assessing this situation, one UNCTAD report commented: "There is little disagreement among the producing countries on the need to regulate world supplies, but there are wide differences on how to share the export market."[123] Further discussion of market control took place in 1974 within the FAO, but little was accomplished, for the same reasons that had undermined agreement before and also because of the sharp increases in tea prices then being registered.[124]

The first years of the UNCTAD-sponsored IPC negotiations (1976–77) were exceptionally buoyant ones for the tea market, with current prices almost doubling from their 1975 level. A session of the FAO Intergovernmental Group in 1977 and the first IPC meeting in January 1978 saw the producers display no real sense of urgency about intergovernmental action. The UNCTAD Secretariat did present a proposal for an ICA with a buffer stock and export quotas, but during the discussions several African producers (notably Kenya) were hostile toward quotas. The problems of relying on a buffer stock—such as the storage costs, the need to rotate stocks and to include different types of teas, the question of quality standards, and the setting of a single indicator price—were also raised. But it was generally recognized, as explicitly stated in the UNCTAD report, that the chief impediment was basic disagreement among producers on the desirability of supply management.[125]

Tea prices dropped precipitously in 1978 and then fell more slowly between 1979 and 1982. From late 1979 to mid-1982 a number of producer-consumer meetings took place in UNCTAD, and on several occasions the producers also met on their own. The producers and many developed-country importers were now supportive of an ICA to be based mainly on export quotas but which might also include a buffer stock. The producers even managed to agree on a global quota, but they could not decide how to allocate national shares. At the heart of this impasse was the traditional dispute between India and Sri Lanka, on the one hand, and Kenya, on the other. With its rapidly expanding production, Kenya was not satisfied with the quota proposals advanced by the major South Asian exporters. Had

Kenya agreed to an export quota, it might have proved possible to obtain the agreement of other African producers as well as of those in other regions. China, which exports limited volumes of black tea, was also prepared to back an ICA. The United States regularly voiced opposition to proposals for an ICA for tea, and countries such as Canada and West Germany also had reservations. However, the positive attitude of the largest importer, Britain, likely would have influenced many developed countries—especially those in the EC—to accept an ICA if the producers had been able to reach agreement. In fact, a more serious obstacle might well have come from the developing-country *importers,* who now account for about 40 percent of world imports, although the absence of clear statements from them makes a firm judgement on this issue difficult.[126]

Over 1983 and 1984 the UNCTAD Intergovernmental Group of Experts on Tea met to review the various problems relating to an ICA. Informal meetings of producers, consumers, and officials of international organizations also took place.[127] The likelihood of progress appeared remote, in large part because tea prices, which began to move upward in 1982, skyrocketed in 1983 and 1984. This development was mainly traceable to a substantial increase in India's domestic consumption, which led it to slash its projected exports. Indeed, in December 1983 the Indian government was compelled to ban exports of certain teas. In addition, Sri Lankan production was stagnating because of poor weather and managerial problems, while African production was not growing fast enough to make up for the projected decline in India's sales. In these circumstances, most exporters were no longer anxious to promote price stabilization, and many importers put aside their previous concern about the plight of tea producers.[128]

The UNCTAD tea negotiations came closer to success than those on most of the other commodities in this chapter. But there is only a slim chance that producer-consumer talks will succeed in the near future. Even if Kenya attains what it regards as a satisfactory market share, other producer "revisionists" may rise to take its place. The willingness of many developed importers to support an ICA is likely to fade as long as the market remains robust. Although the U.S. argument that tea does not need an ICA because its market is relatively stable has been weakened by the events of the last decade, Washington can always find other reasons to oppose market intervention and resource transfers to countries that are not viewed as central to its strategic concerns. And as noted above, there is also the issue of developing-country importers, some of which may be reluctant to accept an ICA that is seen to transfer resources to tea producers.

Jute

The Market. Jute and allied fibers (e.g., kenaf) are used primarily as textile raw materials in the manufacture of cloth, sacks, carpet-backing, and household and industrial wrapping material and cordage. Kenaf, a coarser fiber than jute, is used to make sacks and is grown mainly in Thailand. Farmers often switch back and forth between jute and kenaf and other crops (rice in Bangladesh and casava and maize in Thailand), depending on the prices of the respective commodities. For almost all uses there are synthetic substitutes; since the 1960s these have undermined demand for jute and kenaf, particularly in the industrialized countries.[129]

The volume of jute fiber exports climbed in the 1960s but then dropped markedly from the late 1960s to 1982 because of the substitution of synthetics and increased processing in the fiber-producing countries, especially Bangladesh. Trade in jute manufactured products rose to over 70 percent of total trade in jute fiber and products by the early 1980s, versus about 50 percent in the mid-1960s.[130] The two largest jute producers, India and China, export very little *raw fiber*. India, however, does export a substantial quantity of jute *manufactures*. As for raw fiber exports, Bangladesh occupies a "quasi-monopoly position,"[131] with about two-thirds of the market in recent years. Other lesser exporters include Nepal, Burma, India, and Thailand (table 5.19). Next to Bangladesh, raw fiber exports are most important to Nepal (table 5.20). The pattern of jute fiber imports has altered considerably in recent decades. The developing countries accounted for less than 30 percent of global imports in the 1960s, but since 1980 this has risen to about 50 percent (table 5.21).

Jute fiber prices have been quite unstable, but not to the same extent as those for a number of other tropical agricultural commodities. In constant U.S. dollars, jute prices in the early 1980s were less than half of their level during most of the 1960s.[132] Fluctuations in prices have been caused by changes in supply due to weather; the varying prices of other crops (notably rice); misestimations of demand; changes in demand traceable to the economic cycles in importing countries; the fluctuating cost of synthetics; and the price-support and stocking programs used in producing countries, especially Bangladesh. The depressed market in the early 1980s was mostly attributable to Bangladesh's decision to terminate its guaranteed price for growers and its minimum export price because of the high cost of holding stocks.[133]

TABLE 5.19

Jute and Allied Fibers: Exports by Main Countries and Groupings

Countries	% of World Exports					
	1960	1965	1970	1975	1980	1982
Developed (including centrally planned)	2.6	6.1	4.1	4.3	3.2	3.0
Developing	97.4	93.9	95.9	95.7	96.8	97.0
Bangladesh	95.3	87.3	64.5	49.6	65.0	68.3
Burma	0.1	0.2	0.3	7.8	8.4	0.8
China	0.3	0.1	—	—	6.8	8.1
India	0.4	3.0	2.7	8.3	3.4	7.9
Nepal	0.1	1.2	—	4.4	4.9	8.7
Thailand[a]	0.1	—	25.9	24.9	5.7	1.6
	Exports by Weight (Thousand Tons)					
World	795	868	991	563	526	508

[a]The FAO tables excluded Thai kenaf in the 1960s. This explains the large jump for Thailand in 1970.

Source: Food and Agriculture Organization, Trade Yearbook (various years). Only the larger exporters in the group of developing states are included.

TABLE 5.20
Percentage of Export Earnings of Developing Countries from Jute Fiber

Countries	1976–78	1980–82
Bangladesh	22.9	16.0
Nepal	8.0	10.3
Burma	0.9	1.5

Source: World Bank, *Commodity Trade and Price Trends* (1980), table 11 and (1985), table 9.

Negotiations. The early 1960s witnessed a drastic decline in jute prices that prompted producers to press the FAO's Committee on Commodity Problems to create a group to address their concerns. In 1963 the Study Group on Jute, Kenaf, and Allied Fibers (retitled the Intergovernmental Group in 1972) was formed. In the following year it convened a Working Party on Stabilization that examined a variety of schemes to promote price stability. In 1965 the Study Group adopted an informal, nonbinding agreement with an indicative price range for jute. The agreement has been renegotiated regularly since then except for the 1966–67 and 1974–75 seasons, when shortages led producers to demand higher price ranges than the developed consuming states were prepared to accept. The

TABLE 5.21
Jute and Allied Fibers: Imports by Main Countries and Groupings

Countries	% of World Imports					
	1960	1965	1970	1975	1980	1982
Industrial	68.2	64.3	72.3	41.5	34.5	27.0
North America	6.3	4.3	3.9	4.0	1.8	3.4
Western Europe	55.0	50.0	54.2	32.8	23.3	18.3
Japan	6.1	9.0	12.4	1.9	3.7	1.7
Centrally planned	7.3	7.9	11.6	14.5	16.4	21.9
Developing	24.2	27.9	16.1	43.8	49.1	51.1
Asia	19.8	22.3	8.0	20.2	29.2	34.6
Africa	3.4	4.0	6.6	16.6	13.6	15.2
Latin America	1.1	1.2	1.6	7.0	6.4	1.3
	Imports by Weight (Thousand Tons)					
World	891	1041	837	573	566	526

Source: Food and Agriculture Organization, *Trade Yearbook* (various years). Only the larger importers in the three groups of states are included.

United States has not been involved in these agreements (or other "informal" FAO accords) because the Department of Justice has judged that participation in talks on pricing agreements that are *not* subject to Senate ratification would be contrary to American antitrust legislation.[134] Until the post-1978 period, during which time prices have remained below the floor, export prices tended to be within the range. This was basically due to Bangladesh's minimum export price and stocking policy; it had little to do with the FAO arrangement. As an FAO study analyzing the informal arrangement noted: "The main reason for this success was the close integration between established ranges and the national export and buffer stock policies implemented by the major supplying country."[135]

As noted by one Western official who participated in many of the FAO talks, the FAO scheme may have helped to convince the Bangladesh government to establish prices that respected both market trends and the need to maintain jute's competitiveness vis-à-vis synthetics.[136] But this view is difficult to substantiate, and overall it is not possible to ascribe much importance to the FAO jute arrangement. At one point in the early 1970s the FAO Intergovernmental Group did consider the creation of a buffer stock, but the producers could not agree on its characteristics, while the consuming countries expressed little interest in financing such a scheme given the increasing role of synthetics in the market.[137]

When the list of core commodities for UNCTAD'S IPC was drawn up in the mid-1970s, jute was a natural candidate for inclusion because the fiber is storable, it has relatively uniform grades, and is produced solely by developing countries. In fact, jute was the subject of the very first IPC meeting on an individual commodity in October 1976. In the early sessions, the producing states and the G77 assumed an aggressive negotiation posture, calling for an internationally financed buffer stock for raw jute *and* jute products; the harmonization of the production of synthetics with that of jute; limitations on research into synthetics; a reduction in shipping costs; and more research into productivity and marketing.[138] Producers were deeply concerned about the encroachment of synthetic polypropylene in the jute market, and several developing-country delegations harshly attacked the prospect of further work on synthetics by the developed countries. The Bangladesh representative charged that "There could only be one aim for such a massive expansion programme [of synthetics], namely, the quick displacement of jute from whatever ground it still held."[139]

From the beginning of negotiations through three meetings in 1977 and a single one in 1978, most of the developed consuming states resisted the producers' demands, although the EC, perhaps influenced by Britain's desire to assist Bangladesh, was more forthcoming than the United States. Consuming countries were adamantly opposed to the inclusion of manufactured jute products in any stabilization plan; to restrictions on research on synthetics; and to the harmonization of synthetics production with that of jute (i.e., controls on the manufacture of synthetics). Group B spokesmen argued that a buffer stock was unlikely to work because of the ability of farmers to switch between jute and rice production and because of the competition from synthetics. The U.S. delegate stressed that it made little sense to create an ICA to regulate just one country's exports; it could do that perfectly well on its own. The EC, led by Britain, proposed that the committee consider strengthening the FAO informal arrangement and international financing (up to $80 million) for national stocks, which would, of course, flow largely to Bangladesh. This, however, was viewed as inadequate or undesirable by most of the participants, and particularly by India, which wanted processed jute products included in any international arrangement.[140] (Originally Bangladesh had consented to the inclusion of jute products in order to ensure India's support.)

Serious negotiations on market regulation essentially ended in 1978. Most states had never been very optimistic about the prospects for an accord.[141] After 1978 the UNCTAD jute meetings focused almost exclusively on the creation of an International Jute Organization (IJO) that would be concerned solely with information sharing, research, and technical assistance. The difficult negotiations to create the IJO were successfully concluded in October 1982, and its treaty entered into force provisionally in January 1984.[142]

Since 1980 meetings have also occurred among the producers under the auspices of the UN Economic and Social Commission on Asia and the Pacific (ESCAP) in a body known as the Government Consultation Among Jute Producing Countries. At first some discussions took place on a possible pricing strategy for jute products and on the establishment of a more formal producers' organization. These talks came to naught because of political tensions and economic competition between Bangladesh and India, and reservations regarding the likelihood of progress on the part of the smaller producers. Bangladesh, in particular, was uninterested because its jute mills were generally more efficient than those of India and the two countries were then "engaged in cut-throat competition to gain entry into what [was] essentially a buyer's market."[143] Given this impasse, the ESCAP has instead focused on sharing and generating information on such issues as grading, production, and manufacturing techniques and marketing.[144]

Despite numerous producer-consumer meetings over the past two decades, the likelihood of a formal ICA for jute was never very great. Developed importing countries have consistently ruled out price regulation for manufactured jute products. With respect to the raw fiber market, the dominance of a single exporter, the tolerable degree of price instability, and the decreasing size of the global market owing to synthetics have all led the developed states to view regulation as inappropriate. It is also probable that developing *importing* states would have been less than enthusiastic about any proposed increase in their import costs—despite the economic plight of Bangladesh—although they never explicitly opposed producer proposals. As for the producers, it is clear that an agreement on raw fibers was a priority only for Bangladesh and, perhaps, Nepal. In addition, all the producers realize that the prices for synthetic subsitutes act as a kind of price regulator for natural fibers and products. No ICA can alter this reality unless it requires the industrialized states to restrict the development of synthetics. This is most improbable, regardless of producers' demands in international forums.[145]

Hard Fibers: Sisal and Henequen

The Market. There are four hard fibers that have often been discussed together in international forums: sisal, henequen, abaca, and coir. Sisal and henequen are quite similar and are mainly employed in the manufacture of harvest baler twine. Abaca, or manila hemp, is used to manufacture heavy marine ropes and specialty papers; while coir, a by-product of coconut husks, is used primarily in mattress and seat fillings. Abaca and coir are not discussed here because their prospects for market regulation were always very poor. Abaca is produced largely by a single country, the Philippines, and thus global supply management has depended basically on the policies adopted by that country. The FAO Intergovernmental Group on Hard Fibers did adopt a nonbinding price range for abaca from 1968 to 1971 and from 1978 to the present. However, this scheme has never been very important to the abaca market; Philippine policies and the price of synthetic substitutes are the real determinants of supply and demand.[146] Coir is mainly produced by India and Sri Lanka, whose governments have sought to ensure remunerative prices by maintaining floor prices and by discouraging overproduction. Neither country has supported intergovernmental intervention in the coir market.[147]

Raw fiber exports of sisal and henequen (the latter comes solely from Mexico) grew steadily in the 1950s and early 1960s. But the increasing popularity of synthetic substitutes, coupled with the decreasing use of twines in harvesting, caused exports to drop by about 75 percent between the mid-1960s and early 1980s. The growth of twine exports from producing countries has also helped to reduce their fiber exports.[148] Raw fiber exports by individual countries can fluctuate greatly from year to year because of weather and changes in production programs and government price-support and stocking policies. Certain export trends are clear, however. From 1960 to the early 1980s Tanzania's share of global exports fell from 35 percent to about 20 percent as a result of the deterioration in its estates and international competition. Over the same period Brazil's share jumped from 26 percent to 40 percent (with some significant variations in the 1980s). Most of the other exporters are African, the biggest one being Kenya, which climbed from 10 to more than 20 percent (table 5.22). Raw fiber exports do not account for a large percentage of the export earnings of any of the producing states (table 5.23). The dominant exporter of harvest baler twine in the early 1980s was Brazil, with over a half of the global market, followed by Mexico (25 percent) and Tanzania (12 percent).[149] The major importers of raw fiber have been the Western European states; the United States is the largest importer of harvest twine (table 5.24).[150]

The sisal market has been subject to many price changes since the 1960s. Political uncertainties in East Africa and fears of shortages saw prices rise markedly in the early 1960s. This stimulated more plantings and accelerated the development of synthetic substitutes. The combination of growing synthetics competition and large harvests caused a sharp decline in prices between 1964 and 1970. The low prices prevailed until 1971, at which time two successive years of drought in East Africa reduced production to well below world requirements and led to an extraordinary ninefold increase in prices from 1971 to 1974. This price hike was short-lived, however, as increased competition from synthetics and falling demand for hard fibers forced prices down by almost one-half in 1975. Between 1976 and 1978 hard fiber prices leveled off, only to rise dramatically once more in 1979 thanks to increased demand. From 1981 to 1984 hard fiber prices fell gradually because of a slackening in demand—partly due to declining prices for synthetic twines—and overproduction.[151] The real price of sisal fiber fell by about two-thirds between 1963 and 1971; rose slightly above its

TABLE 5.22

Sisal and Henequen Fiber: Exports by Main Countries and Groupings

				% of World Exports				
Countries	*1960*	*1965*	*1970*	*1977*	*1980*	*1982*	*1983*
Developed (including centrally planned)	7.0	2.7	1.7	0.7	0.9	1.8	—
Developing	93.0	97.3	98.3	98.0	99.1	98.2	100.0
Latin America	27.1	34.2	35.3	38.1	46.7	26.2	54.5
Brazil	18.4	24.2	25.3	36.5	43.7	23.2	53.9
Haiti	3.3	2.3	2.9	0.7	1.3	1.2	0.6
Mexico	5.2	7.6	6.3	1.0	1.7	1.8	—
Africa	63.0	62.0	63.2	59.9	51.5	72.9	45.5
Angola	10.0	8.1	11.2	6.0	3.5	4.9	1.7
Kenya	9.9	9.4	7.6	10.0	17.5	25.0	23.0
Madagascar	1.9	4.7	3.6	2.7	5.7	9.1	6.7
Mozambique	4.8	5.0	3.9	7.0	3.9	6.1	1.7
Tanzania	35.9	34.6	36.8	30.4	20.5	26.2	12.9
				Exports by Weight (Thousand Tons)				
Total	586	619	589	299	229	164	178

Source: Food and Agriculture Organization, *Trade Yearbook* (various years). Only the larger exporters in the group of developing states are included.

TABLE 5.23
Percentage of Export Earnings of Developing Countries from Sisal Fiber

Countries	1976–67	1980–82
Tanzania	5.4	5.7
Mozambique	2.8	2.9
Madagascar	1.6	2.0
Kenya	—	1.8

Source: World Bank, *Commodity Trade and Price Trends* (1980), table 11 and (1985), table 9. Only countries whose exports of sisal accounted for at least 1 percent of their export earnings are listed.

1963 level between 1972 and 1974; and then declined to 1971 levels by the early 1980s (with one marked jump in 1979).[152]

Negotiations. Attempts to regulate hard fiber prices began in the FAO Study Group on Hard Fibers in 1967 (retitled the Intergovernmental Group in 1972). In light of the persistent oversupply problem and the downward price trend, an informal, nonbinding agreement was concluded in September 1967 under the auspices of the FAO group. Like other commodity accords formulated within the FAO, this was essentially a producers' arrangement, with consumers participating only in an advisory capacity. Designed to deal with an immediate market crisis, the agreement had a limited but difficult goal, namely, to raise and maintain prices above

TABLE 5.24
Sisal and Henequen Fiber: Imports by Main Groupings

	% of World Imports					
Countries	1960	1965	1970	1976	1980	1982
Industrial	86.3	91.9	85.6	73.7	64.7	61.6
North America	21.8	21.5	13.5	7.0	3.6	1.2
Western Europe	59.4	63.1	63.5	60.0	54.5	54.1
Centrally planned	4.4	4.3	7.4	12.3	23.7	23.8
Developing	9.3	3.8	7.0	14.0	11.6	14.5
	Imports by Weight (Thousand Tons)					
Total	591	604	540	285	224	172

Source: Food and Agriculture Organization, *Trade Yearbook* (various years). Only the major importing regions in the group of industrial states are included.

the very depressed 1967 level but *below* the level at which the substitution of synthetics would be encouraged. Its chief components were global and national quotas for sisal and henequen fiber and manufactures, and minimum and target prices for sisal fiber. The informal agreement succeeded in moderately raising market prices during 1968, and its export quotas were at first respected. In 1969, however, its effectiveness was eroded when exporters decided to reduce the global export quota by 9.2 percent in order to raise prices. Before the end of the year, it was apparent that the new quota arrangements had not been respected. Despite quota underfulfillments by Mexico and Kenya, total exports in 1969 exceeded the set global quota by some 2 percent. Competition for market shares eventually led to the collapse of the agreement in January 1970. Brazil was the chief transgressor of the quota arrangement, exceeding its allotment by 20 percent, and it "generally ignored the spirit of the informal agreement."[153] But Brazil was not the only party contributing to the breakdown of the agreement. Several other countries also exported in excess of their quotas and/or sold below the minimum price.[154]

In May 1971 the informal agreement was reactivated. A new, broader global export quota was established in order to accomodate Brazil, with the entire amount of the increase going to that country; all the other individual quotas were left unchanged.[155] But the supply shortages and high prices that prevailed from 1972 to 1975 quickly rendered the informal quota inoperative, and it was not reactivated until 1976. Since then, the agreement has continued to operate under the auspices of the FAO Intergovernmental Group, although the quotas were eliminated in 1978 because of disagreements among producers, leaving solely the indicative price range for sisal fiber. From 1976 to 1983 market prices were sometimes within the range (which was unchanged thoughout the period 1980–83), but the informal arrangement had virtually no effect on them. The dominant characteristic of the market since 1981 has been excessive production, which has tended to keep prices below the floor.[156]

Beginning in 1976 the FAO Intergovernmental Group on Hard Fibers regularly discussed whether the informal arrangement should be extended to cover a price range for harvest twine. A major impediment to an agreement on this issue was the producers' insistence that an accord include not just twines made from sisal and henequen but also those made from polypropylene. The developed states flatly refused to accept this demand, which was then dropped by some of the producers in the late 1970s and early 1980s. The key remaining issue was the possible adoption of supply-management measures that would offer some hope of eliminating over-production and of buoying prices. All the EC countries except West Germany were willing to support a price range if supply-management measures were adopted, but the opposition of a few producers (especially Brazil) precluded agreement. With competitive costs of production, lower transportation costs, and a commitment to support its sisal farmers and industry through a price support and stocking program, Brazil was simply not prepared to contemplate any restrictions—even in the form of a non-binding FAO arrangement.[157]

Parallel to the FAO discussions in the late 1970s and early 1980s meetings on sisal and henequen were held in UNCTAD under its IPC. These revealed that most producers supported a formal ICA that would include a buffer stock and export quotas for raw fiber and for manufactured products (basically harvest twine) and that would also "harmonize" the prices of the natural and synthetic products. During the course of the discussions two major axes of conflict became apparent. The first pitted the majority of producers (mainly African) against the developed consuming states. The latter believed that the priority for the producers should be to improve the efficiency of their production and to maintain fiber prices competitive with those of polypropylene. They argued that a price-regulating accord was inappropriate for a commodity whose prices were so intimately related to those of synthetics. The developed states also noted that a buffer-stock scheme would face serious problems in a situation of decreasing demand. And they were strongly opposed to any attempts to control the prices of synthetic manufactured products or to discourage their development and use.

The second axis of conflict saw Tanzania arrayed against Brazil (which was backed by Mexico). With the deterioration of its sisal estates and rising production costs vis-à-vis its competitors, Tanzania sought a price-stabilization agreement with buffer stocks and export quotas both to prevent price declines and to protect its dwindling share of the market. Brazil, by then the largest exporter of raw fiber and twine, did not want to curtail production and employment in its northeast region, was not interested in having its domestic subsidy programs scrutinized, and feared greater market incursions by synthetics if fiber prices were raised. Nor did Brazil want to allocate production shares among its twine manufacturers, which probably would have been necessary had country export quotas been adopted. The Tanzanian-Brazilian conflict was exacerbated by the fact that under the Lomé Convention, Tanzania escaped the EC's 43 percent tariff on twine—a preference that Brazil wished to see abolished.[158]

At both the 1977 and 1978 UNCTAD meetings on hard fibers, participants debated whether to ask the Secretariat to undertake a study on buffer-stock and export-quota arrangements. The consuming countries and Brazil joined together to raise enough barriers to block a consensus on the terms of reference for such a study. A formal request to the Secretariat to prepare a study was finally made at a 1980 meeting, but Brazil and the developed countries "stated that acceptance of such a study implied no commitment by any country to its conclusions."[159] Produced in 1981, the study identified a number of serious impediments to the formation of an ICA with a buffer stock, although it did not completely eschew the idea. The obstacles mentioned included the close interrelationship between the prices of sisal and henequen and those of polypropylene (and hence oil); the unbalanced situation of falling demand and increasing supplies; and the marked variations in production costs.[160] This report ended any serious diplomatic lobbying for the proposal. It was widely understood that the nature of the market, the fierce competition among producers, and the grave reservations of the consuming states effectively precluded intergovernmental regulation of the hard fibers market.

Cotton

The Market. Cotton is an extremely heterogeneous commodity that is grown in more than 75 tropical and temperate countries. Over 50 of these states are exporters. It is a short-cycle crop, with farmers often switching back and forth between cotton and other crops, depending on prevailing prices. Several substitutes for cotton exist. Rayon, for example, is a natural fiber used as a cotton replacement. Synthetics, especially polyester blended with cotton, have slowed the growth of cotton consumption over the past two decades because their cost has fallen relative to that of cotton during this time.[161]

Since the mid-1960s the developing countries' share of world exports has declined from more than 60 to less than 50 percent. The LDC share is evenly divided among Asian, African, and Latin American countries. The reduced LDC export share is a product of both greater sales by the major developed producers and increased textile manufacturing in some of the developing producing states. The United States and the USSR have boosted their joint export share to close to 50 percent—with the United States exporting almost twice as much as the USSR (table 5.25). (The huge U.S. share in 1979/80 is an anomaly, since China bought large volumes in that year—a practice later discontinued as a result of major increases in Chinese

TABLE 5.25

Cotton: Exports by Main Countries and Groupings

Countries	% of World Exports				
	1964/65	*1969/70*	*1974/75*	*1978/79*	*1979/80*
Industrial	25.9	18.3	23.8	32.9	41.7
United States	24.8	16.2	22.9	31.7	40.2
Centrally planned	12.4	14.1	22.7	19.2	16.5
USSR	12.4	13.5	21.4	18.6	16.5
Developing	61.7	68.2	54.7	48.5	41.8
Asia and Oceania	16.1	17.0	18.1	14.5	14.1
Pakistan	2.9	2.2	6.2	1.3	5.3
Syria	4.2	3.4	2.2	2.8	2.0
Turkey	4.6	6.7	3.4	4.9	2.7
Africa	19.6	25.5	16.6	15.2	13.9
Egypt	9.2	8.3	5.1	3.4	3.6
Sudan	2.8	6.1	2.1	4.2	3.5
Latin America	26.1	25.7	20.1	18.7	13.8
Argentina	.0	.3	.2	1.6	2.4
Guatemala	1.8	1.2	2.7	3.6	2.8
Mexico	9.5	6.9	5.5	5.0	4.0
Nicaragua	3.4	1.6	3.5	2.7	.4
Paraguay	.3	.3	.5	2.0	1.3
	Exports by Weight (Thousand Bales)				
World	16,691	17,797	17,220	19,593	23,063

Source: Cotton: World Statistics (Washington, D.C.: International Cotton Advisory Committee, October 1981),
pp. 30–33. Only countries which accounted for at least 2 percent of world exports in 1978/79 or 1979/80 are
included in the table. An additional 26 developing countries accounted for between 0.1 and 1.9 percent of
world exports.

production.) Of the many producing states, the African countries are the
ones that rely most heavily on cotton sales for export earnings (table 5.26).
The trend of cotton imports has gone in a direction opposite to that of exports. The developing countries have increased their share of global imports since the mid-1960s from slightly more than 20 percent to close to 50
percent—largely owing to the growth of textile manufacturing in Asia (especially South Korea, Hong Kong, Taiwan, Indonesia, and Thailand)
(table 5.27).[162]

The price of cotton, a large percentage of which is traded on the New
York Cotton Exchange,[163] fell gradually from the late 1950s through 1970.
The relative stability of the market was mainly a product of a U.S. policy to

TABLE 5.26

Percentage of Export Earnings of Developing Countries from Cotton

Countries	1976–78	1980–82
Chad	76.4	49.1
Sudan	51.4	28.5
Mali	41.8	41.2
Burkina	38.4	42.5
Yemen Arab Republic	31.4	2.2
Paraguay	30.0	38.2
Egypt	24.0	13.7
Nicaragua	23.3	17.3
Afghanistan	20.0	3.4
Benin	18.2	19.3
Syria	17.8	6.8
Guatemala	12.5	9.6
Tanzania	12.2	12.6
Mozambique	9.9	9.7
Central African Republic	8.8	6.1
El Salvador	8.5	8.0
Pakistan	7.1	14.5
Mexico	5.4	1.4
Peru	3.9	1.9
Uganda	3.7	0.8
Colombia	3.5	2.0
Senegal	3.2	1.6
Burundi	3.1	2.2
Zimbabwe	3.0	6.0
Cameroon	2.5	3.4
Togo	1.7	4.9
Guinea-Bissau	—	7.6

Source: World Bank, *Commodity Trade and Price Trends* (1980), table 11 and (1985), table 9. Only countries whose exports of cotton accounted for at least 3 percent of their export earnings are listed.

hold large cotton reserves and to offer a generous support price to its farmers. Foreign exporters knew that they could sell at close to the American support price. During these years, "the U.S. alone held most of the world's real surplus. In effect, through its price programme, the United States operated a world buffer stock."[164] In 1965 the United States abandoned its stocking policy because of the high costs. It reduced its price-support program, and then began to sell off most of its stocks.[165] The price of cotton, which varies according to the grade and quality, began to rise in the early 1970s, and then increased significantly in 1973, 1976, 1980, and 1983 (with

TABLE 5.27

Cotton: Imports by Main Countries and Groupings

Countries	% of World Imports				
	1964/65	*1969/70*	*1974/75*	*1978/79*	*1979/80*
Industrial	59.9	55.3	50.8	43.7	42.0
North America	2.7	2.2	1.6	1.3	1.3
Western Europe	37.0	33.9	30.5	25.6	24.8
Japan	19.6	19.1	18.7	16.7	14.5
Centrally planned	18.7	20.8	20.1	15.8	13.1
USSR	4.9	6.6	3.8	2.0	1.1
Developing	21.2	23.9	29.2	40.6	46.2
Asia and Oceania	17.7	20.5	24.5	36.8	43.5
Africa	1.3	1.4	2.5	1.8	1.2
Latin America	2.4	1.9	2.1	2.1	1.5
	Imports by Weight (Thousand Bales)				
World	17,519	18,132	17,330	20,325	23,077

Source: Cotton: World Statstics (Washington, D.C.: International Cotton Advisory Committee, October 1981), pp. 26–29. Only the larger importers in the three groups of states are included.

several price decreases recorded between these years). These price shifts were traceable to variations in supply caused by weather and production policy (e.g., switching to other crops); changes in demand caused by altered import policies (e.g., China's purchases in 1979/80); the price of synthetics; economic cycles and speculation; monetary developments; and inflation.[166]

Negotiations. The international body in which producing and consuming states have most frequently discussed the world cotton market is the International Cotton Advisory Committee (ICAC), headquartered in Washington. In the early 1950s the United Nations organ concerned with commodity trade, the ICCICA, asked the ICAC to examine the practicability of using buffer stocks and export quotas to stabilize the cotton market. Following lengthy discussions held between 1952 and 1954, the ICAC concluded that a buffer stock was not feasible because of the expense involved. It also noted that the developing-country producers, many of whom hoped to expand exports, generally opposed export restrictions.

The ICAC did not again examine regulatory arrangements at any length until the late 1960s, when the United States decided to stop holding large cotton reserves and, as a consequence, destabilized the previously stable international cotton market. This shift in American policy prompted considerable discussion of different stabilization schemes within the ICAC between 1966 and 1972. However, no agreement was concluded because of the conflicting positions of many producing countries. Some exporters worried that cotton's competitiveness vis-à-vis synthetic fibers would be seriously weakened by any arrangement that regulated prices. As an UNCTAD report in 1972 observed, the ICAC could not agree to production or export controls because "the general view of interested Governments has been that any agreement would be restrictive in nature and would not favor cotton in its competition with man-made fibers."[167] Developing countries anxious to increase their share of world exports opposed intervention into the market, while developed countries such as the United States favored an unregulated market and rejected proposals to restrict production and/or exports. In addition, it was widely recognized that the heterogeneity of cotton would make the effective use of buffer stocks difficult.[168] In any case, by the early 1970s cotton prices were rising rapidly, and the producers were less concerned about price stabilization.

Before the first UNCTAD meeting on cotton in June 1977, the Secretariat organized regional meetings of the myriad LDC producers. These meetings agreed to request the creation of an international buffer stock or a system of coordinated national stocks, but they did not support export or production controls.[169] The Secretariat also rejected supply management, because of the problems involved in getting producers to agree to quotas, the difficulty of enforcing quotas, and the burdens likely to be put on consumers. Although the Secretariat admitted that national stocks were advantageous because only the largest exporters would have to participate, it suggested that the need to secure ongoing intergovernmental consent to operate such stocks rendered them infeasible as a regulatory instrument. Thus, the Secretariat concluded that an international buffer stock was the preferred arrangement.[170]

Between 1977 and 1982 six UNCTAD meetings on cotton took place. These mainly focused on the UNCTAD Secretariat–G77 proposal for a buffer stock or nationally coordinated stocks. During this period related discussions were also held in the ICAC.[171] The importing states would not support the Secretariat–G77 scheme, although only the developed importers publicly expressed doubts about the need for it. However, they did not have to play a prominent role in criticizing the ICA proposal; major differences between and among the developed and developing producers ensured that it would not get off the ground. Only 16 developing-country producers (including Turkey), collectively accounting for 60 percent of developing-country exports, formally supported the official G77 proposal.[172] While most of the other producers remained silent, a group of Latin American countries, including Brazil, Peru, and Colombia, publicly rejected market regulation because of ideological predispositions, the opposition of their private growers, and a realistic recognition that its broad acceptance was impossible.[173] Commenting on the divisions among LDC producers, the executive director of the ICAC concluded that the possibility of a consensus was undermined by differences in production costs, the use of subsidies by governments, and existing market structures. [174]

Regardless of the conflicts among Third World producers, an ICA could not have been negotiated in any event because of the views of the United States and the Soviet Union. The United States argued that price fluctuations "played a useful role in allowing the adjustment of world supply and demand," and that producers had greatly benefited from the recent 1973 and 1976 price increases.[175] The American cotton industry at this time was quite satisfied with the U.S. price-support system and opposed an international buffer stock because of its possible depressive effect on prices.[176] At one point in the UNCTAD discussions the United States stated bluntly that it "was opposed to any agreement with economic provisions, and was not prepared to enter into negotiations on the basis of price stabilization."[177] The Soviet Union was less strident, but its unwillingness to support an international buffer stock was made clear when it stated that all financial contributions should be voluntary. It also argued that intra-Comecon trade should be excluded from any arrangement.[178] The Soviet Union and the United States would have been required to pay significant sums toward a stocking operation because of their large global exports. At one point in the talks several developing exporters suggested that production restrictions might be the best way to buoy the market, but both superpowers quickly came down hard on this idea. Aware that the Third World countries would expect them to bear the burden of any restrictions, they were not about to open the door to that possibility.[179]

In 1982 the UNCTAD Secretariat launched discussions on the establishment of a producer-consumer body that, inter alia, would encourage the exchange of information and consider possible market regulatory arrangements. The Secretariat provided some draft proposals on the possible scope and form of such a body.[180] But the antipathy of many importing and some exporting states to any agreement that could lead to the discussion of market regulation doomed the proposal. The collapse of these talks was followed in 1982 and 1983 by the formulation of a constitution for an International Cotton Producers' Association (ICPA) by a number of developing-country producers;[181] this was opened for signature in 1983. The association has many purposes, including the development of positions for international negotiations concerning market management. Even if it does formally come into existence, it is not likely to affect the prospects for market regulation.

The obstacles to the creation of an ICA for cotton have been and remain formidable. The heterogeneity of grades and the existence of substitutes pose problems, although they are not insuperable. More serious is the vast number of exporters with differing costs of production, few of whom are willing to contemplate restrictions on their own production and exports. This is certainly true of the United States and Soviet Union, but it is also the case for some developing producers opposed to proposals that could curtail employment and risk losses in export earnings. These producers would like the Americans and Soviets to finance a buffer stock and control their own production to support international prices, although such producers have little influence on the policies of developed cotton growers. Vis-à-vis the importing states, developing producers lack market power because of the alternative sources of supply and their own heavy reliance on cotton export earnings (table 5.27). Japan and the major European states are not receptive to arrangements that might increase cotton prices. The same is probably the case for the developing Asian importers whose textile industries have grown rapidly. The fact that shares of global exports and global imports are so evenly divided between industrialized and Third World countries also creates difficult problems for those anxious to conclude an ICA.

Bananas

The Market. Bananas are a permanent crop with little seasonality in production in most countries . Replanting is done annually. Although over 100 countries produce bananas, only 16 are significant exporters. Indeed, less than one-fifth of total world production usually reaches the international marketplace, and the varieties grown for export and domestic consumption are generally different.[182] Brazil, India, Indonesia, Ecuador, the Philippines, and Thailand are the major banana producers, but only Ecuador and the Philippines have sizable export sales. The developing countries controlled virtually the whole global export market in 1980, with Latin American producers alone accounting for 76 percent. Ecuador, the biggest exporter, accounted for 18 percent of the world total in 1982. Costa Rica (with 13 percent of world exports in 1982), Honduras (12 percent), Colombia (11 percent), Panama (8 percent), and Guatemala (6 percent) are the other major exporters in the region. Asia (14 percent) and Africa (3 percent) are smaller exporting areas, with the Philippines (13 percent) being by far the biggest contributor (table 5.28). Banana exports are quite important to the economies of some of the Latin American producing states. The dominant importers are the United States and the EC, accounting for close to two-thirds of the total (table 5.29).

Over four-fifths of international banana trade is conducted on the free market. The remaining 15 percent or so is governed by preferential arrangements, particularly between the European Community and former colonies (most of them from the Caribbean).[183] Banana prices vary some-

TABLE 5.28
Bananas: Exports by Main Countries and Groupings

Countries	% of World Exports				
	1961	*1970*	*1975*	*1980*	*1982*
Industrial	0.3	3.4	3.4	3.6	6.1
Centrally planned	0.1	0.1	0.1	0.1	1.5
Developing	99.6	96.5	96.5	96.3	92.4
Asia	3.5	6.7	15.8	15.7	14.1
Philippines	—	1.8	12.9	13.4	13.3
Africa	11.1	6.8	5.6	3.9	2.7
Latin America	81.3	81.8	75.0	76.6	75.6
Ecuador	24.8	21.4	21.7	20.8	18.0
Costa Rica	5.8	14.9	17.5	14.5	13.2
Honduras	10.8	14.0	5.7	12.5	11.8
Panama	6.9	10.4	7.8	7.2	8.1
Colombia	5.2	4.5	5.8	8.2	10.9
Guatemala	4.1	3.8	4.0	4.8	5.5
	Exports by Weight (Thousand Tons)				
World	3,967	5,805	6,371	6,912	6,973

Sources: Food and Agriculture Organization, *Trade Yearbook* (various years); FAO Doc. CCP: BA/ST 84/3 (1984), appendix H. The figures for 1983 are in the latter document, but some of them are not representative of recent trends because of weather damage in that year. Only the larger exporters in the group of developing states are included.

TABLE 5.29
Bananas: Imports by Main Countries and Groupings

Countries	% of World Imports				
	1961	*1970*	*1975*	*1980*	*1983*
Industrial	88.7	88.2	84.3	83.7	89.5
United States	29.8	32.9	31.2	36.3	36.5
EC-10	38.0	32.1	30.4	28.1	27.6
Japan	1.9	15.0	14.2	10.9	9.3
Centrally planned	1.4	1.8	4.2	4.0	2.6
Developing	9.9	10.1	11.4	12.3	7.9
Asia	1.6	1.8	4.7	4.3	4.9
Latin America	6.9	5.7	3.7	6.0	2.8
	Imports by Weight (Thousand Tons)				
World	3,932	5,618	6,306	6,676	6,205

Sources: Food and Agriculture Organization, *Trade Yearbook* (various years); FAO, Doc. CCP. BA/ST 84/3 (1984), table 2. Only the larger importers in the three groups of states are included.

what among points of origin and destination, but they have been more stable than those of most other commodities. From 1963 until 1974 there was little fluctuation in current prices, although the real or deflated price dropped steadily. Current prices rose dramatically in 1975 and 1976 following a hurricane in the Caribbean in 1974, and then increased further in 1980–81 and 1983—again because of weather damage. In deflated U.S. dollars, prices fell in the early 1970s, rose in 1975–76, declined through 1979, and then increased in the 1980s.[184]

An important characteristic of the banana industry is the critical role of three multinational corporations—Standard Fruit, United Brands, and Del Monte. The extreme perishability of the commodity—a maximum of five weeks can elapse between picking and consumption—lends itself to the efficient coordination of all related activities under one management team. This has stimulated the development of vertically integrated firms that are involved in almost every facet of the industry: plantation ownership, trucking, shipping, distribution, and wholesale activities. The MNCs largely dominate production and other sectors of the industry in Central America—with the exception of Nicaragua since 1982—and the Philippines. They have considerable influence in Colombia, but in Equador they are excluded from production and control only a modest portion of the marketing. In some producing countries all three big MNCs are present (e.g.,

Costa Rica and the Philippines), while in others only one operates (e.g., Panama and Guatemala). The multinational corporations are frequently involved in conflicts with local governments and organizations over production costs and taxes. The power of these MNCs is based on their financial and technical resources and on their control of distribution systems in the importing countries.[185]

Negotiations. The banana market has been discussed regularly over the past two decades in the Food and Agriculture Organization. In 1965 the FAO established a Study Group (renamed the Intergovernmental Group on Bananas in 1972), whose objectives are to provide a forum for talks on the problems of exporters and importers and to work toward finding solutions.[186] In the late 1960s and early 1970s the major issues were trade barriers—with several large exporters opposed to the preferential access enjoyed by smaller producers in the Western European market—and the problem of oversupply, which was causing a downward trend in real prices. No consensus was reached on the oversupply/price issue among the exporters, partly because of policies adopted by and competition among the multinational corporations. Several exporters were unwilling to contemplate any production restraints.[187]

Beginning in the early 1970s, the producing countries also began to meet and collaborate on their own. Apart from establishing a Sub-Group of Exporters within the FAO body in 1971, they discussed the possible creation of a producer organization in 1972. This resulted in the establishment of "Union de Paises Exportadors de Banana" (UPEB) in 1974. The original members were Costa Rica, Colombia, Guatemala, Honduras, and Panama; subsequent additions have been the Dominican Republic (1976), Nicaragua (1979), and Venezuela (1982). The goals of UPEB include expanding markets, encouraging consumption, achieving a balance between supply and demand, securing remunerative prices for exporters, and promoting the exchange of information. The most important members of UPEB were and still are those Central American countries whose industries are dominated by the MNCs. Ecuador and the Philippines are not members. Ecuador sells some of its produce to the MNCs and is not interested in alienating them; it also has lower production costs and higher transportation costs to many markets. The Philippines produces mainly for the Japanese market. Also noteworthy is the fact that Colombia—whose national company, Uniban, controls a large portion of its production—joined UPEB for reasons of regional solidarity but has not collaborated

closely with the other members, in part because of an ambitious pro-
duction-expansion program begun in the mid-1970s.[188]

UPEB members explored the possibility of raising prices through national quotas, but the absence of several important producers from the
organization and the reluctance of some members to limit production
meant that little progress could be made. They then shifted their attention
and agreed to impose a tax on the export of bananas ($1.00/carton). The
multinationals reacted angrily by cutting production, by refusing to buy
from independent or government producers, and by threatening to reduce
investment. Colombia never imposed the tax, while the others later cut
their taxes in order to placate the multinationals.[189] Without a united front
among all or almost all regional producers, the pressure to compromise
was overwhelming.

In the mid-1970s the producers also sought to improve their market
positions by getting agreement within the FAO Intergovernmental Group
to hold producer-consumer discussions on the negotiation of an ICA. The
U.S. representative expressed reservations about the desirability of this enterprise, arguing that there was no problem of price instability. But an
eleven-nation Working Party on the Elements of an International Banana
Agreement was formed and met on three occasions between 1976 and
1978. These meetings were seen as part of UNCTAD's IPC once bananas
had been included in that program in 1976. The negotiations continued at a
meeting of the FAO Intergovernmental Group on Bananas in 1980.

During this period the producers expressed differing views on the
desirability of an ICA with a price range and export controls, with some
even altering their preferences from one meeting to the next. Colombia, in
the midst of an expansion program, consistently lobbied against any
supply-management measures. Guatemala, Honduras, and the Philippines
tended to be fence sitters; they were fearful of alienating the companies and
thus risking the assured market outlets they enjoyed. However, they did
not publicly rule out an ICA. According to participants, the MNCs clearly
indicated their opposition to an ICA, believing that it would force them to
buy fruit of low quality at high prices, discourage the maintenance of
"reserve production" grown in case of weather damage, and erode their
market shares. Ecuador, Panama, and Costa Rica were favorably disposed
to an ICA based on supply management, but Costa Rica changed its position at the 1980 meeting, since it had just embarked on an expansion program. Other factors tended to restrain the enthusiasm of some producers
for an ICA, especially the price increases that occurred in 1975–76 and

1980–81 after weather damage and the expansion of producers' earnings from other commodities (notably coffee). Periodic supply shortfalls owing to weather have had a notable impact on producers' willingness to support supply management.[190]

Following the 1980 FAO meeting, and a 1980 UNCTAD meeting on bananas that confined itself to discussing developmental assistance,[191] banana prices were reasonably strong. In 1982, however, they began to drop. Consumption growth rates were slipping at the time, and the producers were discouraged by the difficulty of opening up new markets, finding new uses for bananas, and persuading some developed countries to lower trade barriers—areas where they had long hoped progress might be made.[192] With these market conditions producers tended to scale back their expansion plans and expressed renewed interest in an ICA with supply management.

Two meetings of groups of producing states in the first half of 1983 saw resolutions passed calling for the creation of an ICA, the freezing of acreages, and respect for existing market shares. These positions were adopted despite the fact that in the early months of 1983 floods in Ecuador, windstorms in Guatemala and Honduras, and droughts in Colombia and the Philippines destroyed crops, resulting in an 11 percent decline in world production that year. The producers obviously had concluded that severe structural problems existed in the banana industry whose solution required international cooperation.[193] However, at this time almost all the producers were reducing taxes because of mounting pressure from the MNCs, and the value of UPEB was increasingly being brought into question. The new executive director of UPEB remarked in mid-1984 that "UPEB is going through a critical phase because of its members' disinterest in the organization."[194] Disarray among the producers in confronting the multinationals and their doubts about the efficacy of collaboration in UPEB did not bode well for the possibility of mounting a common producer front in any future negotiations with consumers on an ICA. Their long-standing competition for market shares, the differences in their costs of production,[195] and the varied roles of the multinationals in their countries all make it difficult to develop unifed producer policies.

In October 1984 the FAO Working Party, established in 1975 to consider the possibility of creating an ICA for bananas, convened its fourth session, the last one having been in 1980. The participants had before them a model agreement and a proposal for establishing export quotas drafted by the FAO Secretariat. At the beginning of the session the executive director of

UPEB, speaking on behalf of its members and Ecuador, proclaimed their support for an ICA, but he did not make any specific proposals for a price range or export quotas. The producers had obviously been unable to resolve the issue of market shares, and most were unwilling to back specific schemes opposed by the MNCs. The majority of the consumers stated that they would be willing to discuss any concrete proposals backed by the producers, but the United States finally ended the drawn-out dialogue when it announced that it would not support any agreement with economic provisions. The Working Party consequently decided to report to the Intergovernmental Group on Bananas that it had failed in its endeavor to agree on a price-regulatory agreement.[196] The Intergovernmental Group meeting in May discussed the possibility of creating an expert group that would discuss a wide range of international measures to assist producers, but the members could not even agree on its establishment.[197]

The demise of the negotiations on an ICA for bananas certainly did not take many observers by surprise. It was always clear that the producers would face a tremendous amount of difficulty in agreeing to market shares. The developed consuming countries have always been adverse to creating ICAs for commodities such as bananas whose prices are fairly stable. The United States, in addition, is sensitive to the opposition of the three big multinationals to market regulation. Although the United States is concerned about maintaining good political relations with the banana-exporting countries of Latin America, it has a variety of other means of assisting them. It does not have to set a dangerous precedent by supporting market regulation for a commodity with a stable price trend.

Tropical Timber, Oils and Oilseeds, and Bovine Meat

Tropical timber exports originate mainly in Asia (about 75 percent), with approximately 20 percent coming from Africa and the rest from Latin America. The two dominant exporters, Malaysia and Indonesia, each have market shares of about 35 percent. At UNCTAD meetings in 1977 and 1978 the producers expressed an interest in nonbinding price ranges for certain types of logs and in improved coordination of production. The developed states did not object to the idea of recommended price ranges, but reports by the UNCTAD Secretariat and the subsequent statements of exporting and importing countries revealed numerous impediments to intergovernmental regulation. First and most important, there is the vast array of different types of tropical timber, many with interchangeable uses and some with nontropical timber substitutes. "Even on a conservative reckoning . . . the umbrella term 'tropical timber' covers at least several thousand individually recognizable commodities."[198] For an intergovernmental body to set and adjust price ranges for all these types of tropical timber would be almost impossible. Second, production costs vary greatly within and among the producing countries.[199] Lastly, prices in any case have been quite stable over the years and have actually increased steadily in constant dollars. As a Secretariat report noted: "The main problem of stability appears to be that of occasional falls in the earnings of producing countries and large price increases for consuming countries . . . "[200] Given this situation, the idea of a price-regulating ICA for tropical timber was not treated seriously.

More international collaboration would be valuable, however, in such areas as market information, research, and technical assistance on forest management and wood processing in the producing countries. Strong consumer demand and the attrition of tropical forests because of log farming and the expansion of areas of human settlement led the consuming states to take an interest in forest management and reforestation. Japan, in particular, took a leadership role in supporting the establishment of an international organization concerned with these issues. In 1983 the International Tropical Timber Agreement was signed, with a mandate to deal with forest management, information sharing, and related issues.[201] Along with the International Jute Organization, this body stands as a modest product of the lengthy negotiations carried out under the IPC.

Oils and oilseeds, like tropical timber, come in many varieties and are often interchangeable in their uses. Many are also interchangeable with animal fats (e.g., butter) and with synthetic products. Oils and oilcakes are extracted from over one hundred varieties of oilseeds, although only 15 to 20 types yield significant quantities. The developed countries have garnered close to 60 percent of the global export earnings from these products, two-thirds from sales of soybeans and soybean products, with the United States being the major supplier. The developing countries dominate the markets for coconuts, palm, groundnuts, and linseeds and their products.[202]

The international oils and oilseeds markets have been discussed at length in the FAO since 1965 and in UNCTAD since 1972. But no serious negotiations on an ICA have taken place because of the multiplicity of commodity types and the plethora of producers.[203] At the start of the UNCTAD IPC deliberations in 1977 the Secretariat suggested that producers might wish to consider coordinated national stocking to boost and stabilize prices,[204] but this idea elicited no response. A Secretariat report noted: "There seems to be no desire on the part of the major exporting countries to engage in negotiations leading to stabilization agreements. Each of these major producing countries has had some success in carrying out production programs, and has achieved relatively high levels of competitiveness. Their policies have been directed more to increasing their market shares than to stabilizing prices."[205] At one point it was agreed that "conventional formal arrangements involving international buffer stocking mechanisms were not practicable for a heterogeneous group of competing vegetable oilseeds and oils."[206] That was clearly the chief impediment to an ICA, with the competition among and between developed and developing producers also playing a role.

Bovine meat was included in the IPC solely because the developing-country exporters—mainly the Latin Americans—hoped to create another forum in which to pressure the developed countries to reduce their trade barriers and subsidies. These issues had regularly been discussed in the FAO since 1969. In the late 1970s trade barriers and beef subsidies were being negotiated in the GATT's Tokyo Round. The two UNCTAD IPC meetings in 1978 and 1980 discussed what should be negotiated in the GATT and what the results of the GATT Tokyo Round meant for LDC exporters, respectively. Both the UNCTAD Secretariat and the developing-country producers themselves explicitly eschewed a price-regulating arrangement, citing the impossibility of buffer stocking. But the fact that developing countries only accounted for about 20 percent of global beef exports—down from around 40 percent in 1960—also influenced their views on the prospects for commodity control.[207]

Conclusion

Five agricultural commodities were examined in detail in this section. In the case of one, cotton, the most significant obstacle to the adoption of an ICA was the opposition of the two major developed producers, the United States and the USSR. The question of developed exporters did not arise for the other four. In these cases producer-consumer and/or interproducer differences undermined the negotiations. Most industrialized importing nations were unsympathetic to regulation of jute and hard fibers because of the growing role of synthetic substitutes in the market. In addition, the desire of the producing countries to include manufactured products and to place restraints on the production of competing synthetics increased developed-country disenchantment with Third World demands. Proposals to establish ICAs for tea and bananas did not meet with outright opposition from most consuming countries, but the United States assumed a negative posture, which would certainly have been crucial to the fate of a banana agreement given the large U.S. share of the global market. The opposition of the three American multinationals involved in the banana industry also undermined the prospect of an ICA; only a strong, united stance among all the producers could conceivably have overcome this barrier.

Divisions among developing-country producers did not pose a major problem during the negotiations on jute because Bangladesh dominated the market for fiber exports. Nor did producer divisions appear to be insuperable in the case of cotton so long as a pure buffer-stock agreement was under consideration. Had a more effective type of agreement involving export quotas been considered, the divisions among LDC cotton exporters would have been more serious, because few were prepared to countenance restraints on their production and exports. With respect to the other three agricultural commodities, the splits among the LDC producers ran very deep: between Brazil and Tanzania on sisal; between Kenya and the South Asians on tea; and among a variety of producers on bananas. Typically, those with expansion programs and lower production costs were wary of supply restrictions.

One interesting issue that never really had to be confronted directly concerned the views and policies of Third World *importing* states, which now account for 40–50 percent of global imports of tea, jute, and cotton. It is doubtful whether LDC importers would have been willing to support ICAs that entailed higher import prices. LDC importers have demonstrated no inclination to accept commodity schemes designed to channel resources to LDC producers. If it were possible to organize trade-offs involving a range of commodities, the picture could change. But such complex bargaining packages have not emerged, and are unlikely to in the foreseeable future.

6

DEVELOPING-COUNTRY POLICIES, BARGAINING OUTCOMES, AND INTERNATIONAL REGIMES

Throughout the postwar period the developing countries have tried to change the norms, rules and institutions that have governed—or, more accurately, partly governed—international trade in primary commodities. Their most concerted effort to transform the global commodity regime occurred in the 1970s, in connection with the ambitious UNCTAD-sponsored Integrated Program for Commodities and after the spectacular success of the oil-producing countries in 1973–74. However, as was emphasized in previous chapters, the Third World's unhappiness with the operation of unregulated commodity markets is by no means a recent phenomenon. Many specific proposals advanced by developing countries to change the conditions under which their commodities are sold on the world market have a long history. It is a singular deficiency of much of the recent literature on North-South relations that it generally lacks a historical perspective, and one of the goals of this book has been to provide such a perspective in one important area.

Examination of the politics of postwar international commodity regulation suggests that three broad sets of questions need to be addressed. The first group of questions focuses on the *policies of the developing countries* toward international commodity issues. What general normative or programmatic reforms have been advocated by the less developed countries? Why have they usually been able to reach agreement on broad reform proposals? In light of their enthusiasm for extensive changes in the major norms that have shaped international commodity policy, why have producers often failed to agree on regulatory schemes for particular products?

A second set of questions probes the *outcomes of bargaining between developed and developing nations* on commodity issues. What successes have the developing countries enjoyed in their efforts to refashion the normative-institutional structure established in the early postwar years? What factors account for their few successes and many failures? On specific commodities, why has the long-standing struggle to establish ICAs yielded only a handful of agreements? In particular, why have Third World producers had so little leverage during the bargaining?

A final set of questions relates to the *strength and nature of the regulatory regime* governing international commodity trade. To what extent has it constrained state behavior? What principles have influenced its design? And what factors explain its weak and market-oriented character?

POLICIES OF THE DEVELOPING COUNTRIES

Norms and General Rules of the Commodity Trade Regime

A striking feature of the developing countries' approach to international economic diplomacy has been their ability to maintain a broad consensus on basic proposals for change. Few would deny that the heterogeneous collection of states that comprise the Third World have been successful in formulating and vigorously articulating ambitious demands regarding the norms and institutions that characterize the international economic order.

Major LDC Proposals. Several proposals designed to alter the postwar commodity regime have enjoyed widespread and fairly consistent Third World support over many years.

1. Intergovernmental action is required to stabilize prices and to increase the export earnings of developing-country producers. From the time of the Havana Charter onward, Third World producers have sought to liberalize the charter's stipulation that ICAs should only be created in very unstable markets when there are situations of "burdensome surplus" and/ or "widespread unemployment or underemployment." They have wanted to legitimize intervention whenever market prices fell precipitously or decreased in real terms. This position is consistent with the general proclivity

of Third World states to favor international regimes based more on "authoritative" than on "market-oriented" modes of allocation.[1]

2. International commodity policy and commodity agreements should embrace the idea of indexing the prices of LDC commodity exports to an indicator which will prevent a loss in purchasing power.[2] Although this issue did not receive sustained attention until the 1970s, it did appear periodically on the United Nations agenda in the 1950s and 1960s.[3] In comparison with other general Third World proposals, indexation has had somewhat weaker LDC support. Nonetheless, an admittedly fragile and vague G77 consensus on the issue was sustained during most of the 1970s.[4]

3. The industrialized countries should contribute to or otherwise subsidize the costs of operating international commodity agreements (for example, by contributing to ICA stocking operations). Beginning in the 1960s the LDCs argued that the developed importing countries should assume an obligation to pay an equal share of the cost of buffer stocks. In the late 1970s they suggested that the developed world not only accept equal cost-sharing in individual ICAs but also assume a proportionally larger financial burden through the creation of the Common Fund.

4. Developed-country importers should compensate developing countries for shortfalls in their commodity export earnings—preferably for the sum of the shortfalls from all the commodities they export. Developing-country representatives first called for such a program in the 1950s. In 1963 the IMF created the Compensatory Financing Facility, but it only provided loans to countries with shortfalls in *total* export earnings that led to balance-of-payments deficits. Over the years the developing countries have sought (so far unsuccessfully) in the IMF, UNCTAD, and other global forums to obtain a compensatory-financing arrangement that either is geared specifically to shortfalls in individual commodity export earnings or separated from balance-of-payments deficits.

5. Developing countries should have greater power in the decision-making bodies of international organizations, and the authority of universal organizations in commodity markets should be expanded. In the 1950s and early 1960s commodity policy was addressed by the UN Economic and Social Council, in which the developed countries enjoyed votes disproportionate to their percentage of the UN's membership. Third World states largely succeeded in transferring the issue to UNCTAD in 1964, although the developed countries refused to bestow binding legal authority on the new organization. UNCTAD's mandate, voting arrangements, and the bias of the Secretariat were all deemed likely to facilitate the promotion of Third

World interests. A more recent strategy pursued by the LDCs to expand their influence over international commodity markets has been to create an organization that is mandated to financially assist bodies administering ICAs and in which the Third World would enjoy substantial voting power (i.e., the Common Fund). They hoped that such an organization would encourage the formation of ICAs and accord Third World countries greater influence over ICAs.

6. Commodity producers should have the right to establish producer cartels and to seek to affect the conditions governing their exports. The developing countries opposed the normative restraint against the formation of cartels implicitly included in the Havana Charter. They maintained this position through the 1950s and 1960s. In the 1970s they proposed UN resolutions legitimizing cartels (e.g., the Charter of Economic Rights and Duties of States) and created a host of new commodity cartels and producer associations.

Explanation of LDC Consensuses. The vast majority of Third World states have consistently supported these basic ideas for regime change. Several reasons may be adduced to explain this. Some are related to the South's perceptions of commodity price trends and market performance; others are linked to environmental conditions or factors that are for the most part extrinsic to commodity markets per se.

Throughout the period reviewed in this book, the developing countries have emphasized that commodity *price fluctuations* are both common and harmful to their economic welfare. This is an issue on which virtual unanimity has prevailed among Third World states. The first chapter noted that some economists have disputed the proposition that commodity price instability necessarily harms producing countries in the long run. But judging from the record of LDC statements and proposals at diplomatic conferences and during commodity negotiations, the developing countries have not been dissuaded by the various complexities that attend the analysis of commodity price stabilization. They seem to accept that price and producer income fluctuations are endemic in unregulated commodity markets; that such fluctuations undermine the development prospects and economic welfare of LDC commodity exporters; and that international schemes to stabilize commodity prices through the establishment of ICAs and other devices will yield results favorable to producers' welfare. It should be emphasized that much respectable scholarly opinion does in fact support many of the views of the South on this matter.[5]

A second key issue concerns the *real price trends* of primary commodity exports. According to LDCs and the UNCTAD Secretariat, there has been a persistent tendency for the commodity terms of trade of developing countries to deteriorate since the early 1950s. Economists have differed on the merits of this stance. Nonetheless, the developing countries generally have continued to evince faith in the declining-terms-of-trade thesis, and their perception of the argument's validity conditions their bargaining stance. Moreover, once again it is necessary to note that much empirical economic work can be cited to bolster their view. The first half of the 1970s undoubtedly witnessed a temporary improvement. But it remains the case that for the vast majority of commodities largely or significantly exported by LDCs, real price trends have been unfavorable during much of the postwar period, with some of the most dramatic price declines occurring in the early 1980s.

Another important factor prompting the developing countries to press for a transformation in regime norms is their inability to secure new regulatory arrangements for individual commodities, i.e., their *lack of bargaining power*. Despite much rhetoric about the Third World's alleged "commodity power" in the 1970s, developing-country producers have not been able to change the fundamental conditions governing international trade in their commodities, with oil being a notable exception. Stephen Krasner suggests that limited Southern leverage characterizes the entire range of international economic issues. He argues persuasively that international weakness in terms of relative "national material-power capabilities" has encouraged the Third World to press for negotiated regime change at the global level:

Their small size and limited resources, even in specific issue areas . . . has led them to attempt the fundamental alteration of international regimes. Conventional statecraft based upon national material attributes is unlikely to reduce vulnerabilities. A . . . strategy designed to alter rules, norms, and institutions offers an attractive alternative, if only by default.[6]

The question of producer bargaining power in commodity markets is taken up more directly later in this chapter. What needs to be stressed in this context is the effect of the Third World's international weakness, namely, that finding themselves unable to force the Western nations to make major concessions in the short run, they turned their attention to trying to gain acceptance of a new set of norms that would help in the attainment of specific changes in the long run.

Yet another feature common to most developing countries that has motivated them to seek intergovernmental regulation of markets is that they lack *the diversity and mobility of resources* characteristic of modern industrial societies. This is due not just to an absence of economic modernization in many sectors but also to rigidities in their political systems.[7] As Albert Hirschman noted in an important treatise published four decades ago, the more immobile a country's resources, the greater will be the difficulties it faces when forced to adjust to changes imposed by external economic forces.[8] Developing economies are typically poorly integrated internally and unable to respond effectively to external shocks. Similarly, political institutions and cohesiveness are weak in many Third World states. As Klaus Knorr has observed, "the need of societies to learn and adjust to external stimuli, which increasing international interdependence demands, is a seemingly overpowering load in populations that in most cases have achieved little political integration . . . and are usually encased in states that, although possessing the trappings of sovereignty, are still extremely weak structurally."[9] Of course, political instability and economic flexibility vary significantly among Third World states. For example, some of the OPEC countries and several of the newly industrializing countries (NICs) of the South may be exceptions to the generalized condition of domestic vulnerability found in the Third World as a whole.[10]

The situation facing most LDCs can be contrasted with that of smaller, politically mature industrial powers. Small industrial states have successfully pursued a number of strategies to deal with their vulnerability to the external economic world, including diversification, domestic adjustment, "invisibility," and manipulation of larger powers.[11] For these strategies to be employed successfully, states must possess certain attributes, including well-developed and coherent political systems and flexible economies. Unfortunately, few developing countries can be placed in the category of "self-directed small states."[12] Given this limited ability to alter their domestic societies and economies to adjust to changes in international markets, Third World governments are naturally drawn to advocating normative positions suggesting that the external world should act to prevent or mitigate hardship in their countries.

Another factor, closely related to the two just discussed, is the pervasiveness of a *dependency belief system*.[13] Many developing countries have embraced the view that their relatively low level of economic development is attributable to the international economic system, not the shortcomings of their own societies. From this perspective, it matters little whether the potpourri of theories uneasily stitched together into the modern dependency-school approach to development are in fact accurate. Far more important is the apparent belief of some Third World elites that the contemporary international economy inherently operates to their disadvantage and to the benefit of the Western capitalist states.

Third World criticism of existing international regimes may have reached its apogee in the post-1973 period, but by no means all the key Southern complaints are of recent vintage. The core of the Third World argument—at least with respect to international trade—was articulated by Raul Prebisch as far back as the late 1940s. It hinges on the proposition that there is a "systematic bias in the distribution of benefits from international trade, a bias favoring the powerful industrial exporters of the 'center' and disadvantaging the weak producers of raw materials in the 'periphery'."[14] So deeply ingrained has this belief become that efforts by the developed countries and economic scholars to refute it are often dismissed by some LDCs as self-serving sophistry. Thus, LDCs' unhappiness with the postwar commodity regime has been but one element of their broader assault on the alleged unfairness of the international market system generally.[15] And, as has been pointed out, widespread acceptance of a "dependency orientation" has been critical to the maintenance of Third World unity in demanding general regime reform.[16]

Another part of the explanation hinges on the simple fact that the reform proposals favored by the South would entail considerable costs for the developed states but no costs or only *minor costs* for the LDCs themselves. This, of course, is scarcely surprising. States that insist on the need for major reform of international regimes do not normally advocate changes that would be highly costly for themselves. Proposals to expand compensatory financing, to increase intergovernmental regulation of commodity markets, to obtain financial support from consuming nations for buffer stocks, and to create the Common Fund and endow it with substantial resources largely contributed by developed states—these demands were seen by LDCs as requiring large financial outlays only by developed countries. In the case of indexation, on the other hand, a number of developing countries grew wary of the proposal precisely because they feared that indexing commodity prices could prove costly to their own economies.

Another reason for the Third World consensus stems not from the weakness of LDCs but rather from the opportunities that the extant international system has afforded them. Here the *role of international institutions* warrants particular attention. As Robert Keohane and Joseph Nye write:

International organizations are frequently congenial institutions for weak states. The one-state-one-vote norm of the United Nations system favors coalitions of the small and powerless. Secretariats are often responsive to Third World demands. Furthermore, the substantive norms of most international organizations, as they have developed over the years, stress social and economic equity as well as the equality of states. Past resolutions expressing Third World positions, sometimes agreed to with reservations by industrialized countries, are used to legitimize other demands. These agreements are rarely binding, but up to a point the norms of the institution make opposition look more harshly self-interested and less defensible.[17]

In the case of commodity trade policy, the clear mandate of the United Nations (particularly UNCTAD after 1964) to be the central global commodity institution and the absence of competing organizations dominated by the developed states—like GATT, the IMF, and the IBRD—meant that the developing countries were able to set the negotiating agenda. As on many other international issues, in commodity trade "The North has been compelled to respond rather than initiate" discussions.[18]

The bargaining positions taken by the Group of 77 often have closely reflected the beliefs and ambitions of the UNCTAD Secretariat. "In fact, the Group of 77 frequently adopts proposals of the UNCTAD Secretariat as its own positions and can thus capitalize on the entire preparatory work undertaken in this respect."[19] This influence on the policies pursued by the Third World is well illustrated by the Secretariat's role in the development of and debates over the IPC.[20] UNCTAD officials conceived of the IPC and drafted the studies relating to it. They labored assiduously—and with remarkable success—to keep the G77 coalition united on the rough outlines of the extensive IPC package. More generally, the existence of UNCTAD (and, to a much lesser extent, the FAO and the UN itself) has been instrumental in whatever success the Third World has achieved in its efforts to alter the commodity regime. Without a standing institution in which to debate general norms and specific schemes, a strategy of regime change would have been more difficult to pursue. And likewise the absence of such a forum would undoubtedly have made more problematic the hammering-out of a Third World consensus on the basic direction of reform.

A final important factor is the nature of *G77 and UNCTAD decision-making.* As noted in chapter 2, many observers have commented on the tendency of the group-negotiating system enshrined in UNCTAD to produce polar bargaining positions.[21] For the developing countries, the need to accommodate the constituent elements of the G77 has typically produced reform proposals that are both vague and maximalist. Only then has it seemed possible to knit together a Third World consensus. In the words of one critic:

The commitment to group unity and the group bargaining process at UNCTAD tends to compel an emphasis within the G77 on grand principles in the dirigiste model, inflated expectations of likely gains, a deliberate de-emphasis on exactly who gains what, and a rigid negotiating stance. Individual demands simply are added together; potential losers are pacified by tacit promises of compensation.[22]

It is also true that many developing states feel strongly pressured to refrain from publicly breaching official G77 positions once the latter have been devised.[23]

From the perspective of LDCs unhappy with particular G77 positions, the fact that proposals are normally couched in terms of "general principles, shared aspirations, and commitments to the way the world ought to be"[24] may actually increase their willingness to support them. Such countries know full well that when they endorse broad G77 positions, they are not accepting concrete, legally binding commitments. They will subsequently have an opportunity to oppose implementation in specific contexts if they judge them to have negative implications for their own interests. Thus, for example, Brazil has lent rhetorical support to the "official" G77 goal of establishing more commodity agreements, but in many instances has worked to prevent the conclusion of agreements for commodities of which it is an important exporter. Similarly, LDCs opposed to particular G77 positions may believe they can afford to keep silent because the firm opposition of Group B ensures that they will never be implemented. This may help to explain the behavior of some LDCs opposed to price indexation in the 1970s. The internal dynamics of G77 decision-making, the pressure on members not to break with the group, and the knowledge that specifics probably will be negotiated later all contribute to the maintenance of what appears to be a consensus on many proposals for regime change.

Regulatory Arrangements for Individual Commodities

While it is indisputable that developing countries have collectively endorsed greater intervention in international commodity markets, it is equally clear that actual attempts to fashion agreements often have been bedeviled either by a distinct lack of Third World enthusiasm or by serious divisions among LDC exporters. To a significant extent, the failure to develop producer-consumer agreements for many of the more than 25 commodities that have been subject to negotiation in UNCTAD, the FAO, and other international bodies is traceable to a lack of producer support. When governments are required to sit down and hammer out an agreement that may actually affect market prices, production plans, export shares, government revenues, employment, and other tangible economic variables, their agreement on general principles may fail to prevent the emergence of sharp conflicts. Translating a vague normative consensus into agreement on specific rules and regulations is always problematic in international negotiations.

LDC Differences on Individual Commodities. The pattern of LDC policies toward individual commodities can be categorized under three basic headings. First, in the case of a few commodities there has been a general lack of interest on the part of LDC producers in joint producer-consumer market regulation. This has been true for meat, vegetable oils and oilseeds, tropical timber, and bauxite. It also seems to have been the case for iron ore, despite India's occasional expressions of interest in some type of market intervention.

On a second and larger group of commodities, negotiations witnessed the emergence of conflicting Third World producer attitudes toward the creation of ICAs. In the case of manganese, Gabon and Brazil—the two major Third World exporters—differed on the desirability of an ICA, with the former supporting and the latter vigorously opposing the idea. Discussions concerning regulation of phosphates saw most smaller developing-country exporters (such as Algeria, Togo, Tunisia, and Senegal) anxious to achieve regulation but Morocco, by far the largest LDC producer, equally determined to avoid it. Peru, Zambia, and to a lesser extent Zaire all wanted to negotiate an ICA for copper, but Chile was an avowed opponent. On sisal, while Tanzania and small African producers favored the conclusion of an accord, Brazil had little interest. On tea, support for an ICA came from India and Sri Lanka, but Kenya and several small African producers would not accept any arrangement that threatened to slow their quest for larger market shares. Countries accounting for over half of LDC cotton exports agitated for an ICA, but other Third World exporters either opposed this or displayed no interest. Finally, in the case of bananas, the proponents and opponents of control varied over time, but policy differences among LDC producers always existed.

For a third group of commodities, a broad producer consensus in support of producer-consumer market regulation has been evident during much of the postwar period, although differences over the nature of agreements have remained. Third World exporters of coffee, cocoa, sugar, tin, and natural rubber have generally favored ICAs for these commodities throughout the past three decades and even earlier in some instances. At times, however, disagreements over the nature of ICAs have undermined accords (e.g., sugar in 1961 and 1984). In the case of some ICAs, particular producers have refused to join accords acceptable to the majority (e.g., the Ivory Coast and the 1980 International Cocoa Agreement and Bolivia and the 1980 International Tin Agreement). Developing-country producers of jute also supported the creation of an ICA in the IPC negotiations.

Explanation of LDC Differences on Individual Commodities. As is evident from the preceding chapters, many considerations have affected the attitudes of developing-country producers toward international market regulation in general, and ICAs in particular. At least six judgments have been critical in shaping their policies: the feasibility of market regulation by an international commodity organization; satisfaction with market price; satisfaction with current output and market shares; the sanctions that might follow from nonparticipation in an ICA; the viability of pursuing alternative strategies, especially unilateral producer collaboration; and the likely impact of the specific regulatory instruments that might be incorporated into an ICA. Typically, LDC policies have been influenced by all or several of these factors, and it is difficult to measure the impact of any one of them over time. Nonetheless, it is possible to provide a general picture of how LDC attitudes toward ICAs have been conditioned by the judgments listed above as well as by the market and nonmarket conditions underlying them.

The *feasibility* of attempting to regulate an international commodity market depends on several factors, the most important being the variety of commodity types and their degree of interchangeability. When a commodity has many different types or grades, some of which are interchangeable, both producers and consumers have tended to recognize the problems inherent in designing an effective pricing system and thus eschewed ICAs.[25] This was understood early on in the IPC negotiations on tropical timber and on vegetable oils and oilseeds. The problem of multiple grades also created doubts about the feasibility of market regulation among some producers of manganese ore, iron ore, bauxite, tea, and cotton, although the difficulties were not on the same scale.

A related factor is the existence of substitutes. If a commodity's price is closely tied to that of a synthetic, as is true for hard fibers, jute, and natural rubber, it may be difficult for an ICA (or producer association) to regulate market prices effectively. The 1979 International Natural Rubber Agreement proves that the existence of substitutes need not preclude an ICA, but it should be recalled that synthetic rubbers cannot be substituted for the natural commodity in some important uses. In the case of hard fibers, the UNCTAD Secretariat finally admitted in 1981 that the possibility of regulating the market was slight given the extent to which the various fibers are intertwined with and dependent upon the markets for their substitutes.

A commodity characteristic that rules out the use of a buffer stock—although it may not preclude an ICA with supply-management provisions—is perishability or the inability to store a product for long periods of time. A number of IPC commodities not included in the core group were excluded for this reason, in particular, bananas, beef, and tropical timber.

Market structure can also affect the feasibility of ICAs. For several of the IPC commodities, widespread reliance on contracts, often of lengthy duration, and transfer pricing within vertically integrated industries tend to lessen the problem of price volatility. They also mean that no single, publicly known price exists because of the absence of an open international exchange. Thus, an ICA could not act to stabilize the price within a prescribed range. As Walter Labys has commented, in such cases "Market price information is not readily available, and one must search for other measures of value."[26] Such "other measures" would have to include information provided by the various sellers and buyers active in negotiating contracts. The difficulties involved in trying to obtain this price information and then in regulating the price would be considerable. Iron ore provides a good example of the problem. Most trade in iron ore occurs on the basis of contracts of varying duration, and there is a good deal of vertical integration in the industry because of the investments made by steel companies in "captive" mines.

Of the 18 IPC commodities, all 8 excluded from the "core" group—they were deemed unsuitable for buffer-stock operations—lack open international market exchanges. If producers of such commodities wish to improve their economic returns, policies other than ICAs are likely to prove more effective. Producers of minerals whose markets are dominated by long-term contracts and/or vertically integrated multinational firms can instead try to negotiate with customers or with MNCs to increase prices and revenues. LDC producers of bauxite, bananas, iron ore, and phosphate rock have pursued these strategies, with varying degrees of success.

Critical to an LDC producer's interest in market management is its *satisfaction with the price*, in terms of both stability and real purchasing power. Historically, the prices of most of the commodities that have been subject to international regulation by ICAs have been quite unstable (although this does not mean that the existence of ICAs has guaranteed stable prices).[27] However, interest in market regulation among LDC exporters has been stimulated not so much by instability per se, but by real or anticipated market downturns. The first tin and sugar agreements, for example, were sought and subsequently formulated in 1953, at a time when prices had dropped following the boom period in the early years of the Korean War. (The prices of both had also been very unstable before the Second World War.) The efforts of LDC sugar producers to reactivate the International Sugar Agreement (ISA), which had collapsed in late 1961, between 1965 and 1968 were related to the prevailing depressed market. Likewise, their lack of interest in renegotiating the ISA in 1973 was largely due to a significant rise in the free market price. The agreement was then revived in 1977 with strong LDC producer support because of a dramatic fall in prices. Most LDC producers were also anxious for a new accord in 1983–84 when the market was very weak. Very similar patterns can be seen in the ICA negotiations for coffee and cocoa.

The first International Natural Rubber Agreement (INRA) was negotiated during a period (1977–79) when rubber prices were actually quite buoyant. However, the talks occurred in the wake of a very serious downturn in 1974–75 that badly hurt growers and caused riots in Malaysia. The prospect of future downward swings and a keen desire to prevent dramatic price falls were therefore prominent in the thinking of producer governments. During the 1985–87 negotiations to renew INRA the price was low for most of the time, and producers, especially Malaysia, pressed hard for a new accord.

Interestingly, the most serious price problem for most of the commodities for which ICAs were *not* created has been falling real prices, not instability. A decline in constant prices occurred over 1960–85 for iron ore, manganese ore, phosphate rock, copper, bananas, tea, sisal, jute, and cotton. Several of these experienced significant price instability during certain periods as well.[28] The downward real price trends for tea, jute, cotton, copper, and phosphate rock in the late 1970s help to explain the interest shown by some producers in ICAs during the IPC meetings. The increase in constant prices for bauxite and tropical timber, on the other hand, was a key reason behind the absence of concerted producer pressure to establish ICAs for these two commodities.

The most important factor influencing the policies of Third World producers toward regulation of particular markets is the perceived compatibility of regulatory provisions with their goals on *output* and *market shares*. Low-cost producers, confident about their future market prospects, tend to oppose international regulation because they are better able to weather periods of low and unstable prices, and because they wish to avoid being locked into existing market shares. Conversely, high-cost producers, especially if they are worried about suffering reductions in market shares, are apt to be strong proponents of ICAs with export quotas. For mineral commodities, the reserve positions of various producers will affect their attitude toward regulation. Countries enjoying abundant reserves are likely to be more interested in long-term market expansion and less oriented toward maximizing immediate returns than those with declining or small reserves.[29]

The way in which divergent production costs and concerns about market shares can combine to thwart producers' efforts to reach a consensus on a commodity control scheme is well illustrated by the case of copper. Chile enjoys the largest reserves and lowest production costs, while Peru has sizable reserves and production costs almost as low. On both criteria, Zaire and Zambia fare rather poorly. Chile has consistently opposed export quotas, and Peru supported Chile until the late 1970s, when Chile embarked on a large expansion scheme. Zambia and Zaire, in contrast, have always been receptive to export control schemes.

The IPC deliberations on manganese ore witnessed a conflict between Gabon and Brazil (and to a lesser extent other producers) over the former's desire to create an ICA that would protect its market share at a time when its production costs were rising. Brazil, a low-cost producer with large reserves, did not share Gabon's outlook on the market. The supporters of an ICA for phosphate rock—mainly such African producers as Algeria, Tunisia, and Togo—were also motivated by a desire to protect their market shares from incursions by Morocco, which enjoys substantially larger reserves and lower costs of production. Quite expectedly, Morocco showed no interest in their proposal, and even refused to attend the IPC meetings.

Tin, the only mineral for which an ICA has been created, provides an interesting comparison to the commodities discussed above. Until the 1980s four exporters dominated the market. Malaysia, Thailand, and Indonesia, all with roughly comparable production costs and reasonably stable shares, coordinated their policies toward the International Tin Agreement. The fourth major producer, Bolivia, faced steeper production costs and lower reserves and thus sought higher price ranges than the other producers. However, Bolivia hesitated to scuttle the ITA because the agreement provided some price support and protection for its market share. With the beginning of the sixth ITA in 1982, interproducer differences intensified and finally led to the demise of the agreement. Increased exports by two traditional nonmembers (China and especially Brazil), combined with Bolivia's refusal to join for fear of having its exports reduced, brought about an increasing problem of oversupply and then the ITA's collapse in the fall of 1985.

Conflicts over market shares were also evident in the case of several agricultural commodities. The unwillingness of Kenya and various East African tea-producing countries to curtail their expanding exports, coupled with Sri Lanka and India's desire to stabilize market shares, has been a constant source of tension in international tea negotiations. Kenya was largely responsible for the breakdown of the informal FAO regulatory arrangement in 1969. Its vigorous opposition to quotas during the UNCTAD talks in the late 1970s and early 1980s, stemming from the quadrupling of its market share since 1961 and its intention to expand production further, prevented agreement on an ICA.

International negotiations on sisal in the 1960s and 1970s also testify to the potency of interproducer conflicts over market shares. Here the main protagonists were Tanzania, which wanted an export quota arrangement, and Brazil, which opposed the idea. Brazil's lower production costs and rapidly growing output have caused it to reject any scheme by which the international market is divided up on the basis of past export performance. It undermined an FAO quota arrangement for sisal and henequen in 1968–69 by exceeding its assigned quota, and then in the late 1970s resisted attempts by Tanzania and several smaller exporters with declining or stagnant market shares to negotiate an ICA.

In the negotiations on commodities for which ICAs have been created, conflicts also often occurred among developing producers over market shares. In the case of sugar, coffee, and cocoa before 1980, such conflicts were generally resolved because of widespread fears of market collapse and the willingness of developed consuming countries to exclude or limit imports. With regard to coffee, interproducer differences did, however, lead to a failure to reintroduce quotas in early 1987. The cases of natural rubber under the 1979 agreement and cocoa under the 1980 agreement are somewhat different because both excluded export quotas and relied on buffer stocks. Competition for shares of the export market could not have a strong effect on states' support for such ICAs because they do not limit foreign sales. In the 1986 cocoa agreement a whole new element was introduced with the creation of a withholding scheme (i.e., obligations by producers to store cocoa when the market price is near the floor of the range). Such a scheme could influence producing states' willingness to join an international commodity agreement, since it will affect volumes of exports and thus market shares. The withholding requirements have not, however, deterred almost all the key cocoa producers from accepting the 1986 ICCA.

Another consideration affecting the policies of producers toward commodity agreements is their judgment of the *sanctions* that may result if a scheme is rejected. Sanctions may originate with consumers or with other producers. The chief sanction available to producers is the threat to flood the market and thus drive down prices. This strategy is only available to large producers in oligopolistic positions who have the stocks, and usually the financial resources, to embark on such a punitive course. Both Cuba during the sugar negotiations of the 1950s and Brazil during coffee talks in the 1960s had the ability to make good on this threat. In the case of tin and, even more so, rubber, Malaysia's prominence as an exporter may have caused some other Third World producers to think carefully before opposing regulatory provisions favored by Malaysia.

Some of the most influential threats of sanctions for nonadherence have originated with consuming states prepared to stand behind an ICA. The 1962 coffee agreement, for example, probably would not have won the reluctant support of African producers if the United States had not explicitly threatened to deprive nonsignatories of access to its market. Consuming-country signatories to ICAs have often been willing to undertake obligations to exclude, or more commonly to limit, imports from nonmember producing states. This unquestionably has encouraged some producers to accept the coffee and sugar agreements.

A final judgment affecting the willingness of producers to negotiate ICAs is the perceived feasibility of *alternative market-regulation strategies,* especially the establishment of a successful producer association or cartel. Producers generally would prefer to regulate a market on their own rather than complicate matters by dealing with consumers. Frequently, however, they encounter the unfortunate truth that consuming countries are needed to help enforce compliance with rules, and sometimes to provide financial resources for the operation of the accord. For many of the commodities examined in this book, Third World producers seriously considered an ICA only after producer collaboration had been tried and failed.

Failures of producer collaboration have frequently preceded the conclusion and renewal of ICAs. In the case of coffee there were unsuccessful cartels prior to the 1962, 1975, and 1982 agreements, and the same was true for cocoa before the 1972 and 1980 ICCAs. Cooperation among sugar producers has always been viewed as difficult because of the large number of sugar-growing states. The major attempt at producer collaboration, which occurred in the mid-1960s when the ISA was suspended, quickly failed and drove producers back to the bargaining table with consumers. The price-support scheme of natural rubber producers in 1976 (the Jakarta plan) was accompanied by a statement of interest in an ICA—indicating doubts about the success of producer-only action.

Looking briefly at some of the commodities for which ICAs were *not* accepted, interest in some form of producer-consumer accord was also often stimulated by the failure of producer cooperation. For example, CIPEC's inability in 1974–75 to stem the precipitous decline in copper prices through its export control scheme led LDC producers to focus their efforts on talks with consumers under UNCTAD's auspices. Producer-only deliberations on control schemes occurred for bananas and iron ore before the IPC meetings. In both instances, producers' inability to agree on export controls heightened interest in a producer-consumer accord.

The factors discussed above have shaped the views of producers concerning the possible creation of commodity agreements. It is also worth considering briefly *producers' evaluations of the impact of different regulatory measures*. LDC commodity producers have usually favored the inclusion of export quotas in ICAs, since the only effective role of such quotas is to protect floor prices. All the agreements analyzed in this book contained export-quota provisions until the United States pressured other conference participants to exclude quotas during the 1979 rubber and 1980 cocoa conferences. With respect to buffer stocks, most LDC producers have appreciated their influence in maintaining prices above floor levels—especially when the costs are borne equally by consumers. But because stocks can be used to moderate price increases as well as declines and also require financial contributions, producers have not always been enthusiastic about them. Fears that buffer stocks could "overhang" the market, and concerns over the costs of stock purchases and storage, have typically sufficed to convince producers that stocks should be kept small. It is noteworthy that when the United States proposed during the IPC copper negotiations that a huge and very expensive pure buffer-stock scheme be considered, LDC producers reacted very negatively, as did developed producers such as Canada and Australia. The high costs and potential price-depressing effects of a large buffer stock were uppermost in their minds.[30] During the rubber and cocoa negotiations in 1979–80, LDC producers also inveighed against the big buffer stocks initially advocated by the United States. Eventually they succeeded in convincing Washington to accept smaller stocks.

Developed-country critics of LDC policies toward ICAs are correct when they suggest that most Third World producers are really interested in protecting floor rather than ceiling prices. Given their vulnerability to external shocks and their long-standing search for ways to stabilize global markets, it would be surprising if LDC exporters were not preoccupied with guaranteeing minimum prices. Beyond this, Third World commodity producers have normally sought as high a price range as possible. A pervasive theme in the history of virtually all ICAs has been the producer-consumer struggle over the price levels to be written into agreements. During periods when market prices are above the ceiling of an ICA range, producers usually argue that the buoyant market will continue and that the range should be raised to reflect this. The almost inevitable cycles of commodity markets often prove these assessments wrong.

The above analysis casts doubts on assertions that Third World unity has been "robust" and that all developing countries' policies "are antithetical to those that inform liberal regimes."[31] Third World states often adopt consensual positions on matters of general policy, but when negotiations focus on specific regulations that could significantly affect their national economic well-being, this unity tends to fracture. Often LDCs do not perceive themselves as having identical interests, and only rarely are they willing to make sacrifices on behalf of fellow Third World nations. Nor do they always seek to dismantle the liberal elements of the international economic order. Instead, their general normative proposals usually envisage modifications of that order to allow greater wealth redistribution through intergovernmental intervention into markets. During negotiations on individual commodities, some developing countries have openly espoused the cause of free competition and the survival of the fittest. As Robert Rothstein has noted, both the IPC and the entire basket of proposals included in the New International Economic Order sought to promote Third World development both by working within existing regimes and by modifying them.[32]

A final point warrants mention. Considerable stress has been put on the conflicts among LDC commodity producers with respect to actual or potential agreements for specific commodities. This contrasts with the relative harmony prevailing within the G77 on broader questions of regime change. The distinction between the two realms, and particularly the importance of interproducer differences, has been drawn rather sharply in order to highlight the chasm that often separates the vague rhetoric of Third World unity from the complex patterns of conflict and cooperation that characterize developing countries' approaches to more concrete, issue-specific negotiations.

While we believe the divisions among LDC commodity producers deserve more attention than they have received in much of the literature on North-South relations, we most definitely do *not* mean to suggest that the absence of such differences would have led to the successful negotiation of a host of new commodity agreements. Even if Third World countries had been united in favoring ICAs for many commodities, opposition from developed states would have thwarted their efforts in many cases.

DEVELOPED COUNTRIES AND BARGAINING OUTCOMES

Norms and General Rules of the Commodity Trade Regime

This chapter has highlighted the durability of a consensus within the Third World on the major proposals to transform the postwar global commodity regime. Unfortunately for the developing countries, their unified position has not yielded them much in the way of tangible results, even during the period of intense commodity diplomacy in the 1970s. Third World advocacy of new principles and norms has been consistently rebuffed by the developed capitalist countries, often joined by the communist states. Only rarely did the Third World successfully challenge aspects of the regime. Even then the changes agreed to have not really altered its basic normative character, which largely continues to reflect the noninterventionist, market-oriented philosophy originally enshrined in the commodity chapter of the Havana Charter. In what follows, the fate of the developing world's demands is reviewed and some reasons for the negotiating results are adduced.

Bargaining Outcomes. Two central issues on which the developing countries have sought normative changes are, first, the market conditions that should prompt the formation of ICAs and, second, the price objectives of these ICAs. The Third World has failed to dislodge the industrialized nations from the position that only severe price instability and producer hardship justify the creation of ICAs. The developed countries have rejected the view that all instances of price instability require intergovernmental intervention. They have displayed an even more hostile stance toward the proposition that a decline in real prices requires intergovernmental market regulation.

The industrialized states accepted the norm that ICAs should promote price stabilization at the time of the Havana Charter negotiations. Since the late 1940s, and especially during the last half of the 1970s, the developing countries sought "an increased share of income generated by existing wealth, to be achieved through higher prices for commodity exports."[33] They suggested that ICAs should aim at assuring LDC producers a higher level of economic development and stable purchasing power. By and large the developed countries have regarded LDC price-policy proposals as virtually nonnegotiable.[34] They have been willing to accept price levels that are "remunerative to producers," but only when qualified with "equitable to consumers" and other phrases indicating a basic respect for market forces (e.g., prices should not be so high as "to encourage structural over-supply, resort to substitute products, or economies of use").[35] At times the G77 was able to have references to indexation written into UNCTAD resolutions, but often the relevant provisions were qualified by the inclusion of market-oriented objectives and were later opposed by some of the Group B states in separate statements.[36] The intransigence of the developed states on this matter did not rule out their occasional support for ICAs that promoted higher prices. As a matter of principle, however, they would not offer across-the-board endorsement for such a policy.

The closest the Third World came to convincing the developed countries to use ICAs as resource-transfer mechanisms was when the latter agreed to provide financial assistance to ICA buffer-stock funds. In 1969 Group B's support for the IMF's Buffer Stock Financing Facility, which provides low-interest loans to countries contributing to ICA buffer-stock funds, signaled a small step toward the G77 position. Then, in the context of the Common Fund negotiations, all Group B states finally accepted joint producer-consumer financing of ICA buffer stocks. They refused, however, to go beyond the principle of equal cost-sharing when they rejected the "source model" for the fund.

The G77 has also demanded that the developed states take steps to discourage the manufacture of synthetics that compete with LDC exports of natural products. The South has registered absolutely no progress on this issue. The industrialized countries have supported research into the production and marketing of natural products in order to boost LDC exports. But they have resolutely rejected any international controls on the development and manufacture of cheaper and better synthetic substitutes.

One issue of general principle on which the LDCs have achieved some success is compensation for shortfalls in commodity export earnings. This was largely as a result of the creation of the IMF's Compensatory Financing Facility in 1963 and the subsequent revisions of it. The CFF provides short-term loans at below-market rates to countries experiencing shortfalls in export earnings that lead to balance-of-payments deficits. Contrary to what the G77 has requested, the CFF does *not* cover shortfalls specifically in commodity export earnings —although commodities tend to be the dominant exports of most LDCs. The sums available under the IMF scheme have not been of the magnitude sought or needed by the Third World. However, the substantial amounts dispersed since the mid-1970s have provided significant assistance to many LDCs. Recent attempts to negotiate a well-funded "globalized STABEX" that would provide compensation for the total of shortfalls in commodity export earnings in *real* terms have been thwarted by the opposition of several key industrialized countries.

The LDCs have made modest progress in increasing their influence in universal international organizations concerned with commodity policy. The creation of UNCTAD afforded the South greater control of the international agenda pertaining to commodity issues. But because UNCTAD resolutions are nonbinding, and because legally binding treaties formulated at special conferences still require the acceptance of each party, the South cannot use its voting strength to force the North to accept its proposals. The G77's major victory in this area was the adoption of the Common Fund treaty in 1980, which granted the G77 47 percent of the votes, compared with 42 percent for Group B. Nonetheless, since the biggest Group B members together retain an effective veto over important decisions, the increase in Third World decision-making power is perhaps more apparent than real.

Another G77 "success" was the demise of the norm against producer cartels. From the Havana Charter negotiations until the early 1970s, the developed countries argued that unilateral producer intervention in markets was contrary to international law, even though they did not really react against collaboration among tea and coffee producers in the 1950s, and tolerated the existence of OPEC in the 1960s. Whatever vestige of illegitimacy may have attached to producer collaboration disappeared in the 1970s with the passage of UN resolutions supporting the legitimacy of cartels, the success of OPEC, the proliferation of other attempts by LDC producers to regulate commodity markets, and the revelations about the secret uranium cartel developed by key industrialized countries. Third World countries were able to undermine the Havana Charter norm concerning producer collaboration because, unlike the issues discussed above, the elimination of this constraining norm did *not* require either an explicit decision by Group B to accept a transfer of resources or its formal approval of a new policy in an international body. Maintenance of the norm proscribing producer cartels would have required that the industrialized countries apply sanctions against LDC producers to force them to abandon their efforts, and this they were unable or unwilling to do.

Explanation of Outcomes. This pattern of negotiating results on regime norms portrays the South's limited achievements after almost four decades of global commodity bargaining. Explaining these outcomes is relatively straightforward: the principal explanatory factors are the attitudes and bargaining power of the developed capitalist states. Although the latter have made some concessions to the Third World, on the whole they have resisted the basic thrust of key LDC proposals. This thrust has been that the developed nations should transfer large-scale resources to Third World countries. LDCs have based this claim on grounds of both morality and mutual interest, but they have not made significant progress. In this respect it might be argued that the Northern countries have attached little importance to the development or wealth-distribution principle in shaping the commodity regime. For Third World countries, on the other hand, "the development objective was not only added to the other aims of commodity agreements but, in fact, became the most important."[37]

All the general reform proposals that were turned down outright involved large-scale direct or indirect transfers of financial resources to developing producers. Where the West exhibited some willingness to reform the prevailing regime, minor financial outlays were involved. The developed countries were, for the most part, very sensitive to "the bottom line," and when they agreed to anything, it was usually a scaled-down version of what producers had demanded.

When the OECD nations accepted some modifications in the general regime guidelines, it had little to do with the "resource power" of Third World countries or their ability to withhold exports needed by the developed world. Rather, the industrialized nations viewed complete intransigence as a politically unwise response that might court a serious political confrontation with at least the more radical developing countries. They did not want to create feelings of hostility and alienation that could spill over into a number of international realms. Moreover, the rhetoric of interdependence regularly espoused by Western leaders would have sat uncomfortably alongside unambiguous failure in commodity diplomacy, particularly since the G77 had placed so much emphasis on commodity trade during its quest for a NIEO. Better, then, to compromise on some issues and to agree to those elements of the Third World's reform package most compatible with the continued operation of competitive markets and requiring minimal financial outlays to global commodity organizations.[38]

In explaining the positions of the developed countries toward LDC proposals, it is worth pointing out that they were not and are not a monolithic group. Some Group B countries exerted considerable pressure toward compromise. The Scandinavian countries and the Netherlands, the so-called like-minded states, were favorably predisposed toward many NIEO proposals. Norway, in particular, regularly pressed for Group B concessions in the 1970s. In the eyes of one observer, it hoped to achieve nothing less than "a future world welfare state displaying two related goals: effective international management of world markets and fair distribution of the goods produced in the international economic system." However, many of its Group B colleagues saw Norway more as a "progressive free rider" than a "devoted internationalist."[39] France also at times took positions sympathetic to LDC demands. It had long argued that "the prices of commodities should not be solely governed by the law of supply and demand." France was also influenced by the views of the African states.[40] Sensitivity to the concerns of former colonies also affected British policy, and Britain's support for a modified Common Fund in 1977 unquestionably had an impact on the American posture. The "like-minded" countries and, more important, France and Britain occasionally convinced the United States, West Germany, and Japan to adopt more accommodating positions. It would be wrong, however, to conclude that any of the major Western powers were ever prepared "to give away the store."[41] With the partial exception of the 1974–75 period, the divisions among the major developed nations on key NIEO issues were not deep enough to undermine agreement on common strategies.[42] And during the mid-1980s the European countries drew closer to the American position that ICAs should not seek to raise price trends but rather be limited to stabilization. This was clearly illustrated during the sugar, cocoa, and natural rubber negotiations during the years 1983–87.

Other factors affecting negotiating outcomes included differences within the G77 and within individual LDC governments, although these were not as important as the preferences and policies of the industrialized states. As was noted previously, most G77 members opposed to general regime changes believed that "pro forma adherence to essentially rhetorical principles [was] a small price to pay for remaining in [the] good graces of the Group of 77."[43] Some LDCs (especially the newly industrialized countries) never really shared the overall antimarket, interventionist bias of most of the G77 and paid little more than lip service to most G77 positions. The developed countries unquestionably were aware of this, and thus felt they could afford to be less concerned about alienating the Third World by rejecting G77 positions.

Another reason for the relative lack of concern felt by many Group B states stemmed from their perception of a gap between the stated policies of LDC spokesmen at North-South conferences and the real policies of their governments in Third World capitals. Relevant to this point is Robert Rothstein's report of the results of a survey of Third World governments conducted by the U.S. State Department:

There is persuasive evidence that the Dialogue looks considerably different from Lima, Accra, or New Delhi than it does from Geneva or New York. In the majority of developing countries . . . the government elites in the capital know very little about the substance of the Dialogue and in some cases are not even aware of the implications for themselves of the proposals in debate. In part, this reflects technical capacity, but perhaps in greater part it reflects the feeling of most of the elites that the meaning of the Dialogue is essentially political and symbolic—talking on equal terms with the developed countries symbolizes the new status of the South. For tangible economic returns, virtually all elites surveyed put primary (and in some cases exclusive) emphasis on bilateral relationships with various developed countries.[44]

Rothstein suggests that Western governments were made aware of the "real" views and expectations of many developing-country governments through private communications and information transmitted on a direct capital-to-capital basis (i.e., not channeled through UN or UNCTAD diplomats involved in the commodity discussions). A perception that the true position of those in charge differed from what was being heard in Geneva or New York led the developed countries to be more sanguine about the consequences of negotiating outcomes far removed from what the G77 was "officially" demanding.[45]

A theme underlying much of the discussion so far is the Third World's inability to challenge successfully the basic norms of the global commodity regime. Only the LDC oil producers were in control of a commodity of sufficient importance to the developed world that they could, for a time at least, have wielded real power on behalf of fundamental transformation. However, for the most part the OPEC countries were unwilling to follow this course, despite much rhetoric to the contrary. They were apparently satisfied that the commodity discussions of the 1970s led to the de facto acceptance of producer cartels. Third World oil producers were not prepared to take concrete actions to bring about major regime changes that would substantially benefit the majority of Third World primary commodity exporters.

Individual Commodity Negotiations

In international negotiations on specific commodities, both the subjects that arose and the approaches adopted by the participants were typically quite different from the bargaining over general policy. As one observer has remarked, even during the highly charged IPC discussions "The negotiations on individual commodity agreements . . . tended to display less political posturing than the Common Fund dialogue . . . to be attended by delegates and advisers relatively more familiar with commodity-market problems, and to be influenced more by economic as opposed to political bargaining positions."[46] Thus, while UN and UNCTAD debates and resolutions on general normative and programmatic issues have exerted some influence over individual commodity negotiations, the latter generally have remained quite distinct.

Bargaining Outcomes. Previous chapters have documented the rather meager results of postwar producer-consumer negotiations on individual commodities. Of the six mineral commodities examined above, only tin has had an ICA, and even it collapsed in 1985. Of the twelve agricultural commodities, price-regulating ICAs have been established for just four—sugar (1953), coffee (1962), cocoa (1972), and natural rubber (1979). The sugar agreement was suspended from 1962–68 and 1973–77, and again in 1985. The same was true of the coffee accord in 1973–75. In addition, during certain periods all these agreements were inoperative because the market price was outside the official price range.

There are eight agricultural commodities examined above for which ICAs have not been negotiated. For two of these, jute and hard fibers, informal nonbinding agreements, concluded through the FAO, existed during part of the period since the mid-1960s, but they have had little impact on market developments. The other six agricultural commodities were discussed within both the FAO and UNCTAD. With the exception of tea, there was never much possiblility of reaching a producer-consumer agreement. The negotiations on hard fibers, jute, cotton, tea, and bananas did at times entertain serious proposals for ICAs, but the same cannot be said for those on meat, tropical timber, or oils and oilseeds. Negotiations on a number of these commodities are continuing, but they are now focused on such questions as information exchange and development projects rather than on price regulation at the international level.

Explanation of Bargaining Outcomes. For some commodities disagreements among LDC commodity producers were sufficient to undermine the possibility of an ICA—regardless of the positions taken by the developed countries. For oils and oilseeds, tropical timber, beef, bauxite, and to a large extent iron ore, Third World producers displayed little interest in ICAs. On phosphate rock, manganese, copper, tea, sisal, bananas, and also sugar (between 1961 and 1967) the divisions among producers on either the desirability or the preferred character of an ICA were such that agreement probably would not have been reached even if the majority of developed states had been willing to go along. In the case of cotton, a few minor cotton producers opposed market regulation, while a larger group did not explicitly express their views. On jute, however, there was outward agreement among the major producing parties.

The major explanations for bargaining outcomes concern the policies of the developed states and the bargaining power of LDCs. Few indeed are the developed countries who have actively lobbied for the creation of ICAs for any of the thirteen commodities discussed in chapter 5 for which agreements were not reached. Developed-country opposition to international regulatory agreements for the five mineral commodities—bauxite, iron ore, manganese ore, phosphate rock, and copper—was quite strong. For a short time the United States was willing to discuss the possiblility of a pure buffer-stock scheme for copper, but the other major developed states did not share this view.

Of the eight agricultural commodities for which accords were never reached, Group B took an even more negative position than the LDC producers in the discussions on oils and oilseeds, tropical timber, and beef; took strong exception to the positions of most LDC producers on cotton, sisal, and jute; and (excluding the United States) espoused neutral or only moderately skeptical views on bananas and tea. With respect to sisal and jute, the developed states' main criticisms focused on the producers' desire to include manufactured products within an ICA, and on the practicability of regulating the price for a product that had closely competing synthetics. During the IPC talks the commodity that the developed countries felt was most suited to an ICA was tea, although there were reservations about certain LDC proposals.

The negotiations on the five ICA commodities have also witnessed serious conflicts between developed countries and Third World producers. The refusal of key consuming countries to accept price ranges as high as those being sought by LDC exporters led to the demise of the sugar and coffee agreements on various occasions and made it impossible to conclude an accord for cocoa until 1972. Sharp conflicts occurred from the late 1970s through the mid-1980s over demands by developing producers for the inclusion of export quotas in ICAs. Quotas were excluded from the 1979/1987 rubber and 1980/1986 cocoa agreements; and differences over their desirability and character were partly responsible for the demise of the sugar accord in 1984. What this brief overview of developed-country policies indicates is that even if all Third World producers had wanted ICAs for all the commodities discussed above, such proposals would frequently have been vetoed by the industrialized nations.

As with LDC policies, those of the developed countries have been shaped by several major judgments. The question of an ICA's *feasibility* is obviously as important for them as for Third World countries. In fact, the developed states tend to have an even gloomier view of the impediments to international regulation posed by such factors as the multiplicity of grades, the existence of substitutes, and the absence of open international exchanges. Other salient considerations for the industrialized nations relate to the implications of ICAs for: their own commodity exports industries, the cost of their imports, the adequacy of future investment in an industry, the general performance of their economies (particularly as regards inflation), domestic and informal international stabilization arrangements, and their broader political and foreign policy interests vis-à-vis the Third World.

A major reason why some industrialized nations have opposed international commodity agreements is that they are *exporters of the commodities in question* and fear that regulatory schemes would have a negative impact on their positions as exporters. Several factors may contribute to this belief. First, unlike the majority of Third World exporters, capitalist and communist developed countries usually depend on a given commodity for only a tiny fraction of their export earnings, employment, government revenues, and aggregate economic activity. Governments are unlikely to view market instability or falling international prices for a particular commodity as a threat to their overall national economic welfare, or indeed even as an urgent problem. Thus, incentives to seek international regulation are weak. Exceptions to this generalization can, of course, be found. Both Canada and the United States, for example, at times favored an ICA for wheat in order to lessen instability and protect prices for a commodity critical to the agricultural sector of their domestic economies.[47] Still, the broad picture indicates that industrial-country commodity exporters are much less vulnerable to the vicissitudes of international markets than are the vast majority of Third World primary commodity suppliers.

A second reason for the reluctance of the developed capitalist countries in particular to participate as exporters in ICAs flows from the hostility of their domestic industries and corporations to such agreements. Although developed countries have a long history of both extensive government regulation of many commodity industries—notably in agriculture—and officially sanctioned commodity cartels and ententes of various sorts, business interests normally have opposed participation in intergovernmental regulatory accords. They have often viewed ICAs as harbingers of greater control by their own governments over their commercial activities.

The most important reason that developed exporters oppose ICAs is their fear that they will be pressured by Third World members to bear the brunt of any required export cutbacks to prevent hardships for LDC producers. This fear is not unfounded. At UNCTAD III in 1972, for example, India called on developed iron ore producers to desist from expanding production and to refrain from actions detrimental to the competitive position of India and other Third World exporters.[48] Similarly, during the IPC talks on cotton, developing-country producers "argued that responsibility for assuming obligations under an agreement lay with the big producers, such as the United States and the Soviet Union. Developed country producers . . . were, according to their view, responsible for market price fluctuations and should bear the burden of adjustment and the cost of any control programme."[49] This factor was taken into account by Canada when the question of affiliating with the copper-producers' association, CIPEC, arose in the 1970s, and again during the IPC negotiations on that commodity.[50] It is also instructive in this context that the European Community has stayed out of the sugar agreements since 1968 because of government and industry opposition to export restrictions.

This attitude has not been solely restricted to capitalist countries; it has also influenced the policies of the Soviet Union. As the second largest cotton exporter, it joined the United States in opposing the proposal for a cotton agreement supported by the majority of developing-country producers during IPC talks. Nor did the Soviets lend support to the attempts of some LDC producers to establish ICAs for iron ore, manganese, or phosphates—commodities for which it then accounted for about 10 percent of global sales. While the Soviets and their allies have offered ample rhetorical support for Third World efforts to refashion both the global commodity regime and other areas of international economic policy, they typically have adopted hard nosed, conservative positions when the time has come for concrete bargaining. As one critic has put it, the Soviet approach involves "backing the poor on matters of high principle and the rich on matters of substance."[51]

As the major consumers of LDC exports, an obvious concern of the developed countries has been the *impact of international agreements on commodity prices*. While some literature posits that consuming countries will benefit from commodity stabilization agreements in certain circumstances,[52] the developed countries have not shown much faith in this theory, mainly because of their skepticism about the ability of such agreements to protect ceiling prices. They recognize that LDCs are overwhelmingly concerned with increasing price levels and obtaining guaranteed floor prices. In practice, once an agreement begins to operate, any sharp increase in prices will galvanize LDC producers to exert pressure to raise the price range in order to "capture" the market. Conversely, if prices fall toward or through the floor, this will generate LDC demands for action to support the floor through quota cuts or buffer-stock purchases. Any suggestion of a downward adjustment of a previously agreed price range is fiercely resisted by Third World exporters. Moreover, the majority of commodity pacts—both before World War II and since then—have been better equipped to support floor than ceiling price levels. While the members of an agreement can always mandate export cuts to boost market prices, it is much more problematic whether they can successfully order that output or sales be increased to protect a ceiling, particularly once full quotas have been reached.

A buffer stock can, of course, strengthen an ICA's ability to dampen price rises, but most of the agreements that have been negotiated or even seriously considered (at least before the late 1970s) have relied wholly or primarily on export controls. And the record of the tin agreement does not lend much support to the notion that ICAs with a buffer stock are effective in protecting ceiling prices. It was basically periodic sales of U.S. surplus tin, not the ITA buffer stock, that played the major role in moderating rising prices.[53] The 1979/87 natural rubber and 1980/86 cocoa agreements, which have buffer stocks and no export controls, have not had their ability to control escalating prices tested because of the very depressed prices of the early 1980s. In sum, it must be concluded that the developed countries have sound reasons to question the likelihood that ICAs will actually improve their welfare through "price stabilization."

Developed countries have at times concluded that price stabilization would *encourage needed investment* in new capacity and hence provide a more stable flow of supplies to consumers. This is especially true for two ICA commodities—tin and natural rubber. For several decades few new significant deposits of tin were brought into production, and consuming states worried that additional investment for exploration and development was needed.[54] (This belief has disappeared in the situation of oversupply of the mid-1980s.) Several importing countries saw the ITA as a useful device for spurring investment in the tin industry.[55] Developed-country members of the Tin Council regularly agreed to increase the price range of the agreement, at least partly on the strength of producing countries' claims that the costs of production had risen to the point where marginal capacity would be lost and new investments precluded. With respect to natural rubber, the major developed countries participating in the UNCTAD negotiations in the late 1970s evidently believed that an ICA would increase investment and boost supply by moderating price fluctuations and providing a minimum price guarantee.[56] The fact that the price of petroleum-based feedstocks used to produce synthetic rubbers increased sharply during the 1970s made importers of natural rubber more sensitive to the need to promote investment.

Another alleged economic benefit of ICAs for importing states is *their impact on inflation* and inflationary expectations. This argument did not become prominent in international commodity diplomacy until the 1970s, a time of escalating inflation throughout the Western world. According to some economists, oligopolistic market forces in developed countries work both to increase the prices of many goods by more than the inflation rate of commodity inputs and then to reduce the prices of final goods during an economic downturn by less than the rate at which commodity prices are declining. "In this way, primary-commodity price increases may cause a ratchet-type inflation that has long-term unfavourable effects on developed countries. . . . "[57] Exponents of this view posit that price-stabilization agreements will dampen price increases and hence inflation.

As was mentioned above, there is little evidence that developed-country negotiators have been convinced that commodity agreements offer significant protection against price increases. Nonetheless, the "ratchet effect" argument did become part of the intellectual arsenal of some American officials anxious to see their government take a more positive approach to ICAs in the 1970s. Both C. Fred Bergsten and Richard Cooper, two influential figures in the Carter administration responsible for economic relations with the Third World, accepted the ratchet thesis, although it did not have much currency elsewhere.[58] U.S. officials involved in forming American commodity policy hoped that the ratchet thesis would prove helpful in seeking to convince a skeptical Congress of the wisdom of affiliating with a larger number of ICAs. Other Western governments, less hostile to international commodity schemes than the United States, did not pay much attention to this argument in formulating policies after 1973. And as memories of the extraordinary 1972–74 boom in commodity prices faded, references to the ratchet effect grew less frequent.

Other factors that deserve mention here are the *existence of nongovernmental mechanisms for international market stabilization* and *the impact of domestic pricing and export schemes.* Developed-country governments have often benefited from the fact that multinational corporations based in their countries are powerful actors in many commodity markets. Both corporations and governments are interested in commodity market stability and in assured supplies of needed raw materials. "For political leaders in advanced importing states, the basic objective of raw materials policy is to avoid the unexpected, not to maximize economic welfare through perfect competition."[59] This is particularly true for minerals such as bauxite.[60] Through such devices as long-term contracts, transfer pricing mechanisms internal to vertically integrated firms, and the ownership of foreign supplier industries, multinational companies have structured international commodity markets to provide stability and guaranteed supplies for developed importing countries. Their ability to do so has attenuated the need for formal, intergovernmental agreements in the eyes of many Western governments (and some from the developing world as well). Some analysts argue that the strength and control of multinational resource firms operating in the Third World has been declining, and that this trend is eroding their ability to stabilize commodity markets.[61] This may eventually lessen the stability of markets for mineral commodities such as bauxite and iron ore, which traditionally have been subject to control by large firms and thus experienced fairly stable prices.

Informal agreements among private firms in an oligopolistic industry can also help to stabilize domestic markets. Until the late 1970s, for example, a "two-price" system for copper existed. Prices outside the North American market were determined by trading activity on the London Metals Exchange, while the oligopolistic U.S. copper industry operated a producer price system. As a result, copper prices in the United States—to whose market Canadian copper producers enjoyed easy access—were far less volatile than those determined on the LME.[62] In this situation, neither American nor Canadian copper producers were affected by international market instability to the same extent as LDC exporters, and thus they were less disposed to favor international regulation.

National price support, subsidy, and import quota schemes in the developed states have also affected perceptions of the need for international regulation. As long as domestic producers are assured of minimum prices or subsidies by governments, they are unlikely to see much need for global stabilization. This has generally been the case for European and American sugar producers, and for U.S. cotton growers as well. Government financial assistance to farmers is pervasive in developed countries. Domestic import-quota schemes, such as those maintained by the United States and the European Community for sugar, also reduce political support for ICAs, since they allow the developed countries to assist particular producing states whose economic well-being and goodwill are very important to them. These national programs, as well as informal international stabilization arrangements, can serve as surrogates for formal ICAs.

The evident weakness of the various economic arguments in support of developed-country participation in ICAs begs the question of what actually has motivated the North to participate in certain regulatory schemes. Examination of postwar commodity diplomacy suggests that support for ICAs has been determined mainly by *political and broad foreign policy considerations*. Concern over the political consequences of price instability and, more particularly, of very low and declining commodity prices has sometimes convinced developed countries of the need for international action to assist Third World exporters.

Fisher's study of the International Coffee Agreement, for example, lays bare Washington's deep concern about potential communist inroads in Latin America if the extremely depressed coffee market were allowed to collapse.[63] In the absence of this overriding foreign policy consideration, it is doubtful that the United States would have agreed to the ICFA and given such strong support to it since the early 1960s. U.S. concern about relations with Latin American sugar producing states was also central to its support for several sugar agreements. And, likewise, its desire to maintain amicable ties with Southeast Asian countries influenced it to join the natural rubber accord and to collaborate tacitly with the Tin Council in supporting a floor price for tin. Conversely, in the case of cocoa, which is primarily produced in West Africa, the United States has rarely demonstrated much interest in taking part in an ICA and has been quite indifferent to the political consequences of its nonparticipation. Economic and political relations with Latin American countries, and to a lesser extent with Southeast Asian states, have loomed larger in U.S. policymaking than have relations with African commodity producers.

While the United States has sometimes refused to join ICAs, the Western European states, Canada, Japan, and most other developed countries have participated in almost all the postwar commodity agreements. They have seen these agreements as a relatively inexpensive way to demonstrate goodwill and to promote good political relations with the Third World. The major exception—the failure of the European Community to join recent sugar agreements—is explained by the potency of its countervailing interest as a large and growing *exporter.*

For the Western Europeans, close historical ties to many commodity-exporting LDCs often have persuaded them to adopt an accommodating stance. As L. N. Rangarajan observes, compared to the United States, "the Community's approach . . . is generally less dogmatic and doctrinal and more pragmatically oriented towards finding specific solutions. The reason is historical association."[64] In the case of two long-standing ICAs, those for tin and sugar, many of the producing countries were still under colonial rule when the first postwar agreements were negotiated. With regard to cocoa, France's desire to maintain strong economic and political links with French-speaking West Africa has underpinned European backing for an accord. Not all community members have been equally sympathetic to ICAs for commodities produced by former European colonies. West Germany has adopted a more skeptical view toward commodity agreements than most of its European allies, and in many respects its policies have mirrored those of the United States. Like the United States, West Germany generally prefers to examine the merits of proposed ICAs primarily by assessing their economic impact and feasibility, rather than simply their political or foreign policy appeal.[65] Occasionally, however, it has muted its economic criticisms under pressure from other European states in order to facilitate the development of a common community policy.

The divergences among the main developed commodity-importing countries should not be exaggerated, however. It is true that the United States has refrained from joining ICAs of which its Western allies have been signatories. Yet in many ways *all* the developed market economies have viewed ICAs in a similar fashion. A perception of strong political reasons to join in international market regulation normally has been required to induce developed countries to accept agreements for the commodities considered in this book. The political argument in support of joining ICAs has not been as influential in the United States as in most of its fellow Group B members, but in part this may be attributable to the fact that the U.S. Congress possesses a frequently exercised veto power over international agreements. This tends to publicize proposed agreements and to provide an open forum for critics to launch attacks on ICAs. Other developed governments are able to adhere to commodity agreements without such extensive publicity or legislative opposition.

The key factors affecting developed-country support for ICAs can be summarized briefly. First, the industrialized nations are apt to be hostile to an ICA for a commodity of which they are also important exporters. Indeed, their interests as exporters will likely override any other economic or political interests they may have. Second, they are unlikely to back an ICA for a commodity in the absence of serious price instability, or to accept proposals designed to correct a declining real price trend. Third, developed importers usually must conclude that broad political and foreign policy goals will be furthered through their acceptance of an agreement. Finally, although they may be willing to join an ICA for largely noneconomic reasons, most developed-country negotiators will insist both that a reasonable price range be written into an agreement and that the market be given wide scope to operate before regulatory instruments are utilized. In fact, since the late 1970s the Western nations have become less willing to support ICAs that attempt to alter market trends.

Producer Power and Bargaining Outcomes. Any explanation of the bargaining outcomes resulting from Third World demands for commodity accords must rest not just on the policy preferences of the developed countries, but also on the power of developing producers. Consumers' fear that commodity producers might collaborate and extract huge price increases from importing states has a long history. But not until OPEC's spectacular success in 1973–74 did the perception begin to grow in the developed world that Third World commodity producers had become "a newly emerging political and economic force ominously aligned against the consumers in the industrialized nations."[66] Before the OPEC embargo, concern over the adequacy of the world's mineral resource base was already on the increase. This was fueled by the gloomy scenarios outlined in studies done by the Club of Rome and other neo-Malthusian groups as well as by the sharp rise in commodity prices in the early 1970s.[67] These trends, coupled with the rude shock administered by OPEC, led a number of analysts to focus on the growing "commodity power" or "resource power" of the South as a whole.[68]

Not surprisingly, analysts writing about the alleged strengthening of the bargaining power of Third World commodity producers were primarily interested in nonrenewable mineral commodities, although some concern was expressed about agricultural commodities as well. Lists of non-oil minerals likely to be subject to producer cartels were produced, and the need to work out some form of accommodation with the South was stressed.[69] To be sure, as discussed in previous chapters, a number of developments over the period 1973–75 did appear to validate Western fears. Bauxite producers established the IBA, and several of them proceeded to impose much higher taxes and levies on the multinational firms and to nationalize some of their mines; the price of phosphates almost quadrupled, increasing fertilizer prices sharply; Third World copper exporters, under the aegis of CIPEC, moved to institute supply cutbacks to support prices; a number of coffee exporters sought to collaborate to regulate the market outside the producer-consumer International Coffee Agreement; and banana producers created their own producers' association, UPEB, and moved to levy higher taxes on the multinational companies dominating the industry.[70] These developments certainly did not appear auspicious for the developed importing countries.

In retrospect, however, it is somewhat surprising that fears of Third World resource power gained such a respectable hearing. The preconditions for the exercise of market power by a large number of LDCs across a range of commodities were generally far from being met, even in the panicky atmosphere of the early 1970s. There were, and are, a variety of reasons.[71] It is clear that the widespread fears of resource exhaustion were greatly exaggerated and flowed from a misunderstanding of both mineral economics and the actual state of mineral reserves. (Fear of exhaustion, of course, was not a factor affecting appraisals of bargaining power in agricultural markets.) The notion that the world is quickly running out of nonrenewable resources—what John Tilton terms the "physical view" of resource scarcity[72]—is difficult to square with the fact that, despite massive increases in mineral consumption, "reserves of nearly all mineral commodities are larger today than in the early postwar period."[73]

Even those more sophisticated observers who adopted an "economic view" of resource exhaustion were also at least partly mistaken in their assumption that production costs would rise inexorably as known deposits were depleted, thus rendering other deposits inaccessible.[74] True, there has been a trend toward the exploitation of progressively lower-grade ores, but technological improvements have helped to reduce costs, thus offsetting, to some extent, the higher costs attendant upon mining lower-grade deposits. Also, technological developments have helped to reduce *demand* for many minerals by permitting substitution.[75] The substitution of plastics for tin and fiber optics for copper are good examples. Increasing production costs and prices are likely for a variety of minerals over the long run, but these developments in themselves do not necessarily pose a threat to mineral-importing countries. Higher prices promote the development of new reserves, encourage consumers to switch to other raw materials, and otherwise economize on the intensity of resource use.[76] Thus, there is little reason to question Raymond Mikesell's conclusion that, for the foreseeable future, "world supplies of non-fuel minerals should be able to grow roughly in relation to the increase in demand."[77]

Not only has scarcity seldom been serious enough to afford LDC producers significant leverage, but other conditions conducive to producer power have also been absent. The conditions or aspects of market structure that promote producer power have been analyzed at length by economists. Their insights are briefly reviewed below within the context of the commodity markets covered in this book.

First, demand for producers' exports must be price inelastic, the more so the better. In practical terms, this means that a commodity should be truly essential for an economy and should have few or no close substitutes for its major uses. Among the commodities covered in the previous chapters, the demand for and prices of natural rubber, sisal, cotton, copper, and a number of others have been seriously affected by substitutes. Also, most agricultural commodities are not "essential," and imports of them tend to fall as prices rise.

Second, supply should be relatively price inelastic, especially in the case of supply outside the control of any producer group. If this is not the case, nonmembers can undermine the price policies of a producer association by bringing forth new output, in response perhaps to the higher prices temporarily engineered by the association. The more price elastic is supply, the more quickly will the benefits of producer collusion be eroded. In this connection, it is worth recalling the many attempts by groups of producers to manage various commodity markets and their failure as a result of increased exports by states outside the cartels (and sometimes the noncompliance of members). This has happened with regard to coffee, cocoa, sugar, copper, tin, sisal, and tea. Also, for certain commodities significant shares of global exports and production are accounted for by developed countries. This is the case for all the minerals discussed in this book except tin, as well as for cotton and oils and oilseeds.

Third, the commodity should be relatively homogeneous. For a homogeneous product, price is the only real dimension of producer competition, and this facilitates producer coordination. As one eminent theorist of market structure has written: "When products are heterogeneously differentiated, the terms of [producer] rivalry become multi-dimensional, and the coordination problem grows in complexity by leaps and bounds."[78] The problem of product heterogeneity has been evident for several of the commodities considered in this book, notably tropical timber and oils and oilseeds. It has also posed problems for the International Coffee Agreement, and complicated the development of unified producer positions in discussions over commodities such as tea and bauxite.

Fourth, a small number of suppliers should dominate the export market. This not only facilitates coordination but also lessens the risk that nonmembers will thwart efforts to affect output and prices. The more sellers there are, the more difficulties they will face in seeking collectively to maintain prices above marginal costs. As F.M. Scherer notes, this is the case for three principal reasons: (1) with larger numbers of suppliers, "individual producers are increasingly apt to ignore the effect of their price and output decisions on rival actions and the overall level of prices"; (2) the more suppliers there are, the greater is the probability "that at least one will be a maverick, pursuing an independent, aggressive pricing policy"; and (3) different suppliers will probably adopt different views of what constitutes the "most advantageous price," particularly to the extent that they face varying production costs.[79] There is some validity to the hypothesis that small numbers facilitate collaboration, but its importance can be overestimated. The small number of important producers of tin, natural rubber, and to a lesser extent cocoa has at times facilitated the conclusion of ICAs, but it has not prevented serious divisions among producers. Also, although there are small numbers of key LDC producers of commodities such as manganese ore, phosphate rock, and tea, they were seriously divided in negotiations on market regulation.

Finally, the governments involved should not be heavily reliant on the commodity in question. A high level of dependence on commodity exports for foreign exchange earnings, government revenues, and employment in a major economic sector makes producers reluctant to cut production and hence seriously curtails their bargaining power.[80] They cannot afford to accept large short-term losses, especially when significant long-term gains are problematic. One economist has pointed to this reality as a major cause of the failure of collaboration among copper producers,[81] but such vulnerability unquestionably was and still is fundamental to the bargaining weakness of Third World producers in many commodity markets (see table 1.2 in this regard).

Overall, the global markets on which Third World producers sell the bulk of their primary products have not been characterized by these conditions associated with strong producer leverage. Most attempts by exporters to control markets have failed. The relative inelasticity of demand and supply typical of most commodity markets in the short run does not provide a firm basis for the excercise of significant producer market power over the longer run. Barriers to entry into many commodity industries are low. Most primary products have substitutes in their major uses. Technological developments have altered the markets for many commodities. The large number of exporters of most of the commodities discussed in international forums since the late 1940s has created impediments to collective action, a problem particularly acute in cases where industrial countries are also important exporters.

In large part the leverage Third World producers do possess has derived from the explicit or implicit threat that a failure by the industrialized world to accept market regulatory schemes could lead them to adopt less amicable policies toward developed countries on a number of fronts. The influence of this factor has varied over time and by region, but overall it appears to have attenuated since the late 1970s.

THE GLOBAL COMMODITY TRADE REGIME

After decades of negotiations and the expenditure of significant human and financial resources by developing countries, the global commodity trade regime today remains remarkably similar to that during the immediate postwar years. The number of intergovernmental regulatory agreements is small (and with the collapse of the tin agreement, getting smaller), while the centerpiece of the South's regime-change proposals of the late 1970s, the Common Fund, will probably be a rather weak institution following the treaty's entry into force. The IMF's Compensatory Financing Facility has been liberalized on several occasions during the past decade, but the G77's proposal for a very different type of compensatory financing arrangement has so far been rebuffed. In any case, compensatory financing has never been the principal focus of Third World reform efforts in the commodity sphere. Rather, greater intergovernmental market regulation, the deliberate structuring of commodity trade in ways designed to benefit LDC exporters, and the establishment of new international institutions in which LDCs would have a dominant voice have long been the central goals of the developing world. For the most part, these goals have not been realized.

As was mentioned in chapter 1, within the set of regulatory arrangements that constitutes a distinct international regime, substantive and procedural rules are basically designed to implement various norms. Two features of the commodity regime will be highlighted here—its strength and its nature. The former refers to the extent to which the regime constrains state behavior, and the latter to those general principles or values that are promoted by the regime's norms and rules.

A word must be said about what constitutes a "strong" regime. In examining regulatory arrangements that help to govern states' behavior in international issue-areas, scholars are primarily interested in the extent to which they require states to follow particular policies and/or refrain from taking various kinds of action. Clearly, international regulatory arrangements that possess strong prescriptive or proscriptive qualities will have more influence on behavior than arrangements that essentially grant states unfettered freedom to pursue whatever course they believe is most likely to promote their national interests.

In the commodity issue-area, a strong regime would be characterized by straightforward prescriptions and proscriptions that, inter alia, would clearly define the conditions under which international regulatory agreements are to be established; set forth the goals that commodity organizations are to pursue; impose limits on the use of national policies to assist domestic commodity industries; and allow the majority of states to legislate agreements applicable to all states. All these features would amount to constraints on states' latitude for independent policymaking on key issues.

Analyzing the "nature" of the regime, in the case of international commodity trade, requires evaluating the extent to which the regime has reflected the general principle of wealth redistribution, or Third World development, or the alternative principle of free international markets. If wealth redistribution were the most important value underlying the regime, then commodity agreements and other regulatory schemes that affect commodity trade would be designed explicitly to further the economic development of Third World states. In contrast, a commodity regime dominated by the free-market principle would be characterized by a reluctance to countenance intergovernmental interventions into commodity markets except in unusual circumstances.

Overall, the injunctions of the international commodity regime have not imposed substantial constraints on state policies, although they have had some degree of influence in a few areas. No regime prescriptions concerning support to domestic commodity producers have been widely accepted, for example. Nor do constraints on the formation of cartels any longer play a role in the regime. Much inconsistency has been evident in the policies adopted by states toward these issues; even in cases where many governments have voiced disapproval of producer subsidies or cartels, they have failed to take concrete steps to pressure states to alter their behavior.

Two substantive issues for which regime constraints have existed relate to ICAs and to financial assistance to commodity-producing countries facing declining export earnings. As was discussed earlier, at a normative level ICAs have been viewed as acceptable only when created to correct marked instability in commodity markets. They have also mainly been restricted to price stabilization around the market trend. Sustained efforts to raise prices have generally been eschewed, although on occasion the developed countries have been willing to use ICAs for this purpose. Moreover, although instability has been a prerequisite, states have not assumed any obligation to negotiate regulatory agreements for all unstable markets. Most countries have insisted on maintaining wide scope for independent policy judgment on whether to participate in ICAs, regardless of market conditions. Only if a clear regime norm prevailed requiring the establishment of ICAs for all unstable markets in which LDCs are principal producers would it be plausible to argue that a strong constraint had developed on this issue.

The actual impact of ICAs may reveal something about the intentions of the states that created them. Studies of the influence of ICAs are not extensive, but most of those that have been undertaken suggest that their ability to stabilize prices has been limited. ICAs have had some success in defending the floors of price ranges but very little in defending ceilings. At times the coffee, tin, and sugar agreements have clearly affected markets, especially in protecting floor prices, but overall their role in shaping market developments has not been great. In short, ICAs have not transformed the character of global commodity markets.[82]

The norm concerning compensatory financing holds that LDC producing states should be offered financial assistance when decreases in their export earnings lead to balance-of-payments deficits. The European Community has given the ACP states either grants or no-interest loans when the latter experience shortfalls in commodity export earnings, but the community has not sought to fashion a *global* scheme along the model of STABEX. The international community has accepted only limited responsibility for assisting LDCs with reduced export sales receipts. States (in effect, the developed nations) will only provide loans if the producing states are in a position where they may not be able to pay for the goods they import. This commitment is not unimportant, but it would be inaccurate to describe it as a strong behavior-constraining norm.

The substantive dimension of the regime overall has been porous and weak. States have preserved most of their freedom to decide when and how regulatory agreements should be formed, and they have made few commitments to assure stability in LDC export earnings. The strongest substantive provisions of the regime are found in the individual ICAs, but these have existed for just six commodities (including wheat), only three of which are currently operating.

The nature of these regime injunctions clearly reflects the free market rather than the development or wealth-redistribution principle. While ICAs would not have been negotiated in the absence of concerted Third World pressure, the commodity agreements place greater emphasis on respecting market forces than on assuring improved producer welfare. Particular ICAs have sometimes raised prices, but the general picture, especially over the last ten years, has been one of adherence to price stabilization around market trends.

Turning now to the procedural dimension, to determine regime strength in this area one must ask to what extent states have committed themselves to accept decisions of international institutions where they lack the power to block such decisions on their own or in collaboration with a small group of allied countries. In fact, states are not obligated to sign or abide by a treaty (e.g., an ICA) once it has been formulated by an international conference or entered into force. No incursions on the principle of sovereign equality have been accepted here. The decisions of institutions administering ICAs or dispensing funds to producing states are binding. However, a small group of states with the largest market shares or providing most of the finances can veto such decisions. (The ability of these states to block decisions is perhaps less of a weakness in the procedural dimension of the commodity trade regime than is the fact that organizations exist in so few commodity markets.)

The nature of the procedural dimension of this regime hinges on the roles of what can be termed the principles of "democracy" (majoritarianism) and "power" (elitism) in shaping the decision-making system.[83] In commodity conferences, the basic rule is that two-thirds of the states attending can create a treaty. This may appear to be a decisive victory for the principle of democracy until one realizes that no country is obligated to accept a treaty with which it disagrees. This fact frequently leads conference participants to structure agreements so as to ensure their acceptance by major actors, whose cooperation is essential. The requirements for the entry-into-force of ICAs and other commodity treaties generally recognize the need for the participation of states accounting for large shares of imports and exports. In organizations involved in administering ICAs and dispensing funding, both "democratic" and "power" principles are given some weight: decisions require the support of both the major actors and a majority of the members. But the cornerstone of the system is the fact that the former group (and usually a small number of them) possesses a veto. Seldom will a proposal advanced by the most powerful countries be opposed by a majority of members. On the other hand, a small group of the most powerful nations can often block proposals favored by the majority.

The commodity trade regime mainly consists of injunctions that do not heavily constrain state behavior, and that reflect the free market rather than the development principle, and more the power principle than democratic majoritarianism. Several factors help to explain the character of the regime. First, certain features of the issue-area have affected the strength of the regime. The prices of commodities and the earnings of exporting nations are at the heart of the international competition for wealth. These issues do not relate merely to the facilitation of exchange relations; in this they differ from many other international economic issue areas. Given that rules concerning commodity prices and earnings in large part define the terms of competition, it is difficult to develop a set of rules that all parties will view as beneficial—any scheme is likely to produce economic winners and losers. In fact, if the creation of ICAs depended solely on states' judgments of their economic impacts, it is probable that none would have been created.

One issue-area characteristic has had a positive influence on market regulation, although compared to other factors it has not loomed large. What the ICAs produce, namely, more stable or higher prices, is not a very "public" good. Thus, the benefits of collaboration usually can be denied to states that fail to comply with the resulting arrangements. If states reject ICAs or choose to violate their provisions, in theory they can be prevented from enjoying better price trends by being excluded from the markets of the consuming members or by having their export quotas cut. The availability of these sanctions has been crucial to the success of several ICAs that have existed in recent decades.[84]

The strength and nature of an international regime obviously are affected by the distribution of capabilities among states and their varying policy preferences. In the case of the commodity regime, the unquestioned dominance of the United States in the immediate postwar years was etched into the norms and institutions that evolved in the 1940s. The United States made clear that it wanted some reasonably strong obligations to respect competitive markets and to limit intergovernmental interventions to producer-consumer accords in very unstable markets. At the same time, it did not want the conditions requiring ICAs to be specified too precisely and objected to any restrictions on assistance to domestic producers. For the most part it was successful in fashioning a set of arrangements that met this conception. Since these early postwar years, mutual interests and congruent policy goals among the developed industrial states as a group (rather than just the power of the United States) have been instrumental in defining the character and the limits of the regime. Commodity trade is not an area in which the United States would have found it easy to employ fully its dominant economic and political power in the face of strong resistance from other Group B states. Fortunately for Washington, it usually has not had to do so. Perceived U.S. interests and policy objectives have generally been shared by most Western states, and the level of agreement has, in fact, increased in the 1980s. Also, Soviet policies have not differed significantly from those of the Western nations. This developed-country consensus has been important, since in virtually no individual commodity market did the United States (or any other country) possess sufficient leverage to dictate negotiating outcomes. And although the United States is an enormous force in world commodity trade as a whole—as an importer and, in some commodities, as a major exporter—its power has not been on a par with the influence it has wielded in, for example, the international monetary regime.

Recent scholarship on international collaboration has emphasized the role of regimes in facilitating the negotiation and maintenance of agreements.[85] It is argued that by improving communications and transparency and by promoting "customary" or "habit-driven" ways of addressing issues and regulating transactions, regimes help to fashion some order and predictability in the world political economy. Moreover, governments, reluctant to abandon existing regimes because they fear the consequences, are apt to engage in "mutual policy adjustment" in an effort to maintain the arrangements they previously negotiated,[86] even though a narrow calculation of state self-interest may indicate that compliance with regime injunctions is not an optimal short-term choice.

In the area of commodities, the existence of various United Nations institutions (notably UNCTAD) as well as the ICOs has undoubtedly facilitated regulatory accords and provided for greater transparency. These institutions have also promoted compliance with the rules of agreements by monitoring states' behavior and offering forums in which the subject can be discussed. However, as was emphasized above, neither these institutions nor other aspects of the regime have fundamentally altered international commodity trade or prompted states to change their policies to any significant degree. There is some evidence that states have continued to support ICAs for short periods of time because of a desire to avoid the political crises attendant on their collapse. But it is also clear that when important trading states realize that accords are definitely contrary to their interests, they are not reluctant to withdraw.

Before considering the future of the international commodity regime, we should ask how it fits into the larger context of North-South relations. The "dialogue" between developed and developing countries, which intensified in the 1970s, served to transform the agenda of international politics by placing issues on the agenda that otherwise would not have been there or would have had much less salience. This certainly describes the situation with respect to commodities. In the absence of concerted Third World pressure, the commodity negotiations of the 1970s and early 1980s would not have taken place. Furthermore, the North-South debate on commodities has ensured both that the subject of commodity policy will remain on the global agenda and that negotiations on commodity issues will continue into the future. Commodity policy has thus joined such topics as trade barriers, international capital flows, and monetary/exchange-rate relations as an ongoing part of the international policy process. And this has happened even though the commodity regime itself has not changed fundamentally as a consequence of the protracted negotiations between North and South in recent decades.

In looking to the future, we see no political or economic trends that appear likely to threaten the continuation of the rather weak, market-oriented commodity regime. For it to evolve toward a stronger or more development-oriented regime, either the developed countries would have to judge that it had become necessary to employ commodity agreements to transfer substantially more assistance to Third World states, or else LDC commodity producers would have to acquire greater bargaining power in resource markets or in global politics more generally. Neither prospect is likely, but neither one can be dismissed out of hand. It is conceivable that the international debt crisis and the structural economic problems confronting many developing states could induce the governments of the rich northern countries to channel additional resources to the Third World via commodity schemes. However, several factors would appear to militate against this.

First, a growing share of world imports of many commodities is now accounted for by Third World states, who so far have demonstrated no inclination to support agreements designed to raise the prices of their raw-material imports or to benefit selected LDC producers. Second, and more important, the developed countries have other means available to assist individual Third World states or groups of states. Trade preferences, regional economic arrangements, and bilateral quotas are among the instruments that northern countries (including the Soviet bloc) have used. These devices allow an industrial country to direct its assistance to client states or preferred political allies. Global commodity arrangements, in contrast, are generally less effective in targeting assistance. However, when a commodity is produced mainly by LDCs favored by the major Western powers, an ICA may be viewed as a useful mechanism for conferring benefits on these producer states.

The likelihood that LDCs will acquire substantially greater leverage in global resource markets (or in world politics generally) must similarly be judged small at present. It is, of course, hazardous to offer firm predictions. Nonetheless, it is worth noting that current trends seem likely to weaken further the position of many Third World producers. Structural oversupply now characterizes a number of commodity markets of interest to the Third World. Moreover, new industrial technologies and materials (for example, in fiber optics or ceramics) cloud the prospects for more than a few primary commodities.[87] Technological change is not only eroding traditional markets for some raw materials, but it is also allowing significant economies in the use of natural resources. The intensity of resource use in industrial countries has declined markedly in recent decades, and this trend is certain to continue.

Another factor working against enhanced Third World leverage in resource markets is the increasing heterogeneity of the developing countries as a group. Growing variation among developing countries will serve to magnify differences in interests and policies, a development already evident in the greater importance of LDCs as commodity importers and the diversity in industrial structure among developing countries. This clear trend is virtually certain to make the Third World less cohesive as a political coalition, and it may attenuate many LDCs' interest in global regime change.

Regardless of the pace of these and other trends, there will doubtless always be a few commodity agreements. If producers of a commodity with unstable prices are willing to enter into a fairly pure price-stabilization arrangement (such as the current ICAs for cocoa and natural rubber), importers will likely conclude that they must consider joining, in line with the general norm of the postwar regime. Some developed countries may occasionally turn to ICAs or other commodity arrangements as a way to provide benefits for favored LDC producers; ICAs may even be used to raise prices for particular commodities, at least on a temporary basis. But the practice certainly will not become widespread. The ongoing dialogue within UNCTAD and the IMF concerning compensatory financing could eventually lead to a larger, more generous global facility similar to STABEX, although at present there is little evidence that developed states are prepared to allocate large new sums for this purpose.

The failure to create substantial numbers of new agreements or a well-financed Common Fund, endowed with an ambitious mandate to intervene in global markets, has probably persuaded some developing countries to consider ways other than the direct regulation of prices and supplies to address their continued vulnerability to fluctuating markets. Compensatory financing is certainly one such alternative. Another is to negotiate bilateral or regional arrangements with importing countries that provide some protection. The renegotiation of the EC-ACP Lomé Convention and the U.S. Caribbean Basin Initiative point to the growing importance of regional programs. Still another strategy that holds promise for developing countries is to focus on improving management and direction in their own domestic commodity industries. Many LDCs are currently seeking to do this, often with the support of the World Bank and other international agencies. For most, however, the inclination to search for international solutions to the problems they face in world markets will remain strong, despite the fact that previous efforts have yielded only marginal benefits for Third World commodity producers.

NOTES

1. INTERNATIONAL COMMODITY POLICY AND THE NORTH-SOUTH DIALOGUE

1. Carmine Nappi, *Commodity Market Controls* (Lexington, Mass.: Lexington Books, 1979), p. 14; Rachel McCulloch and Jose Pinera, "Alternative Commodity Trade Regimes," in Ruth W. Arad, et al., *Sharing Global Resources,* (New York: McGraw-Hill, 1979), pp. 107-8.

2. GATT, *International Trade, 1982/83* (Geneva: GATT Secretariat, 1983), table A-22; UNCTAD, *Handbook of International Trade and Development Statistics, 1986* (Geneva: UNCTAD, 1986).

3. See also World Bank, *Commodity Trade and Price Trends* (1981), table 11.

4. I.S. Chada, "North-South Negotiating Process in the Field of Commodities," in Arjun Sengupta, ed., *Commodities, Finance, and Trade: Issues in North-South Negotiations* (Westport, Conn.: Greenwood Press, 1980), pp. 31–34.

5. OECD, *The Impact of the Newly Industrializing Countries on Production and Trade in Manufactures* (Paris: OECD, 1979). Key Third World "newly industrialized countries," or "NICs," include Brazil, Singapore, Taiwan, South Korea, India, and Mexico. The OECD also classes as NICs several Western European countries (Portugal, Spain, and Greece) as well as Yugoslavia. In addition, Hong Kong is, of course, a major source of Third World manufactured exports, although it is not a sovereign state.

6. David L. McNicol, *Commodity Agreements and Price Stabilization* (Lexington, Mass.: Lexington Books, 1978), p. 16; William R. Cline, "A Quantitative Assessment of the Policy Alternatives in the NIEO Negotiations," in William R. Cline, ed., *Policy Alternatives for a New International Economic Order* (New York: Praeger, 1979), p. 15; Constantine Michalopoulos and Lorenzo Perez, "Commodity Trade Policy: Initiatives and Issues," in Gerard Adams and Sonia Klein, eds., *Stabilizing World Commodity Markets: Analyses, Practice, and Policy,* (Lexington, Mass.: Lexington Books, 1979), p. 247; Ezriel Brook, Enzo Grilli, and Jean Waelbroeck, "Commodity Price Stabilization and the Developing Countries," *Banca Nazionale del Lavoro Quarterly Review* (March 1978), 124:80; and the joint study by the World Bank and the IMF,

The Problem of Stabilization of Prices of Primary Products (Washington: IMF-IBRD, 1969).

7. Joseph D. Coppock, *International Economic Instability* (New York: McGraw-Hill, 1962), p. 15.

8. McNicol, *Commodity Agreements and Price Stabilization*, p. 18.

9. Alexander J. Yeats, *Trade Barriers Facing Developing Countries* (London: Macmillan, 1979), pp. 28–29.

10. Jere R. Behrman, "International Commodity Agreements: An Evaluation of the UNCTAD Integrated Commodity Programme," in William R. Cline, ed., *Policy Alternatives for a New International Economic Order* (New York: Praeger, 1979), p. 87.

11. This discussion draws from the following sources: Alton D. Law, *International Commodity Agreements* (Lexington, Mass.: Lexington Books, 1975), pp. 3–6; Behrman, "International Commodity Agreements," pp. 87–88; G. K. Helleiner, *International Trade and Economic Development* (London: Penguin, 1972), pp. 35–43; and John E. Tilton, *The Future of Nonfuel Minerals* (Washington: Brookings, 1977), pp. 65–68.

12. Coppock, *International Economic Stability;* and Alasdair MacBean, *Export Instability and Economic Development* (Cambridge, Mass.: Harvard University Press, 1966).

13. Cline, "A Quantitative Assessment of the Policy Alternatives in the NIEO Negotiations," p. 15. See also Christopher P. Brown, *The Political and Social Economy of Commodity Control* (New York: Praeger, 1980), p. 158; Yeats, *Trade Barriers Facing Developing Countries,* p. 46; McNicol, *Commodity Agreements and Price Stabilization,* p. 21; and Behrman, "International Commodity Agreements," for confirmation regarding the existence of this consensus. Odin Knudsen and Andrew Parnes, while critical of conventional assumptions concerning Third World export instability, also conclude that export earnings for LDCs are more unstable than those of developed states; *Trade Instability and Economic Development* (Lexington, Mass.: Lexington Books, 1975), p. 29. Reviews of the literature on export instability may be found in David Lim, "Export Instability and Economic Growth," *Oxford Bulletin of Economics and Statistics* (1978), 38:311–22; Peter Wilson, "The Consequences of Export Instability for Developing Countries: A Reappraisal," *Development and Change* (January 1983), 14:39–59; and Elio Lancieri, "Export Instability and Economic Development: A Reappraisal," *Banca Nazionale del Lavoro Quarterly Review* (June 1978), 125:135–52.

14. Behrman, "International Commodity Agreements," p. 89.

15. Brown, *The Political and Social Economy of Commodity Control,* pp. 151–52; Michalopoulos and Perez, "Commodity Trade Policy," p. 248; and Paul D. Reynolds, *International Commodity Agreements and the Common Fund* (New York: Praeger, 1978), p. 35.

16. See Brook, Grilli, and Waelbroeck, "Commodity Price Stabilization," p. 81 and passim; Brown, *The Political and Social Economy of Commodity Control,* pp. 151–54; and Behrman, "International Commodity Agreements," pp. 71–75 for an elaboration.

17. Brown, *The Political and Social Economy of Commodity Control,* pp. 151–53; Brook, Grilli, and Waelbroeck, "Commodity Price Stabilization," pp. 97–99.

18. For reviews of the debate concerning export earnings instability, see Wilson, "The Consequences of Export Instability"; Guy Erb and S. Schiavo-Campo, "Export Instability, Level of Development, and Economic Size of Less Developed Countries," *Oxford Bulletin of Economics and Statistics* (May 1979), 31:263–83; C. Glezakos, "Export Instability and Economic Growth: A Statistical Verification," *Economic Development and Cultural Change* (July 1973), 21:670–78; Geoffrey N. Soutar, "Export Instability and Concentration in the Less Developed Countries: A Cross-Sectional Analysis," *Journal of Development Economics* (1977), 4:279–97; Lancieri, "Export Instability and Economic Development," pp. 135–52; and Knudsen and Parnes, *Trade Instability and Economic Development*, ch. 3.

19. Brown, *The Political and Social Economy of Commodity Control*, p. 161.

20. United Nations Economic Commission for Latin America, *The Economic Development of Latin America and Its Principal Problems* (New York: United Nations, 1950); Joseph L. Love, "Raul Prebisch and the Origins of the Doctrine of Unequal Exchange," *Latin American Research Review* (1980), 15:45–72; and Ragnar Nurske, "Patterns of Trade and Development," in J. Theberge, ed., *Economics of Trade and Development* (New York: Wiley, 1968), pp. 85–102.

21. Helleiner, *International Trade and Economic Development*, pp. 34–35; Yeats, *Trade Barriers Facing Developing Countries*, p. 47

22. Law, *International Commodity Agreements*, pp. 21–23; Paul Bairoch, *The Economic Development of the Third World Since 1900* (Berkeley: University of California Press, 1975), pp. 129–34.

23. Law, *International Commodity Agreements*, ch. 2; David Evans, "International Commodity Policy: UNCTAD and the NIEO in Search of a Rationale," *World Development* (1979), 7:264–68; Michalopoulos and Perez, "Commodity Trade Policy"; William Loehr and John P. Powelson, *Threat to Development: Pitfalls of the NIEO* (Boulder, Co.: Westview Press, 1983). pp. 15–23.

24. Yeats, *Trade Barriers Facing Developing Countries*, pp. 47–48; Evans, "International Commodity Policy," p. 264; and Jere R. Behrman, *Development, the International Economic Order and Commodity Agreements* (Reading, Mass.: Addison-Wesley, 1978), pp. 55–56.

25. Bairoch, *The Economic Development of the Third World Since 1900*, pp. 126–27.

26. Kenzo Hemmi et al., *Trade in Primary Commodities: Conflict or Cooperation?* (Washington: Brookings, 1974), p. 9.

27. Behrman, "International Commodity Agreements," p. 111 and table 3.

28. Evans, "International Commodity Policy," p. 264; McNicol, *Commodity Agreements and Price Stabilization*, p. 19; Nappi, *Commodity Market Controls*, p. 23. For a recent review of commodity price trends and policy issues, see K. Y. Chu and T. K. Morrison, "World Non-Oil Primary Commodity Markets: A Medium Term Framework of Analysis," *IMF Staff Papers* (March 1986).

29. Michalopoulos and Perez, "Commodity Trade Policy," p. 250; Reynolds, *International Commodity Agreements and the Common Fund*, p. 79; and J.W.F. Rowe, *Primary Commodities in International Trade* (Cambridge: Cambridge University Press, 1965), p. 195.

30. L. N. Rangarajan, *Commodity Conflict: The Political Economy of International*

Commodity Negotiations (Ithaca, N.Y.: Cornell University Press, 1978), p. 92; and G. K. Helleiner, "World Market Imperfections and the Developing countries," in Cline, ed., *Policy Alternatives for a New International Economic Order*, p. 370.

31. Rowe, *Primary Commodities in International Trade*, p. 196.

32. McNicol, *Commodity Agreements and Price Stabilization*, p. 67; Rangarajan, *Commodity Conflict*, p. 221.

33. Rowe, *Primary Commodities in International Trade*, p. 191.

34. Ibid., p, 192.

35. Reynolds, *International Commodity Agreements and the Common Fund*, p. 86; McNicol, *Commodity Agreements and Price Stabilization*, p. 77; and Helleiner, *International Trade and Economic Development*, p. 57.

36. Reynolds, *International Commodity Agreements and the Common Fund*, pp. 87–88.

37. McNicol, *Commodity Agreements and Price Stabilization*, ch.4; Law, *International Commodity Agreements*, pp. 73–74; Alasdair MacBean, "Commodity Policies in a New International Order," in Arjun Sengupta, ed., *Commodities, Finance, and Trade: Issues in North-South Negotiations* (Westport, Conn.: Greenwood Press, 1980), p. 71; and Mordechai Krenin and J. M. Finger, "A New International Economic Order: A Critical Survey of the Issues," *Journal of World Trade Law* (November–December 1976), 10: 493-512.

38. Helleiner, *International Trade and Economic Development*, p. 52; Law, *International Commodity Agreements*, p. 73; Loehr and Powelson, *Threat to Development*, pp. 24-26.

39. Law, *International Commodity Agreements*, p. 73.

40. Rowe, *Primary Commodities in International Trade*, pp. 163-66; Kabir-Ur-Rahman Khan, *The Law and Organization of International Commodity Agreements* (The Hague: Martinus Nijhoff, 1982), pp. 222-23; UN Doc. TD/B/C.1/258 (1985).

41. Rangarajan, *Commodity Conflict*, p. 238.

42. Ibid., p. 239.

43. In 1967 the European Economic Community (EEC), the European Coal and Steel Community (ECSC), and the European Atomic Energy Community (Euratom) were combined into a single organization, the European Communities. However, this body soon became known as the European Community (EC). We will refer to EEC only in discussing policy actions of the members between 1957 and 1966.

44. Brown, *The Political and Social Economy of Commodity Control*, pp. 160-61.

45. For an elaboration on the nature of regimes and on the analysis of regimes, see Stephen D. Krasner, ed., *International Regimes* (Ithaca, N.Y.: Cornell Univeristy Press, 1983); and Robert O. Keohane, *After Hegemony: Cooperation and Discord in the World Political Economy* (Princeton: Princeton University Press, 1984).

46. Richard Gardner, *Sterling-Dollar Diplomacy in Current Perspective: The Origins and Prospects of Our International Economic Order* (New York: Columbia University Press, 1980).

47. When it was first established in 1963, the Group of 77 was actually known as the Group of 75. It became the Group of 77 at the first UNCTAD conference in the spring of 1964.

48. Branislav Gosovic, *UNCTAD: Conflict and Compromise* (Leiden: A. W. Sijthoff, 1972), p. 34.

49. Edward L. Morse, "Introduction: The International Management of Resources," in Ruth W. Arad et al., *Sharing Global Resources*, p. 8.

50. Gosovic, *UNCTAD*, p. 29; Joseph S. Nye, "UNCTAD: Poor Nations' Pressure Group," in Robert W. Cox and Harold K. Jacobson, eds., *The Anatomy of Influence: Decision Making in International Organizations* (New Haven, Conn.: Yale University Press, 1973), p. 335.

51. Law, *International Commodity Agreements*; McNicol, *Commodity Agreements and Price Stabilization*; Adams and Klein, eds., *Stabilizing World Commodity Markets*; Behrman, *Development, the International Economic Order, and Commodity Agreements*; Stuart Harris, Mark Salmon, and Ben Smith, *Analysis of Commodity Markets for Policy Purposes* (London: Trade Policy Research Centre, Thames Essay Number 17, 1978).

52. Knudsen and Parnes, *Trade Instability and Economic Development*; Nappi, *Commodity Market Controls*; Geoffrey Goodwin and James Mayall, eds., *A New International Commodity Regime* (London: Croom Helm, 1980); Law, *International Commodity Agreements*, chs. 2 and 3.

53. Christopher P. Brown, *The Political and Social Economy of Commodity Control* (New York: Praeger, 1980); Robert L. Rothstein, *Global Bargaining: UNCTAD and the Quest for a New International Economic Order* (Princeton, N.J.: Princeton University Press, 1979); Rangarajan, *Commodity Conflict*; and Fiona Gordon-Ashworth, *International Commodity Control: A Contemporary History and Appraisal* (London: Croom Helm, 1984).

54. The literature related to these issues is cited in chapter 6.

2. NEGOTIATIONS ON COMMODITY TRADE NORMS AND PROGRAMS

1. On the respective views of the United States and other industrial countries during the early postwar reconstruction period, see Richard N. Gardner, *Sterling-Dollar Diplomacy* (New York: Columbia University Press, 1980).

2. William A. Brown, *The United States and the Restoration of World Trade* (Washington, D.C.: Brookings, 1950), pp. 152–58.

3. J.W.F. Rowe, *Primary Commodities in International Trade* (London: Cambridge University Press, 1965), chapter 12.

4. Ibid., p. 137.

5. Brown, *The United States and the Restoration of World Trade*, pp. 119–20.

6. Clair Wilcox, *A Charter for World Trade* (New York: McGraw-Hill, 1949), pp. 117–18.

7. Ibid., p. 118.

8. Cited in Ervin Hexner, *International Cartels* (Chapel Hill, N.C.: University of North Carolina Press, 1946), p. 123.

9. J. M. Keynes, "The International Control of Raw Materials," *Journal of International Economics* (August 1974), 4:301 and passim. This is a reprint of his original 1942 article.

10. Wilcox, *A Charter for World Trade*, p. 119; Brown, *The United States and the Restoration of World Trade*, p. 122.

11. Brown, *The United States and the Restoration of World Trade*, p. 122.

12. See the proposed amendments of the underdeveloped countries to the Geneva draft in UN Docs. E/CONF.2/C.5/3, Adds. 3, 6-8, and 11–12 (1948).

13. UN Doc. E/CONF.1/C.5/SR.7 (1948).

14. UN Doc. E/CONF.2/C.5/3/Add. 8 (1948).

15. UN Doc. E/CONF.2/C.5/3/Add. 8 (1948).

16. UN Doc. E/CONF.2/C.5/SR.11 (1948).

17. Art. 63; and UN Docs. E/CONF.2/C.5/9, E/CONF.2/C.5/SR.7 and 13 (1948).

18. Article 57.

19. UN Doc. E/CONF.2/C.5/SR.4 (1948).

20. John H. Jackson, *World Trade and the Law of GATT* (New York: Bobbs-Merrill, 1969), p. 722.

21. Rowe, *Primary Commodities in International Trade*, p. 160.

22. Edward S. Mason, *Controlling World Trade: Cartels and Commodity Agreements* (New York: McGraw-Hill, 1946), pp. 247–48; Brown, *The United States and the Restoration of World Trade*, p. 27.

23. Kenneth W. Dam, *The GATT—Law and International Economic Organization* (Chicago: University of Chicago Press, 1970), p. 11.

24. ECOSOC Resolution 39(IV) (1947).

25. The procedures and activities of ICCICA from 1947–64 are described in UN Doc. E/CONF.46/141 (1964), pp. 113–39. The Commission on International Commodity Trade and the debates concerning its character are described in ECOSOC Resolutions 512(XVII) (1954), 557F(XVIII) (1955), and 691A and B(XXVI) (1958); and UN Docs. E/2588 (1954), E/2623, and Adds. 1–3 (1955), E/2649 (1955), E/3124 (1958), and E/3171 (1958).

26. On developments leading up to UNCTAD I, see Branislav Gosovic, *UNCTAD: Conflict and Compromise* (Leiden: A.W. Sijthoff, 1972), ch. 1; Diego Cordovez, "The Making of UNCTAD," *Journal of World Trade Law* (May–June 1967), 1:243–79; and Robert A. Mortimer, *The Third World Coalition in International Politics* (New York: Praeger, 1980), ch. 2.

27. Mortimer, *The Third World Coalition in International Politics*, pp. 16–17.

28. For the proposals, see UN Doc. E/CONF.46/141, vol. I (1964), pp. 230–87.

29. See UN Doc. E/CONF.46/141, vol. I (1964), pp. 58–62 for the UNCTAD I conference resolution on institutional arrangements.

30. In addition to the Committee on Commodities, UNCTAD also created Committees on Manufactures and on Invisibles and Financing. The Committees on Commodities and on Manufactures had 55 members, the Committee on Invisibles and Financing had 45. A Committee on Shipping, also with 45 members was established by the Trade and Development Board at its first session. In 1972, membership in the Committee on Commodities was thrown open to all interested UNCTAD members.

31. On the UNCTAD decision-making process, see Gosovic, *UNCTAD*, pp. 218–

344; Diego Cordovez, *UNCTAD and Development Diplomacy: From Confrontation to Strategy* (Twickenham, Eng.: Journal of World Trade Law, 1972), pp. 150–63; Robert L. Rothstein, *Global Bargaining: UNCTAD and the Quest for a New International Economic Order* (Princeton, N.J.: Princeton University Press, 1979), chs. 5 and 6; Mortimer, *The Third World Coalition in International Politics*, pp. 75–81; and R. Krishnamurti, "UNCTAD as a Negotiating Institution," *Journal of World Trade Law* (January–February 1981), 15:3–40.

32. China is the sole country that is not a member of any UNCTAD group.

33. Gosovic, *UNCTAD*, pp. 299–300.

34. On the evolution of the UN's membership, see Harold K. Jacobson, *Networks of Interdependence: International Organizations and the Global Political System* (New York: Knopf, 1980), p. 118.

35. Karl P Sauvant, *The Group of 77: Evolution, Structure, Organization* (Dobbs Ferry, N.Y.: Oceana, 1981), pp. 36–38.

36. Mortimer, *The Third World Coalition in International Politics*, p. 75; see also Sauvant, *The Group of 77*, pp. 45–47.

37. Rothstein, *Global Bargaining*, p. 198.

38. Sauvant, *The Group of 77*, p. 198.

39. Rothstein, *Global Bargaining*, p. 200.

40. Robert L. Rothstein, "The North-South Dialogue: The Political Economy of of Immobility," *Journal of International Affairs* (Spring–Summer 1980), 34:4.

41. Gosovic, *UNCTAD*, pp. 301–3; Toby Trister Gati, "The Soviet Union and the North-South Dialogue," *Orbis* (Summer 1980), 24:241–70; Padma Desai, "The Soviet Union and the Third World: A Faltering Partnership?" in Jagdash N. Bhagwati and John Gerard Ruggie, eds., *Power, Passions, and Purpose: Prospects for North-South Negotiations* (Cambridge, Mass.: MIT Press, 1984), pp. 261–86.

42. Rothstein, *Global Bargaining*, p. 202.

43. UN Doc. TD/B/175/Add. 3 (1969), pp. 6–7; and also see Sauvant, *The Group of 77*, pp. 17–18 on problems afflicting the group decision-making system in UNCTAD.

44. TDB Resolution 19(II) (1965).

45. Cordovez has remarked that UNCTAD implementation reviews were "transformed into an additional 'general debate' and [did] not involve an exercise in international appraisal and evaluation of policies." Neither the Conference nor the TDB tried to draw up agreed conclusions on the basis of these reviews since "there were insurmountable difficulties in that respect." Cordovez, *UNCTAD and Development Diplomacy*, pp. 14 and 8–14.

46. Members of the ICAs for tin and sugar, as well as those involved in the protracted efforts to negotiate an ICA for cocoa, agreed to have their conferences sponsored by UNCTAD. However, the members of the International Coffee Council took the position that the ICA for coffee should be renegotiated by the council itself. Negotiations aimed at establishing an ICA for wheat were jointly sponsored by UNCTAD and the International Wheat Council, although UNCTAD had a purely pro forma role. Ibid., pp. 22 and 61; Gosovic, *UNCTAD*, pp. 206–7.

47. UNCTAD was even less successful, however, in gaining authority over other international trade-related issue areas. See Jock A. Finlayson and Mark W

Zacher, "International Trade Institutions and the North-South Dialogue," *International Journal* (Autumn 1981), 36:744.

48. UN Doc. E/CONF.46/141, vol. I (1964), 118–20.

49. UN Doc. E/CONF.46/141, vol. I (1964), pp. 9–12 and 60–62.

50. UN Doc. E/CONF.46/C.1/SR.26 (1964), pp.6–7.

51. UN Doc. E/CONF.46/C.1/SR.10 (1964), p. 10 for the statement of the Japanese delegate; and UN Doc. E/CONF.46/C.1/SR.40 (1964), p. 7 for the British view.

52. UN Doc. E/CONF.46/C.1/SR.41 (1964), p. 7.

53. Ibid.

54. UN Doc. E/CONF.46/141, vol. I (1964), p. 20.

55. UN Doc. E/CONF. 46/141, vol. I, 26. Also, see ibid., p. 135 for developed-country positions.

56. UN Doc. E/CONF.46/C.1/SR.13 (1964), p. 13.

57. UN Doc. TD/97, vol. I (1968), p. 433.

58. UN Doc. TD/II/C.1/SR.11–14 (1968).

59. UN Doc. TD/II/C.1/SR.9 (1968), pp. 112–13.

60. UN Doc. TD/97, vol. I (1968), p. 235; Gosovic, *UNCTAD*, pp. 165–66.

61. After discussions extending over several years a resolution on price policy was accepted by the Trade and Development Board in 1970. However, as expected, it was vague and did not represent a departure from Havana Charter norms. UN Doc. TD/B/327, annex I (1970), pp. 6–8.

62. Mortimer, *The Third World Coalition in International Politics*, p. 34. On results of UNCTAD III in the commodity field, see UN Doc. TD/180, vol. I (1972), p. 386; and J. Robert Vastine, "United States International Commodity Policy," *Law and Policy in International Business* (Summer 1977), 9:410–11.

63. UN Doc. E/CONF.46/141, vol. I (1964), pp. 23 and 32–33. This was known as "Special Principle Six."

64. UN Doc. TD/97, vol. I (1968), p. 436.

65. UN Doc. TD/II/C.1/SR.18 (1968), p. 228.

66. Gosovic, *UNCTAD*, pp. 112–13.

67. UN Doc. TD/180, vol. I (1972), p. 387.

68. Ibid., pp. 171–73 and 180.

69. UN Doc. E/CONF.46/141, vol. I (1964), pp. 27 and 135.

70. UN Docs. TD/B/C.1/49 and addenda; UN Doc. TD/II/C.1/SR 1–9; and TD/97, vol. I (1968), pp. 17, 36, and 235.

71. UN Doc. TD/180, vol. I (1972), p. 386.

72. UN Doc.TD/133, supp. 1 (1970), pp. 7–8; UN Doc. TD/127 (1970); UN Doc. TD/III/C. 1/18 (1972), p. 202; TD/180 vol. I (1972), p. 166. UNCTAD III simply called for "intensive intergovernmental consultations" on various *individual* commodities. UN Doc. TD/180, vol. I (1972), p. 81.

73. Mortimer, *The Third World Coalition in International Politics*, pp. 25–29.

74. UN Doc. TD/97, vol. I (1968), p. 433. At UNCTAD II in 1968 Group B was strongly opposed to unilateral producer collaboration, and no agreement was reached on this issue.

75. UN Doc. TD/B/317 (1970), pp. 8–19.

76. Ibid., p. 31; and UN Doc. TD/B/327 (1970), p. 31.

77. UN Doc. TD/180, vol. I (1972), pp. 182–221 and 385–86.

78. UN Doc. E/CONF. 46/141, vol. I (1964), p. 23.

79. Gosovic, *UNCTAD*, pp. 107–8.

80. Ibid., p. 108; see also UN Doc. TD/97, vol. I (1968), pp. 240–42 and 248–54.

81. UN Doc. TD/B/327, annex I (1970), p. 9.

82. Vastine, "United States International Commodity Policy," p. 410. The G77's Declaration of Lima is in UN Doc. TD/180, vol. I (1972), pp. 373–407.

83. General Assembly Res. 3201 and 3202 (S-VI) (1974).

84. General Assembly Res. 3281 (XXIX) (1974). The negotiations on this charter were launched by UNCTAD in 1972, but were transferred to the UN General Assembly, whose imprimatur, it was felt, would give the charter greater legitimacy.

85. Christopher P. Brown, *The Political and Social Economy of Commodity Control* (New York: Praeger, 1980), p. 74.

86. General Assembly Resolution 3202 (S-VI) (1974). Two good analyses of the NIEO are Jeffrey A. Hart, *The New International Economic Order: Cooperation and Conflict in North-South Economic Relations* (New York: St. Martin's Press, 1983); and Craig Murphy, *The Emergence of the NIEO Ideology* (Boulder, Colo.: Westview, 1984).

87. The key Secretariat studies were TD/498 (1974), and UN Doc. TD/B/C.1/166 and supplements (1974).

88. Secretariat arguments in support of the Common Fund appear in note 87 and are summarized in Brown, *The Political and Social Economy of Commodity Control*, pp. 75–76. On the major criticisms, see ibid., pp. 112–20.

89. Rothstein, *Global Bargaining*, p. 55.

90. Brown, *The Political and Social Economy of Commodity Control*, p. 80; also see Rothstein, *Global Bargaining*, p. 45.

91. Rothstein, *Global Bargaining*, pp. 134–35; Brown, *The Political and Social Economy of Commodity Control*, pp. 85 and 91–94; and Raymond R. Mikesell, *New Patterns of World Mineral Development* (Washington, D.C.: British North American Committee, 1979), pp. 25–29.

92. UNCTAD Resolution 93 (IV) (1976).

93. L. N. Rangarajan, *Commodity Conflict: The Political Economy of International Commodity Negotiations* (Ithaca, N.Y.: Cornell University Press, 1978), pp. 133–34.

94. Interviews.

95. General Assembly Res. 3281 (XXIX) (1976), article 5 of chapter 2.

96. Vastine, "United States International Commodity Policy," p. 415.

97. Ibid., pp. 424–26; Charles R. Johnston, Jr., *Law and Policy of Intergovernmental Commodity Agreements* (Dobbs Ferry, N.Y.: Oceana 1976), pp. 39–43.

98. General Assembly Res. 3281 (XXIX) (1974), article 28. On the developed countries' reaction to this proposal, see Robert F. Meagher, *An International Redistribution of Wealth and Power: A Study of the Charter of Economic Rights and Duties of States* (New York: Pergamon, 1979), p. 29 and passim.

99. UN Doc. TD/B/504, supp. 1 (1974).

100. UN Doc. TD/498 (1974), pp. 1–2.

101. UN Doc. TD/B/528, (1974), p. 39.

102. UN Doc. TD/B/563 (1975); and Meagher, *An International Redistribution of Wealth and Power*, p. 69.

103. Rangarajan, *Commodity Conflict*, p. 299; Rothstein, *Global Bargaining*, pp. 100–1. Indexation was publicly supported by the 19 developing-country delegations invited to the Conference on International Economic Cooperation; 7 of these were OPEC members, while another 5 were producers of strong mineral commodities. Mortimer, *The Third World Coalition in International Politics*, p. 102.

104. Resolution 93 (IV), para. (III) (2) (c) (1976). Developed-country reservations are in UN Doc. TD/217 (1976), p. 101.

105. Brown, *The Political and Social Economy of Commodiy Control*, pp. 101–6.

106. In addition to the previously cited documents released prior to UNCTAD IV, see UN Docs. TD/B/IPC/CF/2 (1977) and /4 (1977); TD/IPC/CF/3 (1977); and TD/B/IPC/CF 14, part I (1977).

107. Brown, *The Political and Social Economy of Commodity Control*, p. 128. A good discussion of Western policymaking on the fund is in Barbara B. Crane, "Policy Coordination by Major Western Powers in Bargaining with the Third World: Debt Relief and the Common Fund," *International Organization* (Summer 1984), 10:399–428.

108. UN Doc. TD/B/IPC/CF/14 (part I) (1977), pp. 14 and 19.

109. Brown, *The Political and Social Economy of Commodity Control*, p. 126.

110. Rothstein, *Global Bargaining*, p. 144.

111. UN Doc. TD/B/IPC/CF 14 (part I)(1977), pp. 7 and 15–17.

112. Ibid., p. 9.

113. Ibid., pp. 5 and 13.

114. UN Doc. TD/B/C.1/166/supplement (1974), p. 14.

115. Rangarajan, *Commodity Conflict*, pp. 296–97; Brown, *The Political and Social Economy of Commodity Control*, p. 123.

116. UN Doc. TD/B/C.1/185 (1975), p. 25.

117. UN Doc. TD/B/IPC/CF/8 (1975), pp. 4–5.

118. UN Doc. TD/IPC/CF/CONF/14 part II (1978), annex II, 2.

119. Mortimer, *The Third World Coalition in International Politics*, p. 119. Also see Brown, *The Political and Social Economy of Commodity Control*, pp. 89, 121, 126, and 134.

120. UN Doc. TD/B/IPC/CF/8, annex I (1977), pp. 4–9.

121. Paul D. Reynolds, "A Common Fund to Finance Commodity Agreements," *Law and Policy in International Business* (1978), 10:923–24.

122. UN Doc. TD/B/IPC/CF/8, annex I (1977), p. 14. The original UNCTAD Secretariat statement on the issue is in UN Doc. TD/B/C.1/196 (1975), p. 21.

123. Reynolds, "A Common Fund to Finance International Commodity Agreements," p. 932.

124. Interviews.

125. UN Doc. TD/B/IPC/CF/CONF/14, part II (1978), annex II.

126. UN Doc. TD/B/IPC/CF/CONF/24 (1980), articles 7–17 and schedule D. This document is the Common Fund Treaty. Another issue of dispute that was resolved in favor of the developed countries was the matter of what assets the fund

could draw on in the event of a default by a commodity organization ("the fungibility problem"). The G77 wanted the fund to be able to tap the assets of all affiliated ICOs. Group B demanded that only the contributions of members of the defaulting ICO to other ICOs should be used to cover any debts (article 17).

127. UN Doc. TD/IPC/CF/11 (1977), pp. 3–6.

128. UN Doc. TD/IPC/CF/CONF/14, part II (1980), p. 5.

129. UN Doc. TD/IPC/CF/CONF/24 (1980), articles 10 and 18.

130. UN Doc. TD/IPC/CF/CONF/19 (1980), annex I, p. 5 and annex III, p. 2.

131. Interviews.

132. UN Doc. TD/IPC/CF/CONF/24 (1980), articles 11, 12, 14, 35, and 51.

133. Interviews.

134. UN Doc. TD/B/IPC/AC/27 (1980), p. 3.

135. Ursula Wasserman, "UNCTAD: Agreement on the Common Fund," *Journal of World Trade Law* (December 1980), 14:543.

136. Mortimer, *The Third World Coalition in International Politics*, p. 119.

137. For an excellent discussion of this point, see Robert L. Rothstein, "The North-South Dialogue: The Political Economy of Immobility," *Journal of International Affairs* (Spring–Summer 1980), 34:1–17.

138. Interviews.

139. UNCTAD, press release, January 17, 1986.

140. Interviews.

141. Interviews.

142. Charles Ries, "The New International Economic Order: The Skeptics' Views," in Karl P. Sauvant and Hajo Hasenpflug, eds., *The New International Economic Order* (Boulder, Colo.: Westview Press, 1977), p. 73.

143. A. W. Hooke, *The International Monetary Fund: Its Evolution, Organization, and Activities* (Washington, D.C.: IMF, 1981), pp. 71–75.

144. Ibid., passim; and Louis M. Goreux, *Compensatory Financing Facility* (Washington, D.C.: IMF, 1980).

145. The international discussions concerning the creation of the CFF are described in J. Keith Horsefield, *The International Monetary Fund, 1945–1965* (Washington, D.C.: IMF, 1969), 1:531–36, and 3:442–57; and Margaret G. de Vries and J. Keith Horsefield, et al., *The International Monetary Fund, 1945–1965* (Washington, D.C.: IMF, 1969), 2:416–24.

146. UN Doc. E/CONF.46/C.1/SR.31 (1964), p. 4.

147. Ibid., p. 11.

148. Ibid., p. 6; UN Doc. E/CONF.46/C.1/SR.34 (1964), p. 6.

149. UN Doc. E/CONF.46/141, vol. I (1964), p. 23.

150. Ibid., p. 52.

151. On the 1966 discussions see de Vries and Horsefield, et al., *International Monetary Fund*, pp. 424–27; and Margaret G. de Vries, *The International Monetary Fund, 1966–71* (Washington D.C.: IMF, 1976), 1:261–63.

152. UN Doc. TD/97, vol. I (1968), p. 437.

153. UN Doc. TD/B/C.1/166, supp. 4 (1974); UN Doc. TD/B/C.1/195 (1975); and Paul D. Reynolds, *International Commodity Agreements and the Common Fund: A Legal and Financial Analysis* (New York: Praeger, 1978), ch. 8.

154. Meagher, *An International Distribution of Wealth and Power,* pp. 135–36.

155. Ibid., pp. 137–39.

156. UN Doc. TD/195 (1976), p. 12.

157. The rather general resolution on compensatory financing passed by the UNCTAD IV is in UN Doc. TD/217 (1976), p. 5.

158. Goreux, *Compensatory Financing Facility,* p. 52.

159. Good analyses of STABEX and MINEX are in John Ravenhill, "What Is to Be Done for Third World Commodity Exporters? An Evaluation of the STABEX Scheme," *International Organization* (Summer 1984), 38:544–46; Goreux, *Compensatory Financing Facility,* pp. 80–84; Reynolds, *International Commodity Agreements and the Common Fund,* pp. 165–69; J.D.A. Cuddy, "Compensatory Financing in the North-South Dialogue: The IMF and STABEX (EEC) Schemes," *Journal of World Trade Law* (January/February 1979), 13:66–76; and John Ravenhill, *Collective Clientism: The Lomé Conventions and North-South Relations* (New York: Columbia University Press, 1985). The original commodity groups were groundnuts, cocoa, coffee, cotton, coconuts, palm oil and palm kernels, leather and skins, wood, bananas, tea, sisal, and iron ore.

160. Several commodities were added during the life of Lomé I: vanilla, cloves and clove oils, wool, mohair, gum arabic, pyrethrum, niaouli, ylang ylang, and sesame seeds. Under Lomé II yet more commodities were added: cashew nuts, pepper, shrimps and prawns, rubber, squid, cotton seeds, oil cake, peas, beans, and lentils. Also, when Lomé II was negotiated, a new Mineral Insurance Export Scheme, MINEX, was adopted, covering iron ore, copper, cobalt, phosphates, manganese, bauxite/alumina, and tin. Unlike STABEX, however, MINEX compensation is geared to decreases in export capacity, not earnings declines. This reflects the concern of the European Community states about access to minerals and metals required by many of their industries and not found in Western Europe itself. MINEX, also unlike STABEX, offers low-interest loans, not interest-free loans or grants.

161. John Ravenhill, "What Is to Be Done for Third World Commodity Exporters?" pp. 544–46.

162. MINEX allocated another 280 EUA, which amounted to slightly more than U.S. $250 million in November 1982.

163. Ravenhill, "What Is to Be Done for Third World Commodity Exporters?" pp. 546–50; UN Doc. TD/B/AC.37/3 (1984), pp. 30–36.

164. However, MINEX does require that the funds be directed to projects or programs in the affected mining sectors.

165. UN Doc. TD/B/AC.37/3 (1984), p. 33.

166. Ravenhill, "What Is to Be Done for Third World Commodity Exporters?" pp. 540–43.

167. UN Doc. TD/236 (1979), p. 53; Resolution 128 (V), TD/268 (1979), p. 32.

168. Goreux, *Compensatory Financing Facility,* pp. 50–51. A further change occurred in May 1981, when the IMF board agreed that the CFF could extend additional assistance to members experiencing balance-of-payments difficulties caused by the temporary rising costs of cereals imports. *IMF Survey,* June 1981, pp.165 and 177–79.

169. Goreux, *Compensatory Financing Facility*, pp. 4, 40–41, and 52; Sidney Dell, "The Fifth Credit Tranche," *World Development* (1985), 13:245–49; interviews with IMF officials.

170. Resolution 124 (V), UN Doc. TD/268 (1979), p. 11.

171. The Secretariat studies prepared for UNCTAD V are in UN Doc. TD/229, supp. (1979). References to the proposals of Sweden and West Germany are on p. 7.

172. UN Doc. TD/B/C.1/214 (1980).

173. UN Doc. TD/B/C.1/222 (1981).

174. UN Doc. TD/B/C.1/221 (1981); interviews.

175. Department of State, *IMF Effectiveness During the Present Commodity Slump* (Washington D.C.: U.S. Department of State, March 1982), pp. 4–5.

176. UN Doc. TD/B/C.1/234 (1982).

177. UN Doc. TD/B/C.1/243 (1983). pp. 15–16.

178. UN Doc. TD/325 (1983), p. 18.

179. Dell, "The Fifth Credit Tranche"; *IMF Survey*, January 12, 1983, p. 7; September 1984, pp. 7–8; and September 1985, p. 13.

180. UN Doc. TD/B/1029 (1984).

181. Ibid.; UN Docs. TD/B/1112 and TD/B/AC.43/4 (1986); and interviews.

3. THE TIN AND NATURAL RUBBER AGREEMENTS

1. World Bank, *Commodity Trade and Price Trends* (1985), table 7.

2. World Bank, *Tin Handbook* (1981), pp. I-1–5; William L. Baldwin, *The World Tin Market: Political Pricing and Competition* (Durham, N.C.: Duke University Press, 1983), pp. 8–21; William Fox, *Tin: The Working of a Commodity Agreement* (London: Mining Journal Books, 1974), ch. 1.

3. World Bank, *Tin Handbook*, pp. I-1–15 and II-9; Fox, *Tin*, p. 17.

4. Production figures for the 1980s are in *Financial Times*, November 1, 1985, p. 22; and *Mineral Commodity Summaries 1986* (Washington, D.C.: U.S. Department of the Interior, 1986), p. 167. Information on production costs is in Baldwin, *The World Tin Market*, pp. 184–85 and 214–15; and *Far Eastern Economic Review*, January 23, 1986, pp. 66–67.

5. Baldwin, *The World Tin Market*, pp. 22–45 and 152–83; Fox, *Tin*, pp. 23–69; World Bank, *Tin Handbook*, pp. III-1–2; John Thoburn, "Policies for Tin Exporters," *Resources Policy* (June 1981), 7:75–79.

6. Baldwin, *The World Tin Market*, pp. 192–206; J. Chhabra, E. Grilli, and P. Pollak, *The World Tin Economy: An Econometric Analysis* (World Bank Staff Commodity Paper No. 1, June 1978), p. 23; *Far Eastern Economic Review*, March 20, 1986, p. 30.

7. World Bank, *Commodity Trade and Price Trends* (1985), p. 114. Over 1955–81 the average annual change in constant dollars was quite moderate—10.4 percent (table 1.4). The drastic fall in price from £10,000/ton in early 1985 to below £4,000 in the spring of 1986 is described later in this chapter.

8. World Bank, *Tin Handbook*, pp. II-1–5, III-1–5 and IV-1–3.

9. Supply and demand elasticities are analyzed in Baldwin, *The World Tin Market*, pp. 103–29; see also World Bank, *Tin Handbook*, pp. IV-1–4; Zuhayr Mikdashi, *The International Politics of Natural Resources* (Ithaca, N.Y.: Cornell University Press, 1976), pp. 129–30; Jere R. Behrman, "International Commodity Agreements: An Evaluation of the UNCTAD Integrated Commodity Programme," in William R. Cline, ed., *Policy Alternatives for a New International Economic Order: An Economic Analysis* (New York: Praeger, 1979), pp. 118–19. On developments leading up to the October 1985 crisis, see *Financial Times*, November 1, 1985, p. 22; *Far Eastern Economic Review*, November 7, 1985, pp. 114–15; and the text discussion.

10. Klaus Knorr, *Tin Under Control* (Stanford, Calif.: Food Research Institute, Stanford University, 1945), p. 74.

11. Fox, *Tin*, p. 117. See Knorr, *Tin Under Control*, pp. 77–79, and Baldwin, *The World Tin Market*, pp. 63–65 for reservations about its positive effects.

12. Fox, *Tin*, pp. 187–90; Baldwin, *The World Tin Market*, pp. 69–74.

13. Fox, *Tin*, p. 196; Baldwin, *The World Tin Market*, p. 75.

14. Linda Cahn, "National Power and International Regimes: United States Commodity Policies, 1930–1980" (Ph.D. dissertation, Stanford University, 1980), pp. 256 and 262–63; Fox, *Tin*, p. 228.

15. J.W.F. Rowe, *Primary Commodities in International Trade* (London: Cambridge University Press, 1965), p. 170.

16. Baldwin, *The World Tin Market*, pp. 79–82; Fox, *Tin*, p. 256.

17. The 1953 agreement is in United Nations, *Treaty Series*, 256:31.

18. Fox, *Tin*, pp. 223–24 and 283–84. Provisions regarding adjustment of shares are in article 7 of the 1953 ITA, article 7 and annex G of the 1960 and 1965 ITAs, article 34 and annex G of the 1970 ITA and article 34 and annex F of the 1975 and 1981 ITAs.

19. Fox, *Tin*, pp. 224–25; UN Doc. TD/TIN.6/3 (1980), p. 14; Rowe, *Primary Commodities in International Trade*, p. 171.

20. Rowe, *Primary Commodities in International Trade*, p. 170.

21. Baldwin, *The World Tin Market*, pp. 81–82; Cahn, "National Power and International Regimes," p. 260.

22. Fox, *Tin*, pp. 254 and 266.

23. Rowe, *Primary Commodities in International Trade*, p. 171; Kerstin Barkman, "Costs and Finance of the Tin Buffer Stock," *Journal of World Trade Law* (March–April 1976), 10:499; Fox, *Tin*, p. 281.

24. Barkman, "Costs and Finance of the Tin Buffer Stock," p. 500; Fox, *Tin*, pp. 282–89.

25. Fox, *Tin*, p. 300; Rowe, *Primary Commodities in International Trade*, p. 172; Baldwin, *The World Tin Market*, pp. 83–84.

26. The 1960 agreement is in United Nations, *Treaty Series*, 403:3.

27. Baldwin, *The World Tin Market*, pp. 84–86; Fox, *Tin*, p. 312.

28. UN Doc. E/CONF.32/5 (1960), pp. 23–24.

29. UN Doc. E/CONF. 32/5 (1960), pp. 13–17 for the views of consumers.

30. Fox, *Tin*, pp. 314–16.

31. Ibid., pp. 328–29; UN Doc. TD/TIN.6/3 (1960), p. 5.

32. Fox, *Tin*, pp. 320–52; Cahn, "National Power and International Regimes," p. 296.

33. The 1965 agreement is in United Nations, *Treaty Series*, 616:317.

34. Fox, *Tin*, pp. 354–58.

35. UN Doc. TD/TIN.3/5 (1965), p. 26.

36. International Tin Council, *World Tin Statistics, 1964–74* (London: ITC, 1976), p. 12.

37. Cahn, "National Power and International Regimes," p. 296.

38. Fox, *Tin*, pp. 348–49.

39. Ibid., p. 348; see also Cahn, "National Power and International Regimes," p. 273.

40. Cahn, "National Power and International Regimes," p. 296.

41. UN Doc. TD/TIN.6/3 (1980), p. 6.

42. UN Doc. TD/TIN.6/3 (1980), pp. 6 and 16; Fox, *Tin*, pp. 370–71.

43. Fox, *Tin*, pp. 370–71.

44. Christopher Gilbert, *The Post War Tin Agreements and Their Implications for Copper* (London: Commodities Research Unit, March 1976), pp. 17–18; L. N. Rangarajan, *Commodity Conflict: The Political Economy of International Commodity Negotiations* (Ithaca, N.Y.: Cornell University Press, 1978), pp. 228–29.

45. Fox, *Tin*, p. 373.

46. The U.S. tin objective was raised to 200,000 tons in 1968 and then to 232,000 tons in March 1969; this slashed the GSA's disposable "surplus" to only 25,000 tons. Mikdashi, *The International Politics of Natural Resources*, pp. 120–21; Cahn, "National Power and International Regimes," p. 296.

47. Cahn, "National Power and International Regimes," pp. 276–77.

48. UN Doc. TD/TIN.4/SR.1–8 (1970), pp. 10–11.

49. UN Doc. TD/TIN.4/C.1/SR.1–24 (1970), p. 72 and passim.

50. The 1970 ITA is in UN Doc. TD/TIN.4/7 (1970).

51. Fox, *Tin*, pp. 255 and 260; Mikdashi, *The International Politics of Natural Resources*, p. 120.

52. The council had shifted from the long to the metric ton in January 1970, resulting in a reduction in the previous ceiling of £1,630.

53. Fox, *Tin*, pp. 374–75.

54. UN Doc. TD/TIN.6/3 (1980), pp. 7 and 15.

55. Baldwin, *The World Tin Market*, p. 89.

56. Fox, *Tin*, p. 382.

57. Ibid., p. 386; UN Doc. TD/TIN.6/3 (1980), pp. 8 and 14–15; Carmine Nappi, *Commodity Market Controls* (Lexington, Mass.: Lexington Books, 1979), p. 67.

58. UN Doc. TD/TIN.6/3 (1980), pp. 8 and 14.

59. The 1975 agreement is in UN Doc. TD/TIN.5/10 (1975).

60. U.S. General Accounting Office, *The Fifth International Tin Agreement—Issues and Possible Implications: Report to the Congress by the Comptroller General of the United States* (Washington, D.C.: Government Printing Office, August 30, 1976), p. 6; Baldwin, *The World Tin Market*, pp. 92–93; J. Robert Vastine, "United States International Commodity Policy," *Law and Policy in International Business* (Summer 1977), 9:436–42; interviews.

61. Cahn, "National Power and International Regimes," p. 287; U.S. General Accounting Office, *The Fifth International Tin Agreement,* p. 33.

62. Interviews.

63. C. R. Ostrom, "Third World Producers vs. Developed World Consumers: A Comparison of the International Agreements for Tin and Natural Rubber" (paper presented to twenty-first annual convention of the International Studies Association, Los Angeles, March 18–22, 1980), p. 17.

64. UN Doc. TD/TIN.6/3 (1980), p. 9; U.S. General Accounting Office, *The Fifth International Tin Agreement,* pp. 22–24.

65. *Far Eastern Economic Review,* January 21, 1977, p. 98, and March 18, 1977, p. 96.

66. UN Doc. TD/TIN.6/3 (1980), p. 9.

67. *Far Eastern Economic Review,* March 18, 1977, pp. 96–97.

68. Ibid., p. 97.

69. *Latin American Commodities Report,* March 11 and April 18, 1977.

70. *Far Eastern Economic Review,* July 29, 1977, p. 80; interviews.

71. Ibid., p. 80; interviews.

72. Cahn, "National Power and International Regimes," p. 289.

73. *Latin American Commodities Report,* January 27, February 10, and July 21, 1978; interviews.

74. Interviews; UN Doc. TD/TIN.6/3 (1980), p. 10.

75. *Far Eastern Economic Review,* August 3, 1979, p. 47; *Latin American Commodities Report,* July 27, 1979.

76. *Far Eastern Economic Review,* January 18, 1980, p. 57; *Mining Journal,* March 28, 1980, pp. 245–46.

77. The 1981 ITA is in UN Doc. TD/TIN 6/14 (1981).

78. *Latin American Commodities Report,* February 22, 1980; *Far Eastern Economic Review,* February 29, 1980, p. 37; interviews.

79. Interviews.

80. Interviews; *Far Eastern Economic Review,* May 23, 1980, p. 63; *Latin American Commodities Report,* April 18 and May 12, 1980.

81. *Latin American Commodities Report,* December 19, 1980.

82. *Latin American Commodities Report,* January 9 and April 17, 1981; *Far Eastern Economic Review,* May 1, 1981, pp. 46–47; interviews.

83. Baldwin, *The World Tin Market,* pp. 3–4 and 222–24; interviews.

84. These developments in the last half of 1981 and the first half of 1982 are described in Baldwin, *The World Tin Market,* pp. 5–7; Ursel Baliol Scott, "Tin," *Mining Annual Review—1983,* p. 44; *Latin American Commodities Report,* February 5, March 19, May 7, May 21, July 2, July 16, and August 13, 1982; *Mining Journal,* April 30, 1982, p. 324; May 21, 1982, p. 371; June 18, 1982, pp. 449 and 453–54; June 25, 1982, p. 465; July 2, 1982, pp. 8 and 13; July 9, 1982, p. 34; and July 16, 1982, p. 8; *Far Eastern Economic Review,* May 7, 1982, pp. 50–51, and June 25, 1982, pp. 71–72.

85. Scott, "Tin," pp. 41–42; International Tin Council, *Notes on Tin,* August 1983, p. 405.

86. *Far Eastern Economic Review,* June 3, 1983, pp. 51–53; *Mining Journal,* April 1,

1983, p. 211, and November 25, 1983, p. 386; *Latin American Commodities Report,* February 25 and April 15, 1983, and January 27, 1984; interviews.

87. International Tin Council, *Notes on Tin,* October 1983, p. 459, and April 1984, p. 649; *Mining Journal,* July 1, 1983, p. 8, and February 10, 1984, p. 88; *Financial Times,* November 1, 1985, p. 22; *Far Eastern Economic Review,* May 9, 1985, pp. 94–96; Robert Gibson-Jarvie, *The Tin Crisis: The Final Chapter* (Cambridge: Woodhead-Faulkner, 1986), passim; and interviews.

88. *Far Eastern Economic Review,* May 9, 1985, pp. 94–95 and November 7, 1985, pp. 114–15. The best accounts of the development of "the tin crisis" are in articles by Stephan Wagstyl in the *Financial Times* from October 1985 through May 1986. Gibson-Jarvie's monograph *The Tin Crisis* also provides much valuable information. Information was also obtained from interviews.

89. The changes in tin production are described in *Financial Times,* November 1, 1985, p. 22.

90. The borrowing and forward buying practices of the buffer-stock manager are highlighted in Gibson-Jarvie, *The Tin Crisis,* esp. pp. 32–35; and *Far Eastern Economic Review,* May 9, 1985, pp. 94–96, and November 7, 1985, pp. 114–15.

91. Gibson-Jarvie, *The Tin Crisis,* pp. 40–44; and interviews.

92. *Financial Times,* December 4, 1985, p. 30 and February 4, 1986, p. 36; Gerald-Jarvie, *The Tin Crisis,* pp. 14–23; *Far Eastern Economic Review,* February 20, 1986, pp. 74–75.

93. Interviews; *Financial Times,* April 4, 1986, p. 34; *Far Eastern Economic Review,* March 20, 1986, p. 154.

94. *Financial Times,* May 1, 1986, p. 30; Gibson-Jarvie, *The Tin Crisis.*

95. World Bank, *Rubber Handbook* (1981), pp. I-1–13 and II-1–4; P. W. Allan, *Natural Ruber and the Synthetics* (London: Crosby Lockwood, 1972), pp. 9–10 and 57–59; Economist Intelligence Unit, *Natural Rubber: A Dovetailed Examination of Aspects of the International Natural Rubber Agreement and Its Wider Implications* (London: Economist Intelligence Unit, 1980), pp. 50–51.

96. Ostrom, "Third World Producers vs. Developed World Consumers," p. 11; Allan, *Natural Rubber and the Synthetics,* p. 76; World Bank/FAO, *World Rubber Economy: Structure, Changes, Prospects* (Washington, D.C.: World Bank, June 1978), pp. 16–19.

97. World Bank, *Commodity Trade and Price Trends* (1985), p. 90.

98. World Bank, *Rubber Handbook,* p. IV-7.

99. World Bank, *Rubber Handbook,* pp. IV-1–7 and V-1–4; Behrman, "International Commodity Agreements," p. 119; Ostrom, "Third World Producers vs. Developed World Consumers," p. 8; World Bank/FAO, *The World Rubber Economy,* p. 7.

100. Analyses of developments in the interwar period can be found in Alton D. Law, *International Commodity Agreements* (Lexington, Mass.: Lexington Books, 1975), pp. 61–62; Rowe, *Primary Commodities in International Trade,* pp. 123–24; P. T. Bauer, *The Rubber Industry: A Study in Competition and Monopoly* (Cambridge, Mass.: Harvard University Press, 1948), passim.

101. For accounts of deliberations during these years, see FAO Docs. CCP 53/83 (1983), p. 8; CCP 56/20 (1956), pp. 27–28; and CPP 61/33 (1961), p. 43; and CCP

53/83 (1983), p. 8; UN Docs. E/CONF.46/106 (1964); TD/B/C.1/121 (1972); and TD/B/C.1/SYN. p. 56 (1971); World Bank/FAO, *The World Rubber Economy*, pp. 198–99; Rangarajan, *Commodity Conflict*, p. 188.

102. World Bank/FAO, *The World Rubber Economy*, pp. 15, 19, 59, and 199.

103. Economist Intelligence Unit, *Natural Rubber*, p. 19. On the 1974–75 crisis and producer responses, see Richard Stubbs, "Malaysia's Rubber Smallholding Industry: Crisis and the Search for Stability," *Pacific Affairs* (Spring 1983), 56:86–93.

104. World Bank/FAO, *The World Rubber Economy*, pp. 190 and 199.

105. UN Doc. TD/B/IPC/RUBBER/L.3 (1977), p. 5.

106. UN Doc. TD/B/IPC/RUBBER/L.3 (1977), passim; Karen Mingst, "Economic Determinants of International Commodity Regulations," *Journal of World Trade Law* (March–April 1979), 13:165.

107. Stubbs, "Malaysia's Rubber Smallholding Industry," pp. 84–105; C. P. Brown, *The Political and Social Economy of Commodity Control* (New York: Praeger, 1980), p. 193.

108. UN Doc. TD/B/IPC/RUBBER/L.3 (1977), p. 6.

109. UN Doc. TD/B/IPC/RUBBER/4 (1977), p. 3.

110. UN Doc. TD/B/IPC/RUBBER/5 (1977), p. 4; Brown, *The Political and Social Economy of Commodity Control*, p. 195; interviews.

111. UN Doc. TD/B/IPC/RUBBER/5 (1977), passim; interviews.

112. UN Doc. TD/B/IPC/RUBBER/5 (1977), passim; interviews.

113. Ostrom, "Third World Producers vs. Developed World Consumers," p. 18; *Latin American Commodities Report*, December 15, 1978; interviews.

114. Interviews.

115. Interviews; Ostrom, "Third World Producers vs. Developed World Consumers," pp. 16–25: *Latin American Commodities Report*, April 6, and April 17, 1979; *Far Eastern Economic Review*, April 27, 1979, pp. 106–7.

116. The 1979 INRA is in UN Doc. TD/RUBBER/15/Rev. 1 (1979).

117. Kabir-Ur-Rahman Khan, "The International Natural Rubber Agreement," *Resources Policy* (September 1980), 6:259–60; interviews.

118. U.S., House of Representatives, *International Natural Rubber Agreement* (Hearings and Markup before the Committee on Foreign Affairs and Its Subcommittee on International Economic Policy and Trade, Ninety-Sixth Congress, 2d sess., April 16, 22, and 24, and May 8, 1980) (Washington, D.C.: Government Printing Office, 1980), p. 62.

119. Ibid., p. 79.

120. Stubbs, "Malaysia's Rubber Smallholding Industry," pp. 86–92 and passim.

121. U.S., House, *International Natural Rubber Agreement*, pp. 16, 33, 61–62, and 73–79.

122. U.S., House, *International Natural Rubber Agreement*, p. 33.

123. Interviews.

124. *Far Eastern Economic Review*, August 14, 1981, p. 45.

125. Richard Stubbs, "The International Natural Rubber Agreement: Its Negotiation and Operations," *Journal of World Trade Law* (January/February 1984), 18:27–30; Stubbs, "Malaysia's Rubber Smallholding Industry," pp. 99–101; *Far Eastern Economic Review*, April 23, 1982, pp. 87–88; April 9, 1982, pp. 59–62; May 14, 1982, p. 101;

November 5, 1982, pp. 76–78; and November 26, 1982, p. 10; Frederic W. Siesseger, Director, International Resources Division, U.S. Department of Commerce, "Address to the Washington Rubber Group" (November 3, 1982) (mimeo); interviews.

126. *Financial Times*, April 25, 1985, p. 40, and June 13, 1985, p. 36; *UNCTAD Bulletin*, April 1984, pp. 4–6.

127. *Far Eastern Economic Review*, August 29, 1985, p. 48.

128. *Far Eastern Economic Review*, June 12, 1986, p. 134; interviews.

129. A draft of the 1987 INRA is in UN Doc. TD/RUBBER.2/16 (1987). Information on the conference was obtained from interviews and *The Economist*, March 21, 1987, pp. 76–77.

130. Gordon W. Smith, "U.S. Commodity Policy and the Tin Agreement," in David B. H. Denoon, ed., *The New International Economic Order: A U.S. Response* (London: Macmillan, 1979), p. 190. On the political concerns of the developed states, see Baldwin, *The World Tin Market*, pp. 99–101.

4. THE SUGAR, COFFEE, AND COCOA AGREEMENTS

1. World Bank, *Commodity Trade and Price Trends* (1985), table 7.

2. World Bank, *Sugar Handbook* (1981), pp. V-1–14; D. Gale Johnson, *The Sugar Program: Large Costs and Small Benefits* (Washington: American Enterprise Institute, 1974); Abdessatar Grissa, *Structure of the International Sugar Market and Its Impact on Developing Countries* (Paris: OECD Development Centre, 1976), pp. 24–27; Michael Moynagh, "The Negotiation of the Commonwealth Sugar Agreement, 1949–1951," *The Journal of Commonwealth and Comparative Politics* (July 1970), 16:170–90; Ian Smith, "Structure and Policy Changes in World Sugar," *Journal of World Trade Law* (May–June 1977), 15:228–47; Ian Smith, "Prospects for a New International Sugar Agreement," *Journal of World Trade Law* (July–August 1983), 17:308–24.

3. World Bank, *Sugar Handbook*, pp. IV-1–8 and V-10–13.

4. F. O. Licht's *International Sugar Report*, November 16, 1982, p. 581. Trend data can be found in the annual volumes of World Bank, *Commodity Trade and Price Trends*.

5. World Bank, *Sugar Handbook*, pp. VI-1–4; F. O. Licht's *International Sugar Report*, November 16, 1982, pp. 581–92.

6. J. W. F. Rowe, *Primary Commodities in International Trade* (London: Cambridge University Press, 1965), p. 125.

7. Ibid., pp. 146–47; Carmine Nappi, *Commodity Market Controls* (Lexington, Mass.: Lexington Books, 1979), p. 35.

8. Vincent A. Mahler, "The Political Economy of North-South Commodity Bargaining: The Case of the International Sugar Agreement," *International Organization* (Autumn 1984), 38:709–32.

9. *The World Sugar Economy: Structure and Policies* (London: International Sugar Council, 1963), 2:211.

10. Ibid., 2:211–12; Rowe, *Primary Commodities in International Trade*, pp. 147–48.

11. Nappi, *Commodity Market Controls*, pp. 50–52.

12. The agreement is in United Nations, *Treaty Series* (1957), 258:153.

13. *World Sugar Economy,* 2:213–15.

14. *World Sugar Economy,* 1:126.

15. *World Sugar Economy,* 2:213.

16. *World Sugar Economy,* 1:175 and 191; Rowe, *Primary Commodities in International Trade,* p. 175. Albert Viton, "Towards a New I.S.A.," *F. O. Licht's International Sugar Report,* May 1983, p. 25.

17. Albert Viton, "The Once and Future ISA Negotiations," *F. O. Licht's International Sugar Report,* January 1985, p. 4.

18. *World Sugar Economy,* 1:243.

19. Ibid., pp. 279, 293 and 303–4.

20. Interviews; Ian Smith, "The New International Sugar Agreement: The Search for Effective Market Control," *F. O. Licht's International Sugar Report,* May 1983, p. 8; Viton, "Towards a New I.S.A."; Smith, "Prospects for a New International Sugar Agreement," pp. 319–20.

21. C. P. Brown, *The Political and Social Economy of Commodity Control* (New York: Praeger, 1980), p. 21.

22. *World Sugar Economy,* 2:212.

23. *New York Times,* May 23, 1956, p. 39.

24. *World Sugar Economy,* 2:216; Rowe, *Primary Commodities in International Trade,* p. 176.

25. Viton, "Towards a New I.S.A.," p. 28.

26. Smith, "The New International Sugar Agreement," p. 8.

27. *World Sugar Economy,* 2:214.

28. Interviews; Viton, "Towards a New I.S.A.," p. 25.

29. *New York Times,* September 23, 1958, p. 13; International Sugar Council, *Annual Report and Accounts, 1958* (1960), pp. 6–7.

30. The 1958 agreement is in United Nations, *Treaty Series* (1961), 385:137.

31. Rowe, *Primary Commodities in International Trade,* p. 176.

32. Grissa, *Structure of the International Sugar Market and Its Impact on Developing Countries,* pp. 31–34.

33. Linda A. Cahn, "National Power and International Regimes: United States Commodity Policies, 1930–1980" (Ph.D. diss., Stanford University, 1980), ch. 5.

34. UNCTAD, *Commodity Survey, 1966* (1966), p. 44.

35. *World Sugar Economy,* 1:124; *Economist,* October 21, 1961, p. 280.

36. John Southgate, "World Trade in Sugar," *Journal of World Trade Law* (November–December 1967), 1:609; L. N. Rangarajan, *Commodity Conflict: The Political Economy of International Commodity Negotiations* (Ithaca, N.Y.: Cornell University Press, 1978), p. 215; Nappi, *Commodity Market Controls,* p. 52; Grissa, *Structure of the International Sugar Market and Its Impact on Developing Countries,* p. 17.

37. Southgate, "World Trade in Sugar," p. 631; Nappi, *Commodity Market Controls,* p. 71; Grissa, *Structure of the International Sugar Market and Its Impact on Developing Countries,* p. 57; FAO, *Commodity Review and Outlook, 1968* (1969), p. 104.

38. F. O. Grogan, *International Trade in Temperate Zone Products* (Edinburgh: Oliver and Boyd, 1972), p. 110.

39. *New York Times,* January 6, 1965, p. 11, and March 4, 1966, p. 43; Grissa,

Structure of the International Sugar Market and Its Impact on Developing Countries, pp. 31 and 34.

40. Nappi, *Commodity Market Controls*, p. 71.

41. UNCTAD, *Commodity Survey, 1966* (1966), p. 69; *Economist*, March 19, 1966, p. 1164.

42. Grogan, *International Trade in Temperate Zone Products*, p. 112.

43. Ibid., p. 118.

44. A similar, though more complicated, undertaking was provided with respect to Cuban exports to East Germany and China, which were ineligible to accede to the accord because of their absence from the United Nations. Ibid., p. 119; "The International Sugar Agreement, 1968," *Journal of World Trade Law* (March–April 1969) 3:219–20.

45. "The International Sugar Agreement, 1968," p. 220.

46. Ian Smith, "Sugar Markets in Disarray," *Journal of World Trade Law* (January–February 1975), 9:48.

47. The 1968 agreement is in United Nations, *Treaty Series* (1969), 654:3.

48. Grogan, *International Trade in Temperate Zone Products*, p. 115; Smith, "Structure and Policy Changes in World Sugar," p. 244.

49. Grogan, *International Trade in Temperate Zone Products*, p. 116; Smith, "Sugar Markets in Disarray," pp. 47–48.

50. Grogan, *International Trade in Temperate Zone Products*, p. 122.

51. Rangarajan, *Commodity Conflict*, p.149; Smith, "Sugar Markets in Disarray," pp. 50–53.

52. Grissa, *Structure of the International Sugar Market and Its Impact on Developing Countries*, p. 63.

53. Smith, "Structure and Policy Changes in World Sugar," p. 245; Grissa, *Structure of the International Sugar Market and Its Impact on Developing Countries*, pp. 63–64.

54. Smith, "Structure and Policy Changes in World Sugar," p. 244.

55. FAO, *Commodity Review and Outlook, 1971/72* (1973), p. 88.

56. Smith, "Sugar Markets in Disarray," pp. 48–49.

57. Ibid.; Brown, *The Political and Social Economy of Commodity Control*, p. 23; *New York Times*, October 13, 1972, p. 31.

58. FAO, *Commodity Review and Outlook, 1975/76* (1977), pp. 73 and 78.

59. Smith, "Structure and Policy Changes in World Sugar," p. 236; interviews.

60. *New York Times*, November 19, 1974, p. 61.

61. Vincent A. Mahler, "Britain, the European Community, and the Developing Commonwealth: Dependence, Interdependence, and the Political Economy of Sugar," *International Organization* (Summer 1981), 35:482–83.

62. Ian Smith, "EEC Sugar Policy in an International Context," *Journal of World Trade Law* (March–April 1981), 25:96.

63. FAO, *Commodity Review and Outlook, 1979–80* (1981), p. 23; Smith, "Structure and Policy Changes in World Sugar," p. 233.

64. The 1977 ISA is in UN Doc. TD/SUGAR/9/10 (1977).

65. Smith, "The New International Sugar Agreement," p. 6; Brown, *The Political and Social Economy of Commodity Control*, p. 181; interviews.

66. Viton, "Towards a New ISA," p. 26; Brown, *The Political and Social Economy of Commodity Control*, p. 180; interviews.

67. *Latin American Commodities Report*, July 15, August 19, and September 9, 1977; Brown, *The Political and Social Economy of Commodity Control*, p. 184; interviews. Some producers were concerned that a high price could spur production of high fructose corn syrup in developed countries—thus reducing future demand for sugar.

68. *Latin American Commodities Report*, September 9, September 16, September 23, and October 21, 1977; Mahler, "The Political Economy of North-South Commodity Bargaining," pp. 721–22; interviews.

69. Article 41; Kabir-ur-Rahman Khan, "The International Sugar Agreement, 1977," *Food Policy* (May 1978), 3:107; interviews.

70. Article 34; H. Ahlfeld, "Elements of an International Sugar Agreement," *F. O. Licht's International Sugar Report*, May 1983, p. 17; Smith, "The New International Sugar Agreement," p. 5; Viton, "Towards a New I.S.A.," p. 36; Smith, "Prospects for a New International Sugar Agreement," pp. 316–18; interviews.

71. Khan, "The International Sugar Agreement, 1977," p. 109; Brown, *The Political and Social Economy of Commodity Control*, p. 181; interviews.

72. *Latin American Commodities Report*, February 3, 1978 and March 9, 1979.

73. Prices for 1978–81 are in International Sugar Organization, *Annual Report for the Year 1982* (1983), pp. 30–31.

74. *Latin American Commodities Report*, April 6, 1979; FAO, *Commodity Review and Outlook, 1979/80* (1981), p. 22; Viton "Towards a New I.S.A.," p. 41; and interviews.

75. On what were actually a series of bumper crops beginning in 1979, see Smith, "The New International Sugar Agreement," pp. 7–9.

76. *F. O. Licht's International Sugar Report*, May 28, 1982, pp. 289–90, and December 9, 1982, p. 636; Smith, "Prospects for a New International Sugar Agreement," p. 319.

77. Smith, "Prospects for a New International Sugar Agreement," pp. 314–15; W. D. Bensen, "The Geneva Conference: A Look Backwards and a Look Forwards," *F. O. Licht's International Sugar Report*, January 1985, p. 17; Comptroller General of U. S., *U.S. Sweetner/Sugar Issues and Concerns* (Washington, D.C.: U.S. General Accounting Office, November 15, 1984); interviews.

78. Viton, "Towards a New I.S.A.," p. 27.

79. Viton, "The Once and Future ISA Negotiations," pp. 5–6.

80. The negotiations during 1983 are described in *F. O. Licht's International Sugar Report*, February 8, 1983, pp. 79–87; March 25, 1983, pp. 173–75; May 18, 1983, pp. 264–66; July 15, 1983, pp. 359–61; September 7, 1983, pp. 455–57; October 27, 1983, pp. 545–48; November 11, 1983, pp. 587–88; November 28, 1983, p. 498; January 31, 1984, pp. 68–69. See also Smith, "The New International Sugar Agreement," pp. 5–10; and Smith, "Prospects for a New International Sugar Agreement," pp. 308–24. Information also obtained from interviews.

81. The 1984 conference is analyzed in: *Latin American Commodities Report*, June 11, 1984 and July 6, 1984; Gill and Duffus Ltd., *Sugar Market Report No. 16*, July 1984, pp. 1 and 11–13; and C. Czarnikow Ltd., *Sugar Review No. 1707*, June 18, 1984, p. 119 and *Sugar Review No. 1708*, July 5, 1984, p. 123; Viton, "The Once and Future ISA

Negotiations," pp. 3–11; Bensen, "The Geneva Conference," pp. 17–22; R. Holland, "International Sugar After Geneva," F. O. Licht's International Sugar Report, January 1985, pp. 23–24; and Ian Smith, "World Sugar Market Without Controls: Freedom or Anarchy?" F. O. Licht's International Sugar Report, January 1985, pp. 35–42. Information was also obtained from interviews.

82. The text is in F. O. Licht's International Sugar Report, January 1985, pp. 43–57.

83. Viton, "The Once and Future ISA Negotiations," pp. 3–11.

84. Shamshir Singh, Jos de Vries, John D. L. Mulley, and Patrick Yeung, Coffee, Tea, and Cocoa: Market Prospects and Development Lending, World Bank Staff Occasional Papers 22 (Baltimore: Johns Hopkins University Press, 1977), p. 25.

85. Bart S. Fisher, The International Coffee Agreement: A Study in Diplomacy (New York: Praeger, 1971), p. 4; Singh et al., Coffee, Tea, and Cocoa, pp. 15, 25, 30, and 43; L. T. Galloway, "The International Coffee Agreement," Journal of World Trade Law (May–June 1973) 7:357.

86. Singh et al., Coffee, Tea, and Cocoa, pp. 35–38; R. Edwards, "The Stabilization of the International Coffee Market," Food Policy (1977), 2:188.

87. Edwards, "The Stabilization of the International Coffee Market," p. 188; Nappi, Commodity Market Controls, p. 56; Paul Streeten and Diane Elson, Diversification and Development: The Case of Coffee (New York: Praeger, 1971), p. 15.

88. Thomas Geer, An Oligopoly: The World Coffee Economy and Stabilization Schemes (New York: Dunellen, 1971), pp. 167–68. See also Simon G. Hanson, "The International Coffee Agreement," Inter-American Economic Affairs (Autumn 1963), 17:63; Simon G. Hanson, "The Experience with the International Coffee Agreement," Inter-American Economic Affairs (Winter 1965), 19:52; Streeten and Elson, Diversification and Development, p. 16.

89. On the classic boom-bust cycle, see Derek J. Ford, "Simulation Analyses of Stabilization Policies in the International Coffee Market," in F. G. Adams and J. R. Behrman, eds., Econometric Modeling of World Commodity Policy (Lexington, Mass.: Lexington Books, 1979), p. 128; Singh et al., Coffee, Tea, and Cocoa, p. 31. For a recent general analysis of the market, see Takamasa Akiyama and Ronald C. Duncan, Analysis of the World Coffee Market, World Bank Staff Commodity Working Papers 7 (Washington, D.C.: World Bank, 1982).

90. Geer, An Oligopoly, p. 76.

91. Singh et al., Coffee, Tea, and Cocoa, p. 39.

92. Stephen D. Krasner, "The Politics of Primary Commodities: A Study of Coffee, 1900–1970" (Ph.D. diss. Harvard University, 1971), p. 250; Joe Norton Short, "American Business and Foreign Policy: Cases in Coffee and Cocoa Trade Regulation" (Ph.D. diss. Columbia University, 1974), pp. 57–58 and 65.

93. Krasner, "The Politics of Primary Commodities," pp. 200–3; Fisher, The International Coffee Agreement, p. 24; V. D. Wickizer, Coffee, Tea, and Cocoa: An Economic and Political Analysis (Stanford: Stanford University Press, 1951), pp. 80–82.

94. Fisher, The International Coffee Agreement, p. 15.

95. Ibid., pp. 15–16; Wickizer, Coffee, Tea, and Cocoa, pp. 95–113.

96. Singh et al., Coffee, Tea, and Cocoa, p. 40.

97. Streeton and Elson, Diversification and Development, p. 15; Brown, The Political and Social Economy of Commodity Control, pp. 16–17.

98. Fisher, *The International Coffee Agreement,* pp. 16–19.

99. Ibid., pp. 19–20; Richard B. Bilder, "The International Coffee Agreement: A Case History in Negotiation," *Law and Contemporary Problems* (Spring 1963), 28:337.

100. Interviews; Krasner, "The Politics of Primary Commodities," pp. 207–8.

101. Ibid., pp. 208–10; Fisher, *The International Coffee Agreement,* pp. 20–25.

102. Fisher, *The International Coffee Agreement,* p. 24.

103. Ibid., p. 25; Krasner, "The Politics of Primary Commodities," pp. 210–11; Bilder, "The International Coffee Agreement," pp. 334–38.

104. Article 27. The 1962 ICFA is in United Nation, *Treaty Series,* 469:169.

105. Fisher, *The International Coffee Agreement,* p. 47.

106. Ibid., 45–55; Bilder, "The International Coffee Agreement," pp. 340–41; Krasner, "The Politics of Primary Commodities," p. 285; Short, "American Business and Foreign Policy," p. 45.

107. Bilder, "The International Coffee Agreement," p. 360; Fisher, *The International Coffee Agreement,* p. 61; Krasner, "The Politics of Primary Commodities," pp. 210–11.

108. Fisher, *The International Coffee Agreement,* pp. 59–60. Also on these issues see ibid., pp. 50–51 and 57–58; and Bilder, "The International Coffee Agreement," pp. 345 and 361.

109. Bilder, "The International Coffee Agreement," pp. 362–63; Fisher, *The International Coffee Agreement,* pp. 66–67; Krasner, "The Politics of Primary Commodities," pp. 232–33.

110. Interviews; Fisher, *The International Coffee Agreement,* p. 242.

111. Hanson, "The International Coffee Agreement," p. 77.

112. Interviews; Fisher, *The International Coffee Agreement,* pp. 50–51 and 62; Bilder, "The International Coffee Agreement," pp. 347 and 358–59; Krasner, "The Politics of Primary Commodities," pp. 233 and 281–84.

113. Singh et al., *Coffee, Tea, and Cocoa,* pp. 40–41.

114. Fisher, *The International Coffee Agreement,* pp. 72–79; Rangarajan, *Commodity Conflict,* p. 108.

115. Fisher, *The International Coffee Agreement,* pp. 81–99 and 109–10; Rangarajan, *Commodity Conflict,* pp. 247–48.

116. They rejected UNCTAD's offer to provide the institutional framework since they did not want any political intrusions into their negotiations. Diego Cordovez, *UNCTAD and Development Diplomacy: From Confrontation to Strategy* (Geneva: Journal of World Trade Law, 1972), p. 22.

117. Fisher, *The International Coffee Agreement,* p. 118; Brown, *The Political and Social Economy of Commodity Control,* p. 31.

118. Krasner, "The Politics of Primary Commodities," p. 346.

119. The 1968 ICFA is in United Nations, *Treaty Series,* 647:3.

120. C. F. Marshall, *The World Coffee Trade: A Guide to the Production, Trading, and Consumption of Coffee* (Cambridge: Woodhead-Faulkner, 1983), pp. 117–18.

121. The information on these negotiations came from interviews and Fisher, *The International Coffee Agreement,* pp. 121–29.

122. Ibid., pp. 121 and 133–39; Short, "American Business and Foreign Policy,"

ch. 5; President of the United States, "Third Annual Report on the International Coffee Agreement Transmitted to Congress, January 22, 1968," *Department of State Bulletin* (March 4, 1968), 58:338; Stephen D. Krasner, "Business-Government Relations: The Case of the International Coffee Agreement," *International Organization* (Autumn 1973), 27:513–15.

123. Fisher, *The International Coffee Agreement*, p. 157.

124. Ibid., p. 156–57; Comptroller-General of the United States, *The International Coffee Agreement: Its Impact on Coffee Prices; Its Ability to Deal with Unforeseen Supply and Demand Conditions; and the Soluble Coffee Controversy* (Report to the Committee on Finance of the U.S. Senate, July 1973), p. 20; Julius L. Katz, "The 1968 International Coffee Agreement at the Halfway Mark," *Department of State Bulletin* (March 1, 1971), 64:262.

125. Vernon Yorgason, "The International Coffee Agreement: Prospect and Retrospect," *Development and Change* (1976), 7:214–16; Ursula Wasserman, "1972 Geneva Coffee Agreement," *Journal of World Trade Law* (September–October 1972), 6:612–13; Comptroller-General of the United States, *The International Coffee Agreement*, p. 23.

126. Yorgason, "The International Coffee Agreement," pp. 216–17.

127. C. F. Marshall, "Coffee: The 1973–74 Coffee Year," *Bank of London and South America Review* (1974), 8:695.

128. War in Angola and poor weather in Colombia also reduced production. Singh et al., *Coffee, Tea, and Cocoa*, p. 42; Nappi, *Commodity Market Controls*, pp. 77–79.

129. The 1975 ICFA is in *United States Treaties and Other International Agreements* (Washington, D.C.: Government Printing Office, 1979), 28, pt. 6, p. 6401.

130. C. F. Marshall, "Coffee in 1975: The Brazilian Frost and a New Agreement," *Bank of London and South America Review* (1975), 9:677.

131. Robert J. Vastine, "United States International Commodity Policy," *Law and Policy in International Business* (1977), 9:466; Rangarajan, *Commodity Conflict*, pp. 161–62; interviews.

132. Articles 30–32; K. R. Khan, "International Coffee Agreement, 1976: Issues of Selectivity, Regulation, and Reciprocity," *Food Policy* (1978), 3:180–90; Julius L. Katz, "International Commodity Policy," *Department of State Bulletin* (March 1978), 78:5; U.S. Congress, House of Representatives, *United States Commodity Policies, Commercial Stabilization Agreement: Coffee, Cocoa, and Tin* (Hearings before the House Committee on International Relations and Sub-Committees, Ninety-fourth Congress, 2d sess., April 19, 1976), pp. 49–51.

133. Edwards, "The Stabilization of the International Coffee Market," pp. 197 and 191–92; Nappi, *Commodity Market Controls*, p. 78; interviews.

134. Nappi, *Commodity Market Controls*, p. 79.

135. *Latin American Commodities Report*, January 14, 1977; *New York Times*, January 10, 1976, p. 36, and February 17, 1977, p. 56.

136. Marshall, "Coffee in 1978," pp. 3–6; *Latin American Commodities Report*, August 11, 1978.

137. C. F. Marshall, "Coffee in 1976: The Post Gelidal Boom," *Bank of London and South America Review* (1978), 12:5; Marshall, "Coffee in 1978," p. 5; C. F. Marshall,

"Coffee in 1979: The Effect of the Bogota Group," *Bank of London and South America Review* (1980), 14:2–6.

138. *Latin American Commodities Report,* October 12, 1979, June 16, 1980 and October 10, 1980; interviews.

139. *Latin American Commodities Report,* October 10, 1980; Akiyama and Duncan, *Analysis of the World Coffee Market,* p. 35; interviews.

140. *Latin American Commodites Report,* October 9, 1981; Akiyama and Duncan, *Analysis of the World Coffee Market,* pp. ix and 35.

141. The ICFA was supposed to expire in September 1982. In 1980 it was extended for one year through September 1983.

142. *Latin American Commodities Report,* February 19, April 16, June 18, July 16, and September 27, 1982; *Coffee and Cocoa International,* (1982), no. 5, p. 21; *Third World Quarterly* (January 1983), pp. 165–68; interviews.

143. Interviews.

144. *Coffee and Cocoa International,* (1982), No. 6, pp. 36-37; *Latin American Commodities Report,* September 17, and October 29, 1982; interviews.

145. *Latin American Commodities Report,* January 28, April 29, September 30, October 14, 1983, January 27, and March 23, 1984; *Coffee and Cocoa International* (1983), no. 2, pp. 42–43; (1983), no. 2, p. 24; and (1983), no. 6, p. 23; *Wall Street Journal,* October 2, 1984, p. 51.

146. *Financial Times,* October 3, 1985, p. 40; interviews.

147. *Financial Times,* February 20, 1986, p. 36; interviews.

148. Interviews.

149. G.A.R. Wood, *Cocoa,* 3d ed. (London: Longman, 1975), pp. 2 and 241; Short, "American Business and Foreign Policy," pp. 17–18.

150. Singh et al., *Coffee, Tea, and Cocoa,* p. 76; interviews.

151. Singh et al., *Coffee, Tea, and Cocoa,* pp. 95–96; Rolf Hanisch, "Confrontation Between Primary Commodity Producers and Consumers: The Cocoa Hold-up of 1964-65," *Journal of Commonwealth and Comparative Politics* (November 1975), 13:244; Wayne A. Schutjer and Edward Jide Ayo, "Negotiating a World Cocoa Agreement: Analysis and Prospects," *Pennsylvania Agriculture Experimental Station Bulletin* (October 1967), 74:11–13; Wood, *Cocoa,* pp. 257–59.

152. Wood, *Cocoa,* pp. 353–57; International Cocoa Organization Doc. PCA/3/6 (1984), "An Analysis of the World Cocoa Industry"; and interviews.

153. Hanisch, "Confrontation Between Primary Commodity Producers and Consumers," p. 246; UN Doc. TD/B/C.1/164 (1975), pp. 13–18.

154. Price data are in World Bank, *Commodity Trade and Price Trends* (annual); and International Cocoa Organization Doc. PCA/3/6 (1984).

155. Wood, *Cocoa,* pp. 242–43; UN Doc. TD/B/C.1/164 (1975), pp. 13–18.

156. Schutjer and Ayo, "Negotiating a World Cocoa Agreement," pp. 6–10; F. Helmut Weymer, *The Dynamics of the World Cocoa Market* (Cambridge, Mass.: MIT Press, 1968), chs. 1 and 2; Singh et al., *Coffee, Tea, and Cocoa,* p. 8; interviews.

157. See Wickizer, *Coffee, Tea, and Cocoa,* passim; and T. Kofi, "The International Cocoa Agreements," *Journal of World Trade Law* (January–February 1977), 11:33–41.

158. J. D. Coppock, *International Economic Instability* (New York: McGraw-Hill 1961), p. 46; Schutjer and Ayo, "Negotiating a World Cocoa Agreement," p. 16.

159. Short, "American Business and Foreign Policy," p. 254.

160. Schutjer and Ayo, "Negotiating a World Cocoa Agreement," p. 16; Kofi, "The International Cocoa Agreements," p. 43; Hanisch, "Confrontation Between Primary Commodity Producers and Consumers," pp. 247–48.

161. For an excellent overview of cocoa discussions and the activities of the CSG in the 1956–63 period, see Schutjer and Ayo, "Negotiating a World Cocoa Agreement," pp. 18–28. Also, see Hanisch, "Confrontation Between Primary Commodity Producers and Consumers," pp. 247–48.

162. Short, "American Business and Foreign Policy," pp. 260–62; Schutjer and Ayo, "Negotiating a World Cocoa Agreement," pp. 24–26.

163. Short, "American Business and Foreign Policy," p. 263.

164. Hanisch, "Confrontation Between Primary Commodity Producers and Consumers," p. 255. For analyses of the CPA scheme, see ibid., pp. 248–55; Schutjer and Ayo, "Negotiating a World Cocoa Agreement," pp. 27–30.

165. Ursula Wasserman, "Towards an International Cocoa Agreement?" *Journal of World Trade Law* (November–December 1969), 3:526–28; Schutjer and Ayo, "Negotiating a World Cocoa Agreement," pp. 30–32.

166. Short, "American Business and Foreign Policy," p. 295.

167. *West Africa*, July 2, 1966, p. 749.

168. Short, "American Business and Foreign Policy," p. 268; Wasserman, "Towards an International Cocoa Agreement?" pp. 537–38.

169. Short, "American Business and Foreign Policy," pp. 268 and 297.

170. See Karen Ann Mingst, "The Process of International Policy Making in the Regulation of Tropical Agricultural Products: Coffee and Cocoa" (Ph.D. diss., University of Wisconsin, 1974), pp. 140–44, on the 1967 conference.

171. *West Africa*, November 8, 1969, p. 1344, May 31, 1969, p. 619, and June 13, 1970, p. 637.

172. The 1972 agreement is in: UN Doc. TD/COCOA.3/8 (1972).

173. Thomas C. Papson, "The International Cocoa Agreement," *Law and Policy in International Business* (1973), 5:1007.

174. Short, "American Business and Foreign Policy," p. 269; UN Doc. TD/COCOA.3/EX/SR.14 (1972).

175. Papson, "The International Cocoa Agreement," *Law and Policy in International Business* (1977), 9:558.

176. Papson, "The International Cocoa Agreement" (1973), pp. 1011–12; Short, "American Business and Foreign Policy," p. 269.

177. Short, "American Business and Foreign Policy," pp. 276–77.

178. Ibid., p. 269.

179. *West Africa*, September 22, 1972, p. 1263, and October 30, 1972, p. 1462; Mingst, "The Process of International Policy Making in the Regulation of Tropical Agricultural Products," p. 149.

180. Singh et al., *Coffee, Tea, and Cocoa*, pp. 82–84; World Bank, *Commodity Trade and Price Trends* (1981), p. 34.

181. International Cocoa Organization, *Annual Report 1974/75* (1976), p. 13.

182. UN Doc. TD/COCOA.4/2 (1975), pp. 4 and 12.

183. Ecuador, Mexico, Guinea, the Dominican Republic, and Papua New Guinea

joined in late 1972, bringing to 98 percent the alliance's coverage of world cocoa exports.

184. Brown, *The Political and Social Economy of Commodity Control*, p. 51; *West Africa*, October 27, 1975, p. 1267.

185. The 1975 agreement is in UN Doc. TD/COCOA.4/8 (1975).

186. Papson, "The International Cocoa Agreement," (1977), pp. 564–65; Brown, *The Political and Social Economy of Commodity Control*, pp. 51–52.

187. Papson, "The International Cocoa Agreement" (1977), pp. 555–65; interviews.

188. Ibid., p. 563; *Quarterly Bulletin of Cocoa Statistics* (December 1979), vol. 6 and interviews.

189. Brown, *The Political and Social Economy of Commodity Control*, p. 53; *Latin American Commodities Report*, March 1, 11, 18, and 25, 1977; interviews.

190. World Bank, *Commodity Trade and Price Trends* (1981), p. 34.

191. International Cocoa Organization *Annual Report 1976–77*, (1978).

192. *Latin American Commodities Report*, November 3, 1977.

193. Interviews; *Latin American Commodities Report*, February 16 and March 2, 1979.

194. Interviews; *Latin American Commodities Report*, August 10, 1979.

195. *Latin American Commodities Report*, December 7, 1979; Ursula Wasserman, "Breakdown of International Cocoa Agreement," *Journal of World Trade Law* (July–August 1980), 14:360–63.

196. Interviews; "Doubts About Cocoa Agreement," *South* (December 1980), pp. 63–65; "North-South Monitor," *Third World Quarterly* (October 1980), 2:652–53; Wasserman, "Breakdown of International Cocoa Agreement," pp. 360–61; *Latin American Commodities Report*, December 21, 1979.

197. Interviews; "Doubts About Cocoa Agreement," *South* (December 1980), p. 63.

198. The 1980 agreement is in UN Doc. TD/COCOA.6/7 (1980).

199. Interviews; "Doubts About Cocoa Agreement," *South* (December 1980), pp. 64–65.

200. International Cocoa Organization Doc. ICC/25/8 (1983), pp. 4–5.

201. *Financial Times* (London), October 14, 1981, p. 39, and October 21, 1981, p.39.

202. *West Africa*, April 5, 1982, p. 942.

203. *Latin American Commodities Report*, February, 5, April 2, July 30, October 15, November 12, and December 24, 1982, February 11 and April 15, 1983.

204. For the ICO Secretariat's evaluation, see International Coca Organization Doc. ICC/25/8 (1983). The council decisions are in *Coffee and Cocoa International* (1983), no. 1, p. 59, and (1983), no. 5, p. 62.

205. Information on the 1984–86 negotiations was obtained from International Cocoa Organization Docs. PCA/3/4 (1983), PCA/3/E/W.1/Rev.2, PCA/3/6, PCA/3/REP/I, PCA/3/EC/REP/I and PCA/3/EC/REP/II (1984); *Financial Times* (including July 11, 1985, p. 30; February 7, 1986, p. 30; February 11, 1986, p. 36; February 27, 1986, p. 40; March 12, 1986, p. 38; April 4, 1986, p. 36; July 16, 1986, p. 36); *West Africa* (including July 19, 1985, February 17, 1986, March 17, 1986); and interviews.

206. *Financial Times*, February 11, 1986, p. 36; July 16, 1986, p. 36.
207. The draft 1986 agreement is in UN Doc. TD/COCOA.7/22 (1986).
208. *Coffee and Cocoa International* (1984), no. 1, p. 59.
209. Interviews.
210. *Coffee and Cocoa International* (1981), no. 5, p. 23.

5. UNSUCCESSFUL ATTEMPTS TO NEGOTIATE INTERNATIONAL COMMODITY AGREEMENTS

1. Paul D. Reynolds, *International Commodity Agreements and the Common Fund* (New York: Praeger, 1978), pp. 70–71; Christopher P. Brown, *The Political and Social Economy of Commodity Control* (New York: Praeger, 1980), p. 111.
2. UNCTAD Res. 83 (III) (1972).
3. UN Doc. TD/498 (1973), p. 3. The report summarizing the talks on each commodity is in TD/B/504 (1974).
4. Robert L. Rothstein, *Global Bargaining: UNCTAD and the Quest for a New International Economic Order* (Princeton, N.J.: Princeton University Press, 1979), pp. 52, 54, and 112; Brown, *The Political and Social Economy of Commodity Control*, p. 124.
5. Metals Society, *Future Metal Strategy* (London: Metals Society, 1980), p. 59; D. Metzger, *Copper in the World Economy* (New York: Monthly Review Press, 1980), p. 35; H. Labib and A. Ritter, "Stabilizing the International Copper Market: The Viability and Impacts of Alternate Market Management Arrangements," *Canadian Journal of Development Studies* (1981), 2:75; *Copper Handbook* (Washington, D.C.: World Bank, 1981), p. I-1.
6. *Copper Handbook*, p. I-7; Raymond F. Mikesell, "Structure of the World Copper Industry," in S. Sideri and S. Johns, eds., *Mining For Development in the Third World* (New York: Pergamon Press, 1980), p. 65.
7. Leonard S. Fischman, *World Mineral Trade and U.S. Supply Problems* (Baltimore: Johns Hopkins University Press, 1980), p. 214.
8. S. Zorn, "New Developments in Third World Mining Agreements," *Natural Resources Forum* (April 1977), p. 239; Raymond F. Mikesell, *The World Copper Industry: Structure and Economic Analysis* (Baltimore: Johns Hopkins University Press, 1979), pp. 96–97; *Copper Handbook*, p. II-2.
9. World Bank, *Commodity Trade and Price Trends* (1985), pp. 110–11.
10. "World Copper Market, 1973–82, and International Stabilization Policies," *Resources Policy* (March 1984), 9:19–30.
11. *Copper Handbook*, p. III-1; Mikesell, "Structure of the World Copper Industry," p. 17; Mikesell, *The World Copper Industry*, pp. 96–97; "World Copper Market, 1973–82, and International Stabilization Policies," pp. 24–26; *Latin American Commodities Report*, August 31, 1984, p. 1.
12. Mikesell, "Structure of the World Copper Industry," p. 62; *Copper Handbook*, p. V-1.
13. J. Allan, "Two-Tier Market for Copper," *South* (October 1980), p. 63; Karen A. Mingst, "Cooperation or Illusion: An Examination of the Intergovernmental

Council of Copper Exporting Countries," *International Organization* (Spring 1976), 30:263–88.

14. Mingst, "Cooperation or Illusion," pp. 280–81.

15. Sir Ronald Prain, *Copper: The Anatomy of an Industry* (London: Mining Journal Books, 1975), p. 253.

16. The activities of CIPEC are analyzed in Zorn, "New Developments in Third World Mining Agreements," pp. 239–49; Zuhayr Mikdashi, *The International Politics of Natural Resources* (Ithaca: Cornell University Press, 1976), pp. 86–95; Mingst, "Cooperation or Illusion," pp. 271–76; Carmine Napi, *Commodity Market Controls* (Lexington, Mass: Lexington Books, 1979), pp. 113–16; Prain, *Copper*, pp. 248–60.

17. UN Doc. TD/B/C.1/203 (1976).

18. UN Doc. TD/B/IPC/COPPER/2 (1976); C. Fred Bergsten, *The International Economic Policy of the United States: Selected Papers of C. Fred Bergsten, 1977–1979* (Lexington, Mass.: Lexington Books, 1980), p. 281; Brown, *The Political and Social Economy of Commodity Control*, p. 161; and K. N. Bhuskar, C. L. Gilbert and R. A. Perlman, "Stabilization of the International Copper Market: A Simulation Study," *Resources Policy* (March 1979), 4:13–24.

19. A participant in the meetings stated that there was a split between the foreign ministry and the economics ministry in Peru. A Peruvian official working in Peru at the time claimed that the industry would have fought export controls if there had been a serious chance of their acceptance. However, there is little doubt that many Peruvians were angry about Chile's plans to expand production. Interviews. For accounts of the meetings see Brown, *The Political and Social Economy of Commodity Control*, p. 171; UN Doc. TD/B/IPC/COPPER/2–6 (1976–77).

20. UN Doc. TD/B/IPC/COPPER/11 (1978), p. 20. Also see Brown, *The Political and Social Economy of Commodity Control*, pp. 177–78.

21. Interviews.

22. UN Doc. TD/B/IPC/COPPER/16 (1979), p. 5. A study done under contract for Canada's Department of Energy, Mines, and Resources that shows the depressive effects of a pure buffer-stock arrangement on prices is discussed in Labib and Ritter, "Stabilizing the International Copper Market,"pp. 70–116.

23. It accounted for about 25 percent of world consumption, so the United States would have had to pay that portion of the consumer's total share of $1.5 billion—namely, $375 million. As one U.S. official commented, "it would not have had a prayer of getting through Congress." Interviews. The proceedings of the 1979 meeting are in UN Doc. TD/B/IPC/COPPER/16 (1979).

24. J. d'Hainaut, *A Brief Glimpse of CIPEC* (Paris: CIPEC, March 1979).

25. UN Doc. TD/B/IPC/COPPER/19 (1980), p. 32.

26. Mikesell, *The World Copper Industry*.

27. Ibid., p. 195.

28. Ibid., pp. 187–204.

29. Ibid., pp. 204–14.

30. *Latin American Commodities Report*, January 14, 1983. See also *Latin American Commodities Report*, August 31, 1984; *Mining Journal*, September 17, 1982, p. 196.

31. *Mining Journal*, July 16, 1982, p. 43; *Latin American Commodities Report*, August 13, 1982.

32. *Latin American Commodities Report,* December 24, 1982.

33. Interviews.

34. *Mineral Commodity Summaries 1981* (Washington, D.C.: U.S. Department of the Interior, 1981), p. 77; G. Manners, *The Changing World Market for Iron Ore, 1950–80* (Baltimore: Johns Hopkins University Press, 1971), p. 305.

35. Brown, *The Political and Social Economy of Commodity Control,* p. 202; UN Doc. TD/B/IPC/IRON ORE/3 (1977), pp. 3–4.

36. C. D. Rogers, "LDCs and the Marketing and Distribution of Iron Ore," and "Long-Term Procurement Contracts, with Special Reference to Iron Ore," in S. Sideri and S. Johns, eds., *Mining for Development in the Third World: Multinational Corporations, State Enterprises and International Economy* (New York: Pergamon Press, 1980), pp. 70–83 and 146–48; UN Doc. TD/B/IPC/IRON ORE/2 (1977), p. 19 and /16 (1984), pp. 24–25.

37. UN Doc. TD/B/IPC/IRON ORE/2 (1977), p. 19.

38. Ibid.

39. John F. Tilton, *The Future of Non-Fuel Minerals* (Washington, D.C.: Brookings, 1977), pp. 45–46.

40. World Bank, *Commodity Trade and Price Trends* (1985), pp. 118–19; UN Doc. TD/B/IPC/IRON ORE/16 (1984), pp. 14–15.

41. M. Radetzki, "Market Structure and Bargaining Power"; *Resources Policy* (June 1978), 4:117; Rogers, "Long-Term Procurement Contracts, with Special Reference to Iron Ore," p. 148.

42. Table 5.4; and UN Doc. TD/B/IPC/IRON ORE/16 (1984).

43. Rogers, "Long-Term Procurement Contracts, with Special Reference to Iron Ore," p. 145.

44. Rogers, "LDCs and the Marketing and Distribution of Iron Ore," pp. 79 and 75.

45. Ibid., p. 79.

46. Nappi, *Commodity Market Controls,* pp. 146–47.

47. UN Doc. TD/B/C.1/75 (1970), and /125 (1972).

48. UN Doc. TD/B/C.1/125 (1972), p. 5.

49. UN Doc. TD/B/C.1/142 (1974).

50. Nappi, *Commodity Market Controls,* p. 147.

51. Ibid., p. 147.

52. Ibid., p. 148–49.

53. Ibid., p. 148.

54. Brown, *The Political and Social Economy of Commodity Control,* p. 203; UN Doc. TD/B/IPC/IRON ORE/AC/5 (1978), p. 3.

55. UN Doc. TD/222 (1979), p. 21.

56. Brown, *The Political and Social Economy of Commodity Control,* p. 205.

57. UN Doc. TD/B/IPC/IRON ORE/16 (1984).

58. Interviews.

59. Michael W. Klass, James C. Burrows, and Stephen Beggs, *International Mineral Cartels and Embargoes: Policy Implications for the United States* (New York: Praeger, 1980), pp. 2 and 171; Leonard S. Fischman, *World Mineral Trade and U.S. Supply Problems,* p. 249; UN Docs. TD/B/IPC/MANGANESE/2 (1977), p. 3; and TD/B/IPC/MANGANESE/7 (1980), p. 2.

60. Fischman, *World Mineral Trade and U.S. Supply Problems*, p. 249; Klass, Burrows, Beggs, *International Mineral Cartels and Embargoes*, p. 169; UN Doc. TD/B/IPC/MANGANESE/7 (1980), p. 32.

61. UN Doc. TD/B/IPC/MANGANESE/10 (1983), pp. 3–5; table 5.7.

62. UN Docs. TD/B/IPC/MANGANESE/2 (1977), pp. 17–18, and /5/add. 1 (1978), table XII. Third World countries account for about 13 percent of ferromanganese exports.

63. UN Doc. TD/B/IPC/MANGANESE/3 (1977), p. 17.

64. World Bank, *Commodity Trade and Price Trends* (1985), pp. 120–21.

65. UN Doc. TD/B/IPC/MANGANESE/3 (1977), p. 6 and /10 (1983), pp. 2–9.

66. UN Doc. TD/B/C.1/130 (1972); TD/B/C.1/149 (1974), pp. 6–7.

67. UN Docs. TD/B/IPC/AC/20 (1978), p. 29; TD/B/IPC/MANGANESE/3 (1977); Brown, *The Political and Social Economy of Commodity Control*, pp. 205–6; interviews.

68. UN Doc. TD/B/IPC/MANGANESE/8 (1980); interviews.

69. UN Doc. TD/B/IPC/MANGANESE/10 (1983), pp. 6–7. The Secretariat's and states' comments on the market are in TD/B/IPC/MANGANESE/9 (1981) and adds. 1–3 (1982).

70. Fischman, *World Mineral Trade and U.S. Supply Problems*, p. 495. See ibid., pp. 493–96; Klass, Burrows, and Beggs, *International Mineral Cartels and Embargoes*, pp. 6, 9, and 13–14; Brown, *The Political and Social Economy of Commodity Control*, p. 205; interviews.

71. UN Doc. TD/B/IPC/BAUXITE/2, Rev. 1 (1978), pp. 4–5; Ferdinand E. Banks, *Bauxite and Aluminum: An Introduction to the Economics of Nonfuel Minerals* (Lexington, Mass.: Lexington Books, 1979), pp. 3 and 130–42.

72. *Bauxite and Aluminum Handbook* (Washington, D.C.: World Bank, 1981), p. III-4; Ferdinand E. Banks, *Bauxite and Aluminum* (Boston, Mass.: Lexington Books, 1979), pp. 70–74; Alan Litvak and Christopher J. Maule, "The International Bauxite Agreement: A Commodity Cartel in Action," *International Affairs* (Spring 1980), 57:303; Nappi, *Commodity Market Controls*, pp. 17–20; UN Docs. TD/B/IPC/BAUXITE/1/Rev. 1 (1978), pp. 17–20 and /2/Add.1/Rev.1 (1978), table XIII.

73. UN Doc. TD/B/IPC/BAUXITE/2/Add.1/Rev.1 (1978). tables VIIA and XII.

74. UN Doc. TD/B/IPC/BAUXITE/2/Add.1/Rev.1 (1978), table XIV; World Bank, *Commodity Trade and Price Trends* (1985), pp. 108–9; TD/B/IPC/BAUXITE/2/Rev.1 (1978), pp. 21–27; David E. Hojman, "The IBA and Cartel Problems: Prices, Policy Objectives, and Elasticities," *Resources Policy* (December 1980), 6:290–302; Banks, *Bauxite and Aluminum*, p. 101.

75. UN Doc. TD/B/IPC/BAUXITE/2/Rev.1 (1978), p. 25.

76. Hojman, "The IBA and Cartel Problems," p. 290.

77. For discussions of the events leading up to this development see Nappi, *Commodity Market Controls*, pp. 122–23; Mikdashi, *The International Politics of Natural Resources*, pp. 110–12; C. Fred Bergsten, *Managing International Economic Interdependence* (Lexington, Mass.: Lexington Books, 1977), pp. 193–97. Haiti withdrew in the 1980s when it ceased mining.

78. Mikdashi, *The International Politics of Natural Resources*, pp. 113.

79. Banks, *Bauxite and Aluminum*, pp. 69–70.

80. Litvak and Maule, "The International Bauxite Agreement," p. 306; Bergsten, *Managing International Interdependence*, pp. 193 and 197.

81. Nappi, *Commodity Market Controls*, pp. 123–24; Litvak and Maule, "The International Bauxite Agreement," p. 308; interviews.

82. *Mining Journal*, December 3, 1982, p. 391; *Latin American Commodities Report*, December 10, 1982.

83. J. Souare, "The IBA Is Not a Cartel," *IBA Quarterly Review* (January–March 1981),6:40.

84. *IBA Quarterly Review* (December 1980), 6:1.

85. Bergsten, *Managing International Economic Interdependence*, p. 198.

86. *South*, January 1981, p. 70.

87. Hojman, "The IBA and Cartel Problems," pp. 294–302; Litvak and Maule, "The International Bauxite Agreement," pp. 308–11; Klass, Burrows, and Beggs, *International Mineral Cartels and Embargoes*, p. 110.

88. Litvak and Maule, "The International Bauxite Agreement," p. 309.

89. *Mining Journal*, December 18, 1981, pp. 457–58.

90. Litvak and Maule, "The International Bauxite Agreement," pp. 309–10.

91 UN Doc. TD/B/IPC/BAUXITE/2 (1982), p. 16.

92. Bergsten, *Managing International Economic Interdependence*, p. 205.

93. UN Doc. TD/B/IPC/BAUXITE/3 (1982), pp. 3–4.

94. UN Doc. TD/B/IPC/BAUXITE/4 (1982), p. 6.

95. UN Doc. TD/B/IPC/BAUXITE/5 (1983).

96. *Globe and Mail* (Toronto), December 10, 1983, p. B19.

97. UN Doc. TD/B/IPC/PHOSPHATES/2 (1977), p. 2.

98. UN Doc. TD/B/IPC/PHOSPHATES/1 (1977), p. 41.

99. UN Doc. TD/B/C.1/PSC/22 (1981), pp. 54–56; interviews with government and international organization officials.

100. World Bank, *Commodity Trade and Price Trends* (1985), pp. 126–27. These are figures for Moroccan phosphate rock.

101. UN Doc. TD/B/C.1/176 (1974), p. 10; TD/B/C.1/22 (1967), pp. 49–54.

102. UN Doc. TD/B/IPC/PHOSPHATES/3 (1977), pp. 7 and 11.

103. UN Docs. TD/B/C.1/22 (1967), pp. 18–22 and 54–55; TD/B/IPC/PHOSPHATES/2 (1977), p. 38; and TD/B/C.1/88/Rev.1 (1970), p. 15.

104. UN Doc. TD/113/Supp.1/add. 2 (1972), pp. 2–3.

105. UN Doc. TD/B/C.1/150 (1974), p. 203.

106. Ibid., pp. 1–11.

107. UN Doc. TD/B/IPC/PHOSPHATES/3 (1977), pp. 9–11.

108. UN Doc. TD/B/IPC/AC/20 (1978), p. 30.

109. UN Doc. TD/B/IPC/PHOSPHATES/4 (1977), p. 4.

110. UN Doc. TD/B/IPC/PHOSPHATES/4 (1977).

111. Brown, *The Political and Social Economy of Commodity Control*, p. 60; UN Doc. TD/B/IPC/PHOSPHATES/4 (1978).

112. Interviews.

113. UN Doc. TD/B/C.1/241 (1982), p. 1.

114. *Tea Handbook* (Washington, D.C.: World Bank, 1981), pp. II-1–2; Jos de Vries, *Tea: The Possibilities of International Action,* World Bank Commodity Paper no. 28 (January 1977), annex 1, p. 5; UN Doc. TD/B/IPC/TEA/AC/2 (1978), pp. 26–27.

115. UN Doc. TD/B/IPC/TEA/AC/1 (1977), pp. 5, 11, and 30; *Tea Handbook,* p. II-2.

116. *Tea: Current Situation, 1983/84* (Rome: Food and Agriculture Organization, April 1984), pp. 1–2.

117. World Bank, *Commodity Trade and Price Trends* (1985), pp. 48–49.

118. UN Docs. TD/B/IPC/TEA/AC/2 (1978), p. 46; and TD/B/IPC/TEA/3 (1978), p. 3; *Tea: Current Situation, 1983/84;* L. N. Rangarajan, *Commodity Conflict* (Ithaca, N.Y.: Cornell University Press, 1978); pp. 92–94; interviews.

119. UN Doc. TD/B/IPC/TEA/4 (1978), pp. 2–3; Liaquat Ali, "The Regulation of Trade in Tea," *Journal of World Trade Law* (July–August 1977), 4:570–72; *Tea Handbook,* pp. V-12–14.

120. Ali, "The Regulation of Trade in Tea," p. 576; *Tea Handbook,* p. V-14.

121. G. D. Gwyer, "Three International Commodity Agreements: The Experience of East Africa," *Economic Development and Cultural Change* (1976), 21:474–75.

122. Interviews.

123. UN Doc. TD/113/Add.1/Supp. 1 (1972); T. Eden, *Tea* (3d ed.; London: Longman, 1976), p. 205; *Tea Handbook,* p. V-14. For other discussions of these negotiations see UN Doc. TD/B/IPC/TEA/4 (1978), pp. 3–5; FAO Doc. CCP 74/16 (1974); and Brown *The Political and Social Economy of Commodity Control,* p. 196.

124. FAO Doc. CCP 74/16 (1974).

125. UN Docs. TD/B/IPC/AC/23 (1978), p. 9; TD/B/IPC/TEA/4 and 8 (1978); TD/B/IPC/TEA/AC/2 (1978); Brown, *The Political and Social Economy of Commodity Control,* pp. 196–97; interviews.

126. UN Docs. TD/B/IPC/TEA/11 (1979) and 14 (1982); TD/B/C.1/241 (1982), pp. 10–11; *Far Eastern Economic Review,* May 30, 1980, p. 86 and February 19, 1981, p. 6; *The Guardian,* February 8, 1981, p. 20; interviews.

127. UN Doc. TD/B/IPC/TEA/15 (1983); interviews.

128. World Bank, *Commodity Trade and Price Trends* (1985), pp. 48–49; *Tea: Current Situation, 1983/84;* interviews.

129. For analyses of the products and their markets, see Jock Anderson, et al., "A Dynamic Simulation Model of the World Jute Economy," World Bank Staff Working Papers no. 391 (May 1980); W. C. Labys, "Simulation Analysis of an International Buffer Stock for Jute," *Journal of Development Studies* (April 15, 1979), pp. 154–66; and UN Doc. TD/B/IPC/JUTE/WG/2 (1978).

130. FAO Doc. CCP:JU 82/7 (1982), p. 5.

131. Anderson, "A Dynamic Simulation Model of the World Jute Economy," p. 4.

132. World Bank, *Commodity Trade and Price Trends* (1985), pp. 84–85; FAO Doc. CCP:JU 82/7 (1982), pp. 6–9; table 1–4.

133. Anderson, "A Dynamic Simulation Model of the World Jute Economy"; Labys, "Simulation Analysis of an International Buffer Stock for Jute"; FAO Docs. CCP:JU 82/7 (1982) and 83/8 (1983).

134. Interviews.

135. FAO Doc. CCP: JU 82/7 (1982), p. 2.

136. Interview.

137. FAO Doc. CCP: JU 82/7 (1982), p. 2 and passim; UN Doc. TD/B/IPC/JUTE/WG/2 (1978). There has also been an indicative price range for Thai kenaf since 1970 (except for mid-1974 to 1977), but the market price has seldom been in the range. Also, the fact that Thailand now exports little kenaf makes the accord quite irrelevant. FAO Docs. CCP: JU 82/7 (1982), 82/8 (1982), and 83/8 (1983).

138. UN Doc. TD/B/IPC/JUTE/1 (1976), pp. 3–10; Brown, *The Political and Social Economy of Commodity Control,* p. 197.

139. UN Doc. TD/B/IPC/JUTE/1 (1976), p. 10.

140. UN Docs. TD/B/IPC/1 (1976) and /JUTE/3 (1977). A World Bank analysis of the considerable cost of the UNCTAD jute buffer-stock proposal is in Anderson, et al., "A Dynamic Simulation Model of the World Jute Economy," pp. 18–32. The United States prepared extensive studies on its own before the UNCTAD meetings.

141. Reports on the 1976–78 meetings are in UN Docs. TD/B/IPC/JUTE/1 (1976), /3, /7 (1977) and /11 (1978). Information on the meetings also came from interviews.

142. Accounts of the 1979–82 period are in UN Docs. TD/B/IPC/JUTE/20, /22, /23 (1979), /25, and /28 (1980) and TD/JUTE/1/10 (1982); and TD/B/C.1/241 (1982), pp. 9–10. The International Jute Agreement is in TD/JUTE/11 (1982).

143. *Far Eastern Economic Review,* September 11, 1981, p. 51. See also *Far Eastern Economic Review,* October 17, 1980, p. 77 and *South* (March 1981), p. 64. Information was also obtained from interviews.

144. FAO Docs. CCP: JU 82/8, 82/9 (1982) and 83/8 (1983), p. 8.

145. The developed-country views on the synthetics issue are presented in chapter 2.

146. UN Doc. TD/B/IPC/HARD FIBERS/4/add.1 (1976) and /17 (1980); FAO Docs. CCP:HF 78/7 (1978), 78/10 (1978), 81/7 (1981), 82/8 (1982) and CCP 83/5 (1983) and 85/2 (1985).

147. UN Doc. TD/B/IPC/HARD FIBERS/4/add. 2 (1976) and /17 (1980); FAO Docs. CCP 76/5 (1976), 78/2 (1978), 81/5 (1981), 85/2 (1985), and CCP/HF 83/7 (1983).

148. Twine exports grew only marginally from the early 1970s to early 1980s, but by weight they are now almost equal to exports of raw fiber. Table 5.22; UN Docs. TD/B/IPC/HARD FIBERS/3 (1976), p. 17 and /22 (1981), p. 4; FAO Doc. CCP:HF/CE 84/2 (1984), tables 2 and 3; E. R. Grilli, *The Future of Hard Fibers and Competition from Synthetics,* World Bank Staff Occasional Papers no. 19 (Baltimore: Johns Hopkins University Press, 1975), pp. 12–13 and 86–87.

149. FAO Doc. CCP:HF/CE 84/2 (1984), table 3.

150. FAO Doc. CCP:HF/CE 84/2 (1984), table 7.

151. Grilli, *The Future of Hard Fibers and Competition from Synthetics;* UN Doc. TD/B/IPC/HARD FIBERS/4 (1976); FAO Docs. CCP 75/16 (1975) and CCP:HF/CE 84/2 (1984).

152. FAO Doc. CCP:HF 82/6 (1982), annex; World Bank, *Commodity Trade and Price Trends* (1985), p. 86.

153. Brown, *The Political and Social Economy of Commodity Control*, p. 201.

154. Grilli, *The Future of Hard Fibers and Competition from Synthetics*, pp. 26–27; Rangarajan, *Commodity Conflict*, p. 185; Gwyer, "Three International Commodity Agreements," pp. 471–72; UN Docs. TD/B/C.1/90 (1970), TD/113/Supp. 1/Add. 1 (1972); and FAO Docs. CCP 67/27 (1967) and 69/13 (1969).

155. Grilli, *The Future of Hard Fibers and Competition from Synthetics*, p. 30.

156. UN Docs. TD/B/C.1/130 (1972); TD/B/491 (1974); TD/B/IPC/17 (1980); TD/B/C.1/249 (1982), p. 16; FAO Docs. CCP 76/5 (1976), 76/8 (1976), 77/12 (1977), 78/2 (1978), 79/5 (1979), 80/1 (1980), 81/5 (1981), and 85/2 (1985); CCP:HF 82/2 (1982) and 83/6 (1983).

157. FAO Docs. CCP:HF 82/7 (1982) and CCP 85/2, (1985), pp. 5–7; interviews.

158. UN Doc. TD/B/IPC/HARD FIBERS/1–18 (1976–80); Brown, *The Political and Social Economy of Commodity Control*, pp. 200–1; interviews.

159. UN Doc. TD/B/IPC/HARD FIBERS/18 (1980), p. 5.

160. UN Doc. TD/B/IPC/HARD FIBERS/22 (1981).

161. *Cotton Handbook* (Washington, D.C.: World Bank, 1981), pp. I-1–12; UN Doc. TD/B/IPC/COTTON/1 (1977),pp. 8–9; M. Elton Thigpen, *International Cotton Market Prospects*, World Bank Staff Commodity Paper no. 2.(June 1978), passim.

162. Data on production and trade is in *Cotton: World Statistics* (Washington, D.C.: International Cotton Advisory Committee, October 1981).

163. UN Doc. TD/229/supp. 3 (1979), p. 6.

164. UN Doc. TD/B/IPC/COTTON/1 (1977), p. 5.

165. UN Doc. TD/B/IPC/COTTON/2 (1977), pp. 6–11 and /L.1 (1977), p. 5.

166. World Bank, *Commodity Trade and Price Trends* (1985), pp. 80–81; *Cotton: World Statistics*; UN Doc. TD/B/IPC/COTTON/1 and /2 (1977); Thigpen, *International Cotton Market Prospects*.

167. UN Doc. TD/113/Supp.1/add. 1 (1972).

168. ICAC deliberations are described in UN Docs. TD/B/C.1/30 (1967), /90 (1970), and /185 (1975); TD/B/IPC/COTTON/L.1 (1977), pp.18–20.

169. UN Doc. TD/B/IPC/COTTON/3 (1977), p. 5.

170. UN Doc. TD/B/IPC/COTTON/2 (1977), pp. 15–22.

171. The UN documents for the meetings are TD/B/IPC/COTTON/1–21, (1977–81).

172. Fourteen developing-producers (including Turkey) formed the Izmir Group in 1980 at a meeting of producers sponsored by UNCTAD and the UN Development Program. They issued a declaration that simply reiterated support for the proposals they had been backing in UNCTAD meetings since 1977. UN Doc. TD/B/IPC/COTTON/17 (1980), annex V; *Latin American Commodities Report*, April 4, 1980 and March 20, 1981.

173. UN Doc. TD/B/IPC/COTTON/3 (1977), /7 and /12 (1978); Brown, *The Political and Social Economy of Commodity Control*, pp. 190–91; *Latin American Commodities Report*, February 3 and April 14, 1978, and September 28, 1979; interviews.

174. UN Doc. TD/B/IPC/COTTON/9 (1978), p. 10.

175. UN Doc. TD/B/IPC/COTTON/3 (1977). p. 7.

176. Interviews.

177. UN Doc. TD/B/IPC/COTTON/21 (1981), p. 6 Washington was, however, willing to support a study group, provided it did not discuss market regulation.

178. UN Docs. TD/B/IPC/COTTON/3 (1977), p. 8 and /9 (1978), p. 8.

179. Brown, *The Political and Social Economy of Commodity Control*, pp. 188–91; UN Doc. TD/B/IPC/COTTON/3 (1977).

180. TD/B/IPC/COTTON/Misc. 9/Rev. (1982).

181. "Constitution of the International Cotton Producers' Association" (mimeo).

182. *Banana Handbook* (Washington, D.C.: World Bank, 1981), pp. I-1–3.

183. *Banana Handbook*, pp. III-1–2.

184. Table 1.4; FAO Doc. CCP BA/ST 84/2 (1984), tables 6 and 7; World Bank, *Commodity Trade and Price Trends* (1985), pp. 64–65.

185. I. A. Litvak and C. N. Maule, "Transnational Corporations in the Banana Industry: With Special Reference to Central America and Panama" (New York: United Nations, Division of Economic Development, Joint CEPAL/CTC Unit, Working Paper no. 7, August 1977); Carlos Gallegos, "Sectoral Study on the Banana Industry in Latin America and Caribbean Countries and the Role of Transnational Enterprises" (Washington, D.C.: Organization of American States, October 1981); FAO Doc. CCP BA 82/4 (1984), pp. 5 and 12–14.

186. UN Docs. TD/113/supp. 1/add. 1 (1972);TD/B/C.1/153 (1974); FAO Doc. CCP: 74/13 (1974); Litvak and Maule, "Transnational Corporations in the Banana Industry."

187. Gallegos, "Sectoral Study on the Banana Industry in Latin America and Caribbean Countries," pp. 5–6; Litvak and Maule, "Transnational Corporations in the Banana Industry," pp. 114–23 and passim; UN Doc.TD/B/IPC/BANANAS/3 (1980), p. 4; and interviews.

188. Litvak and Maule, "Transnational Corporations in the Banana Industry," pp. 72–75, 89–95, and 117–18; L. Emil Kreider, "Banana Cartel? Trends, Conditions, and Institutional Developments in the Banana Market," *Inter-American Economic Affairs* (Autumn 1977), 31:19; interviews.

189. *Latin American Commodities Report*, February 6, 1981.

190. For information on the FAO deliberations, see FAO Docs. CCP BA 75/3 (1975); CCP BA/WP 76/2 and /4 (1976); CCP BA/WP 77/2 and /5 (1977), CCP BA/WP 78/4, /6 and /7 (1978); CCP BA 80/5(1980); CCP 80/5 (1980); and CCP/ BA/EXPO 83/3 (1983), p. 2; UN Docs. TD/228 (1979), pp. 9–10; TD/B/C.1/240, pp. 15–16; and Brown, *The Political and Social Economy of Commodity Control*, p. 59. Information was also obtained from interviews with participants.

191. UN Doc. TD/B/IPC/BANANAS/7 (1980).

192. On trade barriers, see FAO Doc. CCP BA 82/7 (1982).

193. FAO Docs. CCP BA/ EXPO 83/3 (1983), BA/TC 83/2 and /3 (1983); *Latin American Commodities Report*, January 27, 1984; February 24, 1984; interviews.

194. *Latin American Commodities Report*, August 17, 1984, January 17, 1984, June 11, 1984, July 6, 1984, September 28, 1984.

195. FAO Doc. CCP BA/82/4 (1982), p. 6.

196. The secretariat proposals are in FAO Docs. CCP BA/WP 84/2 and 3(1984). Minutes of the meeting are in FAO Doc. CCP BA/WP 84/5(1984).

197. FAO Doc. CCP BA 86/7(1986).

198. UN Doc. TD/B/IPC/TIMBER/2 (1977), p. 2.

199. UN Doc. TD/B/IPC/TIMBER/21 (1978), p. 26.

200. UN Doc. TD/B/IPC/TIMBER/21 (1978), p. 24. The reports of these and

early meetings are in TD/B/IPC/TIMBER/1–23 (1977–78). Further discussions of the market are in Raj Kumar, "World Tropical Wood Trade," *Resources Policy* (September 1982), 8:177–92; Kenji Takeuchi, *Tropical Hardwood Trade in the Asia-Pacific Region* (Baltimore: Johns Hopkings Univeristy Press, 1974); Ephraim E. Enabar, "Trends and Patterns of the Tropical Hardwood Trade," *World Development* (April 1977), 5:335–48; Brown, *The Political and Social Economy of Commodity Control*, pp. 209–10; and *Far Eastern Economic Review*, May 12, 1978, pp. 36–38 and November 30, 1979, pp. 52–67.

201. UN Doc. TD/TIMBER/11 (1983); "Tropical Timber Now Covered by an International Agreement, "*UNCTAD Bulletin*, no. 198 (December 1983–January 1984). The negotiations leading up to the signing are described in the UN document series TD/B/IPC/TIMBER and TD/TIMBER (1982–83).

202. UN Doc. TD/B/IPC/OILS/2 (1977); World Bank, *Commodity Trade and Price Trends* (1985), tables 7–9 and 14–15.

203. M. P. Cracknell, "Fats and Oils: The Legal Framework of the World Market," *Journal of World Trade Law* (November–December 1970), 4:743–69; Brown, *The Political and Social Economy of Commodity Control*, pp. 106–7; Rangarajan, *Commodity Conflict*, p. 176; UN Doc. TD/B/C.1/151 (1974); and the UN document series TD/B/IPC/OILS (1977–80).

204. UN Doc. TD/B/IPC/OILS/2 (1977), pp. 21–22.

205. UN Doc. TD/B/IPC/AC/17 (1978), p. 7.

206. UN Doc. TD/B/IPC/AC/30 (1979), p. 11.

207. UN Doc. TD/B/IPC/MEAT/1 through 8 (1978–80), esp. Doc. 2 (1978) on the bovine meat market; Brown, *The Political and Social Economy of Commodity Control*, p. 319, *n* 21; FAO Doc. ESC/ME 84/1 (1984); interviews.

6. DEVELOPING-COUNTRY POLICIES, BARGAINING OUTCOMES, AND INTERNATIONAL REGIMES

1. Stephen D. Krasner, *Structural Conflict: The Third World Against Global Liberalism* (Berkeley: University of California Press, 1985), p. 5.

2. Commodity prices could be indexed to the prices of LDC imports, to the prices of manufactured goods that incorporate primary manufactured commodities, or to changes in LDCs' commodity production costs. See J.D.A. Cuddy, *International Price Indexation* (Lexington, Mass.: Lexington Books, 1976), pp. 5–6.

3. Ibid., 87–93.

4. L. N. Rangarajan, *Commodity Conflict* (Ithaca, N.Y.: Cornell University Press, 1978), p. 301; Robert L. Rothstein, *Global Bargaining: UNCTAD and the Quest for a NIEO* (Princeton, N.J.: Princeton University Press, 1979), pp. 100–1; Christopher P. Brown, *The Political and Social Economy of Commodity Control* (New York: Praeger, 1980), pp. 103–9.

5. See, for example, Ezriel Brook, Enzo Grilli, and Jean Waelbroeck, "Commodity Price Stabilization and the Developing Countries," *Banca Nazionale del Lavoro Quarterly Review* (March 1979), 124:passim; Christopher P. Brown, *The Political and Social Economy of Commodity Control* (New York: Praeger, 1980), pp. 150–55 and

sources therein cited; J.D.A. Cuddy, "Commodity Price Stabilization: Its Effects on Producers and Consumers," *Resources Policy* (March 1978), 4:25–30 and sources therein cited; Jere R. Behrman, "International Commodity Agreements: An Evaluation of the UNCTAD Integrated Commodity Programme," in William R. Cline, ed., *Policy Alternatives for a New International Economic Order* (New York: Praeger, 1979), pp. 63–153; David L. McNicol, *Commodity Agreements and Price Stabilization* (Lexington, Mass.: Lexington Books, 1978), pp. 15–21; Robert L. Rothstein, "Consensual Knowledge and International Collaboration: Some Lessons from the Commodity Negotiations," *International Organization* (Autumn 1984), 38:741–44.

6. Stephen D. Krasner, "Transforming International Regimes: What the Third World Wants and Why," *International Studies Quarterly* (March 1981), 25:130; and Krasner, *Structural Conflict*, p. 36.

7. Krasner, "Transforming International Regimes," p. 130; and Krasner, *Structural Conflict*, pp. 38–45.

8. Albert O. Hirschman, *National Power and the Structure of Foreign Trade* (1945; rpt. ed., Berkeley: University of California Press, 1980), pp. 26–28.

9. Klaus Knorr, *The Power of Nations: The Political Economy of International Relations* (New York: Basic Books, 1975), p. 229.

10. Krasner, *Structural Conflict*, pp. 49–51.

11. Robert O. Keohane, "Economic Dependence and the Self-Directed Small State," *Jerusalem Journal of International Relations* (1982), 6:49–60.

12. Ibid.; see also Peter Katzenstein, "Capitalism in One Country: Switzerland in the International Economy," *International Organization* (Autumn 1980), 34:507–40; and Krasner, *Structural Conflict*, pp. 44–45.

13. Krasner, "Transforming International Regimes," pp. 143–45; Krasner, *Structural Conflict*, pp. 81–90.

14. Albert Fishlow, "A New International Economic Order: What Kind?" in Carlos Diaz-Alejandro, Richard Fagen, Albert Fishlow, and Roger D. Hansen, eds., *Rich Nations and Poor Nations in the World Economy* (New York: McGraw-Hill, 1978), p. 19.

15. Robert W. Tucker, *The Inequality of Nations* (New York: Basic Books, 1977), p. 70; Fishlow, "A New International Economic Order," pp. 17–22.

16. Krasner, *Structural Conflict*, p. 88; see also Tucker, *The Inequality of Nations*, pp. 89–90.

17. Robert O. Keohane and Joseph S. Nye, *Power and Interdependence: World Politics in Transition* (Boston: Little, Brown, 1977), p. 36. See also Branislav Gosovic and John Gerard Ruggie, "On the Creation of a New International Economic Order: Issue Linkage and the Seventh Special Session of the UN General Assembly," *International Organization* (Spring 1976), 30:309–45; Krasner, *Structural Conflict*, pp. 72–75.

18. Krasner, "Transforming International Regimes," p. 141.

19. Karl P. Sauvant, *The Group of 77: Evolution, Structure, and Organization* (New York: Oceana Publications, 1981), p. 46. Interviews have substantiated this judgment. Very few LDC governments have the capabilities to develop their own proposals or choose to devote their limited resources to the UNCTAD context.

20. Brown, *The Political and Social Economy of Commodity Control*, p. 46; Rothstein, *Global Bargaining*, pp. 49–54.

21. Robert L. Rothstein, *The Weak in the World of the Strong: The Developing Countries in the International System* (New York: Columbia University Press, 1977), p. 158; Branislav Gosovic, *UNCTAD: Conflict and Compromise* (Leiden: A. W. Sijthoff, 1972), p. 289.

22. Noel Lateef, "Parliamentary Diplomacy and the North-South Dialogue," *The Georgia Journal of International and Comparative Law* (Winter 1981), 11:37.

23. Robert L. Rothstein, *The Third World and U.S. Foreign Policy* (Boulder, Colo.: Westview Press, 1981), pp. 25–27.

24. Brown, *The Political and Social Economy of Commodity Control*, p. 41.

25. Rangarajan, *Commodity Conflict*, pp. 119–22.

26. Walter C. Labys, *Market Structure, Bargaining Power, and Resource Price Formation* (Lexington, Mass.: Lexington Books, 1980), p. 11.

27. Alton D. Law, *International Commodity Agreements: Setting, Performance, and Prospects* (Lexington, Mass.: Lexington Books and D.C. Heath, 1975); UN Doc. TD/B/C.1/270 (1985).

28. See yearly editions of the World Bank's *Commodity Trade and Price Trends* for data. Of the five commodities for which ICAs were created, only rubber experienced a serious decline in constant price over the 1960s and 1970s, and this was largely confined to the 1960s.

29. Christopher P. Brown, *Primary Commodity Control* (Kuala Lumpur: Oxford University Press, 1975), pp. 134 and 151–55; Rangarajan, *Commodity Conflict*, pp. 112–18; H. Hveem, *The Political Economy of Third World Producer Associations* (New York: Columbia University Press, 1978), pp. 84–86.

30. On the cost of buffer stocks and their effects on negotiations to create ICAs, see McNicol, *Commodity Agreements and Price Stabilization*, pp. 45–52; Rothstein, *Global Bargaining*, pp. 87–89.

31. Krasner, *Structural Conflict*, pp. 15, 65–69, 81–92, 308–11 and passim.

32. Robert L. Rothstein, "Regime-Creation by a Coalition of the Weak: Lessons from the NIEO and the Integrated Program for Commodities," *International Studies Quarterly* (September 1984), 28:308.

33. Rachel McCulloch and José Pinera, "Alternative Commodity Trade Regimes," in Ruth W. Arad, Uzi B. Arad, Ann Hollick, Rachel McCulloch, and José Pinera, eds., *Sharing Global Resources* (New York: McGraw-Hill, 1979), p. 114.

34. Rangarajan, *Commodity Conflict*, p. 240.

35. These particular terms come from the 1970 Trade and Development Board resolution on price policy, but the same or equivalent terms appear in other resolutions and statements. UN Doc. TD/B/327 (1970), annex I, pp. 6–8.

36. See the Group B statements following the passage of resolution 93 (IV) at UNCTAD IV, which launched the Integrated Program for Commodities. UN Doc. TD/217 (1976), p. 101.

37. Rangarajan, *Commodity Conflict*, p. 23. Robert Rothstein has argued that "the Group of 77 made a fundamental error of emphasizing too exclusively Third World development as the key norm." He argues that they should have focused on discovering schemes of mutual economic interest. "Regime Creation by a Coalition of the Weak," p. 313.

38. Interviews.

39. Helge Ole Bergesen, "Norway: The Progressive Free-Rider or the Devoted Internationalist," in Helge Ole Bergesen, Hans Henrick Holm, and Robert D. McKinlay, eds., *The Recalcitrant Rich: A Comparative Analysis of the Northern Response to the Demands for a New International Economic Order* (New York: St. Martin's Press, 1982), p. 148; and Krasner, *Structural Conflict,* p. 91–92. One participant in the OECD talks on the IPC observed that some Western delegates were so incensed at the Norwegians that they held private meetings to exclude them. Interview.

40. M. C. Smouts, "France: Egoism bien tempere," in Bergesen, Holm, and McKinlay, eds., *The Recalcitrant Rich,* pp. 125–26.

41. Interviews; Simon Serfaty, "Conciliation and Confrontation: A Strategy for North-South Negotiations," *Orbis* (Spring 1978), 22:47–61.

42. For an analysis of some of the differences and negotiations, see Gosovic and Ruggie, "On the Creation of a New International Economic Order," pp. 309–45.

43. Rothstein, *The Third World and U.S. Foreign Policy,* p. 26.

44. Rothstein, *The Third World and U.S. Foreign Policy,* pp. 24–25.

45. Ibid., pp. 24–25 and 40 (*n* 13).

46. Brown, *The Political and Social Economy of Commodity Control,* p. 166.

47. Carmine Nappi, *Commodity Market Controls* (Lexington, Mass.: Lexington Books, 1978), pp. 43–47 and 61–63.

48. Mikdashi, *The International Politics of Natural Resources,* p. 101.

49. Brown, *The Political and Social Economy of Commodity Control,* p. 190.

50. Interviews.

51. *The Economist,* December 2, 1978, p. 88.

52. Stuart Harris, "The Case for a New International Commodity Regime: Confused Arguments and Unresolved Issues," in Geoffrey Goodwin and James Mayall, eds., *The New International Commodity Regime* (London: Croom Helm, 1979), pp. 43–44; and sources in note 5 above.

53. Gordon W. Smith and George R. Schink, "The International Tin Agreement: A Reassessment," *Economic Journal* (December 1976), 86:715–28.

54. Ruth and Uzi Arad, "Scarce Natural Resources and Potential Conflict," in Arad et al., eds., *Sharing Global Resources,* pp. 35–36; Rex Bosson and Benison Varon, *The Mining Industry and the Developing Countries* (London: Oxford University Press, 1977), p. 223.

55. Interviews.

56. *Natural Rubber: A Dovetailed Examination of Aspects of the International Natural Rubber Agreement and Its Wider Implications* (London: Economist Intelligence Unit, 1980), p. 197.

57. Brown, *The Political and Social Economy of Commodity Control,* p. 154.

58. Richard N. Cooper and Robert Z. Lawrence, "The 1972–1975 Commodity Price Boom," *Brookings Papers on Economic Activity* (1975), 3:671–715; interviews with officials.

59. Stephen D. Krasner, "The Quest for Stability: Structuring International Commodity Markets," in Gerald and Lou Ann Garvey, eds., *International Resource Flows* (Lexington, Mass.: Lexington Books, 1977), p. 40.

60. David E. Hojman, "The IBA and Cartel Problems: Prices, Policy Objectives, and Elasticities," *Resources Policy* (December 1980), 6:290–91.

61. Krasner, "The Quest for Stability," pp. 49–53; Raymond F. Mikesell, *The World Copper Industry: Structure and Economic Analysis* (Baltimore: Johns Hopkins University Press, 1979); G. K. Helleiner, "Structural Aspects of Third World Trade: Some Prospects," in Sheila Smith and John Toye, eds., *Trade and Poor Economies* (London: Frank Cass, 1979), pp. 71–76. For a persuasive argument that multinational corporations still have a great deal of influence, see Kenneth Rodman, *Sanctity versus Sovereignty: The United States and the Nationalization of Natural Resource Investments in the Third World* (New York: Columbia University Press, 1988).

62. Mikesell, *The World Copper Industry*, pp. 88–89; David L. McNicol, "The Two Price System in the Copper Industry," *Bell Journal of Economics* (Spring 1977), 6:50–73.

63. Bart S. Fisher, *The International Coffee Agreement: A Study in Commodity Diplomacy* (New York: Praeger, 1972).

64. Rangarajan, *Commodity Conflict*, p. 253.

65. J. Betz and M. Kreile, "Federal Republic of Germany: The Knights of the Holy Grail," in Bergeson et al., eds., *The Recalcitrant Rich*, pp. 98–121.

66. Bosson and Varon, *The Mining Industry and the Developing Countries*, p. 125.

67. Donella H. Meadows, Dennis L. Meadows, Gorgen Randers, and William W. Behrens III, *The Limits to Growth* (New York: Signet/New American Library, 1972); Cooper and Lawrence, "The 1972–1975 Commodity Price Boom," pp. 671–715.

68. Zuhayr Mikdashi, *The International Politics of Natural Resources* (Ithaca, N.Y.: Cornell University Press, 1976); C. Fred Bergsten, "The Threat from the Third World," *Foreign Policy* (Summer 1973), 11:102–4; C. Fred Bergsten, "The New Era in Commodity Cartels," *Challenge* (September/October 1974); Kenneth Clarfield et al., *Eight Mineral Cartels* (London: Metals Week, 1975).

69. Bergsten, "The New Era in Commodity Cartels"; Clarfield, et al., *Eight Mineral Cartels*; P. Connelly and R. Perlman, *The Politics of Scarcity* (London: Oxford University Press, 1975).

70. Bergsten, "The New Era in Commodity Cartels," pp. 34–35; Robert Dickson and Paul Rogers, "Resources, Producer Power, and International Relations," in Paul Rogers, ed., *Future Resources and World Development* (London and New York: Plenus Press, 1976), pp. 90–91; J. Robert Vastine, "United States International Commodity Policy," *Law and Policy in International Business* (Summer 1977), 9:401–88; and Mikdashi, *The International Politics of Natural Resources*.

71. For analyses of the factors hindering and facilitating producer collaboration and market control, see in particular Krasner, "Oil is the Exception," pp. 183–96; F. M. Scherer, *Industrial Market Structure and Economic Performance* (Chicago: Rand McNally, 1980), chs. 6 and 7; Bosson and Varon, *The Mining Industry and the Developing Countries*, pp. 125–28; Paul Streeton, "The Dynamics of the New Poor Power," *Resources Policy* (June 1976), 2:73–86; John F. Tilton, *The Future of Non-Fuel Minerals* (Washington, D.C.: Brookings, 1977), pp. 82–88; Marian Radetski, "The Potential for Monopolistic Commodity Pricing by Developing Contries," in G. K. Helleiner, ed., *A World Divided: The Less Developed Countries in the International Economy* (London: Cambridge University Press, 1976), pp. 68–73; Benison Varon and Kenji Takeuchi, "Developing Countries and Non-Fuel Minerals," *Foreign Affairs* (April 1974), 52:505–9; and Arad, "Scarce Natural Resources and Potential Conflict."

72. Tilton, *The Future of Non-Fuel Minerals,* pp. 8–15.

73. Ibid., p. 9. Reserves are known mineral deposits that can be profitably exploited with current prices and technology; they comprise only a fraction of a much larger category, mineral resources. See ibid., ch. 1. Tilton cites data which indicate that as of the mid-1970s only tungsten had actually experienced a reduction in reserves since the late 1940s. Substantial additions to reserves have occurred in the case of a number of key LDC mineral exports, including bauxite, copper, phosphate rock, iron ore, and manganese. Ibid., pp. 8–10. See also Arad, "Scarce Natural Resources and Potential Conflict," pp. 32–41; and Mikesell, *The World Copper Industry,* pp. 6–15.

74. Tilton, *The Future of Non-Fuel Minerals,* pp. 11–15.

75. Benison Varon and Kenji Takeuchi, "Developing Countries and Non-Fuel Minerals," *Foreign Affairs* (April 1974), 52:507.

76. Tilton, *The Future of Non-Fuel Minerals,* pp. 11–15; Raymond F. Mikesell, *New Patterns of World Mineral Development* (Washington, D.C.: British North America Committee, 1979), pp. 6–15; Bosson and Varon, *The Mining Industry and the Developing Countries,* pp. 62–63.

77. Mikesell, *New Patterns of World Mineral Development,* p. 9.

78. F. M. Scherer, *Industrial Market Structure and Economic Performance* (Chicago: Rand McNally, 1980), p. 200.

79. Ibid., pp. 199–200. See also Labys, *Market Structure, Bargaining Power, and Resource Price Formation,* pp. 41–43; and Arad, "Scarce Natural Resources and Potential Conflict," p. 42.

80. Helge Hveem, *The Political Economy of Third World Producer Associations* (New York: Columbia University Press, 1978), p. 86.

81. Nappi, *Commodity Market Controls,* p. 114.

82. Some studies that address the general effects of ICAs are "The Role of International Commodity Agreements or Arrangements in Attaining the Objectives of the Integrated Programme for Commodities," UN Doc. TD/B/C.1/270(1985); FAO Doc. ESC MISC. 83/5(1983); *International Commodity Agreements: New Wave or Ebb Tide?* (Washington, D.C.: Bureau of Intelligence and Research, U.S. State Department, May 8, 1981); and Law, *International Commodity Agreements,* pp. 45–51 and 60–61. Interestingly, the first study cited, written in 1985 by the UNCTAD Secretariat, views ICAs as having limited and not completely favorable impacts.

One ICA on which more has been written is the International Tin Agreement. For evaluations of its effects, see Gordon W. Smith, "U.S. Commodity Policy and the Tin Agreement," in David B. H. Denoon, ed., *The New International Economic Order: A U.S. Response* (London: Macmillan, 1979), pp. 191–93; Gordon W. Smith and George R. Schink, "The International Tin Agreement: A Reassessment," *Economic Journal* (December 1976), 86:715–28; and William L. Baldwin, *The World Tin Market: Political Pricing and Economic Competition* (Durham, N.C.: Duke University Press, 1983), pp. 61–64, 138–39, and 226.

83. For a discussion of these principles and voting arrangements in international organizatons, see Stephen Zamora, "Voting in International Economic Organizations," *American Journal of International Law* (1980), 74:566–608; and Inis L. Claude, *Swords into Plowshares: The Problems and Progress of International Organization* (New York: Random House, 1964), ch. 7.

84. Studies that apply public/collective goods theory to international collaboration include John G. Ruggie, "Collective Goods and Future International Collaboration," *American Political Science Review* (September 1972), 66:874–93; Bruce Russett and John Sullivan, "Collective Goods and International Organization," *International Organization* (Autumn 1971), 25:845–65; and Duncan Snidal, "Public Goods, Property Rights and Political Organization," *International Studies Quarterly* (December 1979), 23:532–66.

The ICAs for sugar, coffee and cocoa all had restrictions on imports from nonmembers. UN Docs. TD/SUGAR/9/10(1977), art. 57; and TD/COCOA.6/7(1980), art. 51. Also, International Coffee Organization, "International Coffee Agreement, 1983," art. 45.

85. See Stephen D. Krasner, ed., *International Regimes* (Ithaca, N.Y.: Cornell University Press, 1983), especially the last chapter by Krasner; and Robert O. Keohane, *After Hegemony: Cooperation and Discord in the World Political Economy* (Princeton, N.J.: Princeton University Press, 1984), esp. chs. 4–6 and 11.

86. Keohane, *After Hegemony,* p. 16.

87. Peter F. Drucker, "The Changed World Economy," *Foreign Affairs* (Spring 1986), 64:768–91.

INDEX

WESTMAR COLLEGE LIBRARY

HF 1428 .F56 1988
Finlayson, Jock A.
Managing international
  markets   (88-1109)

DEMCO